The New Abolitionists

SUNY SERIES, PHILOSOPHY AND RACE
Robert Bernasconi/T. Denean Sharpley-Whiting, editors

The New Abolitionists

(Neo)Slave Narratives and
Contemporary Prison Writings

Edited and with
an Introduction by
Joy James

STATE UNIVERSITY OF NEW YORK PRESS

The cover art, "Milk Goddess Talking to Earth," by artist Sundiata Acoli was originally printed in *Hauling Up the Morning/Izando la Mañana: Writings and Art by Political Prisoners and Prisoners of War in the U.S.*, eds. Tim Blunk, Raymond Luc Levasseur, and the editors of Jacobin Books (Trenton, NJ: Red Sea Press). It appears by permission of the artist and Sunni Middleton.

Published by
State University of New York Press, Albany

© 2005 State University of New York

For information, address State University of New York Press,
194 Washington Avenue, Suite 305, Albany, NY 12210-2384

Production by Marilyn P. Semerad
Marketing by Anne M. Valentine

Library of Congress Cataloging in Publication Data

The new abolitionists : (neo)slave narratives and contemporary prison writings /
  edited and introduction by Joy James.
    p. cm. — (SUNY series, philosophy and race)
  Includes bibliographical references and index.
    ISBN 0-7914-6485-7 (hardcover : alk. paper) — ISBN 0-7914-6486-5 (pbk. :
  alk. paper)
    1. Prisoners' writings, American. 2. Prisoners—United States—Social
  conditions. 3. Prisoners—United States—Biography. I. James, Joy. (date)
  II. Series.

HV9468.N48 2005
365'.973'0922—dc22
                                            2004017478

              10 9 8 7 6 5 4 3 2 1

Since this page cannot accommodate all the copyright notices,
the pages that follow constitute an extension of the copyright page.

Permissions

"Folsom, August 11th: A Question of Races" by Pancho Aguila was originally published in Pancho Aguila, *Dark Smoke: Poems* (San Francisco, CA: Second Coming Press, 1977), 4–6.

1. "Prison Etiquette" by Dachine Rainer and Holley Cantine was originally published in *Prison Etiquette: The Convict's Compendium of Useful Information*, edited by Dachine Rainer and Holley Cantine (Bearsville, NY: Retort Press, 1950). It is public domain.
2. "Notes on the Prison Community" by Bernard Phillips was originally published in *Prison Etiquette: The Convict's Compendium of Useful Information*, edited by Dachine Rainer and Holley Cantine (Bearsville, NY: Retort Press, 1950). It is public domain.
3. "The Criminalization of Poverty in Capitalist America" (Abridged) by Jalil Muntaqim was originally published in *Schooling the Generations in the Politics of Prisons*, edited by Chinosole (Berkeley, CA: New Earth Publications, 1996). It is reprinted by permission of the author.
4. "Control Unit Prisons: Deceit and Folly in Modern Dungeons" by Bill Dunne appears by permission of the author.
5. "Trouble Coming Every Day: ADX—The First Year" by Raymond Luc Levasseur was originally published online in *Letters from Exile*, home.earthlink.net/~neoludd/betty.html. It is reprinted by permission of the author.
6. "Behind the Mirror's Face" by Paul St. John was originally published in *Doing Time: Twenty-Five Years of Prison Writing*, edited by Bell Gale Chevigny (New York: Arcade Publishing, 1999). It is reprinted by permission of Arcade Publishing and Francis Goldin Literary Agency.
7. "A Call for the Abolition of Prisons" by Tiyo Attallah Salah-El appears by permission of the author.
8. "Women in Prison: How We Are" by Assata Shakur was originally published in *The Black Scholar* Vol. 9, No. 6 (April 1978) and was reprinted in *The Black Scholar* Vol. 12, No. 6 (November/December 1981). It is reprinted by permission of *The Black Scholar*.
9. "Women Casualties of the Drug War" by Susan Rosenberg was originally published in *Prison Life*, January–February 1996. It is reprinted by permission of the author.
10. "Reflections on the Black Woman's Role in the Community of Slaves" by Angela Y. Davis was originally published in the *The Black Scholar*, Vol. 3, No. 4 (December 1971) and was reprinted in *The Angela Y. Davis Reader*, edited by Joy James (Malden, MA: Blackwell, 1999), 111–128. It is reprinted with permission of *The Black Scholar*. Thank you to Blackwell Publishers for providing this version of the text.
11. "Killers" by Prince Imari A Obadele (Shemuel ben-Yahweh) appears by permission of the author.
12. "Men Against Sexism" by Ed Mead appears by permission of the author.
13. "The American Indian in the White Man's Prisons: A Story of Genocide" by Little Rock Reed was originally published in *Humanity and Society*, Vol. 13, No. 4 (1989). It is reprinted by permission of *Humanity and Society*.
14. "A People's Revolt for Power and an Up-Turn in the Black Condition: An Appeal and a Challenge" by Imari Abubakari Obadele I was originally published in 1977 as a pamphlet. It is reprinted by permission of the author.
15. "To My Baby's Children" by Prince Imari A Obadele (Shemuel ben-Yahweh) appears by permission of the author.
16. "King Tone's Diary" by Antonio Fernandez (King Tone) appears by permission of the author.

17. "Let's 'Gang Up' on Oppression: Youth Organizations and the Struggle for Power in Oppressed Communities" by Yaki (James Sayles) was originally published under the name of Owusu Yaki Yakubu in *Crossroad Newsletter*, Vol. 5, No. 2/3. It is reprinted by permission of the author.

18. Mumia Abu-Jamal's Evergreen State College Commencement Address, "A Life Lived, Deliberately," was originally published in *Radical Philosophy Review*, Vol. 3, No. 1 (2000) is reprinted by permission of Frances Goldin Literary Agency.

19. "Live from the Panopticon: Architecture and Power Revisited" was originally published in *Lingua Franca* (July/August 1993). It is reprinted by permission of Drew Leder.

20. "On Prisons and Prisoners" was originally published as "An Interview with Angela Davis: On Prisons and Prisoners" in *Prison Focus* (Fall 1997/Winter 1998). It is reprinted by permission of Leslie DiBenedetto.

21. "An Interview with George Jackson" was recorded May 16, 1971 at San Quentin State Prison in California. It was first broadcast on KPFA–FM, a Berkeley, California radio station. The interview was published in 1995 in *Black Prison Movements USA: The NOBO Journal of African American Dialogue*, Vol. 2, No. 1 (Trenton, NJ: Africa World Press), where it was misidentified as an interview done August 21, 1971 (the day of Jackson's murder). An edited version of the original interview was also published in the *Michigan Citizen*, Vol. 22, No. 38, August 13–19, 2000. It is reprinted here by permission of Karen Wald.

22. "The Black Panthers: An Interview with Geronimo ji Jaga Pratt" is excerpted from "The Black Panthers: Interviews with Geronimo ji-jaga Pratt and Mumia Abu-Jamal," originally published in *Race and Class*, Vol. 35, No. 1 (July/September 1993). Heike Kleffner's interview with Geronimo ji Jaga (Elmer Pratt) is reprinted here by permission of *Race and Class*.

23. "'You Have to be Intimate With Your Despair': A Conversation with Viet Mike Ngo (San Quentin Prison, E21895)" appears by permission of Dylan Rodríguez and Viet Mike Ngo.

24. "Cruel But Not Unusual—The Punishment of Women in U.S. Prisons" was originally published as "Cruel But Not Unusual: The Punishment of Women in U.S. Prisons, An Interview with Laura Whitehorn and Marilyn Buck" in *Monthly Review*, Vol. 53, No. 3 (July/August 2001). Conducted in 2001, this interview is reprinted by permission of Marilyn Buck, Susie Day, Laura Whitehorn, and *Monthly Review*.

25. "An Interview with Shaka Sankofa (Gary Graham)" was conducted on February 14, 1996, and was originally published in *The Gaither Reporter*, Vol. 4, No. 6 (March/April 2000). It is reprinted by permission of Larvester Gaither.

26. "Engaged in Life: Alan Berkman on Prison Health Care" appears by permission of Susie Day.

27. "'It's Too Bad the Soil Couldn't Cry Out from the Blood Shed Upon It'," an interview with Philip Berrigan, was conducted on March 14, 1998 from inside the Petersburg Federal Penitentiary in West Virginia and first aired on May 27, 2002 on Democracy Now! Radio. An excerpt is reprinted here by permission of Amy Goodman.

"The Attica Liberation Faction Manifesto of Demands and Anti-Depression Platform" is public domain.

"Attica—Thirty Years Later" by David Gilbert appears by permission of author.

Contributors to this volume, as well as *The Black Scholar, Race and Class,* Democracy Now!, *Monthly Review,* and the Francis Goldin Literary Agency granted free access to reprint their respective articles; Arcade Publishing and *History & Society* provided essays and articles for a reduced fee.

To my ancestral kin: Virginia, Mamie, Eddie Mae, Anna

Contents

III. Revolt

IV. Dialogues in Resistance (Interviews)

Preface

This anthology utilizes writings by modern and contemporary imprisoned authors to examine critiques of confinement and enslavement, resistance and emancipation.

Currently there are over two million people incarcerated in U.S. jails, detention centers, and prisons. Over seventy percent of this population are people of color. Over one million of the incarcerated are African American, largely due to racial and class bias in sentencing and the disproportionate policing and punitive measures directed against the poor.

Hence, we witness the construction of a new "racial formation"—the *bête noir*, the savage: that of the prisoner. Whether "social" or "political," prisoners are constructed as "non-citizens" and, given their caste, as uncivil or not civilized. Even racially fashioned and stigmatized peoples regard incarcerated individuals and incarcerated communities as unique among the outcasts—the outlaw commonly viewed not as (anti)hero but as (sub)human. In racial constructs, the "hyper-black"-as-prisoner is slave and so she stands distinctly debased from all other racial formations in society. This racial stigma is shared in varying degrees among those incarcerated.

The moral suasion of old words (and the stench of old wounds), and antebellum memories, surface in contemporary human rights activists' arguments for the end of the "prison industrial complex," and their self-identifications as "abolitionists." The incarcerated refer to themselves as "slaves" (a title claimed not only by imprisoned African Americans).

This collection of writings by Native American, African American, Latino, Asian, and European American prisoners incarcerated in the United States during the twentieth and twenty-first centuries offers (neo)slave narratives and abolitionism that depict and analyze (and at times reproduce) the master narratives of social and state domination. *The New Abolitionists* builds upon scholarly and historical analyses of incarceration, enslavement, and emancipation to explore a continuum of repressive ideologies and practices surrounding penal sites and the "free world."

The continuum encompasses not only slavery but also resistance and insurrection. Historical resistance includes the organization of "secret societies," writing and counseling groups, underground organizations, and educational and human rights advocacy, as well as rebellion. Also part of the continuum of incarceration, enslavement, and the struggle for emancipation are gender and sexuality. Gender and sexual violence, whether directed at or inflicted by captive men or women, manifest under incarceration in particularly virulent forms (as noted by recent human rights reports on gender and sexual violence).[1]

Anarchists, death penalty abolitionists, and political prisoners critique democracy and captivity, capitalism, gender and sexual violence and exploitation, Foucault's "panopticon," and the very nature of "prison writing" itself. They proffer a view of a nation that distinguishes itself by having the highest percentage and numbers of its people incarcerated and executed of all industrialized nations.

Note

1. See Amnesty International USA, *Abuse of Women in Custody: Sexual Misconduct and Shackling of Pregnant Women,* March 2001; Amnesty International USA, *Not Part of My Sentence: Violation of the Human Rights of Women in Custody,* AMR 51/019/1999, March 1999; Human Rights Watch Women's Rights Project, *All Too Familiar: Sexual Abuse of Women in U.S. State Prisons,* December 1996; Human Rights Watch, *No Escape: Male Rape in U.S. Prisons,* April 17 2001; Elihu Rosenblatt, ed., *Criminal Injustice: Confronting the Prison Crisis* (Boston: South End Press, 1996).

Acknowledgments

Robert Bernasconi and Tracy Denean Sharpley-Whiting enabled this book project, providing the opportunity to publish in their series on philosophy and race. Incisive dialogues with Frank Wilderson helped me to develop this project in political theory and social justice activism.

Sundiata Acoli, former Black Panther Party member, incarcerated for some three decades because of his political acts and beliefs—and his daughter Sunni Middleton—kindly provided us with his art to grace the book cover. Michael Hames-Garcia, Robert Allen and *The Black Scholar*, Andrew McNellie and Blackwell Publishing, Claude Marks and "Freedom Archives," the Francis Goldin Literary Agency, and David Brotherton all generously shared materials and resources furthering the development of this anthology. Also, my thanks to Jenny Bourne and Dr. Hazel Waters of *Race and Class*, and Amy Goodman of Democracy Now! for providing interviews for this volume.

At Brown University, working to create some base for "incarceration studies," I benefited from the support of the Hewlett Foundation, the Wayland Collegium for Liberal Learning, and Brown's University Teaching and Research Assistantship (UTRA) program. This volume gained considerably from the research and editorial work of Brown's former students Sam Seidel, Madeleine Dwertman, Tiffany Joseph, Elizabeth Walsh, and Ross Chapman. Elizabeth and Maddy spent many painstaking hours strengthening this text. Maddy, with considerable skill and patience, helped to shepherd the final draft through the "process"; this collection is shaped by her intellect, diligence, and generosity.

The Rockefeller Foundation's Bellagio Center, in 2002, allowed me to discuss this project with an international collective of intellectuals and scholars who provided political challenges and insights. Being befriended by Cindi and John Aldrich enriched my time in reflection in Italy. My thanks to them, and to all of the scholars and staff of the Bellagio. Finally, my deepest thanks and appreciation to Bellagio Director Gianni Chenli, whose gracious support inspired me to continue this journey.

Folsom, August 11th: A Question of Races

IS THIS THE WAY ATTICA WAS
        Days before the massacre
                Thick with hardened/veteran guards
3x
        4x
                5x . . . . . the usual count
                        Shotguns on the gunrails
                        Replacing the carbine
IS THIS THE WAY ATTICA WAS
        In the days before the slaughter
                Vibes everywhere spelling . . .
                        "Be cool n watch your step"
Does brownskin mean
        A target on my back
        Of black fury
Do blackmen think
        I have a dagger with wings
        To baptize in hatred
And do whitemen think
        I am a friend . . .
                Who do they really think I am
And what of the guards
        Grown five times over
                With commanding courtesy
                Shotgun politeness
IS THIS THE WAY ATTICA WAS
        Will massacres now be televised
                Are they the next t.v. spectacular
                Of the coming fall season
                        With the warden in living color
                        Unweaving his vision
                                Of convict politics

IS THIS THE WAY ATTICA WAS
   When a solid cry arose
      From the thick of oppression
         The denseness of frustration
            The heaviness of despair
IS THIS THE WAY ATTICA WAS
   I ask amidst
      The uncertainty of race
         Mixed with politics of guns
            Leveled upon men
               Standing accused
                  Before the guntowers
                     Of the american dream
IS THIS THE WAY ATTICA WAS
   Are the new atticas
      To be televised
         By the zookeepers
            To the great studios
               Of the american livingroom
I mean are we
   The next t.v. sports special
      For the coming fall season
Are we the ethnic quota
   To be met
      By the national broadcasting stations
         A new minority
            Rising from the bowels
I ask the humans
   Who share the cages
      Of my generation
         (Everyone who breathes air)
This generation of guntowers . . .
   This generation of massacres . . .
      This generation of rebellion . . .

—Pancho Aguila, August 11, 1975

Note

Pancho Aguila (Roberto Ignacio Zelaya)was born in Managua, Nicaragua on September 6, 1945, and raised in the San Francisco Bay Area. Active in San Francisco's street life and radical politics during the 1960s, he was arrested in 1969 for shooting a guard during a robbery. Aguila twice escaped from prison, resulting in his sentence being extended to natural life. His poetry and leadership in creative writing workshops in Folsom Prison garnered him public attention. In 1977, Aguila's writing workshop was suspended and he was transferred to solitary confinement where he remained for the next several years. A local movement, partly inspired by his poetry distributed outside of prison, arose and publicized his case. After being released from prison in 1986, Aguila violated parole and went underground; his whereabouts remain unknown. Aguila's publications include: *Hi-Jacked* (San Francisco, CA: Twin Window, 1975); *Anti-Gravity* (Berkeley, CA: Aldebaran Review Press, 1976); *Dark Smoke: Poems* (San Francisco, CA: Second Coming Press, 1977); *The Beast Has Come* (San Francisco, CA: Cloud House, 1978); and *Clash: Poetry* (San Francisco, CA: Poetry for the People, 1980). See Pancho Aguila, *Anti-Gravity*, in *Aldebaran Review*, Vol. 24 (Berkeley, CA: Aldebaran Review Press, 1976); and The Gale Group, *Contemporary Authors Online*, 2001.

Introduction: Democracy and Captivity
Joy James

Neither slavery nor involuntary servitude, except as a punishment for crime whereof the party shall have been duly convicted, shall exist within the United States, or any place subject to their jurisdiction.
—Thirteenth Amendment, Section 1, U.S. Constitution

[T]he post-Civil War southern system of convict lease . . . transferred symbolically significant numbers of black people from the prison of slavery to the slavery of prison.
—Angela Y. Davis

As a slave, the social phenomenon that engages my whole consciousness is, of course, revolution.
—George Jackson

"What Is in a Name?"

From its origins as a democratic slave state or a slave democracy into its current manifestations as a penal democracy, the United States of America has produced a wealth of writings constituting perhaps the world's largest collection of (neo)slave literature. A singular achievement. This literary productivity will continue given that the United States has the greatest incarceration rate in the industrialized world—estimated at about 2.5 million (counting children, nonlegalized immigrants, and the mentally disordered). Overwhelmingly, these detainees are poor and people of African, Latino, Asian, and indigenous ancestry. The United States also possesses the technological means and wealth to record and to preserve (or censor and disappear) its captive/penal discourse as part of its vast warehouse of "(neo)slave narratives."[1]

I thank Brady Heiner, Dylan Rodríguez, and Sharon Luk for their generosity in critiquing drafts of this reflection on democracy and captivity.

The above epigraphs are part of the abolitionist literature that exists as subcategories of a genre that I identify as "(neo)slave narratives." (Neo)Slave narratives emerge from the combative discourse of the captive as well as the controlling discourse of the "master" state. (Neo)Slave narratives focus on the punitive incarceration and containment of designated peoples in the United States (and its "territories," such as the prisons at Guantánamo Bay in Cuba and Abu Ghraib in Iraq). Here, I focus on three categories of (neo)slave narratives: those of the "master-state"; those of the nonincarcerated abolitionist and advocate; and those of the "prisoner-slave." Ideologically, these narratives range from conservative and liberal to radical and revolutionary. The above epigraphs proffer fragments of abolitionist (neo)slave narratives that clash in ideology and political objective as they seek to alter the reality of enslavement in the United States. (Narratives shaping penal/slave democracies intend different, and at times complementary or contradictory, abolitionisms; among African Americans, the most intensely policed in the United States, [neo]slave narratives possess no uniform ideology.[2])

Of the state narratives, the most significant to this discussion is the Thirteenth Amendment to the U.S. Constitution. The Thirteenth Amendment ensnares as it emancipates. In fact, it functions as an enslaving anti-enslavement narrative.[3] In contradistinction, slain prison rebel, author, and theorist George Jackson—his 1971 death at the hands of California prison guards would spark New York's Attica rebellion weeks later—calls into question the very right of the state (as master) to exist.[4] In abolitionists' insurrectionary narratives, such as those offered by Jackson, what is sought is not the mere abolition of penal captivity or slavery, but the abolition of all masters, including the state-as-master or master-state. Not all abolitionists seek the same "freedoms" or even freedom at all.[5] Some seek management and containment of social or state violence. At times, both a visionary freedom and an immediate emancipation are sought.

Advocacy abolitionism and its narratives by nonprisoners—like state narratives—grant only "emancipation." Neither advocacy abolitionism nor state abolitionism can control or create "freedom" for the captive. These terms cannot be fully explored here. Yet, we can note that despite the common assertion that "Lincoln 'freed' the slaves," the President issued proclamation and legislation to establish emancipated people. Emancipation is *given* by the dominant, it being a legal, contractual, and social agreement. Freedom is *taken* and created. It exists as a right against the captor and/or enslaver and a practice shared in community by the subordinate captives. (In fact, as W. E. B. DuBois notes in *Black Reconstruction*, some 200,000 African Americans fought in the Civil War—for emancipation *and* freedom.) Freedom is an ontological status—only the individual or collective—and perhaps a god—can create freedom.

Narratives by penal slaves seek and demand freedom (no matter for how limited a time, in what limited space).[6] However, penal captives or slaves conditioned by the state can see freedom and emancipation as one and the same. As a consequence, not all penal slave narratives offer new visions of freedom. Some yearn for emancipation (parole, clemency) but not *freedom* (liberation from racial, economic, gender repression) and the political agency and risk-taking that could realize it.

Racially fashioned enslavement shares similar features with racially fashioned incarceration. Plantations, historically, were penal sites—prisons for the exploitation of agricultural, domestic, and industrial labor and the dehumanization of beings.[7] Prison is the modern day manifestation of the plantation. The antebellum plantation ethos of dehumanization was marked by master-slave relations revolving about sexual terror and domination, beatings, regimentation of bodies, exploited labor, denial of religious and cultural practices, substandard food, health care, and housing, forced migration, isolation in "lockdown" for punishment and control, denial of birth family and kin. That ethos is routinely practiced and reinscribed in contemporary penal sites.[8] Physical, emotional, sexual, and economic exploitation and violence are visited upon bodies with equal abandon and lack of restraint in sites disappeared from conventional scrutiny. The old plantation was a prison; and the new prison is a plantation. Both reconfigure the (white) rural landscape, receiving and processing bodies forcibly transported, at times from "black" spaces into often culturally unfamiliar territory. In alien terrain, isolated captives witness and participate in a conditioning in which their civil or human rights are reduced to the rights of slaves.[9]

This discussion, by now, will have ignited old and heated arguments about the "legitimate" use of the term "slavery." Certainly, ambiguities exist concerning the definition of "slavery" in modern usage. Most likely the debates center on the deniability of contemporary enslavement—as a noncriminal or legal state enterprise—in a western, democratic nation-state. For example, Matthew Mancini argues in *One Dies, Get Another* that the convict prison lease system emerging in the late 1800s did not constitute slavery. While Orlando Patterson suggests in *Slavery and Social Death*—by his failure to mention the Thirteenth Amendment and to analyze U.S. penal slavery—that "slavery" is not terminology applicable to the post-emancipation United States.[10]

The political and ideological debates seem sharply drawn. However, despite the contributions of these and other noted scholars, the above three epigraphs were chosen to remind readers that the state through legal narratives, the academic through her scholarship, and the prisoner from his cell, all assert the presence of slavery in the United States as a post-emancipation reality. The state has explicitly identified the slave; its narratives, as a subset of (neo)slave narratives, both illuminate and obscure the racialized body of the slave and/or prisoner. According to the U.S. Constitution, "other persons" (racially fashioned without any racial marker in the text to designate them as "black" or African), and later, according to the Thirteenth Amendment, "other persons" (criminally fashioned again with no apparent racial referent) are designated real and potential slaves. I highlight the Thirteenth Amendment to argue this: *The state does not create legal categories in abstraction.* Legal narratives materialize and manifest in political practice(s). Within its possessions and territories, in the very act of (re)naming involuntary servitude, the United States recreated rather than actually abolished slavery.

Generally, most abolitionist discourse (excepting radical discourse) tends to avoid the debate over naming, and to focus on the rights of the incarcerated (or enslaved). Consequently, the important contributions of advocacy organizations such as Human Rights Watch, Amnesty International, and various policy and organizing groups, tend to emphasize the conditions of penalty and servitude (or slavery), not the ontological status of the servant (or slave). If the question of "slave" status is a critical one and not merely an exercise in semantics, then it might be that some types of abolitionism, just like the master-state narratives that they counter, seek less than freedom—the agency of the captive individual or community to chart their humanity through transforming and negating slavery and social death.[11]

Historically, legal discourse and institutions have manufactured illegal or criminal races as slaves. Laws maintained the plantation and reservation as penal camps, and fuel for labor in consumption for those designated as socially living and free. Democracy rooted in captivity and social parasitism meant that the civic body fed itself through the state's legal (criminal) apparatus and procurement and containment of racially fashioned bodies. Although master-state narrators maintained, for moral and political legitimacy, that it was they who suffered the presence of social parasites—the plague of criminal, antisocial savages poisoning the citizenry—still, in the frame of the nation-state, they became engorged. The state fed the master race (constructed by racial supremacy and propertied "free person" status) with the bodies and lands of its captives. The master race fed the state with the fruits of captive labor. Laws codified, regulated, and policed the exchange.

The official narratives of the nation-state itself—which were legally binding and enforceable—proved coercive and fashioned not only the language of (neo)slavery but slavery itself. The narratives reflect the languages of master, slave, and abolitionist. State, master, and slave in an interminable battle over freedom created the language of the fugitive or incarcerated rebel—the slave, the convict. The language of the illegal or criminalized in turn created the conditions for freedom not rooted in captivity.

Law mandated that to be socially alive, to be fully human and part of the civic body, required the marking of the white European body (of course gender, sexuality, and property would have significance as well). Hence it assisted and encouraged the European body (both individual and civic) by developing a relationship of social parasitism through genocidal anti-Indigenous wars and the African slave trade. The white civic body was strengthened by feeding off those designated as socially dead. The encoding of slavery or criminality onto blackness reflected a counterpart construction: the inscription of "whiteness" and nonincarceration as freedom and civility, hence as property or existential wealth.

The currency of white skin with its parasitical relationship to red, black, brown, and yellow skin would spark centuries of antiracist abolitionism. Perhaps it did and does so because racism is best expressed in the violence of penal culture; and the symbolic and real renderings of penology, as a form of [sur]reality, are shatteringly visceral. Penal culture inverts conventional reality to link the presence of torture and abuse to the law abiding civic body, "civil" and "civilized state." It thus places into question where to locate the "savage."

Abolitionists are heirs to their ancestors' strengths and limitations in combating violent captivity. It is impossible to survey here all of the significant and lengthy history of abolitionist discourse. Still, in order to place this anthology by contemporary imprisoned writers advocating and agitating for justice within a historical context, it is useful to review key state legal narratives that shaped both slave and abolitionist narratives.

Law and Master-State Narration

In an European settler colony, in 1661, the Virginia State Assembly became one of the first legislative bodies to equate enslavement with racial standing by legally coding enslavement as ethnicity/race: "Slave" would be synonymous with African/Black. At the time, there were indentured Europeans as well as indentured Africans and Native Americans; so, captivity was a penal designation applicable to all.

One century after the legal codification of slavery as racially driven, the new republic, triumphant in its war for freedom from its British colonial master, issued its guiding laws and principles: the Constitution of the

United States. That document would also codify the socially living and the socially dead, respectively as master (race) and enslaved (race). (White women of course would not garner the franchise until the 1920s and so existed in between both sites, masters of the enslaved race[s], subjects to their male counterparts.)

The Preamble of the U.S. Constitution sets the template for the construction of "we, the people" to be understood as white and propertied. In 1787, Article I, Section 2 of the Constitution establishes the political profit tied to enslavement. Curiously, what is so present in that document—the most famous issue of the founding fathers—is what is unspoken. There is the specter in the subtext; she appears in the disappearance of the words "black," "African," or "slave." No reference to races binary in construction, designated as nonbeing/noncitizen or being/citizen manifests in this document. Yet, without mentioning the phenotyped captive (one must acknowledge that reservations to warehouse and decimate indigenous peoples were also penal sites), race is everywhere:

> Representatives and direct Taxes shall be apportioned among the several States which may be included within this Union, according to their respective Numbers, which shall be determined by adding to the whole Number of free persons, including those bound to Service for a Term of Years, and excluding Indians not taxed, three fifths of all other Persons.

The Constitution's three-fifths clause demarcates social life from social death; thus it created a political opportunism to benefit electoral elites. Those barred from voting could still accrue political power for whites, increasing not only their congressional representation but also their electoral votes.[12] Ironically this would be revisited over a century after the formal abolition of chattel slavery. (For instance, the majority of prisons located in rural upstate New York house a considerable number of men and women shipped in from downstate or urban areas such as New York City; the state employs largely white prison guards and administrators to police largely black and brown bodies; largely conservative, white congressional representatives are elected in rural districts augmented by [re]apportionment expanded by the incarcerated who cannot vote while the urban congressional representation in prisoners' home districts in Harlem, Brooklyn, and the Bronx shrinks with their enforced absence and appropriation or theft of their electoral value.)

For the slave to attain civic identity and power required her to possess freedom. The republic mandated that freedom could not be obtained by virtue of any haven within its borders or act of autonomy by the captives. Linking the prisoner with the slave, Article IV, Section 2 of the Constitution stipulates that there is no "free" space or site for the prisoner or the slave; no place within the nation where the register of social death would be erased by the captive's volition:

> A Person charged in any State with Treason, Felony, or other Crime, who shall flee from justice, and be found in another State, shall on Demand of the executive Authority of the State from which he fled, be delivered up, to be removed to the State having Jurisdiction of the Crime.

> No Person held to Service or labour in one State, under the Laws thereof, escaping into another, shall, in Consequence of any Law or Regulation therein, be discharged from such Service or Labour, but shall be delivered up on Claim of the Party to whom such Service or Labour may be due.

Insurrectionists though would contest the absence of freedom (rejecting the possibility of manumission or purchasing themselves and family from their captors). In 1822, Denmark Vessey led a slave uprising followed in 1831 by the bloody revolt of Nat Turner. In 1857, the U.S. Supreme Court confirmed the absence of free space for blacks with its majority decision in the Dred Scott Case in which a former slave who had moved to free territory and who had lived as a free man returned voluntarily to slave territory only to lose his free status. Two years after the Supreme Court rendered its verdict on the fixed nature of blackness as property, white abolitionist militant John Brown[13] executed the 1859 raid on Harper's Ferry and was summarily executed by the state after forty days in prison. That armed rebellion, as did the earlier Dred Scott ruling, hastened war—apparently the only avenue to resolve the contestations over the disturbing presence of the socially dead amid the larger civic culture populated by those granted social life by the master-state.

In 1861, following the secession of southern states in the wake of the election of Republican Abraham Lincoln as the sixteenth President of the United States, the Civil War commenced. Two years later, President Lincoln issued the Emancipation Proclamation. This pronouncement was to abolish slavery; it garnered for Lincoln—who felt that African Americans had no social life to give to the nation and therefore should be "repatriated" to Africa or shipped to the Caribbean—the title of the so-called great emancipator. On September 22, 1862, Lincoln gave the following declaration, as the 1863 Emancipation Proclamation:

> That on the 1st day of January, AD 1863, all persons held as
> slaves within any State or designated part of a State the people
> whereof shall then be in rebellion against the United States shall
> be then, thenceforward, and forever free; and the executive
> government of the United States, including the military and
> naval authority thereof, will recognize and maintain the free-
> dom of such persons and will do no act or acts to repress such
> persons, or any of them, in any efforts they may make for their
> actual freedom. . . .
>
> And I hereby enjoin upon the people so declared to be free
> to abstain from all violence, unless in necessary self-defense;
> and I recommend to them that, in all cases when allowed, they
> labor faithfully for reasonable wages.
>
> And I further declare and make known that such persons
> of suitable condition will be received into the armed service of
> the United States. . . .

Presidential cautiousness is evident in this abolitionist narrative. All
enslaved people of African descent are not "freed," only those in the territories or states in rebellion against the union. The President furthermore
pledges the use of the government's military force to ensure the "freedom"
of those seeking liberation in the recognized territories, and cautions
blacks to remain "law abiding"—that is, to continue in the work force and
to abstain from (political) violence except in the case of self-defense. Over
two hundred thousand African Americans would serve in the Civil War;
likely their armed status would have prevented any forcible repatriation
after the exhausting and bloody confrontation (a war preceded by the
written and oral narratives of nineteenth-century antebellum abolitionists
such as David Walker, Maria Stewart, Frederick Douglass, Sojourner
Truth, Harriet Tubman, Henry Lloyd Garrison, and John Brown).

Lincoln, the most venerated of the antislavery abolitionists, was assassinated two years after he issued the Emancipation Proclamation. Also that
year, Congress passed the Thirteenth Amendment to the U.S. Constitution;
thus, after two years of wrangling, it reinstated slavery which Lincoln
abolished. Ratified in 1865, the Thirteenth Amendment, Section 1
rebranded the captive: "Neither slavery nor involuntary servitude, except
as a punishment for crime whereof the party shall have been duly convicted, shall exist within the United States, or any place subject to their
jurisdiction." Now, slavery would operate in a restricted fashion. Congress
resurrected social death as a permanent legal category in U.S. life, yet no
longer registered the socially dead with the traditional racial markings.
Breaking with a two hundred-year-old tradition, the government ostensibly

permitted the enslavement of nonblacks. Now not the ontological status of "nigger" but the ontological status of "criminal" renders one a slave. Yet, as became apparent in the convict prison lease system, blackness remained the signifier of social death, although now all those relegated to prisons would be imbued with that pariah race status. Law mandated the transition from chattel slavery to penal slavery, from personal property to "public" property owned by the state (and leased to corporate interests). In doing so, it established new obstacles and challenges for abolitionism.

Constitutional amendments during and following the Civil War, a war ostensibly to resolve institutional captivity, provide a mixture of abolitionist victory and venality, of euphoria and despair. Three years after the passage of the Thirteenth Amendment, the Fourteenth Amendment's Section 1 amplified the parameters of freedom: "No state shall make or enforce any law which shall abridge the privileges or immunities of citizens of the United States; nor shall any state deprive any person of life, liberty, or property, without due process of law; nor deny to any person within its jurisdiction the equal protection of the laws." Yet, contemporary abolitionists recognize that judicial rulings do not allow prisoners full or equal protection under the Fourteenth Amendment.

The Fifteenth Amendment (1870), Section 1 expands the franchise: "The right of citizens of the United States to vote shall not be denied or abridged by the United States or by any state on account of race, color, or previous condition of servitude." Yet, in 1877, federal enforcement was rendered null and void in the Hayes Compromise to secure electoral votes and the presidency of Rutherford Hayes: Social slavery would remain intact and the radical experiment of Reconstruction for a nonapartheid democracy would end. Of the postbellum years, W. E. B. Du Bois's *Black Reconstruction* notes the Hayes Compromise and federal complicity (reminiscent of the compromise reached in the 1787 Philadelphia convention); that compromise promoted the rise of racial terror through the Ku Klux Klan (KKK), an aristocratic invention, romanticized in D.W. Griffith's *Birth of a Nation*, aligning poorer whites with the economic interests of the plantocracy. The government and its deputized civil society, enforced the institutionalization of Black Codes (formerly Slave Codes) to recreate dead bodies—those denied political electoral power, and those bodies subjected to ritualized and routinized violence.[14]

Following the end of Reconstruction and large scale black (male) voter disenfranchisement, began the massive growth of the convict prison lease system. In that system, primarily blacks, arrested in "sweeps" of streets and communities, were worked to death in mining, agriculture, and forestry in joint ventures between the state and private industry, essentially, dying at higher rates than they had during enslavement on plantations.

Coexisting with the convict prison lease system was the racial-sexual terror and policing of lynchings (largely to prevent black political and economic gains) that dominated the land from 1880s to 1920s.[15] Although reform movements were initiated, they were met largely with general indifference by the general society and by Congress (which refused to pass any anti-lynching legislation).

Apparently, terror directed against the captive (black body) appeared as "routine." Normalization of terror and the invisibility of racially fashioned bodies rendered state and master social violence key obstacles for abolitionists searching for narratives to expose the dehumanizing continuation of enslavement in the "post-slavery" era. The narratives of the prisoners themselves would mark and reveal the continuation of violence and degradation and the arguments that legitimized captivity and abuse. Although reform and penitence were ideological and moral motivations for early penitentiary life, the mass introduction of the "slave" body into prisons following the legislative "abolition" of slavery, altered the "reformatory" aspects of incarceration.

Insurgency: Prison-Slave Narratives and the New Abolitionists

John Edgar Wideman's introduction to Mumia Abu-Jamal's *Live from Death Row*[16] cautions the reader and seeks to protect the imprisoned author by demystifying the "reading" of former Black Panther Abu-Jamal as spectacle and entertainment.[17] In his introduction, Wideman argues that many Americans encounter the trials and trauma of black life and political struggles through the "(neo)slave narrative." Here he limits the definition of (neo)slave narrative to that authored only by the captive black woman or man. Traceable to the nineteenth century, this particular narrative is marked by key characteristics connected to enslavement, abolitionism, and consumerism. It is marketed through literature accessible to and desired by (curious or moral) readers. In addition, according to Wideman, such (neo)slave narratives identify fixed sites of freedom and enslavement. They juxtapose the southern plantation with the northern city in the "free" or nonslave state. In these narratives, the triumphal slave must engage in flight—from captivity, penal or plantation misery—in order to triumph through an exchange of social death for civil life. Coded as "north vs. south," this assertion of identifiable sites of freedom and democracy suggests a continual path of warfare or flight. (Neo)Slave narratives can provide illusory landscapes. Romantic evasions assume that the duality is real; that there is a "free zone" in a democratic slave state, that the "north" as haven in fact exists.[18]

In the prison narrative, the successful escape or emancipation and liberation manifest as physical and metaphysical fleeing from the penal site through parole, exoneration, disappearance into fugitive status, or abolitionism. In conventional (neo)slave narratives, or a subcategory, prison narratives, the state, despite its abusive excesses, provides the possibility of emancipation and redemption.[19] According to such narratives, the state cannot therefore be considered or constructed as inherently and completely corrupt; for the state enables and maintains the sites of freedom (open society), as well as those of enslavement (prison). As the sympathetic reader lives vicariously through the dangerous risk-taking that typifies the life of slave-as-prison-rebel and fugitive, these narratives reassure her of reconciliation with prevailing power structures that allow for or provide emancipation and democratic culture. These structures then must be maintained if not revered despite the "dead zones" within which democracy is made incompatible with the life of specific subcultures. The dead zones, such as the penal site, the immigrant detention center, the military camp, the police station, the foreign prison in Cuba or Iraq or Afghanistan—all deny the possibility of "new life" or rebirth. All are manifestations of institutional and rational and irrational violence; all are anti-democratic.

Although terror functions as entertainment, disciplinary performance, and incitement to abolitionist activity, some abolitionist texts fail to record or comprehend such terror inflicted on racially marked bodies and thus erase racist violence. Yet any narrator not (racially) blinded recognizes the body in penal sites, sees its trauma and scarring.[20] The visual sparks reform and revolution—lynchings of personal friends mobilized Ida B. Wells in 1892 to initiate abolitionism. In 1955, months before Rosa Parks sat down and would not voluntarily rise, the Mississippi lynching of fourteen-year-old Emmett Till ignited the Civil Rights movement, not only because he was murdered but because his mutilated corpse was viewed in an open casket in a Chicago funeral that drew thousands; and the image of that tortured body was disseminated to tens of thousands through photographs published in the black magazine *Jet*.[21] Whether expressed in the popular nineteenth- and twentieth-century black-and-white paper postcards depicting lynchings of blacks by whites, as preserved in the exhibit "Without Sanctuary,"[22] or illustrated in the twenty-first century color digital postcards depicting the torture and rape of Iraqi prisoners by their U.S. captors, the violent (racial-sexual) dehumanization and dismemberment of the captive have proven how memorable terror and sexual violence are.[23] This suggests that textual (neo)slave narratives have been buttressed (and may at times be supplanted in their evocative power to affect civil society and mobilize resistance) by visual or pictorial (neo)slave narratives.

Prison narratives as (neo)slave narratives represent border crossings; just as did Charon,[24] they ferry the dead and the living. The lingua franca of (neo)slave narratives is all discourse that posits distinct worlds: that of criminal and civil, that of outlaw and law abiding, that of slave and freeman or freewoman.

Rhetoric instructs that there are contained sites of nonfreedom and freedom. Yet, enslavement is manufactured in the "free" world; "freedom" is imagined and created in the slave world. When the two worlds meet, as they do incessantly and creatively and violently, there is a border crossing, an intermingling of subordinate and dominant narratives. In narratives—of the master race, the state, the slave, the prisoner, the abolitionist, the advocate—redemption and safety continue to appear as a variation of prison success stories tied to "rehabilitation" rather than to rebellion. For instance, in contemporary parole hearings for self-identified political prisoners, supporters are asked to "tone down" their political rhetoric, to emphasize that the individual on trial or up for parole poses no "threat" to general society; and that their contributions to "social service" were exemplary.[25] Advocates are asked to make their letters for clemency and parole abolitionist texts that harmonize with master-state (neo)slave narratives.

Contemporary insurrectionist penal-slave narratives, such as Abu-Jamal's *Live from Death Row* or Assata Shakur's *Assata: An Autobiography*, can question the very premise of rehabilitation, indicting the state and society, contexualizing or dismissing individual acts of criminality by nonelites, the poor and racialized, to emphasize state criminality or the crimes of elites. Some prison narratives issue calls for dissent for a greater democracy. Dual narratives—those of the petitioners and those of the antagonists to state authority—shape political discourse. The narratives are in dialogue. As they debate with each other, they are differently weighted—some abolitionist (neo)slave narratives are considered more "respectable" and more "valued." Yet, when they emanate from the site of the noncitizen, from men and women in cages, regardless of their outlaw and disreputable status, they illuminate past, present, and future possibilities for the reinvention of democracy.

Contemporary Policing and Political Repression

Through their narratives, imprisoned writers can function as progressive abolitionists and register as "people's historians." They become the storytellers of the political histories of the captives *and* their captors. These narratives are generally the "unauthorized" versions of political life, often focusing on dissent and policing and repression. The more contemporary political activists represented in this volume have intimately interwoven their own autobiographical resistance and subsequent capture into their (neo)slave narratives.

Those currently incarcerated were largely politicized either in pacifist activism during World War II, or more recently in the 1960s and the following decades marked by political dissent and unrest. In the 1960s, in response to radical and progressive social movements, the "law and order" rhetoric and campaigns fed the contemporary imprisonment crisis fueled by resistance and backlash to the turbulent decades of protest against the prevailing order. A rapid review of that history will be useful to situate some of the essays and chapters that follow and help us to better understand the writing of incarcerated radicals.

The year of 1963 proved to be a pivotal one. Martin Luther King Jr.'s "Letter from Birmingham Jail"[26] and the triumph of the March on Washington transformed civil rights "troublemakers" and "criminals" into respectable citizens seeking to contribute to a democratic culture. Turmoil and tragedy ensued throughout the year which witnessed: the murder of civil rights leader Medgar Evers; the bombing of a black church in Birmingham, Alabama, which resulted in the deaths of four girls; and the assassination of President John F. Kennedy. President Lyndon Johnson used the national mourning for Kennedy to shepherd civil rights legislation through Congress, ostensibly to abolish the social death of blacks. In 1964, the Voting Rights Act was passed as another emancipatory gesture, part of the state's expanding abolitionist narrative. Yet riots followed in urban communities. That year, GOP (Grand Old Party) presidential candidate Senator Barry Goldwater (R-Arizona), who influenced Richard Nixon's and Ronald Reagan's positions on policing and imprisonment, stated in his acceptance speech at the Republican National Convention: "Security from domestic violence, no less than from foreign aggression, is the most elementary form and fundamental purpose of any government."

By 1966, segregation abolitionism in the Civil Rights movement was being replaced in popular culture by the militancy of younger antiracists in the Student Nonviolent Coordinating Committee and the Black Panther Party. FBI Director J. Edgar Hoover's 1966 Memorandum on COINTELPRO established the parameters for social and political containment, reserving the harshest punishment for rebels who militantly resisted social death: "The purpose of this new counterintelligence endeavor is to expose, disrupt, misdirect, discredit, or otherwise neutralize the activities of black nationalist organizations and groupings, their leadership, spokesmen, membership, and supporters." Hoover's fear that the militancy of black emancipators would "infect" white America was also shared by elected officials.[27] In 1968, the assassination of Robert Kennedy during his presidential campaign was followed several months later by the assassination of Martin Luther King Jr. In the wake of those killings, with a national heightened sense of fear and uncertainty, Congress passed and President Lyndon Johnson signed the "Omnibus Crime and Safe Streets Act." This act led to the Law Enforcement Assistance Administration and created SWAT (Special Weapons and Tactics) teams, setting the stage for Richard Nixon's "law and order" campaigns.

In the 1980s, during the administrations of Ronald Reagan and his former vice president George Bush, the war on drugs,[28] contra wars, and "constructive engagement" with apartheid along with the funding of contra or counterrevolutionary terrorists-insurgents in Latin America and Africa would be normative. These domestic and foreign policies would lead to a growth of both social and political prisoners.[29] The former were/are largely incarcerated for crimes tied to drug use or sale (and poverty); the latter were/are incarcerated for their rebellion against U.S. domestic and foreign policies.[30] In the 1990s, prisons saw an exponential growth in incarceration, largely from drug sale and consumption. During the Clinton administration, the 1996 "Anti-Terrorism and Effective Death Penalty Act" broadened the use of the death penalty and diminished federal habeas corpus; and the 1996 "Immigration Reform and Immigrant Responsibility Act" abolished due process for undocumented persons.[31] Both laws were passed the year after the Oklahoma City Bombing.

The diminishment of free acts—acts that can be engaged in without fear of surveillance or reprisal—signals the shrinkage of free democratic space. The penal state grows not because of the proliferation of prisons per se, but because "free" space diminishes or disappears. Part of this diminishment stems from legislation. The state shrinks, and alternatively can expand, democratic space through its criminal/civil codes. Currently, it has chosen shrinkage as evidenced in the passage of legislation such as the 1996 Omnibus Crime Bill and the 2001 USA Patriot Act.

Despite increasing police powers, and prison, police, and military violence, the narratives and agency of imprisoned political dissidents continue to redefine and revitalize struggles for a greater democracy. In movements influenced by prisoners, gays/lesbians, feminists, antiracists, and peace activists express insurgent desire and discourse; whether pacifist or militarist, they have refashioned (neo)slave narratives. Out of antiwar and social justice movements, insurgency has produced and will continue to produce imprisoned abolitionists and political icons.

However, the state continues to provide the midwifery to rebirth disenfranchisement despite the civil, human rights, and liberation movements of the twentieth century. The status of felon is used to strip tens of thousands of people (from mostly poor or black and brown communities) of the vote. In the 2000 Presidential election, Florida voters, overwhelmingly registered with the Democratic Party, in low-income, high-minority districts were over three times more likely to have their votes discarded than voters in high-income, low-minority districts; and voters in some low-income, high-minority districts were twenty times more likely to have their votes discarded than voters in other districts.[32] In 2004, similar controversy emerged concerning Ohio. Yet to focus on Florida or Ohio and the role of the Republican Party in the disenfranchisement of black voters would miss a crucial point: *Both national parties, Republican and Democrat, routinely undercount African American votes nationwide, jettisoning some one in seven according to a 2004 study.*[33] Hence "voting while black/brown" suggests a rupture with the civic body—some form of nonbeing interjected into restrictive democratic processes. That is, the black body shares a proximity of positionality with the felon/prisoner—that of the suspect or noncitizen. Consequently, contemporary radical penal narratives as (neo)slave narratives denounce the State for manufacturing slavery on both sides of prison walls.

Conclusion

In previous centuries, forging a new language, the modern antislavery movement marked a significant awakening of the public moral conscience in the Western world. In this century, antiprison movements offer the same possibilities: to struggle by dismantling mechanisms of incarceration and dehumanization.

These writings by prisoner-abolitionists (some identify as "slaves," all as former or current captives) focus on the captured rebel, visionary or insurrectionist. New abolitionists shape and contest (neo)slave narratives, and penal democracy. Their projects suggest that in America, as in its Athenian progenitor, there is no free space, as we know it, without penal or slave space, as we fear it.

The New Abolitionists' chapters are organized into four sections interconnecting issues of activism, gender, resistance, dialogue. The narratives presented here depict progressive politics. At times, social inequality is reproduced in this volume through an author's language of class, sexual, or ethnic chauvinism. Yet these pieces reflect humanity struggling to reinvent and assert itself. Such writings and narratives reveal social life amid social death with the urgency and power of the political speech of prisoner and fugitive abolitionists representing historical and contemporary struggles. Often referencing a political present inextricably linked to the past, captives frame a future for abolitionism, emancipation, and freedom.

Joy James

Notes

1. Infused as they are with economic and ethnic-racial bias, the massive incarceration and detention apparatuses constitute a crisis in contemporary American democracy. In critiques of the incarceration industry, what is reasonably contested is not the responsibility and need to contain people to prevent them from harming themselves or others; what is contested is containment fashioned as enslavement and policing and imprisonment shaped by racial and economic status rather than by criminal or criminalized acts.

The most disturbing features of contemporary incarceration are its abuses of humanity and its racially and economically driven punitive characteristics. Poor people comprise the majority of those imprisoned and on death row. Some 70 percent of the more than 2 million incarcerated in U.S. prisons, jails, and detention centers are African American, Latino, Native American, and Asian; approximately 1 million or 50 percent of the incarcerated are African American. The racially driven features of punishment, detention, and imprisonment are documented. The Sentencing Project has noted disparity in sentencing in which blacks convicted of the same crimes as whites are much more likely to be sent to prison. The American Bar Association has advocated a moratorium on executions citing the rampant racial bias in determining death sentences given that the race of both defendant and victim is the primary factor in capital punishment. Those convicted of killing a white person are significantly more likely to receive the death penalty, particularly if they are not white themselves. The abysmal living conditions and treatment of detained immigrants in camps in the United States and "unlawful combatants" at Guantánamo Bay have led to hunger strikes, riots, or attempted suicides. See Joseph Lelyveld, "In Guantánamo," *New York Review of Books*, November 7, 2002.

See The Bureau of Justice Statistics Website (through the Department of Justice) which contains statistics on the U.S. prison/jail system, www.ojp.usdoj/bjs/. Also see, Jerome G. Miller, *Search and Destroy: African American Males in the Criminal Justice System* (New York: Cambridge University Press, 1996); Terry Kupers, *Prison Madness: The Mental Health Crisis Behind Bars and What We Must Do about It* (Indianapolis, IN: Jossey-Bass, 1999); Marc Mauer, *The Race to Incarcerate* (New York: The New Press, 2000).

2. The ways in which (neo)slave narratives are written and spoken by African Americans deserves more careful scrutiny than can be provided here. However, we can note how black Americans reinvigorate old language concerning captivity. For instance, African American families and friends visiting their incarcerated relatives have been known to refer to black guards as "Uncle Toms." And abolitionists in civil society who have married prisoners create new narratives that conflate their experiences as synonymous with those of prisoners and prison rebels.

For an example of the coupling of narratives and the resulting erasure of difference between the captive insurgent abolitionist and the "free" abolitionist, to the enhanced standing of the latter, consider several questions the Washington Square Reader's Club Guide poses at the end of Asha Bandele's *The Prisoner's Wife*: "14. *The Prisoner's Wife* features allusions to *Soledad Brother*, George Jackson's seminal portrait of the struggles, politics, and intricacies of prison life. How has Jackson's book—the work of a brave and embattled man—influenced our culture's perceptions of political imprisonment, racism, and the United States justice system?"; and, "15. In what ways can we view *The Prisoner's Wife*—the work of an equally brave and similarly embattled black woman—as a useful, even indispensable, counterpoint (and complement) to the messages in Jackson's *Soledad Brother?*" See Asha Bandele, *The Prisoner's Wife* (New York: Scribner, 1999).

Bandele's memoir is deployed to refashion the abolitionism of the imprisoned insurrectionist into the liberation narrative of the "free" abolitionist. A quote, taken from *Blood in My Eye* and circulated among radical abolitionists, by George Jackson, a militarist who when killed by guards also had witnessed/participated in the killings of his captors, posits no such compatibility: "If one were forced for the sake of clarity to define [fascism] in a word simple enough for all to understand, that word would be 'reform.'"

3. (Neo)Slave narratives can seek to expand or expel freedom; only those that seek to diminish or destroy slavery are abolitionist. Abolitionist discourse can also refashion shackles as in the Thirteenth Amendment to the U.S. Constitution, which abolished slavery during the Civil War only to legalize it today.

4. See George Jackson, *Soledad Brother: The Prison Letters of George Jackson* (New York: Coward-McCann, 1970; repr., Chicago: Lawrence Hill, 1994); and *Blood in My Eye* (New York: Random House, 1972; repr., Baltimore: Black Classic Press, 1990).

5. In some abolitionist texts, what is sought is not "freedom" per se, because the master-state will not or cannot offer that. It cannot provide what it does not possess. What the master-state grants, and often what the incarcerated acquiesce to, is emancipation. Yet this emancipation cannot fulfill the conditions for a decent life or livelihood.

Consider that in referring to the California Youth Authority, MSW candidates in California universities speak disquietingly about the "emancipation" of children who are wards of the state, in the foster care system (also a prison, according to some who were warehoused there during their youth). One is "emancipated" when one reaches the age of eighteen. Emancipation suggests that prior to that moment, children were in bondage, housed in private or group homes. Upon emancipation, technically no longer on the rolls to have their actions directly dictated, that is, no longer the direct property of the state, they are "free." Essentially at the age of eighteen, whether or not they have matriculated from high school (such students would disproportionately not graduate by age eighteen having had their schooling delayed because of frequent moves, familial disruption, and childhood trauma), formerly captive children, now free adults, are put out—without housing, without advanced schooling, and with no income. As in 1865, slaves would ask, emancipated for what end—subsistence, starvation, or entry into the illegal, underground economy?

6. A study of maroon societies in the United States—e.g., the Seminoles—an amalgamation of indigenous peoples and runaway African slaves, the only entity to defeat the U.S. army on its own soil—the Americas, or the Haitian revolution illustrates the sporadic appearances of freedom struggles. See C. L. R. James, *The Black*

Jacobins (New York: Vintage Books, 1963); and Sibylle Fischer, *Modernity Disavowed: Haiti and the Cultures of Slavery in the Age of Revolution* (Durham: Duke University Press, 2004).

7. Rather than conflate "penal" and "carceral," some scholars coin the term "punitive carceral(ity)," drawing from Foucault in order to foreground the distinction between "punishment" and "incarceration." I find this distinction to be somewhat unnecessary. The United States has rendered the two as synonymous for racialized bodies on or in plantations, reservations, prisons. When the quest for rehabilitation, for the individual as opposed to the collective body, became severed from incarceration, incarceration became reduced to punishment. Incarceration is used as a form of punishment, although the "common sense" language of the United States denies a critical recognition of this in relation to its histories of enslavement, mass imprisonment, and genocide.

8. Robert Jay Lifton, referencing the abuses in Iraqi prisons committed by U.S. personnel, describes warfare and military prisons as an "atrocity producing situation." Atrocity producing situations exist in ordinary civilian prisons and in military prisons. See Robert Jay Lifton, "Mental Aspects of Abuse and War," interview, *Weekend Edition*, National Public Radio, WBUR–Boston, May 9, 2004.

9. Some 40 percent of the nation's prisons are housed in rural areas. Given draconian drug laws, such as the Rockefeller Drug Laws, many prisoners from urban areas serve long prison terms in remote areas that are highly inaccessible to low-income families without private transportation.

10. See Matthew Mancini, *One Dies, Get Another: Convict Leasing in the American South, 1866–1928* (Columbia: University of South Carolina Press, 1996); and Orlando Patterson, *Slavery and Social Death* (Cambridge, MA: Harvard University Press, 1982).

11. Saidiya Hartman argues that emancipation enabled new forms of subjection, and that rather than providing a departure, putative black "freedom" structured a profound and oppressive violence, one seamlessly linked with slavery. See Saidiya Hartman, *Scenes of Subjection* (New York: Oxford University Press, 1997).

12. Political scientist John Aldrich has noted that the 1800 presidential contest between Thomas Jefferson and John Adams, which was determined, as all U.S. presidential elections are, by the electoral college, would have likely been settled in favor of the latter, the loser, if the three-fifths clause were not law.

13. The impact of the abolitionist John Brown, although erased or vilified in conventional memory, would spark continued abolitionist struggle, ranging from the song "John Brown is moldering in his grave . . ." sung by Union soldiers, a song which would later become "The Battle Hymn of the Republic" (and later still, "Solidarity Forever" written in a prison cell by Joe Hill, the labor activist and socialist), to twentieth-century white antiracist/imperialist revolutionaries such as the John Brown/Anti-Klan network of former and current political prisoners such as Linda Evans, Laura Whitehorn, David Gilbert, and Marilyn Buck.

14. See: W. E. B. Du Bois, *Black Reconstruction* (Millwood, NY: Kraus-Thomson Organization, Ltd., 1976); Matthew Mancini, *One Dies, Get Another: Convict Leasing in the American South, 1866–1928*.

15. In 1892, Ida B. Wells published *Southern Horrors* (New York: Arno Press, 1969, repr.). Wells organized antilynching crusades and a British boycott against southern cotton and joined W. E. B. Du Bois in the founding of the National Association for the Advancement of Colored People (NAACP) in 1909–1910. Lynching abolitionists and turn-of-the century activists such as Ida B. Wells and Mary Church Terrell foreshadowed women's leadership in contemporary prison abolitionism.

16. See Mumia Abu-Jamal, *Live from Death Row: This Is Mumia Abu-Jamal* (New York: Avon, 1995).

17. An award-winning journalist, Mumia Abu-Jamal began writing at age fifteen as Lieutenant Minister of Information for the Philadelphia branch of the Black Panther Party. Mumia Abu-Jamal has been incarcerated for over twenty years for a crime for which he maintains his innocence, that of killing a (white) policeman. In 2003, he was declared a Citizen of Paris, an award the city last bestowed in 1971 upon Pablo Picasso.

A May 14, 2004 press release from South End Press, the publisher of Mumia Abu-Jamal's latest work *We Want Freedom: A Life in the Black Panther Party* (Boston: South End Press, 2004), noted prison censorship of their publication. According to the Press, on April 20, 2004, *We Want Freedom* was confiscated by the Security Threat Group Coordinator of the Indiana Department of Correction in Pendleton, Indiana, when a prison official refused its delivery to Zolo Agona Azania, a political activist on death row. South End reports that:

> According to State Form 11984 the book was confiscated in accordance with executive directive 9625 and specifically cited "'The Empire Strikes Back: COINTELPRO,' Chapter Six, page #117" as the reason.
>
> The page in question begins with a quotation from Hugo Black, Associate Justice of the U.S. Supreme Court, which reads, "History should teach us . . . that in times of high emotional excitement, minority parties and groups which advocate extremely unpopular social or governmental innovations will always be typed as criminal gangs and attempts will always be made to drive them out."
>
> . . . Mr. Abu-Jamal challenges historians who claim that only the civil rights model was authentic, positioning the BPP as an ahistorical aberration. . . . He brilliantly locates the Party in a centuries-long tradition of Black resistance, a legacy articulated in Kathleen Cleaver's sharp introduction as a "disfavored history." . . . [one] of resistance to slavery, racial politics in Philadelphia, and the FBI's subversion of justice through COINTELPRO. . . ."

Also see John Edgar Wideman's introduction to *Live from Death Row*; and Joy James, "NeoSlave Narratives and Revolutionary Icons," *Shadowboxing: Representations of Black Feminist Politics* (New York: St. Martin's, 1999).

18. This illusion justifies the forcible "democratization" of other peoples and cultures and nations. Historically the democratic enterprise waged by the United States has meant the concentration of economic wealth and property, the exprop

ation of the material wealth and cultural-political autonomy of those indigenous and African peoples initiated into the "free" world, and the phantasm of civilizing missions which made profitable the discourse of slave trades.

19. Of course, the exception in historical slave narratives would be the Dred Scott case and the Supreme Court ruling that occasioned a mass exodus of black Americans to Canada and elsewhere.

20. The language of academic abolitionists varies in its political intent. Consider only a small selection of Michel Foucault's work: *Discipline and Punish* and the "Attica Interview" (John K. Simon, "Michel Foucault on Attica: An Interview," *Telos,* No. 19 [1974]: 154–61). Elsewhere, I have critiqued the erasure of racial violence, torture, and terror in *Discipline and Punish*. (See Joy James, "Erasing the Spectacle of Racialized Violence," *Resisting State Violence* [Minneapolis: University of Minnesota Press, 1996].) Here, it is sufficient to briefly note that in the interview conducted in 1972, during his tour of Attica, the site of the prison rebellion brutally repressed by then Governor Nelson Rockefeller and the National Guard, Foucault does not once mention the men who rebelled in Attica and who were killed there. He stands in a graveyard and derisively likens the architecture to "Disneyland" but mentions no agency of the insurrectionists, some thirty-nine men, who died there. The erasure of the specificity of black/brown bodies and the risky abolitionist gestures and revolutionary moves for which they were slaughtered is disturbing.

Equally problematic is Foucault's indifference to the state's investment in criminality. Foucault in this interview asserts that crime is a *"coup d'etat* from below" and hence has a "proto-revolutionary" function. Yet, the largest criminals are from "above"—in terms of property theft (white collar crime), drug trafficking (laundering is the most profitable; growers and street dealers garner only a fraction of the take), and organized violence. When the *coup d'etat* from below meets the *coup d'etat* from above one finds the intermix of democracy and captivity. A cursory study of the Bureau of Indian Affairs reveals the structural or state nature of institutional theft and the nation-state as criminal enterprise. It in fact reveals that organized crime and the state have been working together for decades—the state is manifestation of organized criminality.

21. See *Jet,* September 15, 1955.

22. See James Allen, ed., *Without Sanctuary: Lynching Photography in Amer-*'anta Fe, NM: Twin Palms Publishers, 2000).

3. Lynchings, with the racial-sexual terror that accompanies them, are war-
are prisons. Both represent the ultimate spectacles for physical and sexual
onsider for example: the lynching parties that drew thousands in which
\k body parts home for souvenirs; the parading of nude Black Panthers
\ting between police and BPP; the posing of nude Iraqi prisoners in Abu
n. Iraqis have also lynched their occupiers—literally dismembered and
burned bodies, but apparently without the emphasis on the sexual
\ographic. Also, photos have displayed Iraqi boys and young men
arel/possessions of dead U.S. soldiers killed in a Humvee for

24. In Greek mythology, Hermes brings Charon, the ferryman of the dead, the souls of the deceased, and Charon ferries them across the river Acheron.

25. Protesting at the Republican National Convention in Philadelphia in 2000, Camilo Viveiros, a Portuguese organizer with the Massachusetts Alliance of HUD (Department of Housing and Urban Development) Tenants, was arrested for allegedly striking Philadelphia Police Commissioner John Timoney with a bicycle. Of the 420 protestors arrested along with Viveiros, over 95 percent had their charges dismissed for lack of evidence or were acquitted shortly after the arrests. In April 2004, Viveiros, Eric Steinberg, and Darby Landy (known popularly as the "Timoney Three"), were the only three protestors left facing charges. Viveiros, who was being tried on three felony charges and four misdemeanors, faced up to forty years in jail and $55,000 in fines. Activists who rallied around Viveiros's case formed "Friends of Camilo," a group that distributed literature, organized events, and raised money in his support while consistently attesting to the state's unlawful silencing of legal dissent and Viveiros's "exemplary" character. On April 5, 2004, the first day of his trial, Judge William Mazzola exonerated Viveiros and his two codefendants due to inconsistencies in the prosecution's testimony and video footage that showed Viveiros did not resist arrest and was punched on the back of the head by an officer as he was handcuffed. See www.friendsofcamilo.org.

26. The 1950s and 1960s constituted the "second reconstruction," as liberals in Martin Luther King Jr.'s Southern Christian Leadership Conference (SCLC) would refer to it, and the "second civil war," as radicals or the "shock troops" of the Student Nonviolent Coordinating Committee (SNCC) would describe it. Historian Howard Zinn, a former mentor along with Ella Baker of SNCC, documented the important contributions of the young activists in the book *SNCC: The New Abolitionists* (Boston: South End Press, 2002, repr.).

Much of Southern activism centered on the right to vote. The Twenty-fourth Amendment to the U.S. Constitution promised the franchise and hence, theoretically, recognition of full citizenship with the mandate that made the poll tax or any tax as the precondition for voting illegal.

27. As reported in Eldridge Cleaver's obituary, California governor Ronald Reagan, responding to Black Panther Party leader (and former convict) Eldridge Cleaver's invitation to lecture at the University of California-Berkeley, warned: "If Eldridge Cleaver is allowed to teach our children, they may come home one night and slit our throats." See *New York Times*, May 2, 1998, B8.

28. In *Lockdown America*, Christian Parenti notes that during the Reagan administration's "war on drugs," prisons and police departments grew, along with poverty and cuts to grants for child nutrition, education, and urban development. The Federal Crime Bill of 1984 created assets forfeiture laws that enabled police departments to keep up to 90 percent of "drug tainted" property that they confiscated; police revenues from drug forfeiture laws grew from $100 million in 1981 to over $1 billion in 1987. The Anti-Drug-Abuse Act of 1986 created twenty-nine new mandatory minimum sentences and disparity in penalties for ("suburban") powder cocaine and ("urban") crack (100:1). The majority of powder and crack cocaine users are now white "suburbanites," yet the majority of those incarcer-

ated for drug offenses are African American or Latino. Four years later, a new federal crime bill would mandate a "one strike" policy in public housing and transfer counseling and drug rehabilitation to law enforcement. See Christian Parenti, *Lockdown America: Police and Prisons in the Age of Crisis* (New York: Verso, 1999).

29. For a discussion of "social prisoners," "political-econ" prisoners, and "political prisoners," see Joy James, ed., *Imprisoned Intellectuals: America's Political Prisoners Write on Life, Liberation, and Rebellion* (Lanham, MD: Rowman and Littlefield, 2003).

30. Punishment meted out to political prisoners or prisoners of conscience tended to be the most severe. See the Amnesty International reports on torture and sensory deprivation at the Lexington Control Unit for women, and at Marion Prison in Illinois for men. See Amnesty International USA, *Allegations of Mistreatment in Marion Prison, Illinois, U.S.A.*, AMR 51/26/87, May 1987.

31. See Parenti, *Lockdown America*.

Following the September 11, 2001 tragedies, Attorney General John Ashcroft issued directives for "lockdowns" of U.S. political prisoners. The 2001 USA Patriot Act passed later that year provided provisions that enable the government to: detain noncitizens indefinitely at the discretion of the Attorney General; conduct searches, seizures, and surveillance with reduced standards of cause and levels of judicial review; construe guilt by association.

32. See Minority Staff, Special Investigations Division, U.S. House of Representatives, "Income and Racial Disparities in the Undercount in the 2000 Presidential Election," July 9, 2001.

33. See Gregory Palast, "Vanishing Votes," *The Nation*, April 29, 2004.

I. Penal Democracy

1

Dachine Rainer and
Holley Cantine

Born on January 13, 1921, in New York City, Sylvia Newman's early political development was heavily influenced by the executions of anarchists Nicola Sacco and Bartolomeo Vanzetti.[1] By the 1930s, she was a self-declared anarchist and pacifist. She eventually took the *nom de plume* "Dachine Rainer," identifying with poet Rainer Maria Rilke's political and humanitarian views. Rainer studied English literature at Hunter College in 1938, and for the next twenty years she published articles and poems in periodicals such as *The Nation* and *New Republic*, and also published novellas and a novel: *Outside Time* (1948), *A Room at the Inn* (1958), and *The Uncomfortable Inn* (1960). In the 1950s, working with poet e. e. cummings, she formed the Committee for the Liberation of Ezra Pound to protest Pound's impending treason trial for vocally supporting Italian Fascism. In the early 1960s, Rainer moved to England taking British nationality in the 1970s. Dachine Rainer continued publishing political writings and poetry until her death in 2000.

Born in 1891, Holley Cantine, an anarchist and a short story writer, received multiple honors in 1960 for a science fiction short story, "Double Double Toil and Trouble" (1959). He translated Russian anarchist V. M. Eikhenbaum's (Volin) *The Unknown Revolution, 1917–1921* from French into English and, in 1961, published *Second Chance: A Story*. Together, Cantine and Rainer also coedited a quarterly magazine, *Retort*, from 1946 to 1960, and a newspaper, *The Wasp*. Both writers were held in federal prison as conscientious objectors during World War II.[2] From this experience the pair was inspired to edit *Prison Etiquette* (1950), a collection of writings by imprisoned conscientious objectors.

Notes

1. *Editor's note*: Italian anarchists Nicola Sacco and Bartolomeo Vanzetti were convicted, on July 14, 1921, of first-degree murder for their alleged involvement in a shoe factory robbery in South Braintree, Massachusetts, in April 1920. Their case drew international attention and support for the defendants. Despite numerous protests and appeals, Sacco and Vanzetti were

sentenced to death in August 1927, a sentence that was most likely the result of their political involvement and ideals. See Felix Frankfurter, "The Case of Sacco and Vanzetti," *Atlantic Monthly,* March 1927; Howard Zinn, *A People's History of the United States* (New York: Harper & Row, 1980).

2. *Editor's note: Prison Etiquette: The Convict's Compendium of Useful Information* was reprinted by Southern Illinois University Press (SIU) in 2001. According to SIU, Cantine and Rainer were imprisoned as "conscientious objectors" during World War II. See www.siu/edu/~siupress/titles/s01_titles/cantine_prison.html.

References

Cantine, Holley. *Second Chance: A Story*. Bearsville, NY: Retort Press, 1961.
———. "Double Double Toil and Trouble." *The Magazine of Fantasy and Science Fiction,* January 1960.
Rainer, Dachine. *Outside Time*. Bearsville, NY: Retort Press, 1948.
———. *The Uncomfortable Inn*. London: Abelard-Schuman, 1960.
——— and Holley Cantine, eds. *Prison Etiquette: The Convict's Compendium of Useful Information*. Bearsville, NY: Retort Press, 1950.
Volin. *The Unknown Revolution, 1917–1921*, trans. Holley Cantine. New York: Free Life Editions, 1974.

Prison Etiquette
1950

Prison Etiquette is "the convicts' compendium of useful information." We are publishing it neither because we want to reform the Prison System, nor merely to honor the valor and integrity of its contributors who, because of their convictions, spent up to three years in the Federal Penitentiaries of this country.

We are publishing *Prison Etiquette* in order to present the experiences of some of the several thousand Conscientious Objectors[1] to World War II. Many of them salvaged from their years of captivity ideas of immeasurable value to all of us who contemplate in the coming totalitarian days a continual warfare with the state—both in and out of its prisons.

Prison etiquette is a learned art for the radical. Its technique varies with country, time, and political set-up. These young men deal with a prison system that is unknown to us. We must be equipped to evade it, to survive in it if caught, to resist it in the psychologically most economical, and politically effective way. That is, we must learn to remain sane, to survive physically, and at the same time to continue resisting.

This book is not a commemorative exercise. It is a practical book that we have edited in a manner calculated to provide our reader with what may unfortunately become useful information.

II

There is one loss sustained in prison that transcends in poignancy the numerous comparatively trivial pains and material discomforts—it is the idea of being unfree. Imprisonment is a violation of the fundamental nature of human existence which is predicated on a certain amount of freedom of choice and movement. While obviously no such thing as total freedom can exist owing to the biological and intellectual limitations of man, man exists in the Prison in an almost total absence of free motion and choice.

These two qualities are meaningful only if both are present simultaneously. That is, if one can proceed from the idea to the act, or from the choice to the fulfillment. This is almost never the case in Prison. The arbitrary separation and curtailment of these two freedoms that define the individual is the essence of Imprisonment—the entire system is predicated on the conscious and systematic destruction of the Person. When the Prisoner is not under direct surveillance he is confined in a narrow space, and when he is allowed some freedom of motion, he is subjected to the strictest kind of regimentation.

When he is locked into his cell where he is allowed freedom to think, no acts may follow from that thinking that can affect either his Prison environment or the other prisoners—unless he disobeys Prison rules in some manner. When he moves about outside his cell it is under orders—in lines or in work detachments. This abrogation of the essence of the individual destroys not only each single person, but consequently, any possibility of community—except again, when Prison rules are disobeyed. For while the prisoner is Free to think, or perform a limited number of acts involving his own person—even suicide is made very difficult—he is allowed little, if any, interpersonal relationships. The individual prisoner lives either in a dormitory, where he has no privacy, or he lives in relative or absolute isolation, where he has little or no opportunity to communicate with anyone; these two situations can exist alternately for the same individual.

The effect of all this is to produce an intense egocentricity that is almost infantile. It is calculated to create a docile, easily controlled Prison population that is largely incapable of organizing resistance.

III

Prison is the only key political institution that is peculiar to the State form of society. Armies, courts, schools, legislative bodies exist, at least in embryo, in nearly all other social forms. But the Prison exists only in highly centralized systems. It is the most perfect expression of the full implications of Statism. In the Prison the population is subjected to the type of control that State functionaries aspire to impose on the population "at large." The Prison represents absolute freedom of coercion.

The stronger the State becomes, the more laws it passes and the more the area of potential lawbreaking is increased. Old-fashioned notions of guilt and innocence, crime and respectable behavior, become meaningless in the tangled web of the laws and regulations of a totalitarian State.

Everybody is guilty of innumerable offenses and escapes incarceration only through chance. While the United States has yet to achieve this degree of uniformity in the culpability of its population, it is moving in that direction, and many individuals who have little in common with the old concept of the professional criminal may find themselves in trouble with the authorities.

The old-fashioned radical, not unlike the professional criminal, lived in continual expectation of going to prison; if he had not done time on various occasions himself, he was sure to have acquaintances who had, and the experience, when it came, as it was almost certain to, was therefore neither unexpected nor entirely unprepared for, emotionally as well as intellectually. For the past few decades, however, except for those war resisters who spent time in Prison for refusing military service, the number who have been arrested, let alone imprisoned, has been comparatively small in this country. The reasons for this need not be gone into here, but it is obvious that this situation is changing rapidly and the luck of the radical seems about to take a sharp turn for the worse. Therefore, in order to fill at least partially the gap in experience and psychological preparation that was created during the New Deal honeymoon[2] between radicalism and the government, we feel that some current information on Prison conditions should be of considerable service to those who now face imprisonment for their ideas. The old-timers in the movement, while they unquestionably know a great deal about Prison conditions of twenty or more years ago, are probably not so familiar with the current situation, and the younger generation, for the most part, has neither first nor second-hand knowledge of it.

IV

One thing we are not trying to accomplish is Prison reform. The existing Prison system in the United States is, in many ways, the most thoroughly reformed in the world as it is, but we have never heard of anyone whose stay in it was greatly alleviated on this account.[3]

Reforming an institution like Prison is only possible on the most superficial level, and its importance to the individual prisoner is highly questionable. The fact of incarceration is the one thing that can never be removed by reform; that is, the fact that one is confined to a place in which he would much rather not be, and beside this such considerations as food, cleanliness, recreation, etcetera—provided they do not sink to the level where survival itself is endangered—are of distinctly secondary importance.

It may even be harder, for psychological reasons, to endure the new sort of "honor system" Prison, in which the prisoner is made to feel personally responsible for his own captivity, than the old, frankly autocratic and brutally coercive type of institution. Giving the inmates a greater say about how their lives are to be run in Prison is at best hypocrisy, inasmuch as none of them would be there at all if they could help it; and at worst, the sort of horror that existed in the Nazi concentration camps, where nearly all custodial functions were performed by inmates (under supervision of course) with consequences, in terms of brutalization and degradation, that surpass anything in the history of the Prison.

Agitation for Prison reform is a thoroughly futile activity since Prisons never stay reformed. Russian and German Prisons under the relative utopias of the Czar and Kaiser,[4] respectively, provided—at least for their political prisoners—a reasonably comfortable existence, in which it was possible to devote considerable time to study. At this time—that is, prior to and during World War I—conditions for political prisoners in American Prisons were worse than for criminals and among the worst in the world. Living conditions were intolerable, and beatings were common. In the space of a generation the situations have been reversed; conditions in American Prisons have been greatly ameliorated;[5] and everyone knows about the Nazi German and Soviet Russian concentration camps.[6]

V

The contributors to this volume were political prisoners but our opposition to imprisonment extends not merely to their imprisonment, but to the whole concept of the Prison. Imprisonment is gratuitous punishment: except for the liberal penologist—there is no one, neither Prisoner nor guard, who would testify to its rehabilitating effects. Prison fails to discourage "crime"; it insures its increase. Moreover, a great deal of what is considered punishable as "crime" does not deserve to be punished or even discouraged. Obviously it is a clear violation of the most elementary concept of civil liberties to punish people for holding an opinion, no matter how contrary it is to the generally accepted one. But apart from this, and apart from the fact that many individuals are arrested for offenses they never committed—but in order that some cop meet his quota of arrests, and are convicted in order that some Prosecuting Attorney meet his quota of convictions—how much of what is generally considered to be crime is so because of arbitrary definition?

One might agree that it is wrong to imprison people for their ideas, and certainly wrong to imprison them in frame-ups, but might feel the need to put away the "aggressors against society." What constitutes an aggression against society? Is it theft, murder, assault, rape, arson? But is there ever any more arson committed than in the bombing of a city; is there ever any more assault and murder committed than in the course of war? Is there ever any more rape and looting than by occupying troops? Yet the perpetrators of these crimes are held to be guiltless or even heroic and the initiator of the crime of warfare is that same institution, the State, which passes judgment on the relatively piddling crimes of individuals.

The numerous other crimes like counterfeiting and income tax evasion are punished by the State because they undermine its power. But who, conceding that the State is the Arch Criminal, would wish to conserve or increase its power? It might more logically be argued that failure to pay one's income tax, considering the criminal purpose to which it is put, is an obligatory and virtuous act.

We do not wish to imply that the cases of individual social aggression, like arson, theft, etcetera, do not constitute something of a problem, but it is patently absurd to hold that the Great Thief, the Great Arsonist is at all equipped to pass judgment on the lesser ones.[7]

VI

We realize that a book of this sort should be primarily concerned with techniques for escaping, but unfortunately, such techniques are not easy to come by, for obvious reasons. We have had to content ourselves with the poor second best of relating methods by which one's stay in Prison can be alleviated as much as possible, giving as wide a choice of alternative methods as we could obtain. Different personalities will, of course, find different ways of enduring Prison. Pure individualists may find helpful suggestions in Lowell Naeve's example of absolute non-cooperation;[8] more gregarious types, in the various pieces dealing with strikes and group resistance; and all should benefit from the practical ideas for achieving oblivion.

The importance of striking in Prison, whatever its particular objective, lies not so much in the end to be attained, as in the act itself. It is one way, and in some cases the only one, in which the individual can assert himself as an individual (or at least as a member of a group of his own choosing), rather than remain a mere object, to which the whole weight of institutional pressures, both conscious and unconscious, attempt to reduce him.

This, in our opinion, is the most important aspect of enduring Prison: to maintain as much as possible one's sense of being an individual. In some cases, it might even be true that winning a strike—for instance, one for greater democracy in running the Prison—would be worse, from a psychological standpoint, than losing it. For, to the degree one is made to feel responsible for his life in Prison (which is not at all the same as being responsible for his life) he ceases to be an individual and thus ceases to possess those qualities which make survival itself meaningful.

Notes

Originally published as the "Introduction" to *Prison Etiquette: The Convict's Compendium of Useful Information*, eds. Dachine Rainer and Holley Cantine (Bearsville, NY: Retort Press, 1950).

1. *Editor's note:* Information about Conscientious Objectors can be found by viewing the Public Broadcasting Service (PBS) Documentary *The Good War and Those Who Refused to Fight It* by filmmakers Judith Ehrlich and Rick Tejada-Flores. See www.pbs.org/itvs/thegoodwar/.

2. *Editor's note:* The New Deal was implemented by President Franklin Delano Roosevelt in the 1930s–1940s in response to the economic devastation of the Great Depression. From the New Deal emanated programs such as the National Recovery Administration, the Public Works Administration, the Works Progress Administration, the Tennessee Valley Authority, and Social Security. The New Deal signaled the rise of the welfare state and the co-optation of the militant sector of the Labor Movement's demand for economic equity. There was a notable exclusion of African Americans from the national recovery programs that defined the New Deal. See Jacqueline Jones, *Labor of Love, Labor of Sorrow: Black Women, Work, and the Family from Slavery to the Present* (New York: Basic Books, 1985).

3. The improvement in the material conditions in American Prisons in the interval between the First and Second World Wars is considerable. The food is better, there are better accommodations, more light, air, exercise; the beatings, deprivation, and solitary are less frequent, and plumbing is conspicuously present. We do not believe that these gains have occurred through liberal intervention, but probably through such fortuitous factors as the Prohibition Era, which resulted in the imprisonment of high-grade "criminals" who could bribe for improvements, and perhaps the graft involved in getting plumbing contracts for Prison installations.

4. *Editor's note:* There is insufficient published historical data to support this claim about the condition of political prisoners under the Kaiser. For more information about prisoners in Czarist Russia, see Gerald H. Davis, "National Red Cross Societies and Prisoners of War in Russia, 1914–18," *Journal of Contemporary History*, Vol. 28 (January 1993): 31–52.

5. Except in Springfield, Missouri, the Federal Prison system's "mental hospital," where the old order still remains—numerous beatings and psychological terror [sic]. Prisoners who are "difficult"—that is, any prisoner who refuses to submit to the "normal" Prison regime—is "bugged" and sent to Springfield. The threat of being sent there is continually held over the heads of all Federal Inmates.

6. *Editor's note:* The beginning of the twentieth century in the U.S. marked a move toward massive prison reform. This movement is detailed in Matthew J. Mancini, *One Dies, Get Another: Convict Leasing in the American South, 1866–1928* (Columbia: University of South Carolina Press, 1996).

7. The whole concept of guilt and innocence, judgment and punishment is involved here. Judgment (except when it is private AND powerless) coexists with authority, and is an unmitigated evil. Any body of men, by virtue of their numbers and organization towards a common end is able to coerce the single man. It is by this democratic fallacy—which insists that numbers equal RIGHT, when numbers merely signify POWER, that the family may have evolved into the group, the group into the State, each with its inviolable right to judge and to coerce.

It seems that man in the group, even the very small group, perhaps even the family, is more than, and different from the sum total of the individual members of the unit. I do not believe that the status of the individuals involved is significant— MERELY THE FACT OF COLLECTIVITY. Groups persecute individuals. For the survival of the group—the survival of an organization, that is—no matter how loose, how circumscribed in function and power, it is essential that each individual give up a certain degree of individuality—contribute it, so to speak, to the group. The group therefore becomes something out of nothing and each individual that is part of it becomes something less than he was. In extreme cases, like the Prison, the organization is everything; the prisoner AND the guard nothing. —D. R.

8. *Editor's note:* A chapter in *Prison Etiquette* by Lowell Naeve, "A Field of Broken Stones," is taken from a book of the same name by Lowell Naeve and David Wieck, *A Field of Broken Stones* (Glen Gardner, NJ: Libertarian Press, 1950).

2

Bernard Phillips

Research was unable to provide biographical data on the World War II anti-war activist Bernard Phillips. However, this essay, first published by Dachine Rainer and Holley Cantine in their anthology *Prison Etiquette*, offers an incisive reminder of the continuity of penal repression half a century after Phillips's imprisonment, and an illustration of, in Phillips's words, prison's "reproduction of the situation 'outside.'"

Notes on the Prison Community
1950

Recruitment

Prisons are the least-mentioned institutions of the state. Just as one becomes a responsible citizen through learning that nakedness is bad, that elimination should be secret, that masturbation is unspeakably dangerous, so one is led to believe that the prison system is the indispensable but unmentionable cloacal region of the "community." Stereotypes about criminality and criminals utilize much the same terms and ideas as those about sexual perversion, or any other structure associated with nastiness and revulsion, contrary to good taste.

. . . It is valuable to study the prison community not because it varies sharply from the general community, but because it is a total psychosocial organization in a condition of isolation from minor crises of the general society. It is the image of general community, a clean mirror unsullied by the breath of public attention. Truly, an extension of the metropolis, remodeled by its inhabitants to make it better for them than the life they lead "outside." There could be no rejection of the outside, anyway, for its denizens enter daily emphasizing the nearness, and granting as privileges direct contact with the general community—nonprison foods, conveniences, cultural objects (books, radio).

Authoritarian standards implicit in the general community are unmasked in the prison. Power-wielders are clearly defined, as are the limitations of their constructivity, in their own inefficiency. The controlled are very important to the controllers, they are watched, counted and recounted, studied. . . .

Prisons and armies are laboratories for perfecting and smoothing class-authoritarian techniques. The prison, administratively considered, remains despite innovations, an extension of the police force and fulfills in an ordered and contained space the functions of police power in an unordered space.

Controllers and Controlled

The criterion of police efficiency is that no activity of any group or individual should escape scrutiny, and that there is sufficient arsenal and man-
power on hand to stop any group or individual activity at the command of
constituted authority. The problem for the cop, in the gun tower or at the
picket line, is whether or not to take initiative to intervene. Bluntly put, the
cop is beyond all law and restraint except for learned morality. So long as
he goes by the manual (a flexible document) there are no limits on his
action. He is not punished for simple error (infinitely extensible category!)
unless he seriously misjudges latent resources of the person he accosts. Justice costs heavily in time and money, and if the cop has any powers of
observation at all he will select appropriate arrestees, inside or out.

The psychology of police work is not that of unremitting vigilance (so
much has to be overlooked), but, it is *waiting and assaulting*.[1] It is more
obvious when the cop is working in a closed space. His reactions in this
situation impose special problems on inmates accustomed to rigid rou-
tinization, and initiate spasmodic reactions on their part. Man-watching is
a nerve-wracking and exacting task even when the watcher is a competent
individual with some reason to feel superiority to his charges. However,
the ordinary prison guard cannot feel this generalized self-assurance. Many
of his charges are obviously superior to him in intelligence, social effectiveness, or education.[2] His learned morality often leads him to anxiety about
punishment of innocent men. The tendency is to be "as decent as possible," though the employee's manual instructs him never to debase himself
by being familiar with the inmates. As compensation for this illicit inter-
subjectivity, the guard persecutes the inferior human specimens who are
inevitably components in a prison populace.

General Structure

The prison contains two great collectives . . . 1. [with] distinct and non-
transponible memberships, 2. recruited from homogeneous social and distinct psychological types, 3. maintaining definite tension and conflict with
the alter-collectivity. Their differentiation is along typical and ethical lines,
sharply dividing the inmate population into two in-groups (equal, or
almost so, in numbers).

The *rats* are inmates who have frankly made a living out of crimes
against property. They are the robbers, burglars, and the professional
thieves. Among this group the adage "honor among thieves" holds. The rats
have a conscious justification for their life-ways—hatred of work, love of

novelty, travel, adventure, resentment of social constraint which concretely means proletarianization. Many have supported wives and families with the proceeds from their depredations. Characteristically the rats are adequate persons, readily prisonized, logical, generous, and argumentative. They take the roles of leaders and constructive agitators. Their criteria for acceptance or rejection of new inmates are positive, noneconomic, and postjuvenile.

Squarejohns are offenders against the person (except for those instances where the rats' occupational hazards of gun-using have resulted in inadvertent slaying). They include the sex offenders of all kinds, impulse-and-regret murderers, subnormal and inadequate personalities ("dopes" and "goons"), and numerous "frauds" convicted for forgery, insufficient funds, or other business trickery.

The crime is the personal comment on the world. Not everyone is capable of every crime, and there are rats who have never offended against the person no matter how powerful the push of circumstance and opportunity. The reaction of the prisoner is *a posteriori* proof of the nature and reality of the offense. Innocent men and rats do not bellyache. Squarejohns do. Preoccupations also are consonant with the crime. The rat, thinking of future release, wonders whether anybody has cased that good job in Peoria, while the squarejohn wonders if he can get away with it with his next daughter and calculates how old she will be then.

One would call this merely ethical differentiation if it were only a matter of one sort of criminal defending "his" kind of crime and denouncing the "opposition" for committing another type of crime. However, the difference can be regarded as structural, because the squarejohns carry the pattern of personal violence through in their day-to-day relations with their own and other types. They are more prone to show object-aggression, and often this becomes apparent in relation to inanimate objects too—squarejohns burn mattresses, smash radios and light bulbs, stuff up the plumbing system when they are excited.

Socially, the "squarejohns" are the good citizens who maintain the ethics of the general community, as against the rats' defiance of the code. This is the basal paradox (?) [*sic*] and central point of conflict among the inmate population, an absolute contrariety to all the assumptions of the meliorist and reformatory strategy so loudly espoused by the "curing" school among positivist penologists. Those individuals who look and sound the best to the parole boards are the ones who do constitute an actual, walking physical threat in the absence of supervision—while the "bad-risk," serial-offender "tough" is the individual who could, without supervision, reintegrate in the general community easily and without emotional disturbance because of his achieved self-distanciation from the unstable moral codes.

A facile characterization of the whole squarejohn complex would be—conscious guilt, repentance, active striving toward social recognition, and unconditional reinstatement. The johns tend to be older men with unconcealable mental and physical deficiencies, and correspondingly strong reliance on communal sanctions, often with concentrated avoidance of actions to which their abnormalities bring them close. With increasing age they show more rigid scrupulosity in obedience to precepts of religion, patriotism, and other introcepted [sic] codes and props for concealment of constitutional pathologies. Any person who reveals a dependent and inadequate personality is classified in the prison as a squarejohn, and this fact of forcible classification is especially offensive to the good citizens who wish to regain ethical solidarity with the outside community, and fail to see the identity of their moralizing and the behavior of the feeble-minded who are driven into association with them.

The rats, utilitarians and hedonists as they are, feel that the only bar to their success is the process of law enforcement.

In prison where their welfare cannot be advanced by pursuing random ends, but *can* be supported by collective action of the regime of moods dubbed "prisonization," they maintain a peace-tending society that is more effective for securing their group welfare than those available to them in the general community, in part because of the limitations of ends imposed, the advantageous immediacy of concrete individual interaction, and the pre-exposure of alien caste ethics and counterclaims.

This contrast of the two collectivities does not imply that a reversal of function has taken place inside the prison, with the outlaws taking social initiative because the good citizens are prostrated in masochism or *anomie*. The process is more complex, and is known as prisonization.

Basic Demands

The presumption of the inexperienced is that the prisoner is under tremendous pressures, that peculiar distortions of personality must appear, that social adjustments would be below the norms of a "free" community, that pathological reactions would be formed to the constant authoritarian environment, and radiate beyond those affected. This is the romantic perspective of the humanitarian citizen or the typical social scientist—that perennial orthopsychiatrist.

However, the main effect upon the individual prisoner is that he becomes "prisonized"! This is supposedly shown by increased passivity and greater submission to authority, by changes in the gradient of receptivity (toward or away from "socially worthwhile goals")—in general, by heightened suggestibility to stimuli provided both by his associates and by "society."

This interpretation of the prisonization process presumes that discipline in the prison is constructive. However, one cannot measure the prisoner's conduct by his conduct record, because the authority (which he either breaches or does not) is coercive, not constructive. Most problems of discipline arise from trying to feed and house many men where there is room for only few. Breakdown in authority is not a measure of inmate performance but of the laziness and stupidity of the "administration." A great part of misconduct is constructive rebellion against impossible conditions.

For instance, one main effort of "authority" is enforcement of physical filthiness for inmates. Cells have no warm water, washing personal clothing is limited to ten minutes one day per week, washing state clothes is forbidden (the very best that can be hoped for is a weekly change.) The state's soap *will* clean, but it also takes away the skin[;] one thin hand towel (16 x 29 inches) is issued each week—and must be used for the weekly ten-minute shower bath, too. About a third of all rule infractions, for which inmates are sentenced by "summary court" are those which arise from men sneaking a bath (or semi-bath), washing state clothing, or bargaining for haircuts, for laundry service, etcetera. Because cell sinks drain at hourglass speed, everyone must wash up in the toilet bowl—washing is therefore a rare and reluctant process. Rules of order enforced by convicts are made to break down or evade such conditions wherever possible. The conflicts of ethics and status between rat and squarejohn are eliminated by brute necessity. One may dislike the crippled, grizzled sodomist, but if he can get the laundry "fixed" one perforce deals with him.

Geniality and solidarity of the inmate caste rest upon this immediate basis of cooperative rule-breaking and exchanging favors. The mechanical and anonymous regime is not adjusted to humane needs, though it ensures animal survival. Communication for interest serving is taboo, so that all humane response is also rule-breaking. Commands are depreciated by the convict, they appear not worth following [*sic*]. No initiative has been left to the inmate, such would be a threat to "security." Since nothing done in the prison is directed to any rational or productive end, there is no formal freedom for the prisoner to perform meaningful actions. Thus like the citizen on the street he is coerced (or persuaded) to perform nonsense activity. The only difference arises from the fact that the citizen has formal freedom (some command-following may lead to a rational conclusion, while situationally, he finds that his power of personal initiative is meaningless). So the convict follows commands, tempering obedience with contempt for uniformed authority that is creating such a fuss, shouting so loudly, looking over its shoulder in unnecessary uneasiness. The convict regards guard behaviors as interjections of a strange sort of animal caught in the web of his *own* conduct. Realization of this reciprocity is the subjective sign of prisonization.

The objective index of prisonization is that the inmate is affiliated with one or the other of the ethical collectivities and defends its values. It is quite possible for two rats and two "johns" to share the same cell for years without any relations other than contractual (economic) or caste-directed (rule-breaking). The situation cannot be altered by authority, and the tendency is for squarejohns to gravitate to idle companies (a correlate of age, ill-health, and social inadequacy as much as of outraged inability to defend good citizenship against the logical jibes of the rats).

With the inmate's loss of formal freedom to approve or disapprove of plans, authoritarian behavior becomes completely irrelevant to those who are not immediate victims of the caprice, and the inmate turns to the community of his kind. The introversion is not toward the lowest norms of association represented. Scrupulous courtesy is necessary where nobody has freedom to release energy except under the scrutiny of three other men in a 9 x 11 cell. The troublemaker is frozen out as soon as possible, and no great sympathy is felt for the extreme deviate in his segregated quarters, for in nine cases out of ten he was engineered there by collective repression of inmates. The loud agitator must go to preserve the equilibrium of both the adequate and inadequate person. There is nothing more pitiful or disgusting than to be in a cell and hear a stream of blasphemy or a chant of innocence, when minor irritations have summated to the point where one is ready to indulge in the lame behavior—if it were not for having associates who would react violently against, and depersonalize, even such an expression. Depersonalization and equanimity are sought for between inmates. Trouble of any sort can only mean trouble for them.

When everyone wears the same clothing, eats the same food at the same time and place, sleeps in identical beds, in identical rooms, for the same number of hours, and goes to work that is equally unremunerative and uninteresting and unimportant, conflicts between men largely thin down to invariants of social interaction. The organization of activity is not exhausted in object aggressions and manipulations, but develops nuances of individuation. There is heightening of individuality wherever possible, but the limits of this possibility are drawn very tightly, *not by impersonal but by personal forces.* One does not have to guess how business will turn out, or what the boss thinks of one's personality or output. The "business" is recognizably of no value, and for the subjectivity questions one can secure a ready answer since the boss is always in sight, always carries a club, and is trained to despise you. The only difference from "outside" is that here all these relationships are transparent: the paycheck and the theory of courtesy do not obscure interaction between distinct social classes. The displacement of courtesy and convention between convict and keeper would be almost sufficient in itself to intensify display of these forms as between convicts. Learned codes of taste are infused with new life when they facilitate responses to extreme behavior and extreme situations. A partial prescription for reactions to extreme situations lessens tensions and indicates prisonization. One will dispose of the stabber's knife as a mark of courtesy and friendly concealment, as one wipes away the spilled drink of one's guest.

Prisonization, then, is accommodation to out-caste status with active reservation of a distinct ethical position. Primacy must be granted to rule-breaking as the vehicle for caste association. While self-justification is a tempting form of action, it is limited to the squarejohns, for all practical purposes—as a sign of enlistment in their collectivity of thwarted good citizenship. Self-justification is an incomplete tampon to object or environmental aggression. For the entire caste, prisonization is the measure (in the varying forms of introversion and socialization) of adequacy and self-integration that recognizes that general end-following is inappropriate to the social situation. The individual with any social capabilities what[so]ever will make a rapid adjustment to the conditions of unspectacular comradeship in one or the other collectivity. Initiation is by example. Extremes of courtesy, concern, solicitude, at first do give the impression of homosexual overture or pathological reaction. But they are the symptoms of a softened and gentled life and the goodwill is real. The novice interprets special services as special acts of friendship, and then suddenly finds himself going out of the way to do favors for some stranger, often at personal risk. One is always thereafter "giving time" to others—and gladly. Message giving and general coordination devolve as tasks for the range-man who serves several cells in a single range and arranges barter and exchange. Highly socialized persons seek these jobs, and others, such as library delivery boy and mail and commissary delivery. One does not need many close friends: almost anyone who is free enough to reach one's cell will run errands and do jobs that "outside" would be entrusted only to close friends. If he does not, he cannot last long on his pleasant assignment before getting into trouble.

After Prisonization

. . . The convict is always in a hurry—one created by himself—and quite oblivious of the fact that he is rushing in circles. Environmental sameness invests every action with special significance, brevity and uncertainty of friendly contacts makes for infinite planning and replanning of what to do and say in any particular instant, how to bring that instant about, how to preserve inconspicuosity during it. . . . Meanwhile there is time and more time to be filled. One can race with time, by doing this, and this, and. . . . Spasmodicity becomes the way of life, the restless behavior of the untrained or mistrained person, with components of irritability, anxiety, misdirected, or briefly sustained effort. The escape patterns of the weakly motivated individual often closely resemble the states of overwork or job-fatigue of the strongly motivated and usually productive person. Watch the inmate in the dormitory after the day's work. He reads, rushes to a friend's bunk to chat avidly, goes by the card tables and stays for one hand with a casual group, takes a shower, types a letter, reads again, walks swiftly around the whole dormitory a few times, smuggles, makes and distributes a round of tea, then revises his letter, etc. No activities last longer than nine minutes, few less than four. Multiply this behavior by 150 (the number of men in the dormitory) and it is evident that a report on it must reveal either a sociometric chaos or a smoothly functioning community in which the individual has a low but definite and constant stimulus "value" for his associates. The latter is the case. . . .

The Reserve-Mechanisms

. . . All activities introverted toward the prison community make for a radical split between johns and rats. There is active conflict over the recruitment to the collectivities of the new prisoners ("fish"). The squarejohn is not a good argument for his own ethical code, and it is one repulsive to the young offender fresh from strife against it—but the mechanism of the sexual lure is very powerful. If one will only believe in God and country, he can restabilize his sexual life, and this is a powerful attraction for the young man. On the other hand, general courtesy, services, and sociability are provided by the rats. The young man thus undergoes a long period of "wavering" between standards—but has to come down on one side or the other, or be outlawed by everybody. Contrary to public opinion about the mixture of young offenders with "hardened criminals," the hardened criminals often accept the youth as a guest and transient, who is to be converted from criminal activity. "Bub, look at us—it doesn't pay . . ." is the pattern of much recruiting-speech. Rats mute their own extraordinary opinions and convert many youngsters to the ideal of conformity—"for your own sake, you're young and can still choose." The dangers, physical and mental, are, for youth, not offered by the "radicals" or rats, but by the good citizens. This is again a reproduction of the situation "outside."

Individuation

Material for individuality is strictly limited. Every new inmate learns to dog-face, that is to assume an apathetic, *characterless* facial expression and posture when viewed by authority. The dog-face is acquired easily when everyone freezes or relaxes into immobility. The face is that typical of streets, of social occasions, of all concealment. Relaxation comes when inmates are alone: there is an exaggeration of the smiling effervescence of the "friendly" party. The face that is protective by day is aggressively hardened and hate-filled by night, against the stationed or pacing guard. Tensity and dislike follow assumption of the face, guards react with scrupulous relaxedness, holding the face "soft" with an effort often accompanied by slight trembling of hands.

How to express contempt for authority? The manner of "obeying" orders is one way. Resentful alacrity is most common. A dormitory group accustomed to marching into the dining hall in single file, with men finding positions beside their friends, was ordered to march into the hall double-file. (Cell block companies have [a] set order for marching and seating.) After a great deal of scowling and muttering from men hurried from the dormitory, a double line was formed. Thereafter the unpopular guard who first gave the order was always confronted by formation of a double-file line, although a single trial had convinced him of the inconvenience caused to other company guards by his innovation. He did not attempt to reverse his order, and within two weeks every guard who was especially disliked found that the inmates formed double lines for him. The practice spread to another dormitory. Negroes are especially apt at parody, sometimes breaking into a goose step. They seat themselves at table ten at a time, snatching off caps simultaneously and precisely.

Individuation, being impossible on the level of consumption and standards of comfort, develops as ego-strengthening eccentricity. Patterns of eccentricity then fade into desultory acts (with spectators) or circular forms, very unusual in content, but conscious and definitely designed. Spasmodicity favors the apparently desultory act (coenopportune [*sic*] reaction). Examples include *hectoring* and *pseudo-sales*: going into the dining hall, where talk in line is prohibited, one man will stand aside and chant, "Get your programs here, meal program right here, one dime—can't tell one dish from another without a program—also a list of everything served in this room—five lines, 10 cents." The largest sale in 1946 was for Braino: "Clear that clogged brain with Braino, one great truth, fi' cents!" The truth enjoined as Braino was: "All people are just people. Don't let any people tell you they aren't people."

Hectoring usually produces audience response disregarding any threats of interference from authority, and is directed at least obliquely against authoritarianism. Companies saddled with especially oppressive guards show great increase in overt individuation of the men's conduct, and attempts to discipline the "hectors" lead to booing the guard (with resultant collective punishment).

Norms of Disorder

The most striking aspect of criminal thought is the universal maintenance of the "sacredness of the individual." How is it that the social type that orients itself toward aggression against other individuals and their interests should maintain this ideology? Is the conviction simply a verbal attitude arising from imprisonment with its loss of social status, or a factor in the motivation of criminal behavior?

The rat has a profound belief that the people he dubs "citizens" in the prison populace are identical with the man-on-the-street whom the rat robs and dubs "sucker." Note that the citizen or squarejohn is the individual who is spending either a very brief or a very long time in prison, as punishment for an offense either "trivial" or "very serious." He is the nonrepeater typically, or an older man whose offense was [a] simple index of senility. The rat is a serial offender who totals up years in prisons, jails, and workhouses, and lacks any strong familial or friendship ties in the community. He is confined inside and outside to social and "business" relationships with other rats. Exigencies of escape often lead one rat to betray another, indeed *informing* is the characteristic sign of the trapped rat.

The convict can always point to the man on the streets and say truthfully: "He put me here." Rats are vengeful and scornful of all morality—relying on anybody has always meant catastrophe to them. [Objectively, many rats are orphans or neglected children, have never had a family life, are ready to repeat the pattern of illegitimacy-and-abandonment that is the model "background." . . .] [*brackets in original*]

The "citizen" wants out, to renew his old associations and to attempt to pick up living again where he left off. The prison is to him a social blank, not the place where he finds his old friends. Actually, his offenses indicate that rejoining the community will be less easy than he dreams—he is often intellectually and physically inadequate, attracted to old associations that have damaged him in the past. But, emotionally dependent and deficient in self-analysis as he is, the citizen is pointed away from prisonization. The world beyond is habitable and interesting.

The rat is really infuriated by the conservatism and religiosity of the older offenders and sex criminals. He does not perceive that these uneducated men have no other theory of motivation and conduct that has "prestige" in their social circle, and that they will cling to it under the insults of the rats. Further the content of Christian doctrine is excellent solace for anyone wishing to justify what he recognizes (with his critics) as irrational action. The essential plea is that the individual is helpless as against his own affectual makeup. Human nature is sinful, anybody will slip once in a while, I don't think it would happen again [*sic*]. I have paid my debt to society, don't you think they should let me out?"

Convicts are by no means ethically agnostic. The agreement on what it is "ethical" to do, does serve to define one's position in the rat or citizen collectivities—"ethics" and "personality" are perhaps the most overworked words in the prison, nuances in their definition give the trained observer basis for prognosis of the speaker's future, when his actual offense and his speaking circle are known.

Rats deny validity of retribution for their aggressions on two contrary grounds: 1. "Nothing I ever do hurts the common people. . . ." 2. "Somebody ought to ball up those lunchbucket artists, those staunch citizens. . . ." Part of their interest in continuing criminality is that it causes real and observable damage to the interests of others. But the rat often uses the Robin Hood argument, saying that he redistributes property among his friends (who need it most) and that none of his exploitations work hardships comparable to those imposed by "lunchbucket life."

Each group envisions *personality* as a transient "accomplishment" of the actor. The citizens think that personality is activity that is rational performance of any sanctioned action with clear awareness of what one is doing. (Here is a transparent conversion: taking misconduct to be motivated breaking of sanctions, the one-time offender claims that he supports sanctions, his offense was unmotivated, an action "unlike himself," and therefore unreal, something for which he cannot be held responsible.) Rats confuse command-action with "personality." He who commands is a person[;] obeyers are animals. However, the criminal is not as vulgar as the advertiser. He wishes to be conspicuous (in a favorable sense) and to be obeyed. Instead of placing faith in a new suit or a more expensive car, he carries a gun. The gun is an equalizer, the only one available in present-day street life. . . .

Notes

Originally published in *Prison Etiquette: The Convict's Compendium of Useful Information,* eds. Dachine Rainer and Holley Cantine (Bearsville, NY: Retort Press, 1950), 95–109.

1. D.R. & H.C.: The rationale of police work reaches its essence in the guards who wait in hiding, then leap out and club any passing convict. The element of surprise adds much to their pleasure. A disciplinary board for guards has slightly reduced the quantum of "assaulting." More prominent are the controllers who try to pick fights with the unwilling prisoners.

2. D.R. & H.C.: The prison mail office illustrates the extreme low in mentality. It is difficult to get a letter past the censors if any literary expression is used, or any word of more than four syllables. For instance, the writer had one letter returned with a red circle around the word "aposiopesis," with the threatening comment—"Any further vulgar language and we will cancel your mail privileges." Poor "parataxis" later met the same fate.

3

Jalil Muntaqim

Jalil A. Muntaqim (Anthony Bottom) was born on October 18, 1951, in Oakland, California. As an adolescent in the 1960s, he organized with the National Assocation for the Advancement of Colored People (NAACP) and engaged in street riots against racism and police brutality in San Francisco. In high school, Muntaqim was recruited by the Black Student Union (BSU) of San Jose State and City College to participate in "speakouts."

Two nights after the 1968 assassination of Martin Luther King Jr., Muntaqim, the Chair of the BSU, and several high school students were arrested in a car and charged with possession of high-powered rifles and Molotov cocktails. At the age of eighteen, he joined the Black Panther Party and was eventually recruited into the underground Black Liberation Army.

On August 28, 1971, Muntaqim was captured along with the late Albert "Nuh" Washington during a shoot-out with San Francisco police. He was charged with the killings of two New York City police officers; although he maintains his innocence and petitioned for a new trial given government malfeasance in previous trial(s). He is currently serving a virtual life sentence in New York State.

While at San Quentin prison, Muntaqim organized the 1976 National Prisoners Campaign to petition the United Nations to recognize political prisoners in the United States. He also established a revolutionary prisoners' national newspaper, *Arm the Spirit,* and wrote political pamphlets and essays. He is the author of a collection of prison writings entitled *We Are Our Own Liberators: Selected Prison Writings,* an unpublished novel, and a teleplay.

References

Can't Jail the Spirit: Political Prisoners in the U.S.: A Collection of Biographies, fifth edition. Chicago: Committee to End the Marion Lockdown, 2002.

Kaufman, Michael T. "Slaying of One of the Last Black Liberation Army Leaders Still at Large Ended a 7–Month Manhunt." *New York Times,* November 16, 1973, 10.

Muntaqim, Jalil. "On the Black Liberation Army." *Arm the Spirit,* September 18, 1979.

———. *We Are Our Own Liberators: Selected Prison Writings.* Montreal, QC: Abraham Guillen Press, 2002.

The Criminalization of Poverty in Capitalist America (Abridged) 1996

The Poor, Welfare, and Prisons

An anonymous poet in the 1700s wrote about crime: "The law will punish a man or woman who steals the goose from the hillside, but lets the greater robber loose who steals the hillside from the goose."[1]

When talking about "the greater robber," it seemed particularly appropriate in the midst of the biggest financial rip-off in the history of this country to think about the billions of dollars the Savings & Loan criminals stole, and about how most of them have gotten away with it.[2] I thought about the complete insanity of how this country defines crimes in society. If you steal $5 you're a thief, but if you steal $5 million— you're a financier.

Thirty percent of the wealth of this country is controlled by one-half of one percent of the people. Eighty percent of the wealth is controlled by ten percent of the people. I think that is a crime. In the dictionary, the word "crime" means "an act that is against the law." Crime applies particularly to an act that breaks a law that has been made for public good. Crime in one country, the dictionary continued, "may be entirely overlooked by the law in another country or may not apply at all in a different historical period."

That was interesting. What that really said was that concepts of "crime" are not eternal. The very nature of crime is sociopsychological and defined by time and place and those who have the power to make definitions—by those who write dictionaries, so to speak.

The more I thought about that and about those who write the laws, or at least define what law is, the more profound it became. I believe we all will agree that the United States is a nation of criminals. From its inception as a settler nation, exiled British criminals stole the land and lives from Native Americans and Africans. They justified their actions by

29

making and defining the law of the land, for example, defining an African as three-fifths of a man during slavery. Hence the power to define is an awesome power. It is the power of propaganda. It is the ability to manipulate our ideas, to limit our agenda, to mold how we see, and to shape what we look at. It is the power to interpret the picture we see when we look at the world for the American people in general, and New Afrikans, in particular. It is the power to place the picture we see when we look at the world. It is the power to place a frame around the picture, to define where it begins and ends. It is, in fact, the power to define where our vision begins and ends, the power to create our collective consciousness.

That kind of social propaganda is not only tremendously powerful, but it is also mostly invisible. We can't fight what we don't see. Most people accept the images and definitions that we have been taught as true, neutral, self-evident, and for always; so that the power to paint the future, to define what is right and wrong, what is lawful and what is criminal, is really the power to win the battle for our minds—and to win it without ever having to fight it. Simply said, it is hard to fight an enemy who has an outpost in our minds. This indicates the need for revolutionary nationalists to develop a national agitation-propaganda mechanism. Specifically, nationalists need a single national publication and organ that represents the unified development of NAIM (The New African Independence Movement) to which each formation and organization contributes and supports its distribution.[3]

The Social Dynamics of Crime

Though some may question, as did [Karl] Marx, the system's fairness in applying its rules, today most people don't question the basis of the system itself. That is, people don't question the relationship between those who own and those who don't. Though many people vote every four years on who governs, they never vote on and rarely question what governs. People don't challenge the legitimacy of the system; they accept it. The exception, of course, is when the oppressed rebel in insurrections. But usually we don't step outside of the frame around the picture. We don't disconnect the dots. Emile Durkheim argued that crime is "normal" and necessary social behavior.[4]

> According to Durkheim, the inevitability of crime is linked to the differences (heterogeneity) within a society. Since people are so different from one another and employ such a variety of methods and forms of behavior to meet their needs, it is not surprising

that some will resort to criminality. Thus as long as human differences exist, crime is inevitable and one of the fundamental conditions of social life.[5]

In this regard, the conservative view echoes this sentiment inasmuch as it seeks to establish a genetic trait that explains criminal behavior. They argue:

> If liberals have trouble with the idea that people's genes influence their chances of committing crimes, conservatives have trouble with the idea that poverty causes crime. Conservatives do not deny that the poor commit more crimes than the rich. But instead of assuming that poverty causes crime, conservatives usually assume that poverty and crime have a common cause, namely the deficient character or misguided values of the poor.[6]

Concomitantly, the neoliberals are essentially giving credence to the conservatives' position as it pertains to the "underclass." For instance, sociologist William J. Wilson argues that liberal perspectives "on the ghetto underclass" have "become less persuasive and convincing in public discourse principally because many of those who represent traditional liberal views on social issues have been reluctant to discuss openly or, in some instances, even to acknowledge the sharp increase in social pathologies in ghetto communities."[7] Needless to say, such ideas as "genetic traits are the cause of crime" set a dangerous precedent. Trying to discern the social pathologies of the underclass harbors views that purport the wholesale contamination of entire communities. However, if one were to advocate that criminal behavior, especially of the poor, is either caused by genetic traits and/or born of social pathologies, then indisputably, it must be espoused that much of America suffers from these same causes.

In the March 12, 1993 issue of the *Wall Street Journal,* an article entitled "Common Criminals—Just About Everyone Violates Some Laws, Even Model Citizens," by Stephen J. Adler and Wade Lambert, stated: "We are a nation of lawbreakers. We exaggerate tax-deductible expenses, lie to customs officials, bet on card games and sports events, disregard jury notices, drive while intoxicated—and hire illegal childcare workers."[8]

The last of these was recently the crime of the moment, and Janet Reno wouldn't have been in the position to be confirmed unanimously as attorney general yesterday if Zoe Baird had obeyed the much-flouted immigration and tax laws.[9] But the crime of the moment could have been something else, and next time probably will be. This is because nearly all people violate some laws, and many people run afoul of dozens, without ever being considered, or considering themselves, criminals.

When we look at downtown urban centers, we look at the lines of humanity waiting for food or a bed at the missions; if we look at the faces of people living in cardboard boxes on the streets of the cities, we must know that a crime has been committed. When we look at the faces of the dispossessed people, we see faces that look like people who lived in California when it was part of Mexico. In Miami, we see faces of people whose great-great-grandparents were abducted and brought here from Africa.

In America, in the 1990s, as was the case in England in the 1800s, it is a crime to be poor. The poorer you are, the more criminal you are. If you are so poor that you have no place to live, and you live on the pavement or sleep in a car or in a park, you have committed a crime. It's against the law to sleep on the streets or in a park. If we have no home, it's against the law to sleep anywhere. Walter I. Trattner, in *From Poor Law to Welfare State: A History of Social Welfare in America,* observed that at times government policies sought "to dismantle all benefit programs for working-age people except perhaps for unemployment insurance."[10]

Indeed, others argued that structural changes in the economy and the erosion in antipoverty programs were the causes of the problem, and that a strengthening, not dismantling, of the welfare state was essential in order to solve it. Such was the theme of Michael Harrington's *The New American Poverty,*[11] a depressing sequel pronouncement that "The poor are still there." They are poor, however, said Harrington, not because of any personal shortcomings or decisions on their part, but because of changes in the international economy, especially the "de-industrialization" of America, and the way in which they have been treated, or mistreated, here at home. They are the uprooted and the homeless, products of de-institutionalization, cuts in welfare programs, shortages in low-rent housing, and other social and economic forces over which they have no control; undocumented aliens who have become the new sweatshop laborers; unemployed blue-collar workers victimized by the disappearance of steady and relatively well-paying manufacturing jobs in the "smokestack industries" as a result of technological advances and global competition; white-collar workers who lost their jobs due to reorganization schemes in the name of efficiency, plant closings, or moves to new locations in the so-called Sunbelt; hopeless, uneducated, and untrained young blacks unable to get and hold jobs; families headed by poor, unmarried women; uprooted farmers and farm laborers hurt by the elimination of the subsistence farm and the agricultural depression; and millions of others in unskilled, unsteady (and often part-time), low-wage, dead-end benefitless jobs in the service sector of the economy—cooks in fast food restaurants, dishwashers and chambermaids in hotels and motels, janitors and cleaning women in schools, hospitals, nursing homes, and the like. Harrington and others demand that the government spend billions of dollars on social programs to meet the needs of these "rejects" of society.[12]

When the government fails to be responsible to its citizens and ignores the social dynamics of poverty, people are generally forced to seek illegitimate means to eke out an existence. In this case, it is a question of national oppression, whereby the imperialist government maintains exploitative relationships with New Afrikans, Native Americans, Chicanos, and Asians. Too many of these "rejects" of society are caught in the vicious web of the criminal justice system. But the real criminals are those who create the socioeconomic conditions that perpetuate impoverishment. The real criminal is the colonial government itself. It then becomes necessary to assess the pathology of the capitalist and social policy makers that make crime big business and deflect culpability of their criminal behavior.

Crime is Big Business

The political decisions of the bankers are decisions about who will be poor. Corporate decisions made in the late 1950s to remove industry from communities of color were mostly about who would be unemployed. Decisions by developers and bankers about redevelopment (redlining and gentrification) are decisions about who will be homeless. Such decisions affect everyone, but people have no say in the matter. Generally, people, especially the poor, have no say in most social and economic decisions that affect their lives. Somehow that is not part of the democratic method of government, and because people have no say in the process, creating homelessness is not criminal, but being homeless is. Runaway plants and plant closures are legal, but vagrancy is a crime. Trattner says:

> Meanwhile the plight of the nation's hungry and homeless worsened. In November, 1984, in a pastoral letter on "Catholic Social Thinking and the U. S. Economy," American Roman Catholic bishops had called poverty in America a "social and moral scandal that must not be ignored," and stated that "works of charity cannot and should not have to substitute for humane public policy. . . . A little more than a year later, the Physicians Task Force on Hunger in America reported on a two-year nationwide study it had conducted and concluded that, despite fifty-eight continuous months of economic expansion, hunger was more widespread and serious than at any time in the fifteen years (affecting some twenty million Americans), largely, in its words, because of "governmental failure."[13]

Hunger and homelessness are deliberately imposed socioeconomic conditions that disenfranchise large numbers of the American population. This is especially significant when consideration is given to the method and means by which the malfeasance of the powers that be operates to ensure that such conditions stay the same. Thus such pathology ensures the rich get richer, while the poor get prison and early death.

Max Weber[14] has argued that society is structured to function in a specific way to ensure its existence, that the social structure is subject to the mechanics of government, and that governing is all-important above and beyond the immediate needs of the people:

> Weber held that social stratification depends on the distribution of three resources: wealth (economic resources), power (political resources), and prestige (social resources). Thus, in our society wealthy business owners often gain power by contributing to political campaigns and earn prestige by making large donations to charity or to the arts. In other cases, however, the three are not linked. For example, in our society an individual acquires less prestige (in most circles) than someone who acquires comparable wealth by legitimate means. Artists, the clergy, and others may enjoy prestige but not wealth. On occasion people with few economic resources and little social prestige—bureaucrats, for instance—exercise considerable power. . . . Weber held that because stratification is multidimensional, the formation of groups depends on which interests or identities people choose to emphasize. In capitalist societies, for example, ethnic and national identifications have proved more important than economic or class identification.[15]

We are able to determine the social and racial implications of certain classes, then, having a vested interest in crime. It can be argued that because an elite class of criminals is in charge, they commit capital crimes, crimes against society and humanity. The jails are overflowing, but that doesn't seem to help—because the real criminals aren't in jail. They're in the board rooms and in the White House. They are the social policymakers that run this country . . . increasing social repression by building more prisons and creating harsher legal sanctions . . . becoming ever more heedless to the social implications of poverty as an impetus to committing crime.[16]

Crime is big business in America. Annually the laws are changed to ensure profitability in the industry of crime. Social conditions that serve to maintain levels of poverty and feed the industry of crime also put stress on the social stratifications of society. Given the fact that America is a nation of criminals . . . social conflict is inevitable. It then becomes a matter of identifying the real culprits of crime, and seeking the means to have them become accountable for their criminal behavior. This may very well include the redistribution of their wealth and the reorganization of the social contract between the government and the governed.

In response to the stratification outlined above, it requires revolutionary nationalist and socialist efforts to formulate a national political agenda and policy that will challenge the prevailing social contract between the oppressed and the oppressor nation. This means revolutionary nationalists and socialists must have a clear and concise mass-line and political program that identifies and explains the nature of poor peoples' oppression and how they are to be organized to confront their oppression.

Notes

Originally published in *Schooling the Generations in the Politics of Prison,* ed. Chinosole (Berkeley, CA: New Earth Publications, 1996).

1. This quote was taken from an edited version of a speech by Sabina Virgo, given in Los Angeles, California on International Human Rights Day, December 8, 1990.

2. *Editor's note:* The Savings and Loan scandal was surpassed by the 2002 "corporate crime wave" involving Enron, WorldCom, Arthur Andersen, and other major financial institutions, which destabilized investor confidence and marked the greatest economic malfeasance (loss to individual and collective investors) in U.S. history. See Associated Press, "Turmoil at WorldCom: The Overview," *New York Times,* June 27, 2002, A1; Associated Press, "Enron's Many Strands: The Overview," *New York Times,* February 28, 2002, A1.

3. *Editor's note:* The diversity of black nationalists range from cultural nationalists to revolutionary nationalists who embrace Marxist philosophy. See Cedric Robinson, *Black Marxism: The Making of the Black Radical Tradition* (Chapel Hill: University of North Carolina Press, 2000); "Black Liberationists," in *Imprisoned Intellectuals: America's Political Prisoners Write on Life, Liberation, and Rebellion,* ed. Joy James (Lanham, MD: Rowman and Littlefield, 2003).

4. *Editor's note:* The works of Emile Durkheim, the French social scientist regarded as one of the founders of contemporary sociology, include: *The Division of Labor in Society* (New York: Free Press, 1964, repr.); *The Rules of Sociological Method* (Chicago: University of Chicago Press, 1938).

5. Larry Siegel, *Criminology,* fourth edition (St. Paul, MN: West/Wadsworth Publishing Co., 1992), 40.

6. Christopher Jencks, *Rethinking Social Policy: Race, Poverty, and the Underclass* (Cambridge, MA: Harvard University Press, 1992), 11.

7. *Editor's note:* See William Julius Wilson, *The Truly Disadvantaged: The Inner City, the Underclass, and Public Policy* (Chicago: University of Chicago Press, 1990), 6.

8. Stephen J. Adler and Wade Lambert, "Common Criminals—Just About Everyone Violates Some Laws, Even Model Citizens," *Wall Street Journal,* March 12, 1993.

9. *Editor's note:* Zoe Baird was nominated for the position of Attorney General by President Bill Clinton during his first term. Her confirmation was derailed because she had knowingly employed an undocumented immigrant, or "illegal alien," as a childcare worker. See Stuart Taylor Jr., "Inside the Whirlwind," *The American Lawyer* (March 1993): 64.

10. Walter I. Trattner, *From Poor Law to Welfare State: A History of Social Welfare in America* (New York: Free Press, 1989), 335.

11. Michael Harrington, *The New American Poverty* (New York: Holt, Rinehart, and Winston, 1984).

12. Ibid., 336.

13. Trattner, 337–38.

14. *Editor's note:* Max Weber (1864–1920), the German sociologist and political economist, significantly influenced sociology. His key works include *From Max Weber: Essays in Sociology* (New York: Oxford University Press, 1946) and *The Protestant Ethic and the Spirit of Capitalism* (London: George Allen and Unwin, Ltd., 1930).

15. Michael S. Bassis, Richard J. Gelles, and Ann Levine, *Sociology: An Introduction* (New York: Random House, 1999), 238–39.

16. *Editor's note:* Muntaqim's statistics have been updated. For more current data, see "The Sentencing Project," www.sentencingproject.org; "American Civil Liberties Union," www.aclu.org/Prisons/PrisonsMain.cfm.

4

Bill Dunne

I was made a prisoner of the state on October 14, 1979, in Seattle, Washington. Late that evening, I was picked up by paramedics while under the influence of police bullets near a shot-up and wrecked car containing some weapons and a dead jail escapee. According to the ensuing state and federal charges, I and a codefendant and unknown other associates of a San Francisco anarchist collective had conspired to effect a comrade's armed liberation from a Seattle jail and attempted to execute the plot on October 14, 1979. The charges further alleged the operation was financed by bank expropriation and materially facilitated by illegal acquisition of weapons, explosives, vehicles, ID, and other equipment.

After long subjection to atrocious jail conditions and three sensationalized trials, I got a ninety-year sentence in 1980. I subsequently got a consecutive fifteen-years as a result of an attempted self-emancipation in 1983. The aggregate 105 years is a "parole when they feel like it" sort of sentence.

—Bill Dunne, January 1998

37

Control Unit Prisons: Deceit and Folly in Modern Dungeons 1998

Prison authorities have interests in controlling and manipulating prisoner behavior that is not consistent with societal interests. The docile sheep the prisonocracy feels make good prisoners are not good citizens in any society predicated on freedom, democracy, and personal and social responsibility. Prisoncrats operate institutions that are unfree, autocratic, and replace responsibility with orders to be followed. They thus have an interest in suppressing self-motivated activity and individual initiative and attacking attitudes that foster them.

Making sheep out of cats isn't easily done and its mechanisms don't spring readymade into prison administrators' heads, which gives them an interest in psychosocial experimentation and dark concrete corners in which to carry it out. And imprisonment is just one pillar of a larger, reactionary apparatus of repression. Control units[1] also serve as the leading edge of counterinsurgency to the extent [that] their experimental results move laterally within the apparatus. They can then be translated to maintaining social dominance in an outside society characterized by increasing concentration of and disparity in wealth and power and erosion of civil rights.

Understanding the official disinformation upon which the explosion in control units is predicated and the bankruptcy of this repressive model to quell objectionable behavior requires examination of several issues. The most obvious is whether the people subjected to control units are, in fact, the inherently bad and intrinsically disruptive nasties the prisonocracy claims. There is also the ancillary question of whether the reasons given for their being treated thusly are as egregious as officialdom alleges, have the same meaning, and warrant years of lockdown. Next is whether the long-term (individual or small group) isolation characteristic of control units corrects or aggravates behavioral problems.

Control Units

Official propaganda has billed control units as "the end of the line" for "the worst of the worst," a repository for predatory prisoners who have committed (sometimes only "been convicted of") acts of violence in other prisons. Sometimes the phrase "or are escape risks" is included, though it is frequently omitted. The omission is undoubtedly because "escape risk" might entail only suspicion or be easily understandable and not necessarily violent behavior, and is thus tougher to justify draconian control units. Whatever its details, the propaganda suggests that control unit prisoners are so intrinsically nasty, vicious, and disruptive to regular maximum security (a misnomer in light of control units) prisons that their long-term subjection to punitive isolation is warranted.

While some prisoners consigned to control units were involved in some sort of violence (some of which is definitional rather than actual), some consigned were not. Other common, frequently undocumented, nonviolent, and/or nonescape reasons for control unit consignment include:

- Isolating "Mr. Bigs," the especially notorious and the officially despised
- Alleged affiliation with gangs or disruptive groups
- Friendship or associations with people who have committed serious infractions
- Internal exile in other (state) prison systems
- Possession of weapons or drugs or testing positive for drug use
- Preventing placement of prisoners in an open population that might prove problematic
- Mental illness
- Targeting litigators, organizers, and active or influential political prisoners (estimates that the capacity to absolutely control 2 to 5 percent of a population ensures control of the character and direction of society indicate why [these groups are targeted]).

Exceedingly few prisoners in control units have been "convicted" of anything but their original street charge; they are guilty of charges almost always assigned administratively. The standard of proof in such assignments is so low it merits neither the term "standard" nor "proof." Such use of control units results in gross overstatement of the need for them.

Official credibility is compromised by its misrepresentation of the significance of what actual behavior may underlie infractions for which people are sent to control units. The prisonocracy would have the observer believe that any (violent) behavior it brands a rule violation (and, as noted, the standard is low) is evidence of the depravity of all prisoners who would engage in it. It seeks to create the impression that the "transgression" is the expression of prisoners' predatory nature. That leaves force and repression as the only viable responses. Prisoners, however, are not slavering fiends just lurking, like spiders for flies, for a victim.

The Drug Trade

Consider, for example, the drug trade in prisons. It includes some of the prisoners previously described as "probable" transfers to control units but unlikely to be deterred by the prospect. The authorities push potential for violence growing from drug use as emblematic of serious prisoner misbehavior and justification for repression. They also use the stigma of *any* involvement with drugs to dispel liberal notions of prisoners as "hapless victims."

The official picture is a simplistic chain. Drug use is bad. Drug selling is bad. Drug use and selling cause violence. Violence is bad. Bad things are against the rules. Violation of any rules is bad. Prisoners violate rules and are thus bad. Ergo, causation is irrelevant in addressing rule violations and controlling prisoner badness. Bad is bad and must be suppressed. This concatenation for repression is similar to that dynamic that makes it all but impossible for street politicians to consider causes of crime and advocate the less repressive "treatment" solutions. But while many politicians, out of fear of being labeled "soft on crime," may to some extent be victims of the syndrome, prisoncrats are more ideologically committed to a repression model based on "inherent" prisoner "badness." Reality is more complex.

A prison dope fiend might become overextended in debt (either deliberately or otherwise) and feel and be threatened as a result. His or her creditors might feel threatened by the prospective default leaving them unable to meet their own obligations and/or by the eyes of other debtors and/or opportunists on their handling of the situation. Prisoners will, even more than street traffickers, virtually always go to great lengths to resolve such disputes without violence because "doing what one has to do" absent resolution is materially bad for everyone. It pushes the trade to a level of visibility the agents of repression can't tolerate.

Problems are thus almost always resolved privately and without violence. Indeed, debt and its restructuring can be stabilizing because the parties have an interest in jobs and hustles and other economic activity not being disrupted by violence and lockdowns. Occasionally, however, poor communication skills, unavailability of a better solution (frequently caused by guards), the social prescriptions and constraints governing such situations, and asshole-nature (among other factors) intervene. They cause the evasion and dunning interaction to precipitate a fight or worse.

Prisons are particularly social places, and such scenarios are complicated by the extent that they do not and cannot occur solely and secretly between the individuals involved. Within the drug use/trafficker milieu and frequently beyond it, people know what is going on. Prisoners live close together and gossip is endemic. Knowing at least generally who is who and what is up in one's vicinity can be important as well as entertaining. Habits, associations, character traits, economic condition, and hustles and other activities are fairly visible to prisoners.

Drug users know other users at various distances, often get high together, turn each other on, and borrow from, lend to, and deal with each other. In the prison fishbowl, they can't do so in complete invisibility. Drug sellers have to make their wares available and do business within a community. The associations and communities of interest and/or affinity (which also exist for other reasons) can lead to lines being drawn in the foregoing type scenarios (and others) that reach beyond the individuals directly involved and the substance of the transaction. Where gangs, either formal or informal, are involved such lines may be preexisting, extend farther, and include considerations outside the immediate situation. While the social context can defuse problems, it can also exacerbate them.

Environment and Community

Prisoners do not traffic in drugs merely and uniformly because they are bad. Everything happens for a reason that is only subjectively good, bad, or indifferent. Underlying the attraction to drugs is the desire to feel good on several interrelated levels and thus escape an oppressive reality. That attraction is aggravated by an environment that provides few alternative means of fulfilling the desire accessible to many, if not most, prisoners. The material side of feeling good—of being somewhat more comfortable by getting high or having some commissary, sneakers, a radio, etcetera—is an essential but subordinate part of the equation. Psychological comfort is much more important.

Many prisoners, however, do not have the skills to reap sufficient pleasure and fulfillment from absorbing the often heavy time not occupied by jobs with reading or study, or with other intellectual pursuits. Similarly elusive for many is the social connection of maintaining or establishing satisfying outside relationships via correspondence or even inside relationships via stimulating interpersonal interaction, be it as limited as recreational activity like games or sharing the events of the many, many days. Most people are able to do these things for some part of their day and over short to medium periods, but the ability is for many unequal to long hours stretching over long times.

Poverty of Officially Sanctioned Activities

The problem of superficial community is compounded by prisoners' insecurity of location and association: a prisoner may be moved away from his or her inside place or people at any time and on no notice and be barred from communicating with them (legally, anyway) thereafter. Though socialization in the crucible of prison can be much more intense and concentrated than is normal outside, prisoners are often denied the time to develop deep, enduring relationships and consciousness of community. The likely possibility of having communal ties snatched away also inhibits their development under the rubric of pain avoidance.

Other factors also influence the extent of the small group isolation. Some prisoners are afflicted with mental illness that isolates them from other prisoners and impedes or prevents normal pursuit of social needs within the group. Subgroups may form within the larger community and individuals might be excluded to varying degrees for reasons of affinity, race, culture, geography, or affiliation. Time in the group is also important to the extent of integration, as is the range of differences the small group isolation effect must overcome. The conditions of isolation are also influential. The duration and manner of permitted prisoner interaction and the burden of the regime all aggravate negative behavior.

Conclusion

Control unit prisons are a metastasizing cancer that can do a substantial amount of harm to the communities they are supposed to serve. The rationale for them is predicated on official disinformation disguising repression used to create prisoners who will not be good citizens. People are relegated to control units for reasons other than the stated ones. The use of these facilities as instruments of political repression is intrinsically anti-social and exaggerates the meaning, seriousness, and degree of the behavior that purportedly justifies control units. Where control unitization is inflicted on people whose behavior does suggest a need for re-socialization, it is done without addressing the causes of the behavior. Moreover, the means of control unitization—individual and small group isolation—are incapable of positively addressing those causes. Absent such attention to causation, control units cannot achieve the end of eliminating the attitudes underlying the behavior; they tend to aggravate negative behavior instead.

Prisoner behavior defined as objectionable is not the product of some inbred evil, but occurs for reasons learned, consciously or not, in the socialization process. Where the process is faulty, as it frequently is in the face of dysfunctional families, abysmal education, poverty, and oppression, etcetera, what people learn about how to be a good person can and does diverge from social norms. This results in belief systems that allow and require behavior that appears principled and proper, or at least acceptable, to their adherents but is criminal according to the dominant belief system and its norms (or threatening to the ruling class or its apparatus of repression in the case of belief systems motivating illegal political activity). Repressing the behavior by making its perpetrators prisoners (and when the behavior continues in prison, subject to control units) cannot induce adherence to the belief systems that underlie acceptable social norms.

Control units thus do not and cannot reintegrate offenders into a more open prison community or the outside community to which virtually all of them will eventually return. Insistence on their use in light of that fact cannot be mere incompetence. Rather, it is evidence of desire to conduct experimentation toward developing the techniques of social manipulation and control, for use within the archipelago and beyond prison walls.

The future holds promise!

Note

1. *Editor's note:* In 1972, some of the first control units were established in Illinois, New Jersey, and Massachusetts. By 1985, approximately six units were scattered around the country. During the 1990s, control units (disciplinary units within prisons) and supermax prisons began to spread rapidly. Surveys conducted in 1997 by the National Campaign to Stop Control Units found that over forty-five states, the federal prison system, and the District of Columbia have some model of control unit prisons. According to the Human Rights Watch "2001 World Report," more than twenty thousand prisoners were being held in long-term solitary confinement. See Rachael Kamel and Bonnie Kerns, "The Prison Inside the Prison: Control Units, Supermax Prisons, and Devices of Torture" (Philadelphia: American Friends Service Committee, 2003); Elihu Rosenblatt, ed., *Criminal Injustice: Confronting the Prison Crisis* (Boston: South End Press, 1996); and Amnesty International, *2003 Report,* www.amnestyusa.org/home.

5

Raymond Luc Levasseur

Raymond Luc Levasseur was born on October 10, 1946, into a family of poor French Canadian factory workers in Sanford, Maine. While serving in Vietnam in 1967, he witnessed and was radicalized by racism against the Vietnamese people and U.S. soldiers of color. Upon his return, Levasseur began organizing with the Southern Student Organizing Committee (SSOC), which supported antiwar activities, black liberation, and workers' unions. In 1969, he was caught in an undercover police "sting" and received five years for selling seven dollars worth of marijuana, even though he had no prior record.

In 1971, Levasseur was paroled to Maine, where he organized for Vietnam Veterans Against the War (VVAW) and became involved in prisoners' rights organizations, including the Statewide Correctional Alliance for Reform (SCAR), which created community based "survival programs" for prison families.

In March of 1975, Levasseur was arrested in Rhode Island with Students for a Democratic Society (SDS) activist Cameron Bishop. After being released on bail, he went underground. The U.S. government alleges that between 1974 and 1984 Levasseur and his comrades were members of the United Freedom Front (UFF) and the Sam Melville/Jonathan Jackson Unit (SM/JJ), organizations that claimed responsibility for a series of bombings of government and military buildings and corporate offices. No deaths occurred in any of these actions, but there were injuries in the Suffolk County courthouse bombing.[1]

Federal agents apprehended Levasseur on November 4, 1984, in Ohio, and he, along with the "Ohio Seven," were convicted in 1986 of bombings against U.S. military facilities and businesses profiting from South African Apartheid. Levasseur received a sentence of forty-five years. From 1994 to 1999, Levasseur was imprisoned in the Federal Correctional Complex at Florence, Colorado, one of the most high-tech administrative segregation (ADX) units in the United States. In 1999, he was transferred to the Atlanta Federal Prison and was released from solitary confinement for the first time in thirteen years. In 2004, Ray Luc Levasseur was released from prison.

Note

1. According to correspondence with Ray Luc Levasseur in 2002, the only injuries in any SM/JJ and UFF bombing occurred at the Suffolk County courthouse in Boston where authorities considered a telephoned warning to evacuate the facility a hoax. Suffolk was the first bombing. No injuries resulted from subsequent bombings.

References

Levasseur, Raymond Luc. "Dear Betty." *Letters from Exile,* March 1990, home.earthlink.net/~neoludd/betty.html (March 18, 2002).
———. "Death Chambers." *Letters from Exile,* home.earthlink.net/~neoludd/chambers.html (March 18, 2002).
———. "My Blood is Quebecois." *Letters from Exile,* May 1992, home.earthlink.net/~neoludd/qbq.htm (March 18, 2002).
———. "The Trial Statement of Ray Luc Levasseur." *Letters from Exile,* January 1989. (Opening Statement, January 10, 1989: Springfield, MA), home.earthlink.net/~neoludd/statement.htm (18 March 2002).
———. "Raymond Luc Levasseur." In *Can't Jail the Spirit,* fifth edition. Chicago: Committee to End the Marion Lockdown, 2002, 182–83.

Trouble Coming Every Day:
ADX—The First Year
1996

> And so beneath the weight lay I
> And suffered death, but could not die.
> —Edna St. Vincent Millay, "Renascence"

SOCIETY REFLECTS ITSELF in the microcosm of prison. From a class-based, economically driven, racially motivated construct devolves life as a series of Chinese boxes—a set of boxes decreasing in size so that each box fits inside the next larger one. I am in the smallest box.

I AM IN Administrative Maximum (ADX) prison, the Federal government's latest boondoggle to contain prisoners' rebellion and dissent. I am in a "boxcar" cell. Picture a cage where top, bottom, sides, and back are concrete walls. The front is sliced by steel bars. Several feet beyond the bars is another wall. In this wall is a solid steel door. The term "boxcar" is derived from this configuration: a small, enclosed box that doesn't move.

I AM CONFINED to the boxcar cell 157 hours of each 168–hour week. Eleven hours each week I'm allowed into the barren area adjacent to this cell. Each morning begins with the noisy rumble of the steel door opening. A guard steps to the bars and slides food through a small slot. Feeding time. The guard steps back and the door slaps shut with a vengeance.

THE PURPOSE OF A BOXCAR CELL is to gouge the prisoners' senses by suppressing human sound, putting blinders about our eyes and forbidding touch. Essential human needs are viewed with suspicion. Within the larger context of a control unit prison, the boxcar cell is designed to inflict physical and emotional isolation that wears down a prisoner's will to resist. When this regimen undermines a prisoner's health or distorts his/her personality, it's considered the cost of doing business.

IT SEEMS ENDLESS. Each morning I look at the same gray door and hear the same rumbles followed by long silences. It is endless. Subjected to

47

humiliations designed to buckle our knees, we are: bent over, arms clamped behind our backs, pawed, prodded, cell-searched, strip-searched, commanded, marched distances of fifty feet, silenced, and hooked to a chain running through 1,500,000 prisoners. All this is enforced by a porcine abomination called the Goon Squad whose idea of combat is to jump on handcuffed and caged prisoners while applying boots, truncheons, and blasts of chemical agents to faces that are pushed into unforgiving concrete.

I'M DEEPLY CORNERED in their prison. My sight is diminished, but I maintain my vision. I see their hand in the use of four point "restraints" to spread-eagle prisoners, something inherently abusive regardless of the excuse. I see forced feedings, cell extractions, mind medications, and chemical weapons used to incapacitate. I see a steady stream of petty hassles, harassments, verbal barrages, mind-fuck games, disciplinary reports, medical neglect, and the omnipresent threat of violence. Airborne bags of shit and gobs of spit become the response of the caged.

THE MINDS OF SOME prisoners are collapsing in on them. I don't know what internal strife lies within them but it isn't mitigated here. One prisoner subjected to four-point restraints (chains, actually) as shock therapy had been chewing on his own flesh. Why is a prisoner who mutilates himself kept in ADX? Is he supposed to improve his outlook on life while stripped, chained, and tormented by a squad of guards and prison functionaries?

SOME PRISONERS RARELY come out of their cells. Others never come out. I don't know why. Meanwhile, psychologists with heads full of psychobabble roam the tiers supposedly sniffing out pockets of mental instability.

I WAS IN TENNESSEE'S Brushy Mountain penitentiary in 1970–71 when it was locked down. The media (finally!) did a shocking exposé demonstrating that up to one-third of Brushy's prisoners were mentally ill and didn't belong there. Left unanswered was whether they arrived in that condition or whether Brushy drove them over the edge. It never will be answered because Brushy prisoners rebelled in a conflagration that claimed lives on both sides of the bars. The old Brushy Mountain was closed.

ADX WAS DESIGNED the way corporations design schemes to poison the environment while avoiding responsibility for doing so. They cut into sight and sound with ubiquitous walls and boxes. We exercise in something resembling the deep end of a cement-lined pool. Every seam and crack is sealed so that not a solitary weed will penetrate this desolation. Smell and taste are reduced to staleness and sameness. Every guard functions as a spy, watching and listening with prying, voyeuristic eyes, cameras, and microphones. ("Intelligence gathering by the staff is critical."[1]) When they're done with us, we become someone else's problem.

TELEVISION DESERVES SPECIAL mention. Unlike other prisons, every ADX cell is equipped with a small black & white TV, compliments of the Bureau of Prisons (BOP) pacification program. Hollywood and Madison Avenue images are churned out through a barrage of talk shows, soaps, cartoons, and B movies to give us some vicarious social interaction. Feeling rebellious, lonely, angry, miserable, alienated, unskilled, and uneducated? Turn on the face of Amerika. The administration replaces a broken TV quicker than fixing a toilet.

THERE ARE NO JOBS for those in boxcar cells. Like millions of others, we are punished with unemployment. Education is restricted to inadequate videos on the TVs. One such program featured "The Criminal Mind." I was expecting some analysis of U.S. corporate criminals and politicians. Instead, we got a sketch of drug abusers stealing and cavorting in a landscape of dilapidated houses and abandoned factories. A school we had already been through.

RELIGIOUS SERVICES ARE relegated to TV. Recently, the prison chaplain presented his video analysis of the United States's decline caused by homosexuality, AIDS, and women's rights. Lifting this blight would "make America great again"—like in the good old days of land theft and chattel slavery. The chaplain said nothing about the scourge of poverty, racism, unemployment, or killer cops and their connection to the prison industry. The chaplain said nothing about the ADX visiting room where floor-to-ceiling partitions rub "family values" into our wounds. "Christianity" rules. There is no Imam for Muslim prisoners.

EVERY MORNING, I GO through my own ablution. Every morning there is a layer of chalky dust settled about the cell. It comes through the single air vent. It never stops. Each morning I busy myself with a wet rag mopping up all that is not in my lungs.

THE GOVERNMENT SAYS WE don't have much common cause with humanity because we are "the worst of the worst"—an incessant BOP incantation that has become an effective sound bite. The government successfully monopolizes and manipulates information pertaining to crime and punishment. But was the government to be believed about Vietnam or the S&L [Savings and Loan] ripoff? Was Nixon to be believed on Watergate? Was Reagan to be believed about the mass murder in Central America? Was Clinton to be believed concerning the human ashes in Waco? If they were, maybe you'll buy a Brooklyn Bridge named ADX. The government has a major credibility problem, yet tax dollars continue to bleed away into the sordid business of the world's largest prison system.

WHO ARE WE? WE ARE part of the chain gang, a human chain of one and a half million prisoners that runs from the "evil and unnatural construction"[2] of impoverished communities to the evil, unnatural construction of children's prisons, penitentiaries, control units, and death chambers. With each repressive step, the "troublemakers," AKA "the worst of the worst," are removed, as if WE spawned conditions in Roxbury, North Philly, East LA, and Appalachia.

Christianity Rules . . .

WE ARE MEN OF NO property, predominantly black and brown, and increasingly younger, who enter one of the few doors open to us: the penitentiary. We are too uppity, too rebellious, too subversive, and too quick to piss on prison policies. At times we are so outrageous that we destroy government property, and challenge the State's authority to treat us like dogs. We are quick to defend ourselves, our rights, our religions, and our principles. Sure, there are some happy killers and heavy bulk dealers that cashed in on other people's suffering, but they are a small minority. Most of those dealing in crimes against humanity remain on the street. No one in ADX left as many bodies in his wake as Reagan did in Central America.[3] Not even close.

WHO AM I? I AM ONE subjected to the collective punishment within the common ground of ADX. I was sent to prison for political offenses and I was placed in a control unit prison because the State maintains that my radical political beliefs and associations warrant extreme measures. Recently I was cited with a disciplinary infraction for allegedly making a derogatory comment about an ADX administrator during a media interview. The constitutional expression of my views is considered conduct unbecoming within the master/chattel relationship.

"WORST OF THE WORST" is where the illusion clashes with the reality. The illusion—that the criminalization of poverty and the isolation and degradation of prisoners provides an effective, humane response to social ills. The reality—that crimes begin at the top with predatory capitalists profiting grotesquely, while the results of their activities mire the rest of us in economic and social rot.

IN A 1993 COMMEMORATION of the Marion lockdown I wrote that ADX (then under construction and slated to replace Marion) "awaits those who continue to refuse and resist."[4] Sure enough, ADX became the destination for those prisoners held responsible for the recent uprisings throughout the federal system. The best were sent to ADX after running gauntlets of gunshots, beatings, tear gas, and the destruction of their few personal belongings. A baptism into the ranks of resistance.

OTHER UPRISING PARTICIPANTS were sent to Marion, still locked down since 1983. To the public, the BOP maintained that once ADX became operational, the lockdown would end. They lied. They doubled their control unit capacity by keeping both prisons locked down.

FOR YEARS, PRISONCRATS RAVED about the deterrent effect of Marion. If it works so well, why hasn't it put itself out of business? Marion/ADX didn't deter the October uprisings, the most widespread and destructive in the Federal prison system's history. They didn't deter USP Atlanta from grabbing headlines with its high level of violence. They have not deterred prisoners transferred to other prisons or released to the streets from picking up new charges. Control unit prisons are not the solution. They are part of the problem.

LAST YEAR, A PRISONER RELEASED from the isolation and brutality of California's notorious control unit at Pelican Bay killed a cop before he got home and unpacked his bag. Apparently, someone forgot to explain the finer points of deterrence to him. The response of the state representative from the district including Pelican Bay was illuminating. He introduced legislation mandating that released Pelican Bay prisoners be transported directly to their destination, so that when the bodies drop it will be in some other bailiwick and not stain the the Department of Corrections. Prisoncrats, like politicians, are amazingly adept at shielding themselves from the consequences of their policies.

WHERE ARE THE MENTAL CHALLENGES, stimulations, education, recreation, and socialization that are the building blocks of sound minds? The answer lies in the ADX "STEP" program, an insidious operation based on a carrot-and-stick to compliance.

WE ALL BEGIN IN the boxcars. Beyond this initial "STEP," prisoners must pass through three other steps for the ultimate award: transfer to a less degrading prison.

EACH STEP BEYOND THE BOXCARS provides greater mental and physical stimulation and less isolation. Each step provides for a bigger and tastier carrot. Be compliant, lucky, or necessary to fill a quota and you will receive more privileges. Be noncompliant, unlucky, or present any resistance and you will be buried in ADX until you're released, or you find an innovative way to beat them, or die. That's a lot of weight to carry.

ADVANCEMENT IN STEP INVOLVES pseudo debriefings by a review committee, which includes an ADX shrink. The committee expects at least a token degree of compliance, which can range from keeping one's mouth shut to standard shuck and jive. Were I to tell the committee what I am now putting on paper, I would be rejected. The bottom line is the administration's power and agenda; no different, really, than outside.

HERE, THEY ADVANCE WHO they want, when they want, and for whatever reason they want. They just as arbitrarily reject others. Or they ignore
their own "guidelines" whenever it suits their political or personal purpose. They toy with prisoners' lives and compile reams of paper to create
the fiction that the federal prison system, indeed, the country, is a better,
safer place because of their efforts.

Not Quite Slave . . .

THE FINAL STEP IS UNICOR [U.S. Department of Justice Federal Prison
Industries, Inc.]—the factory. Prisoners are required to demonstrate their
readiness to function in a less restrictive environment by laboring for 26
cents an hour (". . . to be treated in such a way as to exploit them to the
highest possible extent at the lowest conceivable degree of expenditure").[5]
Not quite slave labor, but close.

THE ADMINISTRATION CONSIDERS STEP/UNICOR its primary management and control mechanism, which it manipulates at will. They consider
it something of a propaganda coup to have the system's designated recalci-
trants filling the slots. I say this, in part, because shortly after UNICOR
became operational, the ADX segregation unit filled with incoming prisoners from the October uprisings. The irony of having one group of prisoners
set up a primary component of a program that serves to entrap other prisoners entering ADX has not gone unnoticed. If we cannot counter the
administration's strategy of dangling each prisoner from his own rope,
they will turn us into our own worst enemies.

LOCKED DOWN PRISONS are no longer unique. They have erupted
across the country like malignant sores on a diseased organ. The entire
prison gulag vies with gambling as the country's fastest growing industry,
with neither one producing anything of social value. Jails and prisons
compete with fast-food joints for the public appetite. Jails are scattered
among churches. Prisons are scattered among cow pastures. Barges are
converted into jails. Tents are converted into cells. Military bases are converted into prisons. Schools are being looked at next. It all bottoms out in
control unit prisons.

LET'S NOT KID OURSELVES ABOUT the prevailing attitude among the
political and corporate elite and much of the voting public: prisoners are
human waste. The more forbidding the penitentiaries, the more like
garbage they define us. As downsized laborers, outcasts, and outlaws,
there is no room for us at the table. Exterminating us on a mass scale is
not presently acceptable, so plan B is in effect: execute small numbers, cor-

rupt some, co-opt others, drive others mad, and imprison millions. As prisoners, the only value we have is if they can turn a political campaign or a dollar on us.

SO, OUR BODIES BECOME commodities for someone else's gain. Past recidivist rates documented a failed system. Today's recidivist rates read like the Dow Jones Industrial Average—the higher the recidivism, the more various opportunists stand to gain.

THE TRAFFICKERS IN BODIES INSURE a steady supply by slashing at fundamental programs serving our poorest families. They demand more police, more children's prisons and more youth incarceration. More bodies, younger bodies, with increased shelf life due to mandatory sentences. They legislate harsher conditions that make us leaner, meaner, and infinitely more recyclable.

CROWDING THE WASTE ARE PARASITES and scavengers that descend on misery like gulls at a landfill: prison guards, administrators, consultants, contractors, construction companies, maintenance personnel, concessionaires, realtors, social workers, paper shufflers, etcetera, ad nauseam. All of them opt for the government's blue light sale rather than find respectable employment.

ADX GUARDS SAY THEY are just doing their job, which they will gladly do for an annual entry level salary of $32,000; $50,000 with overtime. A nice benefits package and a bully pulpit to boot. Some do it with benign neglect, while others do it with perverse cruelty. In a Faustian contract with the government, they work the cages and in return get to send their kids to college and take Caribbean vacations.

GUARDS, LIKE ALL ENTERPRISING citizens, can buy a piece of the action through tax exempt bonds that underwrite state prison construction. They can do it with the detached air of the postmodern fascist because such purchases do not hold them liable for anything that happens within the prison. No beating, injury, medical neglect, or death will cut into their profit. In the burgeoning private prison industry stock purchases are available through investment companies. Why not? General Motors invested in Nazi Germany.

THERE'S MONEY TO BE MADE in fraud; the government is rife with it, but like most frauds there are a few who profit from prisons while many more are victimized. Taxpayers subsidize most prisons, and it is citizens who pay through the nose. By ANY financial measure, statistic, or body count, the prison system is an abysmal failure. Very high cost, very little benefit.

THERE'S A PARALLEL with the Vietnam War: The government takes your money and children for war while deceiving you into acquiescence. In return we get a divided society, more violence, and an abandonment of the

War on Poverty. And like those years, it appears the present "silent majority" isn't ready for a serious policy review until the cycle of violence drives its stake deeper into middle Amerika's heart, and their pockets have been more thoroughly picked.

> We were the slaves in Pharaoh's land,
> you and he and I.
> And we were serfs to feudal hands
> Now that times gone by.
> Prentices in cities, prisoners for debt,
> Hunted vagrants, parish poor, our life is a lie.
> We move, an invisible army. . . .[6]

THE RULING CLASS MAKES the laws, and there's no shortage of sycophants to wield them like a club. Guards and administrators operate under color of prison law that ranges from court-granted "qualified immunity" to stark terror and murder. The United States Constitution's Thirteenth Amendment allows convict labor to be harnessed like slave labor. A Supreme Court mandate forbids prisoners from forming unions. Circulating a petition is a punishable offense. Interwoven through the letter of the law is five hundred years of white supremacy. Twenty-five lashes. Twenty-five year sentence.

PENITENTIARIES TURN OUT MORE violent, crime-prone, big-attitude men, women, and children who have been told in no uncertain terms that their individual freedom and dignity are worth nothing, and that their futures are nil. The police cannot protect communities from the volatile rage this brings to bear. All the police do is step in after the fact to clean up some of the mess. The Better Business Bureau accepts no complaints about the criminal justice system's grand fraud and toxic emissions.

MILLIONS MORE LIVES IN prison will not improve life on the street. It takes an investment in humanity that provides living wage jobs and other development opportunities to improve the quality of our lives and communities. America doesn't lack the resources. It lacks the will.

THE ATTICA REBELLION AND massacre demonstrated that the State can and will kill us, and that killing us is the ultimate sanction for militant resistance. Twenty-five years of subsequent litigation put the courts' approval on the massacre. The government ALWAYS approves its own slaughter. But the capacity to live in submission and have the lifeblood sucked out of us from one decade into the next has its limits. When we are strong, organized, and ready, we will transcend these limits—as only human beings can.

Notes

Originally published online by Raymond Luc Levasseur in *Letters from Exile,* home.earthlink.net/~neoludd/betty.html.

1. John Vanyur, Associate Warden, ADX, "Design Meets Mission at New Federal Max Facility," *Corrections Today,* Vol. 57, No. 4 (July 1995): 92.

2. Jonathan Kozol, *Amazing Grace: The Lives of Children and the Conscience of a Nation* (New York: Crown, 1995).

3. *Editor's note:* During the administration of President Ronald Reagan in the 1980s, segments of the U.S. government were crucial in securing millions of dollars in legal and illegal funding for paramilitary death squads in El Salvador and Guatemala; and for "contras"—counterrevolutionary terrorists waging war against the socialist Sandanista government in Nicaragua.

4. Raymond Luc Levasseur, "The Fire Inside," in *Letters from Exile,* September 1993, home.earthlink.net/~neoludd/betty.html.

5. Fritz Saukel (Head of Nazi forced labor program, 1942). *Editor's note:* See Joseph E. Persico, *Nuremberg: Infamy on Trial* (New York: Viking, 1994).

6. "All Of Us Together," Southern labor song, 1930s.

6

Paul St. John

Paul St. John was born in 1956, grew up on Long Island, New York and eventually earned an MA in sociology. Incarcerated for a drug offense, St. John began writing fiction while in prison. He won literary prizes for "Peeks by the Gnome of the Slums on the Bad Hardened to the Absolute" and for "Behind the Mirror's Face," which he wrote while at Eastern New York Correctional Facility. St. John has also received multiple honorable mentions in PEN (Poets, Playwrights, Essayists, Editors, and Novelists) contests and has published fiction in *Midnight Zoo*.

Reference

Chevigny, Bell Gale, ed. *Doing Time: Twenty-Five Years of Prison Writing.* New York: Arcade Publishing, 1999.

Behind the Mirror's Face
1999

Charlie says to me, "We gotta get ready for that new facility mag, get us our voices heard." He's chewing on a nip of his cigar, which I despise, the stogie like a pen on the tripod of his hand.

"This is prison, Chuck, not a facility. In here they don't facilitate a friggin' thing." Charlie can't listen and talk in the same context. "Prison writing man, that's where it's at." He's staring at a blank screen above my shoulder.

My brain lines up a reasonable response: How long you been down, you big stupid ape? "It makes no difference, bro," I say instead. This is one redneck I won't offend.

From here on in it's a one-way conversation, two hundred and eighty pounds of duress humming on about Jack Henry Abbott[1] writing his way out of the Joint because he had the guts to speak up, how prison writing breaks down the walls of isolation, how the pen is mightier than . . .

The thoughts begin to soar V-formation:

Funny that in the end the sword proved to be Abbott's master. / With Mailer for an editor I'd write my way out of hell. / He also did a little snitching there, if the truth be told.

But they just dive off and fall away. I wave my hands at the curtains of smoke Charlie has installed in my cell, and he knows that's enough of him for one morning.

I ride the inside track, and within an hour I find out why the warden has seen fit that a few caged birds should go to print. As every con knows, democracy in the prison setting is just another word for "never," so when each inmate group petitions to put out their own newsletters, the warden has an aberration to prevent. (Manifold printing costs, new jobs for x inmate staffs to type, edit, and layout page after page of burning prose and slick graphics on blazing 486 computers. Forget it. They end up smarter than the guards. Then the salaried censorship squad for all whiners who will harp on and on about an evil system and skewed justice, dire living, exploitation, Bill of Rights violations, and conspiracy theories ad nauseam.) So what is a reasonably sly warden to do? He will locate two or three lifers who would have been Nobel laureates if not for lack of opportunity, to offer them the chance of their lifetime. It is time his prisoners be heard!

He will leave out one small detail: This is to be a one-time venture, something he can show the inmate groups so their nagging will rest. You will have one facility-sponsored publication, one single vehicle of choice for all your groaning pains and visions. Come and spill out your guts, dudes, in unity of song!

There will be plenty of Dostoevskis and Malcolms in this number, but from the groups Mr. Warden will hear a single chorus: RUB IT ON YOUR CHEST 'CAUSE WE AIN'T RIDIN' SHOTGUN. His calculated effort will be thus consummated, and he will smile to the portrait of Reagan on his wall. Hey, guys, I handed it to you on a mess hall tray and you declined.

For Charlie it will be the beginning of great things. Charlie got soul. If I could synthesize the heart of his verse it would be this: the longing of looking through iron bars at the real world. Real touching stuff once you get past the trademark ache/break and dove/love rhymes. Next time around he would probably push his more radical stuff, things like "Why the Parole Board Should Be Abolished" and "Why Media Coverage of Violent Crime Should Be Abolished" and "Why the Random Cell Search Should Be Abolished." I just hope he won't start acting up when he discovers there isn't going to be a second time.

Prison Writing. The term reverberates in my brain case like kettle-drums. The anger returns. I can't recall the psychospeak, but I know it's like a form of Pavlov's.[2] People are set off by certain sights, sounds, even smells, that affect them in very special ways.

Suddenly the gallery feels awfully quiet. I stare at my typewriter, which turns into a missile-control board. It's time to fire away.

I will call her Mother Nature, an artist who came into the prison to "find flowers where others saw only weeds." I taped the Author's Release to the wall two weeks ago. I feed a blank sheet to the machine.

Dear Mother Nature,

Thank you for the opportunity you have given us to videotape our work for a showing at the Cultural Center. I think you are a unique spirit for daring to tap into the voices of this miserably dark place. However, I regret to say that you are on the wrong track if your intentions are to use this so-called Prison Writing Experience as a means for reform, simply because prisoners, although they understand what is wrong with the system better than any criminologist, judge, cop, or outsider, have the credibility of elves. In this sense prison writing's dead wood.

The only other way to look at prison writing is as a way of expression. And, frankly, who wants to hear about loneliness, hopelessness, despair, loss of autonomy, harassment, contempt, or civil death, except to feel real good that things aren't as bad out in the world? Please don't think that I will allow myself to be used as consolation for a civilian audience.

Finally, if you are on a true healing mission, seeking to change the minds and hearts of prisoners through a revolution of the pen, I will appreciate it very much if you'd begin with sending me some real food and vitamins to counterbalance the negative effects of the garbage I am fed. I could also use real medical care, you know, the kind that steps right to the business and doesn't doubt the patient, and doesn't wait for *rigor mortis* in order to proceed. That's all I got to say.

> Very truly yours,
> Dr. J.

Sorry, Charlie, I think you better take all your "I hurt" trash and your impossible solutions and rub them on your fat redneck chest. I will be a writer in prison, for now. You be all the prison writer you wish. Be a white gorilla in your cubicle bush with iron fronds and rock-hard soil. Moan your nightly if-onlys and grunt your morning sores of broken luck alone, my man, 'cause I'll be traveling light, with the Daughters of Sin. Their silken manes fall down their rears like pouring silver, and their moans are all I need for a cloak. Their touch is a tingle of mercurial dew, their panting a hot leaden mist, a desert of glass. I won't tell you about their kiss, not tonight, Charlie.

Charlie would never understand that nothing they do here is for his benefit. The language of his philosophical cutlery will be toned down, watered down, rekneaded to retain the basic dignity of the system, or rejected if he doesn't go along. Would any prison foster a printed attack on its own ways? Prison writing is as free as the author. Again I engage the machine and begin to spin out a little speech I have prepared for my prison writing group, which I polish up as I go.

On the Subject of Prison Writing

Good evening, fellow writers. I would like to take a few minutes tonight to discuss prison writing and its place in the larger world of letters.

As we know, writing comes in many kinds. There is fiction writing, journal writing, junk mail writing, copy writing, textbook writing, speech writing, news writing, film script writing . . . you aim, I shoot.

Subject, genre, specialty—the writer enters it by choice. But prison writing is a matter of status. It comes with the bid and that's that. It must take as subject matter life in prison. Prison writing is literally forced upon the writer, who, incidentally, has been stripped of just about everything else. Now, that's supposed to liberate.

Hey, Charlie, you dumb ass! You big cigar-puffin' ignorant crass sack of southern white trash! You bemused witless serf!

A con may write fiction, but everybody will know where it comes from. His fiction wears the stink of prison for a belt. Her fiction is pregnant with loss disguised as possibility. His outlaws always get the better of a wicked status quo. Her heroines grope through a jungle of shame for their stolen womanhood, and perhaps a piece of heaven. A convict may write about Mars, the sea, rebirth, cats, needles and pins; without the "convict point of view" there is no prison writing. Take this goddamned place out of your art is what I am trying to tell you all.

My concentration is assaulted by my boombox-proud neighbor, who jacks up the rapper cacophony until the presence of the guard, like some magical wand, directs him to turn into a punk. (Whatever happened to cool smooth good ol' American jazz?) As soon as the guard leaves the gallery, he is King Kong again.

King Punk is confined to his cell for talking to another inmate two steps out of character. Although he got the brunt of it, violence has no victims here. Self-defense is without justification. If you're hurt, you shouldn't have been there. If you do not defend yourself, you're on a stainless steel table with a sheet over your head, it's that simple.

And yet sometimes I think prison violence is all overstated, amplified, dramatized, *mythicized*, mostly by outsiders. Maybe I'm desensitized but prison life isn't really as dangerous as it's commonly portrayed. Much of the tension on the inside comes more from the perception of danger than from danger itself. That's why the sneak attack is the preferred mode of action—the little guy sticking a pen in the big guy's eye after the latter jokingly threatened to make him his girl. Although most cases of violence involve aggressor and prey, prison managers are unwilling to recognize assault because of the lawsuits. So they do their damnedest to make everyone look guilty or well-deserving.

Their process is succored by an important rule: Never believe what an inmate says except when he's snitching. In the old days, telling was an abomination. Sooner or later the snitch would be found out and have to face the music. Today, telling is something of a sport and the facing up usually doesn't happen, as the snitch may conveniently check his cowardly ass into protective custody.

Underlying this apparent confusion is a beautiful symmetry. In the street, where self-defense is a legitimate act and telling is the bread of concerned citizens, crises tend to ripple off toward agreement. Behind the mirror's face, the littlest disturbance bears the seed of chaos.

After mopping the gallery catwalk that stretches like a giant steel blade past forty cells, I ease into my slippers and robe. On my way to the shower I pass Captain Lafane, whose harrowed look makes me wonder if it's me who is doing the time. He knows that my transition from systems analyst to prison porter has not been easy, but that is not the reason for his grief. His oldest son has AIDS.

◆ ◆ ◆

I awaken to the chirping of birds. With all the nooks on the outside, they had to nest in here. There are dozens of them, lodged in the stone bowers high above the uppermost gallery. Jailbirds. Now it happens that prison is also a state of mind.

Will there be any stabbings today? Any rapes? Who cares? No will ever know the half of it. Just as I rake the stubble off my chin guards rush past my window into the deep of the gallery. A minute later, two more guards go by with a wire mesh stretcher. Here we go.

Except for the crackle of radios, the gallery is dead-still. No one is dead-still. We must have an overnighter. The portable mirrors go into peeking mode.

The guards are slow on the catwalk. Two are old and overweight; one just looks sick and tired. Their walk is like a funeral march without an entourage. As they approach my cell I pull my mirror in and look down at the stretcher. It's Jimmy G. I better hurry up and finish shaving before they yell for chow.

◆ ◆ ◆

Questions are being raised about the night guard's rounds, which should go on every two hours. The coroner has established that Jimmy took his life sometime after two. Even after this leak, we know that nothing will be done beyond tightening up the rounds for a while. No jobs will be in jeopardy, even when Jimmy had been talking suicide a few weeks in advance. Even after he was taken twice for observation to a psychiatric center, and advised that there was nothing wrong with him. Even after he flashed his suicide card to his pastor.

In her letter of thanks to his church for having run a fund collection, his mother stated that Jimmy had a chemical imbalance, foreclosing any possibility of a negligence action. Anyway, thank you, Mrs. G. Now all of us who did nothing to prevent your son from giving up will feel better. It was all in his genes as luck is in the stars, we will say.

Jimmy was four-fifths of the way through a sentence for murder. If the truth be told, I can think of one thousand better candidates for Hades just on the basis of their bearing. Jimmy had found religion. Jimmy had found a good church girl to elope with.

We all knew that he had been distressed over his failed marriage, but in here a man is pretty much left alone with the affairs of his heart. It was a union blessed by God, not to be set asunder by another. Why did she have to have "a male friend" at her house almost every time he called. . . .

It couldn't have been you instead of Jimmy, could it, King Punk, you rappin' tappin' slappin' wind-up moppet-faced big bad mouth cybernaut stooge. Even you, farther down, who would have your voice heard by the prison machine. How much are you willing to renounce? A noun-slice here, a verb-tuck there, perhaps a sentence-graft or two? Why don't you just sing praises to the Beast? Something might click. A new trend. Charlie, it might just make a difference!

Jimmy, perhaps you should have come to me. I would have told you their names.

I saw your humbled heart filling your mouth with hardened bread, and I kept silent. You should have known her, too, the one holding the wineskin, that fine hostess of spoils. Plethora will give you of her sac of ambrosia, and you will be made new. I will not risk offending, else I would bring her to you.

When I heard you smite your chest in penitence, I thought, *Jimmy, that ain't no way of doin' time.* Hedone will give you relish, comfort, a new zest. Frolic between the happy slopes and valleys of her Eden, for no one needs saving from love. Rest, Jimmy, rest now, and pound your chest no more.

But of the three, Cacoethes is the crown. She's the baddest, the good-est, the sweetest, the tartest, the hostess of play. She's the lifeline, the night life, hops, cheers, saturnalia again. Fandago, tango, fling, and boogaloo.

They say that she's full of bad habits. Not true. She's sport, gala, picnic, and game all the same. Overall, she's a labor of love. In a cinch she's Ways and Means, my man. For you, she would have plucked the hand that held the knife of infidelity, before it ripped your heart. When Mars directs the rouge over her lips, and paints her eyes for the battle cry, you know there's no staying and no praying for more. All in all, she'll save you from a two-timer wife. Cacoethes is the blood of my pen, liberation without the prison writing.

You won't be needing religion in the bowels of Earth. Neither do I in the belly of Baal. You may judge me unwise, but at least there is no falling from grace in this bed. One day I might tell you the meaning of their names, if you should resurrect.

But tonight I'm riding with the wind.

Notes

Originally published in *Doing Time: Twenty-Five Years of Prison Writing,* ed. Bell Gale Chevigny (New York: Arcade Publishing, 1999), 119–25.

1. *Editor's note:* Jack Henry Abbott, an imprisoned author who obtained release in 1981 with the help of author Norman Mailer, wrote *In the Belly of the Beast: Letters from Prison* (New York: Random House, 1981). Shortly after his release, Abbott killed a waiter in New York City and was subsequently convicted of second-degree murder.

2. *Editor's note:* Ivan Petrovich Pavlov, a Russian physiologist and experimen-tal psychologist, developed research on the conditioned reflexes of dogs. He won the 1904 Nobel Prize in physiology and authored *Conditioned Reflexes: An Inves-tigation of the Physiological Activity of the Cerebral Cortex* (New York: Dover Publications, 1960).

7

Tiyo Attallah Salah-El

Tiyo Attallah Salah-El is a decorated Korean War veteran, who after being wounded and honorably discharged in 1953, began playing jazz. As he writes, he "also engaged in many negative activities (e.g., drug sales, abusing women, lying, stealing, assault and battery, and shootings)." In 1975, Attallah Salah-El was sentenced to life in prison for murder. Incarcerated for three decades, he has been a member of the prison activist community and abolitionist movement for many years, and is a founder of the organization and newsletter, "The Coalition for the Abolition of Prisons." While in prison, Attallah Salah-El earned a BA in African American history, a MA in Political Science, and appointments such as Program Advisor for Beacon College and Director of the Prisoner Education Program. A graduate of law school, he is a member of the National Lawyer's Guild.

References

Attallah Salah-El, Tiyo. "Attaining Education in Prison Equals Prison Power." *Journal of Prisoners on Prisons,* Vol. 4, No. 1 (1992).

Hartnett, Stephen and Kate Klehr, eds. "Broken Chains." *Coalition for the Abolition of Prisons (CAP) Newsletter* (Summer 2001).

A Call for the Abolition of Prisons
2001

In the history of philosophy, there is perhaps no more powerful image than the "cave" described by Socrates in Plato's *Republic*. This deep, dark hole, we are told, is inhabited by "prisoners" bound in such a way that all they can see is the play of shadows on an interior wall, fleeting shapes that they mistake for reality. Far above these hapless souls, outside their underground dwelling, is the dazzling light of the sun—a sight reached only after an arduous journey upward.

For over a quarter of a century, I have been making that arduous journey, striving and struggling to reach that dazzling light of freedom and justice, not just for myself but also for the two million women and men presently housed in that cave. During that journey, I gained new insight regarding the pain of prisons and the devastation and the brutalizing of people by capitalism and imperialism. From that painful experience, I became an abolitionist.

I may never be able to fully describe the complex dynamic process of how to organize and bring about the abolition of prisons. However, it is my hope that the views and information presented here will help others to further develop their own reasons why they would be willing to undertake the struggle to help abolish prisons. The strength of my vision depended in great measure on what I learned about prison during my twenty-five years of incarceration and how much I am willing to continue learning. This type of learning requires a lifelong commitment to continual inquiry and knowledge in order to arrive at new levels of understanding and insight.

I have learned that there are many different ways of looking at any thing, event, or process. It all depends on how you are looking at it. I continue to look and learn as I live within the rotten, corrupt core of the criminal justice system. The prison has been a teacher for me. It reflects my own mind. The prison has not changed. It is my mind that has changed.

When your mind changes, new possibilities begin to arise. In fact everything changes when you can see things on different levels simultaneously, when you can see fullness and connectedness as well as individuality and separateness. Your thinking expands in scope. This can be a profoundly liberating experience. It has taken me beyond my limited preoccupations with myself. It put things in a larger perspective. It has certainly changed the way I relate to prisons and the criminal justice system. If we hope to see things more clearly as they actually are and thereby perceive their intrinsic meaning, we have to be mindful of the ruts our thinking gets us into, and we have to learn to see and approach things differently.

Facing our problems is usually the only way to get past them. There is an art to facing difficulties in ways that lead to effective solutions. We can, by exercising imagination, intuition, and creativity in our own work, use the pressure of the problem itself to propel us through it. It is incumbent upon us to find new ways to break into the cycle of violence that so much characterizes the present corrections and criminal justice system in this country.

The least controversial observation that one can make about American criminal justice today is that it is remarkably ineffective, absurdly expensive, grossly inhumane, and riddled with ruthlessness and racism. In my view and the views of a growing number of people, it seems clear that the hypothesis that prisons are institutions for control of people of color is a far more viable one than the notion that prisons are an effort to prevent crime. All serious analyses of the history of incarceration reveal the same historical thrust: Prisons and other systems of punishment are for social control, not crime control.

The criminal justice system is a multibillion dollar industry, and also very subversive of democratic principles. This establishment has doubled over the last decade. And its power has mostly been concentrated on the black community. The system is accountable to no civilian oversight. There is no more unaccountable system than a corrections system. The corporate media usually frames the debate over the criminal justice system and that arcane realm of the government contract think tanks, where civilians answerable to no elected official formulate policies and concoct plans that wreak havoc on the poor and minorities, especially on black women and men.

There has been a turning away from looking at the social factors and social issues that create crime. Most people don't want to talk about things like adequate income, employment, and antipoverty programs, all of this now being passé. And so the people are left with the idea that criminals therefore must somehow be simply wicked persons, quite unlike them, and if they can genetically define these criminals, it's made even easier. It's an easy way out. Then one does not have to feel any guilt for what goes on in one's society. The general public wants their pound of flesh. They don't care what happens. They want to prove a point with blacks, and the politicians are going to do it with the criminal justice system.

Race is the big, ugly secret that lies at the heart of U.S. crime policy. The criminal justice system is a system run on sound bites and throwaway lines. The system is not interested in anything that would lower crime, much less in anything decent or human that's going to advance society. It's just a terribly corrupt system. And of course, when you are talking about crime and criminals, it's very, very easy to fall into demonizing and stereotyping. Not only will people accept it, you can build a political career around it.

There is a need to unwind; there's a need to find options, a lot of options, especially for the lesser offenders who have drug problems, but who are now being sent to prison. We must go further than merely condemning prisons and the building of more prisons. We have to point the direction in which the solution lies. We must focus upon what we must put in the place of prisons, and whether what we demand or propose will really eliminate the evils being objected to. We have to create and offer a well thought-out program for accomplishing the change and propose a specific form of alternative with which to replace the present system. We are going to have to face and deal with questions that demand workable and acceptable solutions. How would society function if we abolished prisons? What to do with the dangerous few? Who decides? Who pays? Who benefits? Who will be in charge? Where will this lead us?

This is why we must be clear as to tactics, and above all, armed with a workable program that will enable us to reach our goal. We cannot ignore the lessons that history has already taught us. We must create and project a powerful program for reaching our revolutionary goal of abolishing prisons. I strongly suggest we begin a new way of thinking about abolition.

Justice suggests that we may need to take a broader view of certain problems if we hope to solve them. This approach involves asking us what the extent of the problem actually is and discerning the relationship between the various isolated parts of the problem and the problem as a whole. If we do not identify the system correctly in its entirety, we will never come to a satisfactory solution because a key domain will always be missing, the domain of the whole.

We have to expand beyond our habitual ways of seeing and thinking and acting. If we don't, our attempts to identify and solve our problems will usually be thwarted by our own prejudices and preconceptions. Our lack of awareness of the system as a whole will often prevent us from seeing new options. We will have a tendency to get stuck in our crises and to make faulty decisions and choices. Rather than penetrating through problems to the point where solutions are reached, when we get stuck, there is a tendency to make more problems and to make them worse, and also to give up trying to solve them.

Such experiences can lead to feelings of frustration, inadequacy, and insecurity. Our doubts about our own abilities become self-fulfilling prophecies. They can come to dominate our lives. In this way, we effectively make our own limits by our own thought processes. Then, too often, we forget that we have created these boundaries ourselves. Consequently we get stuck and feel we cannot get beyond them. Therefore, when someone comes forth with the idea of abolishing prisons, most people react and respond with all sorts of self-imposed boundaries. Some will even turn a deaf ear to the words calling for the abolition of prisons.

I took on the challenge and the risks of facing full attack from the criminal justice system. I surprised others and myself with my newfound courage and clarity. In the process, I discovered my limits receding and I found myself capable of doing things that I never thought I could do. The point is that we don't always know what our true limits are.

Prison abolition, like the abolition of slavery, is a long-range goal. Abolition is not simply a moment in time, but a protracted process. Prison abolitionism should not now be considered a pipe dream, but rather a strong strategy that can in time bring about a halt to the building of more prisons. This is why an abolitionist approach demands a solid critical analysis of crime that is juxtaposed with social structures, plus anticrime strategies that focus on the provision of social resources. We must educate the public that prisons need to be abolished as the sole way of attempting to resolve social problems that are better solved by other more human ways and means.

Abolition and revolution are not new. History is replete with stories of the struggles of people on the bottom of the social ladder banding together and organizing to bring radical change for the better in their lives and the lives of future generations. Some struggles succeeded, some failed, and others are ongoing. The questions we face regarding the struggle to abolish prisons are too many to count. I do not know how long it will take to abolish prisons. That is akin to asking me how much air is in the universe. Therein is the real challenge—our search for answers must be incessant.

Shouldn't we ask ourselves how we can build new powers from below? How can we create a new common language to define injustice and to imagine a society without prisons? What are we doing in practice to create the new from within the old? Does such a movement have a chance of surviving and creating change? Survival and victory depend on coordinated action. We must learn how to cooperate quickly and effectively so as to intensify, broaden, and deepen our struggles. We need stronger networks of communication and support. We must develop a process of dialogue and organization unprecedented in the history of America.

We can develop a process of dialogues and organization unparalleled in the history of abolition in America. Let us strive to give hope to many that a new kind of thinking about the abolition of prisons is in the making, one capable of inspiring people to come together, speaking to each other about abolition and revolution. *We must strengthen the hope and dreams of Freedom, Abolition, and Revolution.* [In the words of Subcommandante Marcos of the EZLN (*Ejército Zapatista Liberación Nacional*):]

> Here we are, the dead of all time, dying once again, only now with the object of living. You have to get out of your self to save yourselves. What we seek, what we need and want is that all those people without a party and organization make agreements about what they want and do not want and become organized in order to achieve it (preferably through civil and peaceful means), not to take power, but to exercise it.

Some suggestions for moving ahead:

1. Accept the fact that no one person or organization can keep up even in a cursory manner with all the aspects of struggle; sharing that work through political organizations is necessary, as is developing supportive and cooperative relations among many organizations. Therefore, we should consider supporting, listening, learning, and exchanging knowledge (not just "information") with antideath penalty organizations in their efforts to first bring about a moratorium of the death penalty and the eventual abolition of the death penalty. When such a goal is achieved, we can build upon that success via inviting them to take the next revolutionary step and buttress our struggle to work toward abolishing prisons. We would then have a much broader base of well-seasoned activists, supporters, networks, knowledge, communications, information, and funding.

2. Do not set out with the idea to tear down prisons, but to promote and transform the present prisons into Healing and Caring Centers. The infrastructure is already in place for all the basic needs such as food, clothing, shelter, medications, transportation, and recreation. Retrain prison staff toward becoming in-house teachers, paid at the same pay scale as they are presently being paid. Such a strategy will help placate the various guard unions and other misguided proprison advocates. Present-day prisons could eventually become Healing and Caring Centers for the homeless, shelters for abused and battered women and children, meaningful and productive drug and alcohol treatment centers, meaningful education and

vocation programs for families living in abject poverty. Bring new leadership roles into prisons to work along with most treatment personnel.

3. To the best of my knowledge, there has been little, if any, mention much less serious discussion among abolitionists about what to do with the dangerous few. I think we can all agree that for the over all well-being and safety of society-at-large, detention is and may always be required for the small group of people who cause harm to others. This question must first be acknowledged, studied, discussed, and resolved by not only abolitionists, but also among broad-based groups of doctors, judges, community organizations, corrections personnel, psychologists, legislators, and others on the local, state and federal levels. The general public must be invited to take part in these open discussions. This issue will test the metal of not just abolitionists, but of all involved. Now is the time to begin thinking and planning tactics and strategies regarding this important and sensitive issue.

Creating a new way of "Thinking About Prisons" requires the best efforts, ideas, and experiences and honest, careful, sharp, and critical reflection from all those who are willing to take on this daring and daunting task. We must construct the groundwork for future generations to build a world that is safe and just. Let us begin working at the edges of what is possible. Let us strive toward a new possibility. Let us fight with the weapon of intelligence. *I invite you to join us.*

II. Gendered Captivity

8

Assata Shakur

Assata Shakur (Joanne Chesimard) was born in 1947, in New York. She became involved in antiracist activism in the mid-1960s while attending Manhattan Community College. Upon graduation, Shakur began working with the Black Panther Party (BPP) and then the Black Liberation Army (BLA), an underground military formation. A main target of the Federal Bureau of Investigation's COINTELPRO, Shakur was accused of numerous charges, all of which were eventually dropped or of which she was acquitted.

In a 1973 confrontation with New Jersey state troopers, she was seriously wounded, and BLA co-member, Zayd Shakur, and state trooper Werner Foerster were killed; companion Sundiata Acoli (Clark Squire) escaped but was later apprehended. Despite medical evidence showing she could not have fired a shot given her wounds from police fire, Shakur was convicted as an accomplice to the murder of Foerster and of assault on trooper James Harper. The March 1977 conviction by an all-white jury came after a 1973 change of venue and a 1974 mistrial.

Shakur escaped from New Jersey's Clinton Correctional Facility in 1979, and lives in exile in Cuba where she received political asylum in 1984. Shakur discusses her life and experiences in the black liberation struggle in *Assata: An Autobiography.*

References

Bin Wahad, Dhoruba, Mumia Abu-Jamal, and Assata Shakur. *Still Black, Still Strong: Survivors of the U.S. War Against Black Revolutionaries,* edited by Jim Fletcher, Tanaquil Jones, and Sylvère Lotringer. New York: Semiotext(e), 1993.

Parenti, Christian. "Assata Shakur Speaks from Exile: Post-modern Maroon in the Ultimate Palenque." *Z Magazine,* Vol. 11, No. 3 (March 1998): 27–32.

Perkins, Margo V. *Autobiography as Activism: Three Black Women of the Sixties.* Jackson: University Press of Mississippi, 2000.

Williams, Evelyn. *Inadmissable Evidence: The Story of the African-American Trial Lawyer Who Defended the Black Liberation Army.* Brooklyn: Lawrence Hill, 1993.

Women in Prison: How We Are
1978

We sit in the bull pen. We are all black. All restless. And we are all freezing. When we ask, the matron tells us that the heating system cannot be adjusted. All of us, with the exception of a woman, tall and gaunt, who looks naked and ravished, have refused the bologna sandwiches. The rest of us sit drinking bitter, syrupy tea. The tall, fortyish woman, with sloping shoulders, moves her head back and forth to the beat of a private tune while she takes small, tentative bites out a bologna sandwich. Someone asks her what she's in for. Matter-of-factly, she says, "They say I killed some nigga'. But how could I have when I'm buried down in South Carolina?" Everybody's face gets busy exchanging looks. A short, stout young woman wearing men's pants and men's shoes says, "Buried in South Carolina?" "Yeah," says the tall woman. "South Carolina, that's where I'm buried. You don't know that? You don't know shit, do you? This ain't me. This ain't me." She kept repeating, "This ain't me" until she had eaten all the bologna sandwiches. Then she brushed off the crumbs and withdrew, head moving again, back into that world where only she could hear her private tune.

Lucille comes to my tier to ask me how much time a "C" felony conviction carries. I know, but i cannot say the words. I tell her i will look it up and bring the sentence charts for her to see. I know that she has just been convicted of manslaughter in the second degree. I also know that she can be sentenced up to fifteen years. I knew from what she had told me before that the District Attorney was willing to plea bargain: five years probation in exchange for a guilty plea to a lesser charge.

Her lawyer felt that she had a case: specifically, medical records that would prove that she had suffered repeated physical injuries as the result of beatings by the deceased and, as a result of those beatings, on the night of her arrest, her arm was mutilated (she must still wear a brace on it) and one of her ears was partially severed in addition to other substantial injuries. Her lawyer felt that her testimony, when she took the stand in her own defense, would establish the fact that not only had she been repeatedly beaten by the deceased, but that on the night in question he told her he would kill her, viciously beat her, and mauled her with a knife. But there is no self-defense in the state of New York.

The District Attorney made a big deal of the fact that she drank. And the jury, affected by tv racism, "law and order," petrified by crime and unimpressed with Lucille as a "responsible citizen," convicted her. And I was the one who had to tell her that she was facing fifteen years in prison while we both silently wondered what would happen to the four teenage children that she had raised almost single-handedly.

Spikey has short time, and it is evident, the day before she is to be released, that she does not want to go home. She comes to the Bing (Administrative Segregation) because she has received an infraction for fighting. Sitting in front of her cage and talking to her i realize that the fight was a desperate, last ditch effort in the hope that the prison would take away her "good days." She is in her late thirties. Her hands are swollen. Enormous. There are huge, open sores on her legs. She has about ten teeth left. And her entire body is scarred and ashen. She has been on drugs about twenty years. Her veins have collapsed. She has fibrosis, epilepsy, and edema. She has not seen her three children in about eight years. She is ashamed to contact home because she robbed and abused her mother so many times.

When we talk, it is around the Christmas holidays and she tells me about her bad luck. She tells me that she has spent the last four Christmases in jail and tells me how happy she is to be going home. But i know that she has nowhere to go, and that the only "friends" she has in the world are here in jail. She tells me that the only regret she has about leaving is that she won't be singing in the choir at Christmas. As i talk to her i wonder if she will be back. I tell her good-bye and wish her luck. Six days later, through the prison grapevine, i hear that she is back. Just in time for the Christmas show.

We are at sick call. We are waiting on wooden benches in a beige and orange room to see the doctor. Two young women who look only mildly battered by life sit wearing pastel dresses and pointy-toed state shoes. (Wearing "state" is often a sign that the wearer probably cannot afford to buy sneakers in commissary.) The two are talking about how well they were doing on the street. Eavesdropping, i find out that they both have fine "old men" that love the mess out of them. I find out that their men dress fly and wear some bad clothes and so do they. One has forty pairs of shoes while the other has one hundred skirts. One has two suede and five leather coats. The other has seven suedes and three leathers. One has three mink coats, a silver fox and a leopard. The other has two minks, a fox jacket, a floor length fox, and a chinchilla. One has four diamond rings and the other has five. One lives in a duplex with a sunken tub and a sunken living room with a waterfall. The other describes a mansion with a revolving living room. I'm relieved when my name is called. I had been sitting there feeling very, very sad.

There are no criminals here at Riker's Island Correctional Institution for Women (New York), only victims. Most of the women (over 95 percent) are black and Puerto Rican. Many were abused children. Most have been abused by men and all have been abused by "the system."[1]

There are no big-time gangsters here, no premeditated mass murderers, no godmothers. There are no big-time dope dealers, no kidnappers, no Watergate women. There are virtually no women here charged with white-collar crimes like embezzling or fraud. Most of the women have drug related cases. Many are charged as accessories to crimes committed by men. The major crimes that women here are charged with are prostitution, pickpocketing, shoplifting, robbery, and drugs. Women who have prostitution cases or who are doing "fine" time make up a substantial part of the short-term population. The women see stealing or hustling as necessary for the survival of themselves or their children because jobs are scarce and welfare is impossible to live on. One thing is clear: amerikan capitalism is in no way threatened by the women in prison on Riker's Island.

One gets the impression, when first coming to Riker's Island that the architects conceived of it as a prison modeled after a juvenile center. In the areas where visitors usually pass there is plenty of glass and plenty of plants and flowers. The cell blocks consist of two long corridors with cells on each side connected by a watch room where the guards are stationed, called a bubble. Each corridor has a day room with a tv, tables, multi-colored chairs, a stove that doesn't work and a refrigerator. There's a utility room with a sink and a washer and dryer that do not work.

Instead of bars the cells have doors that are painted bright, optimistic colors with slim glass observation panels. The doors are controlled electronically by the guards in the bubble. The cells are called rooms by everybody. They are furnished with a cot, a closet, a desk, a chair, a plastic upholstered headboard that opens for storage, a small bookcase, a mirror, a sink, and a toilet. The prison distributes brightly colored bedspreads and throw rugs for a homey effect. There is a school area, a gym, a carpeted auditorium, two inmate cafeterias, and outside recreation areas that are used during the summer months only.

The guards have successfully convinced most of the women that Riker's Island is a country club. They say that it is a playhouse compared to some other prisons (especially male): a statement whose partial veracity is not predicated upon the humanity of correction officials at Riker's Island, but, rather, by contrast to the unbelievably barbaric conditions of other prisons. Many women are convinced that they are, somehow, "getting over." Some go so far as to reason that because they are not doing hard time, they are not really in prison.

This image is further reinforced by the pseudomotherly attitude of many of the guards; a deception that all too often successfully reverts women to children. The guards call the women inmates by their first names. The women address the guards either as Officer, Miss __, or by nicknames (Teddy Bear, Spanky, Aunt Louise, Squeeze, Sarge, Black Beauty, Nutty Mahogany, etcetera). Frequently, when a woman returns to Riker's she will make rounds, gleefully embracing her favorite guard: The prodigal daughter returns.

If two women are having a debate about any given topic the argument will often be resolved by "asking the officer." The guards are forever telling the women to "grow up," to "act like ladies," to "behave" and to be "good girls." If an inmate is breaking some minor rule like coming to say "hi" to her friend on another floor or locking in a few minutes late, a guard will say, jokingly, "don't let me have to come down there and beat your butt." It is not unusual to hear a guard tell a woman, "what you need is a good spanking." The tone is often motherly, "didn't I tell you, young lady, to . . ."; or, "you know better than that"; or, "that's a good girl." And the women respond accordingly. Some guards and inmates "play" together. One officer's favorite "game" is taking off her belt and chasing her "girls" down the hall with it, smacking them on the butt.

But beneath the motherly veneer, the reality of guard life is ever present. Most of the guards are black, usually from working-class, upward-bound, civil-service oriented backgrounds. They identify with the middle class, have middle-class values, and are extremely materialistic. They are not the most intelligent women in the world and many are extremely limited.

Most are aware that there is no justice in the amerikan judicial system and that blacks and Puerto Ricans are discriminated against in every facet of amerikan life. But, at the same time, they are convinced that the system is somehow "lenient." To them, the women in prison are "losers" who don't have enough sense to stay out of jail. Most believe in the bootstrap theory—anybody can "make it" if they try hard enough. They congratulate themselves on their great accomplishments. In contrast to themselves they see the inmate as ignorant, uncultured, self-destructive, weak-minded, and stupid. They ignore the fact that their dubious accomplishments are not based on superior intelligence or effort, but only on chance and a civil service list.

Many guards hate and feel trapped by their jobs. The guard is exposed to a certain amount of abuse from coworkers, from the brass as well as from inmates, ass kissing, robotizing, and mandatory overtime. (It is common practice for guards to work a double shift at least once a week.) But no matter how much they hate the military structure, the infighting, the ugliness of their tasks, they are very aware of how close they are to the welfare lines. If they were not working as guards most would be underpaid or unemployed. Many would miss the feeling of superiority and power as much as they would miss the money, especially the cruel, sadistic ones.

The guards are usually defensive about their jobs and indicate by their behavior that they are not at all free from guilt. They repeatedly, compulsively say, as if to convince themselves, "This is a job just like any other job." The more they say that the more preposterous it seems.

◆ ◆ ◆

The major topic of conversation here is drugs. Eighty percent of inmates have used drugs when they were on the street. Getting high is usually the first thing a woman says she's going to do when she gets out. In prison, as on the streets, an escapist culture prevails. At least 50 percent of the prison population takes some form of psychotropic drug.[2] Elaborate schemes to obtain contraband drugs are always in the works.

Days are spent in pleasant distractions: soap operas, prison love affairs, card playing, and game playing. A tiny minority are seriously involved in academic pursuits or the learning of skills. An even smaller minority attempt to study available law books. There are no jailhouse lawyers and most of the women lack knowledge of even the most rudimentary legal procedures. When asked what happened in court, or what their lawyers said, they either don't know or don't remember. Feeling totally helpless and totally railroaded, a woman will curse out her lawyer or the judge with little knowledge of what is being done or of what should be done. Most plead guilty, whether they are guilty or not. The few who do go to trial usually have lawyers appointed by the state and usually are convicted.

Here, the word lesbian seldom, if ever, is mentioned. Most, if not all, of the homosexual relationships here involve role-playing. The majority of relationships are either asexual or semisexual. The absence of sexual consummation is only partially explained by prison prohibition against any kind of sexual behavior. Basically the women are not looking for sex. They are looking for love, for concern and companionship. For relief from the overwhelming sense of isolation and solitude that pervades each of us.

Women who are "aggressive" or who play the masculine roles are referred to as butches, bulldaggers, or stud broads. They are always in demand because they are always in the minority. Women who are "passive," or who play feminine roles are referred to as fems. The butch-fem relationships are often oppressive, resembling the most oppressive, exploitative aspect of a sexist society. It is typical to hear butches threatening fems with physical violence and it is not uncommon for butches to actually beat their "women." Some butches consider themselves pimps and go with the women who have the most commissary, the most contraband, or the best outside connections. They feel they are a class above ordinary women, which entitles them to "respect." They dictate to fems what they are to do and many insist the fems wash, iron, sew, and clean their cells for them. A butch will refer to another butch as "man." A butch who is well liked is known as "one of the fellas" by her peers.

Once in prison changes in roles are common. Many women who are strictly heterosexual on the street become butch in prison. "Fems" often create butches by convincing an inmate that she would make a "cute butch." About 80 percent of the prison population engages in some form of homosexual relationship.[3] Almost all follow negative, stereotypic male/female role models.

There is no connection between the women's movement and lesbianism. Most of the women at Riker's Island have no idea what feminism is, let alone lesbianism. Feminism, the women's liberation movement, and the gay liberation movement are worlds away from women at Riker's.

The black liberation struggle is equally removed from the lives of women at Riker's. While they verbalize acute recognition that amerika is a racist country where the poor are treated like dirt, they, nevertheless, feel responsible for the filth of their lives. The air at Riker's is permeated with self-hatred. Many women bear marks on their arms, legs, and wrists from suicide attempts or self-mutilation. They speak about themselves in self-deprecating terms. They consider themselves failures.

While most women contend that whitey is responsible for their oppression, they do not examine the cause or source of that oppression. There is no sense of class struggle. They have no sense of communism, no definition of it, but they consider it a bad thing. They do not want to destroy Rockefeller. They want to be just like him. Nicky Barnes, a major black dope seller, is discussed with reverence. When he was convicted practically everyone was sad. Many gave speeches about how kind, smart, and generous he was. No one spoke about the sale of drugs to our children.

◆ ◆ ◆

Politicians are considered liars and crooks. The police are hated. Yet, during cop and robber movies, some cheer loudly for the cops. One woman pasted photographs of Farrah Fawcett Majors all over her cell because she "is a bad police bitch." Kojak and Barretta get their share of admiration.

A striking difference between women and men prisoners at Riker's Island is the absence of revolutionary rhetoric among the women. We have no study groups. We have no revolutionary literature floating around. There are no groups of militants attempting to "get their heads together." The women at Riker's seem vaguely aware of what a revolution is, but generally regard it as an impossible dream. Not at all practical.

While men in prison struggle to maintain their manhood, there is no comparable struggle by women to preserve their womanhood. One frequently hears women say, "Put a bunch of bitches together and you've got nothin' but trouble"; and, "Women don't stick together, that's why we don't have nothin'." Men prisoners constantly refer to each other as brother. Women prisoners rarely refer to each other as sister. Instead, "bitch" and "whore" are the common terms of reference. Women, however, are much kinder to each other than men, and any form of violence other than a fistfight is virtually unknown. Rape, murder, and stabbings at the women's prison are nonexistent.

For many, prison is not that much different from the street. It is, for some, a place to rest and recuperate. For the prostitute, prison is a vacation from turning tricks in the rain and snow. A vacation from brutal pimps. Prison for the addict is a place to get clean, get medical work done, and gain weight. Often, when the habit becomes too expensive, the addict gets herself busted (usually subconsciously), so she can get back in shape, leave with a clean system ready to start all over again. One woman claims that for a month or two every year she either goes to jail or to the crazy house to get away from her husband.

For many the cells are not much different from the tenements, the shooting galleries, and the welfare hotels they live in on the street. Sick call is no different from the clinic or the hospital emergency room. The fights are the same except they are less dangerous. The police are the same. The poverty is the same. The alienation is the same. The racism is the same. The sexism is the same. The drugs are the same and the system is the same. Riker's Island is just another institution. In childhood school was their prison, or youth houses or reform schools or children shelters or foster homes or mental hospitals or drug programs and they see all institutions as indifferent to their needs, yet necessary to their survival.

The women at Riker's Island come there from places like Harlem, Brownsville, Bedford-Stuyvesant, South Bronx, and South Jamaica. They come from places where dreams have been abandoned like the buildings. Where there is no more sense of community. Where neighborhoods are transient. Where isolated people run from one fire trap to another. The cities have removed us from our strengths, from our roots, from our traditions. They have taken away our gardens and our sweet potato pies and given us McDonald's. They have become our prisons, locking us into the futility and decay of pissy hallways that lead nowhere. They have alienated us from each other and made us fear each other. They have given us dope and television as a culture.

There are no politicians to trust. No roads to follow. No popular progressive culture to relate to. There are no new deals, no more promises of golden streets, and no place else to migrate. My sisters in the streets, like my sisters at Riker's Island, see no way out. "Where can I go?" said a woman on the day she was going home. "If there's nothing to believe in," she said, "I can't do nothin' except try to find cloud nine."

What of our Past? What of our History? What of our Future?

I can imagine the pain and the strength of my great-great-grandmothers who were slaves and my great-great-grandmothers who were Cherokee Indians trapped on reservations. I remembered my great-grandmother who walked everywhere rather than sit in the back of the bus. I think about North Carolina and my hometown and i remember the women of my grandmother's generation: strong, fierce women who could stop you with a look out the corners of their eyes. Women who walked with majesty; who could wring a chicken's neck and scale a fish. Who could pick cotton, plant a garden, and sew without a pattern. Women who boiled clothes white in big black cauldrons and who hummed work songs and lullabys. Women who visited the elderly, made soup for the sick, and short'nin' bread for the babies.

Women who delivered babies, searched for healing roots, and brewed medicines. Women who darned socks, and chopped wood, and layed bricks. Women who could swim rivers and shoot the head off a snake. Women who took passionate responsibility for their children and for their neighbors' children too.

The women in my grandmother's generation made giving an art form. "Here, gal, take this pot of collards to Sister Sue"; "Take this bag of pecans to school for the teacher"; "Stay here while I go tend Mister Johnson's leg." Every child in the neighborhood ate in their kitchens. They called each other sister because of feeling rather than as the result of a movement. They supported each other through the lean times, sharing the little they had.

The women of my grandmother's generation in my hometown trained their daughters for womanhood. They taught them to give respect and to demand respect. They taught their daughters how to churn butter; how to use elbow grease. They taught their daughters to respect the strength of their bodies, to lift boulders and how to kill a hog; what to do for colic, how to break a fever and how to make a poultice, patchwork quilts, plait hair and how to hum and sing. They taught their daughters to take care, to take charge, and to take responsibility. They would not tolerate a "lazy heifer" or a "gal with her head in the clouds." Their daughters had to learn how to get their lessons, how to survive, how to be strong. The women of my grandmother's generation were the glue that held family and the community together. They were the backbone of the church. And of the school. They regarded outside institutions with dislike and distrust. They were determined that their children should survive and they were committed to a better future.

I think about my sisters in the movement. I remember the days when, draped in African garb, we rejected our foremothers and ourselves as castrators. We did penance for robbing the brother of his manhood, as if we were the oppressor. I remember the days of the Panther Party when we were "moderately liberated." When we were allowed to wear pants and expected to pick up the gun. The days when we gave doe-eyed looks to our leaders. The days when we worked like dogs and struggled desperately for the respect that they struggled desperately not to give us. I remember the black history classes that did [not] mention women and the posters of our "leaders" where women were conspicuously absent. We visited our sisters who bore the complete responsibility of the children while the Brotha was doing his thing. Or had moved on to bigger and better things.

Most of us rejected the white women's movement. Miss ann was still Miss ann to us whether she burned her bras or not. We could not muster sympathy for the fact that she was trapped in her mansion and oppressed by her husband. We were, and still are, in a much more terrible jail. We knew that our experiences as black women were completely different from those of our sisters in the white women's movement. And we had no desire to sit in some consciousness-raising group with white women and bare our souls.

Women can never be free in a country that is not free. We can never be liberated in a country where the institutions that control our lives are oppressive. We can never be free while our men are oppressed. Or while the amerikan government and amerikan capitalism remain intact.

But it is imperative to our struggle that we build a strong black women's movement. It is imperative that we, as black women, talk about

the experiences that shaped us; that we assess our strengths and weak-
nesses and define our own history. It is imperative that we discuss positive
ways to teach and socialize our children.

The poison and pollution of capitalist cities is choking us. We need
the strong medicine of our foremothers to make us well again. We need
their medicines to give us strength to fight and the drive to win. Under the
guidance of Harriet Tubman and Fannie Lou Hamer[4] and all of our foremothers, let us rebuild a sense of community. Let us rebuild the culture of
giving and carry on the tradition of fierce determination to move on closer
to freedom.

Notes

Originally published in the *Black Scholar*, Vol. 9, No. 7 (April 1978); reprinted in
the *Black Scholar* Vol. 12, No. 6 (November–December 1981): 50–57.

1. *Editor's note:* As of 2002, the population of New York jails and prisons
was 84 percent nonwhite. (*Mother Jones, Debt to Society* Special Report, avail-
able online at www.motherjones.com/prisons/index.html; statistics gathered from
Bureau of Justice Statistics, Criminal Justice Institute, and U.S. Census Bureau.)
For more information about women in prison, see Amnesty International, *Abuse
of Women in Custody: Sexual Misconduct and Shackling of Pregnant Women*,
March 2001; Amnesty International *"Not Part of My Sentence": Violations of the
Human Rights of Women in Custody*, 1999, www.amnesty.org.; Martin Greer,
"Human Rights and Wrongs in Our Own Backyard: Incorporating International
Human Rights Protections Under Domestic Civil Rights Law—A Case Study of
Women in United States Prisons," *Harvard Human Rights Journal*, Vol. 13
(Spring 2000), www.law.harvard.edu/studorgs/hrj/iss13/geer.shtml.

2. *Editor's note:* For more information on the use of psychotropic drugs in
prison, see Kathleen Auerhahn and Elizabeth Dermody Leonard, "Docile Bodies?
Chemical Restraints and the Female Inmate," *The Journal of Criminal Law &
Criminology*, Vol. 90, No. 2 (Winter 2000): 599–634; D. Benson, "Getting High
in Jail: Legal vs. Illegal Drugs," *Prison News Service*, No. 52 (September, 1995):
5; J. P. Morrissey, et al., "Overview of Mental Health Services Provided by State
Adult Correctional Facilities: United States, 1988," *Mental Health Statistical
Note*, Vol. 207 (May 1993): 1–13.

3. *Editor's note:* See Wilbert Rideau, "The Sexual Jungle," *The Angolite*
(November/December 1979); reprinted in Wilbert Rideau and Ron Wikberg, eds.,
Life Sentences: Rage, Rape and Survival Behind Bars (New York: Random House,
1992); Don Sabo, Terry A. Kupers, and Willie London, eds., *Prison Masculinities*
(Philadelphia: Temple University Press, 2001). See also Paula C. Rust, *Bisexuality
in the United States: A Social Science Reader* (New York: Columbia University
Press, 2000); Estelle B. Freedman, "The Prison Lesbian: Race, Class, and the Con-
struction of the Aggressive Female Homosexual, 1915–1965," *Feminist Studies*,

Vol. 22 (Summer 1996): 397–423; Christopher Hensley and Richard Tewksbury, "Inmate-to-Inmate Prison Sexuality: A Review of Empirical Studies," *Trauma, Violence & Abuse: A Review Journal*, Vol. 3, No. 3 (2002): 226–43.

4. *Editor's note:* Harriet Tubman (1820?–1913), an escaped slave and abolitionist, led hundreds of slaves to freedom in the North on the "Underground Railroad" between 1850 and 1860. During the Civil War she served as liaison between the army and newly freed African Americans, and following the war she raised money for the education of former slaves and founded a home for the old and poor. Fannie Lou Hamer (1917–1977) was a Mississippi sharecropper who, in 1962, attempted to register to vote as part of the Student Nonviolent Coordinating Committee's (SNCC) voting rights campaign. She was consequently fired from her job, which led her to join SNCC full-time as a fieldworker. Hamer was jailed and severely beaten in Mississippi in 1963. She also founded the Mississippi Freedom Democratic Party (MFDP) in 1963, and made an unsuccessful bid for Congress as a MFDP candidate.

9

Susan Rosenberg

Susan Rosenberg was born in 1955, in New York and is a Doctor of Acupuncture. She became involved with anti-racist activism and the student, antiwar, and women's movements in the early 1970s. The Federal Bureau of Investigation (FBI) targeted Rosenberg for her support of the Black Liberation Army. She went underground in the early 1980s. She was arrested in New Jersey in 1984 on weapons possession charges, convicted, and sentenced to fifty-eight years, sixteen times the national average for such an offense (the judge cited her political ideology as the reason for the lengthy prison term).[1] Rosenberg had been previously charged in the 1981 "Brink's Robbery" case in New York and was accused of participating in the escape of Assata Shakur from prison, but these charges were dismissed for a lack of evidence.[2] In 1988, she was charged in the "Resistance Conspiracy" case; these charges were also later dropped.

In over ten years in isolation and maximum security conditions, Rosenberg continued to organize, teach, and write. Rosenberg, who obtained her master's degree in writing in 2000, was pardoned by President Bill Clinton in 2001. A human rights and prisoner rights activist since her release, she is completing her memoir and taught literature at the John Jay School of Criminal Justice in New York City.

Notes

1. Ann Nicholson, "Commutations gained through work of law faculty, students," *Washington University Record,* Washington University in St. Louis, April 6, 2001.
2. Ibid.

References

Baraldini, Silvia, Marilyn Buck, Susan Rosenberg, and Laura Whitehorn. "Women's Control Unit." In *Criminal Injustice: Confronting the Prison Crisis,* edited by Elihu Rosenblatt. Boston: South End Press, 1996.

Nicholson, Ann. "Commutations gained through the work of law faculty, students." *Washington University Record*. St. Louis, MO: Wasington University, April 6, 2001.

Resistance Conspiracy. San Francisco: Bay Area Committee to Support the Resistance Conspiracy Defendants [distributor]. Oakland: Peralta Colleges Television Production Company, videocassette, 1990.

Rosenberg, Susan. "Reflections on Being Buried Alive." In *Cages of Steel: The Politics of Imprisonment in the United States,* edited by Ward Churchill and Jim Vander Wall. Washington, D.C.: Maisonneuve Press, 1992.

Women Casualties of the Drug War
1996

The war on drugs has become a war on women in the drug trade: the wives and girlfriends of drug dealers, the runners, mules, and drug users. In the long-termer's unit at Danbury FCI [Federal Correctional Institution] for women, many prisoners are serving lengthy sentences with no hope of parole. For the most part, these "losers" are first-time, nonviolent offenders whose convictions are related to drug conspiracies. The majority are black or Latino. They leave their children and families on the outside in ruin.[1]

Though some women are fortunate enough to have family members who remain unscathed by the criminal prosecution—a loved one who can hold some semblance of family life together—many have no one to care for their children. Without family at home, these women lose their children to the state. Gone. In a matter of minutes, everything the woman has known in the making of her life is over and done with. Only prison time lies ahead, at times more prison time than there are years left to live.

The lengthy sentences, and the often great distances family members or friends must travel to visit prisoners, make it nearly impossible for a woman to maintain ties with the outside world. When there is little hope of release, women prisoners quickly lose touch with those they leave behind. If you are thirty-five years old and you get a forty-five year sentence under the new sentencing laws, you must do at least forty years, which means you can walk out free and clear at age seventy-five. If you have a natural life sentence, you never walk out; you die in the women's prison hospital center at Carswell AFB [Air Force Base], Texas.

Many women do the time. They struggle through every day and find a way to cope. Some don't know how to survive in prison; they end up on psychotropic medication. Increasingly, women who have information to trade will use it to get a time cut; others, with no information to trade, end up doing lengthy sentences. The severity of the punishment, the very length of the sentence, is intended to be coercive. As a result, more and more women are targeted by drug agents and pressured into becoming snitches.

The convict code of silence has been dismantled piece by piece by the state. When a woman is a walking "contents under pressure" about to explode, and she finally does, it means she has been broken. She has been bought by the government and can and will be used again and again. Once a defendant gives information in exchange for sentence leniency, the government owns her.

To justify this to themselves, these women end up seeing their captors as all-powerful. It is the government that holds their fate in its hands; it is the government that must be obeyed. Other prisoners are seen as a threat. Building unity among women prisoners becomes close to impossible. Eventually, a more petty form of snitching takes over. The trade of information in prison may not rise to the level of informant trial testimony or "cooperation" as prosecutors euphemistically call it, but it can and does prevent women prisoners from exercising collective power over the actual and difficult conditions of their lives.

The Bureau of Prisons [BOP] plays an active role in this coercion. Although the Bureau claims it is only involved in custody, not in the terms of punishment, and that it is neutral and only carries out the directives of the courts, this is not so. No longer is prison itself sufficient punishment. No longer is the loss of freedom enough. Now the purpose of imprisonment is also to ensure total "cooperation," total subservience to the all-powerful government. While there may be different government agencies—FBI [Federal Bureau of Investigation], DEA [Drug Enforcement Agency], IRS [Internal Revenue Service], BOP and so on—there is only one system.

Most people who get busted don't think they will wind up giving information to the government. But threats of lengthy sentences begin before the indictment and continue into the first several years after conviction. Before the implementation of mandatory sentences, prisoners had a right to request a sentence reduction. The motion was called a Rule 35. There were various grounds on which one could bring this motion, including family hardship. If a prisoner could demonstrate to a judge that her imprisonment was causing her family undue suffering, the judge could reduce the sentence. Though not common, sentence reductions under Rule 35 gave prisoners hope, a chance for a break in the unrelenting prison time.

Now a Rule 35 motion can only be brought by the prosecution. Rule 35 has been transformed into a government tool whereby compliance, or snitching, is the only grounds for sentence reduction. The motion has been reduced to a single-page list of categories with a box for a check mark next to each. Under the first category, "Debriefing," are four subcategories: debriefing on own role; debriefing on other principals; debriefing on general activities of the conspiracy; debriefing on criminal acts. The sentence reduction depends on how many boxes contain check marks.

In the years I was locked up at the maximum-security women's unit in Marianna, Florida, I witnessed many times the process of women prisoners being broken. The unit, called Shawnee, is unique in the federal prison system.[2] It is the only super maximum-security unit for women. Many prisoners are sent there directly from sentencing proceedings. This is not because they are a security threat and need more supervision; few women require maximum-security conditions. Rather, the purpose of Shawnee unit is to subject the women who are sent there to the worst of conditions— maximum isolation—to give them a taste of the way the rest of their lives will be unless they give in to the government. For many, it is unbearable.

The coercive threat is explicit. I saw women with life sentences, one hundred-year sentences, forty-year sentences, pass through Shawnee's five electronically controlled doors. While they lay in their cells, the impact of their new lives hit them. They walked out, transferred to easier prisons, with ten, seven, or four years left to go. They had called the special agents or prosecutors, or responded when law enforcement officials contacted them; Rule 35 motions were offered, prosecutorial powers exercised, accompanied by promises of protection and even money.

Belle is a forty-year-old African American woman who has a life sentence for her involvement in a drug conspiracy. She is the mother of teenagers and youngsters. Before her arrest, Belle was the backbone of her family. She is a large, smiling, expansive woman whose eyes crinkle at the corners when she tells a story. The full life she once knew as a mother is gone; though she tries to stay involved in the lives of her children, the family ties unravel with each passing month.

Along with twelve coconspirators, Belle sold about a kilo of cocaine a week. The Colombian cartel they were not. They didn't make billions of dollars, there were no murders in the case nor any bribes or threats to public officials. They were local people involved in a small-time operation labeled "big-time" by self-serving DEA agents. Several of the people who were convicted and sentenced to decades in prison had no knowledge of the overall conspiracy. They were selling coke on the side to make ends meet.

When [the] DEA busted Belle, they told her they were going to put her away forever. They told her that her best friend had already rolled over on her. They said several others were ready to roll. They brought Belle's teenage daughter in and told her that if her mother failed to rat on others, she would be wheeling her mother's body out in a cheap pine box after she died in prison. "Debrief!" they all screamed at Belle over and over for months. Her options, they explained, were life in prison or cooperation—which meant at most five years in prison, three years with good conduct.

Belle is the first to admit that selling coke was wrong. Like many other mothers who get caught up in the drug trade, Belle told herself she was selling cocaine to give her children a better life. Because of the difficulties she faced in providing for her family, she opted for existence in the underground economy. "It was an easy way out of a bad situation," she says. It was later that her addiction took hold. "I know that crack addiction destroys people, and I'm glad it's over." She says this not to justify her actions, but to place them in context.

As of the present, Belle refuses to get past that first check mark on the Rule 35 motion. Her position is that she did the crime, so she must take the weight for her actions. She refuses to debrief on anyone other than herself. She is four years into a life sentence. She did go back to the authorities and debrief on her own role in the conspiracy, but that wasn't enough for the U.S. Attorney to recommend a sentence reduction. Again, they told her, "Give us what we want and you can walk out in eighteen months."

It is difficult to imagine how one might face such a choice: eighteen months versus life in prison. Belle didn't go for it; and she struggles with this decision every day. I can see it in her face when she thinks no one is looking. When she went back to be debriefed on her own role, and she saw her children in the visiting room, they had grown beyond recognition. At that moment, her beliefs were more deeply challenged than at any previous point in her life. It is the foulest of bribes—your beliefs or your life—an unconscionable action by an all-powerful state.

Soon, Belle will no longer be of any use to law enforcement. If she holds out and resists the pressure to inform on others, her options will close. Her punishment, the forfeiture of her life, so exceeds the crime that it is difficult to comprehend unless you consider the government's agenda to target the most vulnerable defendants and coerce them into snitching. What they are saying is that the crime itself is not so bad; they seek to punish excessively only those who refuse to tell on others.

Belle, like most women casualties of the drug war, was a low-level player. The white men who run the international drug cartels have the power and money to buy and bargain their way out of prison, often by snitching. American society is dominated by white supremacy in its institutions, particularly in the criminal justice system. The government has targeted the African American community with its so-called war on drugs and crime. With the help of a complaisant mass media, we are barraged with images and pronouncements that demonize and criminalize the African American. This disregard for the value of life, and particularly nonwhite life, is part of the fabric of American social relations. The nation was founded upon the destruction of Native American life and the importation of African slave labor. Now the means of dealing with people of color has been relegated to the prison system where it has become a rule that one must either snitch or rot behind bars.

When the most callous and cynical manipulations of sentence length are the main device the government employs in its war on drugs, a total corruption of the system prevails. That the government, through its law enforcement agents, can say to a woman, a mother, a person with a past and a present and hopes for a future, "Your life means shit to us, and your freedom nothing at all," is a betrayal by the state of all basic human rights, and a degradation to the humanity of us all.

Notes

Originally published in *Prison Life* (January–February 1996): 57, 59–61.

1. *Editor's note:* For discussions of the racial implications and injustices of the U.S. domestic war on drugs, see Clarence Lusane, *Pipe Dream Blues: Racism and the War on Drugs* (Boston: South End Press, 1991); Randall Kennedy, *Race, Crime, and the Law* (New York: Pantheon, 1997); David Cole, *No Equal Justice: Race and Class in the American Criminal Justice System* (New York: The New Press, 1999).

2. *Editor's note:* For analyses of the political incarceration of radical women, see Mary K. O'Melveny, "Portrait of a U.S. Political Prison: Lexington Prison High Security Unit," in *Cages of Steel: The Politics of Imprisonment in the United States,* eds. Ward Churchill and Jim Vander Wall (Washington, D.C.: Maisonneuve Press, 1992); Laura Whitehorn, "Resistance at Lexington," and, Silvia Baraldini, Marilyn Buck, Susan Rosenberg, et al., "Women's Control Unit," in *Criminal Injustice: Confronting the Prison Crisis,* ed. Elihu Rosenblatt (Boston: South End Press, 1996). Also see Marilyn Buck, "The Effects of Repression on Women in Prison" and Carol Gilbert, O.P., "Ponderings from the Eternal Now," in *Warfare: Prison and the American Homeland,* ed. Joy James (Durham: Duke University Press, 2006).

10

Angela Y. Davis

Angela Y. Davis was born in 1944, in Birmingham, Alabama. She attended Brandeis University, where she studied with philosopher Herbert Marcuse, took her junior year in France at the Sorbonne, and then returned to the United States to work with Marcuse at the University of California at San Diego. After a period of involvement with the Student Nonviolent Coordinating Committee, Davis worked with the Black Panther Party (BPP) and the Communist Party, USA (CPUSA). In 1969, she was removed from her teaching position in the philosophy department at the University of California—Los Angeles as a result of her social activism and her membership in the CPUSA.

Davis's commitment to prisoners' rights dates back to her involvement in the campaign to free the California prisoners known as the "Soledad Brothers." In 1970, she was placed on the Federal Bureau of Investigation's Ten Most Wanted List on charges connected to seventeen-year-old Jonathan Jackson's attempt to bring attention to dangerous prison conditions for his older brother, George Jackson, and the other Soledad Brothers, by taking hostages at the Marin County courthouse. The confrontation resulted in the deaths of Jonathan, Judge Harold Haley, and prisoners James McClain and Willliam Christmas by guards following official policy to prevent escapes regardless of casualties. Subsequently, Davis became the subject of an intense police search that drove her underground and culminated in one of the most famous trials in recent U.S. history. During her sixteen months of incarceration, a massive international "Free Angela Davis" campaign was organized. Davis was acquitted of all charges in 1972. The following essay by Davis was written during her incarceration.

A professor in the History of Consciousness Program at University of California-Santa Cruz, and an advocate of prison abolition, Davis critiques racism and sexism in the criminal justice system. Her publications include *Women, Race & Class, If They Come in the Morning: Voices of Resistance* (coedited with Bettina Aptheker), *The Angela Y. Davis Reader,* and *Are Prisons Obsolete?*

References

Aptheker, Bettina. *The Morning Breaks: The Trial of Angela Davis.* New York: International Publishers, 1975; repr., Ithaca, NY: Cornell University Press, 1999.

Davis, Angela Y. *Angela Davis: An Autobiography.* New York: International Publishers, 1974.

———. *The Angela Y. Davis Reader,* edited by Joy James. Malden, MA: Blackwell, 1999.

——— and Bettina Aptheker, eds. *If They Come in the Morning: Voices of Resistance.* New York: Third Press, 1971.

Reflections on the Black Woman's Role in the Community of Slaves (Abridged) 1971

The American brand of slavery strove toward a rigidified disorganization in family life, just as it had to proscribe all potential social structures within which black people might forge a collective and conscious existence.[1] Mothers and fathers were brutally separated; children, when they became of age, were branded and frequently severed from their mothers. That the mother was "the only legitimate parent of her child" did not therefore mean that she was even permitted to guide it to maturity.

Those who lived under a common roof were often unrelated through blood. . . . The strong personal bonds between immediate family members that oftentimes persisted despite coerced separation bore witness to the remarkable capacity of black people for resisting the disorder so violently imposed on their lives.

Where families were allowed to thrive, they were, for the most part, external fabrications serving the designs of an avaricious, profit-seeking slaveholder.

The strong hand of the slave-owner dominated the Negro family, which existed at his mercy and often at his own personal instigation. An exslave has told of getting married on one plantation: "When you married, you had to jump over a broom three times."[2]

This slave went on to describe the various ways in which his master forcibly coupled men and women with the aim of producing the maximum number of healthy child-slaves. In the words of John Henrik Clarke,

> The family as a functional entity was outlawed and permitted to exist only when it benefited the slave-master. Maintenance of the slave family as a family unit benefited the slave-owners only when, and to the extent that such unions created new slaves who could be exploited.[3]

101

. . . A great deal has been said about the black *man* and resistance, but very little about the unique relationship black women bore to the resistance struggles during slavery. To understand the part she played in developing and sharpening the thrust toward freedom, the broader meaning of slavery and of American slavery in particular must be explored. Slavery is an ancient human institution. Of slave labor in its traditional form and of serfdom as well, Karl Marx stated:

> The slave stands in absolutely no relation to the objective conditions of his labor; it is rather the *labor* itself, in the form of the slave as of the serf, which is placed in the category of *inorganic condition* of production alongside the other natural beings, e.g. cattle, or regarded as an appendage of the earth.[4]

The bondsman's existence as a natural condition of production is complemented and reinforced, according to Marx, by his membership in a social grouping that he perceives to be an extension of nature. Enmeshed in what appears to be a natural state of affairs, the attitude of the slave, to a greater or lesser degree, would be an acquiescence in his subjugation. Friedrich Engels points out that in Athens, the state could depend on a police force consisting entirely of slaves.[5]

The fabric of American slavery differed significantly from ancient slavery and feudalism. True, black people were forced to act as if they were inorganic conditions of production. For slavery was "personality swallowed up in the sordid idea of property—manhood lost in chattelhood."[6] But there were no pre-existent social structures or cultural dictates that might induce reconciliation to the circumstances of their bondage. On the contrary, Africans had been uprooted from their natural environment, their social relations, their culture. No legitimate sociocultural surroundings would be permitted to develop and flourish, for, in all likelihood, they would be utterly incompatible with the demands of slavery.

Yet another fact would militate against harmony and equilibrium in the slave's relation to his bondage: Slavery was enclosed in a society otherwise characterized by "free" wage-labor. Black men and women could always contrast their chains with the nominally free status of white working people. This was quite literally true in such cases where, like Frederick Douglass, they were contracted out as wage-laborers. Unlike the "free" white men alongside whom they worked, they had no right to the meager wages they earned. Such were some of the many contradictions unloosed by the effort to forcibly inject slavery into the early stages of American capitalism.

The combination of a historically superseded slave-labor system based almost exclusively on race and the drive to strip black people of all their social and cultural bonds would create a fateful rupture at the heart of the slave system itself. The slaves would not readily adopt fatalistic attitudes toward the conditions surrounding and ensnaring their lives. They were a people who had been violently thrust into a patently "unnatural" subjugation. If the slaveholders had not maintained an absolute monopoly of violence, if they had not been able to rely on large numbers of their fellow white men—indeed the entire ruling class as well as misled working people—to assist them in their terrorist machinations, slavery would have been far less feasible than it actually proved to be.

The magnitude and effects of the black people's defiant rejection of slavery has not yet been fully documented and illuminated. But there is more than ample evidence that they consistently refused to succumb to the all-encompassing dehumanization objectively demanded by the slave system. Comparatively recent studies have demonstrated that the few slave uprisings—too spectacular to be relegated to oblivion by the racism of ruling-class historians—were not isolated occurrences, as the latter would have had us believe. The reality, we know now, was that these open rebellions erupted with such a frequency that they were as much a part of the texture of slavery as the conditions of servitude themselves. And these revolts were only the tip of an iceberg: Resistance expressed itself in other grand modes and also in the seemingly trivial forms of feigned illness and studied indolence.

If resistance was an organic ingredient of slave life, it had to be directly nurtured by the social organization that the slaves themselves improvised. The consciousness of their oppression, the conscious thrust toward its abolition could not have been sustained without impetus from the community they pulled together through the sheer force of their own strength. Of necessity, this community would revolve around the realm that was furthermost removed from the immediate arena of domination. It could only be located in and around the living quarters, the area where the basic needs of physical life were met.

In the area of production, the slaves—pressed into the mold of beasts of burden—were forcibly deprived of their humanity. (And a human being thoroughly dehumanized has no desire for freedom.) But the community gravitating around the domestic quarters might possibly permit a retrieval of the man and the woman in their fundamental humanity. We can assume that in a very real material sense, it was only in domestic life—away from the eyes and whip of the overseer—that the slaves could attempt to assert the modicum of freedom they still retained, it was only there that they might be inspired to project techniques of expanding it further by leveling what few weapons they had against the slaveholding class whose unmitigated drive for profit was the source of their misery.

Via this path, we return to the African slave woman: in the living quarters, the major responsibilities "naturally" fell to her. It was the woman who was charged with keeping the "home in order." This role was dictated by the male supremacist ideology of white society in America; it was also woven into the patriarchal traditions of Africa. As her biological destiny, the woman bore the fruits of procreation; as her social destiny, she cooked, sewed, washed, cleaned house, raised the children. Traditionally the labor of females, domestic work is supposed to complement and confirm their inferiority.

But with the black slave woman, there is a strange twist of affairs: in the infinite anguish of ministering to the needs of the men and children around her (who were not necessarily members of her immediate family), she was performing the *only* labor of the slave community that could not be directly and immediately claimed by the oppressor. There was no compensation for work in the fields; it served no useful purpose for the slaves. Domestic labor was the only meaningful labor for the slave community as a whole (discounting as negligible the exceptional situations where slaves received some pay for their work).

Precisely through performing the drudgery that has long been a central expression of the socially conditioned inferiority of women, the black woman in chains could help to lay the foundation for some degree of autonomy, both for herself and her men. Even as she was suffering under her unique oppression as female, she was thrust by the force of circumstances into the center of the slave community. She was, therefore, essential to the *survival* of the community. Not all people have survived enslavement; hence her survival-oriented activities were themselves a form of resistance. Survival, moreover, was the prerequisite of all higher levels of struggle.

But much more remains to be said of the black woman during slavery. The dialectics of her oppression will become far more complex. It is true that she was a victim of the myth that only the woman, with her diminished capacity for mental and physical labor, should do degrading household work. Yet, the alleged benefits of the ideology of femininity did not accrue to her. She was not sheltered or protected; she would not remain oblivious to the desperate struggle for existence unfolding outside the "home." She was also there in the fields, alongside the man, toiling under the lash from sunup to sundown.

This was one of the supreme ironies of slavery: In order to approach its strategic goal—to extract the greatest possible surplus from the labor of the slaves—the black woman had to be released from the chains of the myth of femininity. In the words of W. E. B. Du Bois, "our women in black had freedom contemptuously thrust upon them."[7] In order to function as slave, the black woman had to be annulled as woman, that is, as woman in her historical stance of wardship under the entire male hierarchy. The sheer force of things rendered her equal to her man.

Excepting the woman's role as caretaker of the household, male supremacist structures could not become deeply embedded in the internal workings of the slave system. Though the ruling class was male and rabidly chauvinistic, the slave system could not confer upon the black man the appearance of a privileged position vis-à-vis the black woman. The man-slave could not be the unquestioned superior within the "family" or community, for there was no such thing as the "family provider" among the slaves. The attainment of slavery's intrinsic goals was contingent upon the fullest and most brutal utilization of the productive capacities of every man, woman, and child. They all had to "provide" for the master. The black woman was therefore wholly integrated into the productive force: "The bell rings at four o'clock in the morning and they have half an hour to get ready. Men and women start together, and the women must work as steadily as the men and perform the same tasks as the men."[8]

Even in the posture of motherhood—otherwise the occasion for hypocritical adoration—the black woman was treated with no greater compassion and with no less severity than her man. As one slave related in a narrative of his life: "women who had sucking children suffered much from their breasts becoming full of milk, the infants being left at home; they therefore could not keep up with the other hands: I have seen the overseer beat them with raw hide so that the blood and the milk flew mingled from their breasts."[9]

Moses Grandy, ex-slave, continues his description with an account of a typical form of field punishment reserved for the black woman with child: "She is compelled to lie down over a hole made to receive her corpulency, and is flogged with the whip, or beat with a paddle, which has holes in it; at every stroke comes a blister."[10]

The unbridled cruelty of this leveling process whereby the black woman was forced into equality with the black man requires no further explanation. She shared in the deformed equality of equal oppression.

But out of this deformed equality was forged quite undeliberately, yet inexorably, a state of affairs that could harness an immense potential in the black woman. Expending indispensable labor for the enrichment of her oppressor, she could attain a practical awareness of the oppressor's utter dependence on her—for the master needs the slave far more than the slave needs the master. At the same time she could realize that while her productive activity was wholly subordinated to the will of the master, it was nevertheless proof of her ability to transform things. For "labor is the living, shaping fire; it represents the impermanence of things, their temporality."[11]

The black woman's consciousness of the oppression suffered by her people was honed in the bestial realities of daily experience. It would not be the stunted awareness of a woman confined to the home. She would be prepared to ascend to the same levels of resistance that were accessible to her men. Even as she performed her housework, the black woman's role in the slave community could not be identical to the historically evolved female role. Stripped of the palliative feminine veneer that might have encouraged a passive performance of domestic tasks, she was now uniquely capable of weaving into the warp and woof of domestic life a profound consciousness of resistance.

With the contributions of strong black women, the slave community as a whole could achieve heights unscaleable within the families of the white oppressed or even within the patriarchal kinship groups of Africa. Latently or actively it was always a community of resistance. It frequently erupted in insurgency, but was daily animated by the minor acts of sabotage that harassed the slavemaster to no end. Had the black woman failed to rise to the occasion, the community of slaves could not have fully developed in this direction. The slave system would have to deal with the black woman as the custodian of a house of resistance.

The oppression of black women during the era of slavery, therefore, had to be buttressed by a level of overt ruling-class repression. Her routine oppression had to assume an unconcealed dimension of outright counterinsurgency.

To say that the oppression of black slave women necessarily incorporated open forms of counterinsurgency is not as extravagant as it might initially appear. The penetration of counterinsurgency into the day-to-day routine of the slavemaster's domination will be considered toward the end of this paper. First, the participation of black women in the overt and explosive upheavals that constantly rocked the slave system must be confirmed. This will be an indication of the magnitude of her role as caretaker of a household of resistance—of the degree to which she could concretely encourage those around her to keep their eyes on freedom. It will also confirm the objective circumstances to which the slavemaster's counterinsurgency was a response. . . .

The oppression of slave women had to assume dimensions of open counterinsurgency. . . . As for those who engaged in open battle, they were no less ruthlessly punished than slave men. It would even appear that in many cases they may have suffered penalties that were more excessive than those meted out to the men. On occasion, when men were hanged, the women were burned alive. If such practices were widespread, their logic would be clear. They would be terrorist methods designed to dissuade other black women from following the examples of their fighting sisters. If all black women rose up alongside their men, the institution of slavery would be in difficult straits.

It is against the backdrop of her role as fighter that the routine oppression of the slave woman must be explored once more. If she was burned, hanged, broken on the wheel, her head paraded on poles before her oppressed brothers and sisters, she must have also felt the edge of this counterinsurgency as a fact of her daily existence. The slave system would not only have to make conscious efforts to stifle the tendencies toward acts of the kind described above; it would be no less necessary to stave off escape attempts (escapes to maroon country!)[12] and all the various forms of sabotage within the system. Feigning illness was also resistance, as were work slowdowns and actions destructive to the crops. The more extensive these acts, the more the slaveholder's profits would tend to diminish.

While a detailed study of the myriad modes in which this counter-insurgency was manifested can and should be conducted, the following reflections will focus on a single aspect of the slave woman's oppression particularly prominent in its brutality.

Much has been said about the sexual abuses to which the black woman was forced to submit.[13] They are generally explained as an out-growth of the male supremacy of Southern culture: The purity of white womanhood could not be violated by the aggressive sexual activity desired by the white male. His instinctual urges would find expression in his rela-tionships with his property—the black slave woman, who would have to become his unwilling concubine. No doubt there is an element of truth in these statements, but it is equally important to unearth the meaning of these sexual abuses from the vantage point of the woman who was assaulted.

In keeping with the theme of these reflections, it will be submitted that the slavemaster's sexual domination of the black woman contained an unveiled element of counterinsurgency. To understand the basis for this assertion, the dialectical moments of the slave woman's oppression must be restated and their movement recaptured. The prime factor, it has been said, was the total and violent expropriation of her labor with no compen-sation save the pittance necessary for bare existence.

Secondly, as female, she was the housekeeper of the living quarters. In this sense, she was already doubly oppressed. However, having been wrested from passive, "feminine" existence by the sheer force of things—literally by forced labor—confining domestic tasks were incommensurable with what she had become. That is to say, by virtue of her participation in production, she would not act the part of the passive female, but could experience the same need as her men to challenge the conditions of her subjugation. As the center of domestic life, the only life at all removed from the arena of exploitation, and thus as an important source of survival, the black woman could play a pivotal role in nurturing the thrust toward freedom.

The slavemaster would attempt to thwart this process. He knew that as female, this slave woman could be particularly vulnerable in her sexual existence. Although he would not pet her and deck her out in frills, the white master could endeavor to reestablish her femaleness by reducing her to the level of her *biological* being. Aspiring with his sexual assaults to establish her as a female *animal*, he would be striving to destroy her proclivities toward resistance. Of the sexual relations of animals, taken at their abstract biological level (and not in terms of their quite different social potential for human beings), Simone de Beauvoir says the following:

> It is unquestionably the male who *takes* the female—she is *taken*. Often the word applies literally, for whether by means of special organs or through superior strength, the male seizes her and holds her in place; he performs the copulatory movements; and, among insects, birds, and mammals, he penetrates. . . . Her body becomes a resistance to be broken through. . . .[14]

The act of copulation, reduced by the white man to an animal-like act, would be symbolic of the effort to conquer the resistance the black woman could unloose.

In confronting the black woman as adversary in a sexual contest, the master would be subjecting her to the most elemental form of terrorism distinctively suited for the female: rape.[15] Given the already terroristic texture of plantation life, it would be as potential victim of rape that the slave woman would be most unguarded. Further, she might be most conveniently manipulable if the master contrived a ransom system of sorts, forcing her to pay with her body for food, diminished severity in treatment, the safety of her children, etcetera.

The integration of rape into the sparsely furnished legitimate social life of the slaves harks back to the feudal "right of the first night," the *jus primae noctis*. The feudal lord manifested and reinforced his domination over the serfs by asserting his authority to have sexual intercourse with all the females. The right itself referred specifically to all freshly married women. But while the right to the first night eventually evolved into the institutionalized "virgin tax,"[16] the American slaveholder's sexual domination never lost its openly terroristic character.

As a direct attack on the black female as potential insurgent, this sexual repression finds its parallels in virtually every historical situation where the woman actively challenges oppression. Thus, Frantz Fanon could say of the Algerian woman, "A woman led away by soldiers who comes back a week later—it is not necessary to question her to understand that she has been violated dozens of times."[17]

In its political contours, the rape of the black woman was not exclusively an attack upon her. Indirectly, its target was also the slave community as a whole. In launching the sexual war on the woman, the master would not only assert his sovereignty over a critically important figure of the slave community, he would also be aiming a blow against the black man. The latter's instinct to protect his female relations and comrades (now stripped of its male supremacist implications) would be frustrated and violated to the extreme. Placing the white male's sexual barbarity in bold relief, Du Bois cries out in a rhetorical vein:

> I shall forgive the South much in its final judgment day: I shall forgive its slavery, for slavery is a world-old habit; I shall forgive its fighting for a well-lost cause, and for remembering that struggle with tender tears; I shall forgive its so-called "pride of race," the passion of its hot blood, and even its dear, old, laughable strutting and posing; but one thing I shall never forgive, neither in this world nor the world to come: its wanton and continued and persistent insulting of the black womanhood which it sought and seeks to prostitute to its lust.[18]

The retaliatory import of the rape for the black man would be entrapment in an untenable situation. Clearly the master hoped that once the black man was struck by his manifest inability to rescue his women from sexual assaults of the master, he would begin to experience deep-seated doubts about his ability to resist at all.

Certainly the wholesale rape of slave women must have had a profound impact on the slave community. Yet it could not succeed in its intrinsic aim of stifling the impetus toward struggle. Countless black women did not passively submit to these abuses, as the slaves in general refused to passively accept their bondage. The struggles of the slave woman in the sexual realm were a continuation of the resistance interlaced in the slave's daily existence. As such, this was yet another form of insurgency, a response to a politically tinged sexual repression.

Even E. Franklin Frazier (who goes out of his way to defend the thesis that "the master in his mansion and his colored mistress in her special house nearby represented the final triumph of social ritual in the presence of the deepest feelings of human solidarity"[19]) could not entirely ignore the black woman who fought back. He notes: "That physical compulsion was necessary at times to secure submission on the part of black women . . . is supported by historical evidence and has been preserved in the tradition of Negro families."[20]

The sexual contest was one of many arenas in which the black woman had to prove herself as a warrior against oppression. What Frazier unwillingly concedes would mean that countless children brutally fathered by whites were conceived in the thick of battle. Frazier himself cites the story of a black woman whose great-grandmother, a former slave, would describe with great zest the battles behind all her numerous scars—that is, all save one. In response to questions concerning the unexplained scar, she had always simply said: "White men are as low as dogs, child, stay away from them." The mystery was not unveiled until after the death of this brave woman: "She received that scar at the hands of her master's youngest son, a boy of about eighteen years at the time she conceived their child, my grandmother Ellen."[21]

An intricate and savage web of oppression intruded at every moment into the black woman's life during slavery. Yet a single theme appears at every juncture: the woman transcending, refusing, fighting back, asserting herself over and against terrifying obstacles. It was not her comrade brother against whom her incredible strength was directed. She fought alongside her man, accepting or providing guidance according to her talents and the nature of their tasks. She was in no sense an authoritarian figure; neither her domestic role nor her acts of resistance could relegate the man to the shadows. On the contrary, she herself had just been forced to leave behind the shadowy realm of female passivity in order to assume her rightful place beside the insurgent male.

This portrait cannot, of course, presume to represent every individual slave woman. It is rather a portrait of the potentials and possibilities inherent in the situation to which slave women were anchored. Invariably there were those who did not realize this potential. There were those who were indifferent and a few who were outright traitors. But certainly they were not the vast majority. The image of black women enchaining their men, cultivating relationships with the oppressor, is a cruel fabrication that must be called by its right name. It is a dastardly ideological weapon designed to impair our capacity for resistance today by foisting upon us the ideal of male supremacy.

According to a time-honored principle, advanced by Marx, Lenin, Fanon, and numerous other theorists, the status of women in any given society is a barometer measuring the overall level of social development. As Fanon has masterfully shown, the strength and efficacy of social struggles—and especially revolutionary movements—bear an immediate relationship to the range and quality of female participation.

Notes

"Reflections on the Black Women's Role in the Community of Slaves," which Davis wrote while imprisoned in 1971, was originally published in the *Black Scholar*, Vol. 3, No. 4 (December 1971) and is reprinted in *The Angela Y. Davis Reader*, ed. Joy James (Malden, MA: Blackwell, 1999), 111–128.

1. It is interesting to note a parallel in Nazi Germany: With all its ranting and raving about motherhood and the family, Hitler's regime made a conscious attempt to strip the family of virtually all its social functions. The thrust of their unspoken program for the family was to reduce it to a biological unit and to force its members to relate in an unmediated fashion to the fascist bureaucracy. Clearly the Nazis endeavored to crush the family in order to ensure that it could not become a center from which oppositional activity might originate.

2. [Frederick] Douglass quoted in Andrew Billingsley, *Black Families in White America* (Englewood, NJ: Prentice-Hall, 1968), 61.

3. John Henrik Clarke, "The Black Woman: A Figure in World History," Part III, *Essence* (July 1971).

4. Karl Marx, *Grundrisse der Kritik der Politischen Oekonomie* (Berlin: Dietz Verlag, 1953), 389.

5. Friedrich Engels, *Origin of the Family, Private Property and the State* (New York: International Publishers, 1942), 107.

6. Frederick Douglass, *Life and Times of Frederick Douglass* (New York: Collier Books, 1962), 96.

7. W. E. B. Du Bois, *Darkwater: Voices from Within the Veil* (New York: AMS Press, 1969), 185.

8. Lewis Clarke, "Narrative of the Sufferings of Lewis and Milton Clarke, Sons of a Soldier of the Revolution" (Boston, 1846), 127 [quoted by E. Franklin Frazier, *The Negro Family in the United States* (Chicago: University of Chicago Press, 1966)].

9. Moses Grandy, *Narrative of the Life of Moses Grandy, Late a Slave in the United States of America* (Boston, 1844), 18 [quoted by E. Franklin Frazier, *The Negro Family in the United States* (Chicago: University of Chicago Press, 1966)].

10. Ibid.

11. Marx, 266.

12. *Editor's note:* Maroon societies were comprised (not exclusively) of escaped slaves that successfully created communities of their own in remote areas, away from plantations. These sites became frequent havens for other escaped slaves. See Thomas Wenthworth Higginson, *Black Rebellion* (New York: DaCapo Press, 1998); Richard Price, ed., *Maroon Societies: Rebel Slave Communities in the Americas* (Baltimore, MD: Johns Hopkins University Press, 1996).

13. *Editor's note:* In 2002, 96,000 women were in state or federal prison. An additional 944,000 were on probation or parole. Forty-three percent of women prisoners are African American and 12 percent are Latina. See sentencing project.org/pdfs/1032.pdf. Sexual abuse and violation has been noted by Amnesty International, USA, *Not Part of My Sentence: Violations of the Human Rights of Women in Custody*, 1999; Amnesty International, USA, *Abuse of Women in Custody: Sexual Misconduct and Shackling of Pregnant Women*, 2001.

14. Simone de Beauvoir, *The Second Sex* (New York: Bantam, 1961), 18–19.

15. *Editor's note:* For information on the rape of men in prison, see Human Rights Watch, *No Escape: Male Rape in U.S. Prions,* April 2001; Don Sabo, Terry A. Kupers, and Willie London, eds., *Prison Masculinities* (Philadelphia: Temple University Press). Also, for narratives on the rape of black women by black men, see Aishah Shahidah Simmons, *No!,* (Philadelphia: AfroLez Productions, work in progress), documentary.

16. August Bebel, *Women and Socialism* (New York: Socialist Literature, 1910), 66–69.

17. Frantz Fanon, *A Dying Colonialism,* trans. Haakon Chevalier (New York: Grove Press, 1967), 119.

18. Du Bois, 172.

19. E. Franklin Frazier, *The Negro Family in the United States* (Chicago: University of Chicago Press, 1966 [1st edition, 1939]), 69.

20. Ibid., 53.

21. Ibid., 53–54.

11

Prince Imari A. Obadele (Shemuel ben-Yahweh)

My life begins in the struggle against white supremacy. In the early 1960s as a child at my father's [Imari Abubakari Obadele I] side i marched with Martin Luther King Jr. in Detroit, Michigan where i was born; participated in the Detroit school system boycott led by my father and the Group on Advanced Leadership; belonged to the Frederick Douglass Rifle Club and the Malcolm X Society; soldiered in the 1967 Detroit Rebellion; and, in 1968, was one of the original signers—and the youngest—of the New Afrikan Declaration of Independence, which ushered in the Provisional Government of the Republic of New Afrika and the New Afrikan Independence Movement—all by the time i was twelve years old.

On March 31, 1969, i became a political prisoner of war at the tender age of thirteen, having soldiered against the Detroit police in their armed attack on the Republic of New Afrika and Our annual conference at New Bethel Baptist Church. I was the last of more than 250 people to be released from jail.

By the first week of September 1971, at the age of fifteen, i was captured and charged, and subsequently convicted, for my part in an armed expropriation against whom We were led to believe was a drug dealer, which resulted in the death of a policeman. I stayed imprisoned for that action until I was nineteen. (Having been a juvenile in 1971, i was not tried as an adult.)

After my release, i immediately hooked back up with what remained of my cadre and, as they say nowadays, put some work in. However, one of the brothers new to Our cadre turned out to be my "best friend" and a heroin addict, and police informer. By 1976, at the age of twenty, i too was addicted to heroin and turning twenty-one in the State Prison of Southern Michigan, "Jackson." A revolutionary junky. And, the next fourteen years saw me at times putting in revolutionary work with various members of Our cadre, but just as often with the muggers and druggers, stealers and killers.

By August of 1990, having moved to Houston, TX, i was operating alone attempting to knock up on enough cash to open a survival center based upon the movement models of the late '60s, early '70s and the ideas of Dr. Mutulu Shakur. It was these actions that led to my current captivity as a result of a parole violation.

The last twenty-four years have been a struggle with demons within and demons without. I have lost everything including my son whom i am estranged from. But, i am alive and kicking and rising like the sun to continue to build for independence.

I am currently building a temple with its various ministries (The Latasha Harlins Ministry and The Dr. Mutulu Shakur Ministry) and striving to make these devils allow me to enroll in the Alvin College's Licensed Chemical Dependency Counselor program, since one of my areas of work will be in the treatment of addictions. Needless to say, all of this is intricately linked to the worldwide struggle to end oppression.

The Struggle continues!
Free all Political Prisoners!

Shalom!

—Minister Shemuel ben-Yahweh, a.k.a. Prince I. A. Obadele
January 2001

Killers
2003

Most Texas prisons are filled with burglars, car thieves, armed robbers, drug dealers, drug addicts, and thieves, with sprinklings of rapists, child molesters, and murderers, and two political prisoners: Ana Lucia Gelabert and myself. Texas prisons are also filled with "killers." But these killers aren't killing anything in defense of their rights and persons. They aren't even killing the ratches and roaches. These killers stand in the cell doors and "gun down" any female guard that comes around. They stand behind the walls peeping around the corners "shooting that bitch down." They sit in the classrooms, the infirmaries, dayrooms, and chow halls killing.

"Killers" are what i call "proxy-rapists." They are "taking the pussy" by proxy, in a virtual reality, so to speak.

"Killers" and "killings" are no different in their psychology than rapists and rapings. We are not talking about a prisoner who asks a female guard if she will let him masturbate on her, or "kill" her as some of them state. The killer stares at the guard with his hand in his pants and kills her, whether she allows it or not. Some killers are bold enough to pull their penis out and hope the pig will see it. Then, if the guard doesn't tell them to stop, or write them a disciplinary case, the pig becomes "good." "Is she good, man?" "Yeah, she good." Count-time comes and the killer is standing to block off the killer's cellmate's sight, butt-naked killing. If both celly's are killers they will both be at the cell door, butt-naked killing. Just as often one celly is not a killer and ends up hitting the killer in the back of the head. Or, if the killer is too big and tough for the nonkiller to whip, that celly has to try to get moved or put up with it.

Killing is so prevalent that almost all black prisoners are labeled as killers before We are labeled anything else, by both the pigs and other prisoners. In the eleven plus years i have been imprisoned in Texas prisons, not once have i have had a celly who did not want to know if i was a killer, for one reason or another. Up to the mid-1990s, Texas male prisoners wore pants with pockets and a button-down fly. Killers would cut holes in the pockets and crotches of those pants so that they could kill. One could rarely get a pair of pants that did not have the pockets and/or crotch cut out. The reactionary prisoncrats dealt with that problem by taking male pants away. No more pants with flies and pockets! We now wear the same pants the female prisoners have always worn: elastic waist band, no fly, one pocket in the back. Now when We have to use the toilet We have to pull Our pants down like the wimmin prisoners. Such is the prevalence of killing.

Understand that i don't give a damn what happens to a prison guard. It wouldn't bother me one bit if these same killers were using guns and knives and other instruments of death on these same guards. But they are not. And the culture of killing does not bode well for the safety of little girls and wimmin. The psychology of killings has equated masturbation and autoerotica with violence and death—they are "taking the pussy" and "killing" the wumyn. Most of these killers don't have a revolutionary ideology that guides them. For instance, from my political analysis, the guards are enemy soldiers. They are not "workers" with whom i can find common ground. They are my captors regardless of how well or poorly any individual guard might treat me. It is their sworn job to keep me repressed. It is my sworn duty to resist that oppression; therefore We are sworn enemies at war. However, my revolutionary politics does not countenance rape, whether physical or proxy, as a weapon of war. my politics says that rape is a war crime.

On the other hand, the killer, whose political ideology is counterrevolutionary sees the guard as just another wumyn. So the killer's attitude and actions are transferred to all wimmin: Wimmin are objects upon which to commit violence and to kill.

These same killers, the majority of them, are going to the streets one of these days and they will be peeping at your mothers, daughters, sisters, and wives from behind the walls and around the corners, or swinging from the trees like tarzan snatching up jane.

Killing and all it implies is a problem, among many other problems, that must be addressed by the revolutionary formations, progressive groupings, the reparations movement, and Our friends. In Amistad-March, a prison chapter of N'COBRA [National Coalition of Blacks for Reparations in America], this is one of the psychological damages that We are speaking of when We say that focus on the nonmaterial reparations is just as important as the material reparations. We need your help to address these and other issues pertinent to the repair of those being held prisoner who will, in most cases, be returning to your community.

12

Ed Mead

I was one of six children raised by a single mother who was homesteaded near Fairbanks, Alaska. When I was twelve during the mid-'50s, me and my sisters chopped a crude road into unsurveyed land they were about to homestead. We subsequently built a log cabin, drilled a well, and endured a whole lot of poverty. During the next ten years I pretty much ran wild, without the social or moral restraints imposed on most young men by parents, peers, church, school, and the other means of public information and conditioning. I was first incarcerated at the age of thirteen, at the State Industrial School for Boys in Ogden, Utah (Alaska did not have a juvenile institution at the time so I was subjected to out-of-state banishment at a very young age), for burning down a large structure on school grounds. By the time I was eighteen, I was serving a three-year sentence in the Federal Prison at Lompoc, California, for burglarizing a gas station (Alaska did not have a state prison at the time).

I was subsequently released on parole, violated the conditions of my supervision and was sent back to federal prison. At this point my life became a cliché of recidivism. I was in and out several times, mostly in, doing life on the installment plan. Then during the late '60s, while serving a ten-year attempted escape sentence at the federal prison at McNeil Island, Washington, I came into possession of some radical literature. Until then I supported the war in Vietnam. Not because I believed in the justice of the U.S. cause, but because I had heard some older men say something to the effect of: "We ought to bomb that place into the Stone Age and then pave it over and make a parking lot out of it." In the absence of an opinion of my own, I would have parroted something to that effect. But the anarchist and Marxist literature I was reading enabled me to intelligently choose sides.

Those who supported the war also advocated for longer sentences, the elimination of parole, and favored the death penalty. Those who opposed the war demanded an end to prison construction, freedom for prisoners, and the leftists opposed the death penalty. When McNeil Island prisoners went on a work strike, the singer Pete Seeger and actress Jane Fonda were on the docks with six hundred people demonstrating in support of the striking prisoners. The Weathermen busted Timothy Leary out of prison, and they were bombing the government. Choosing sides was easy, and . . . having done it, I've never looked back.

Released by a federal court order in 1972, I left Alaska and moved to Seattle to "join the revolution." I was active in Seattle's progressive political community for several years, until I was arrested in 1975 during an unsuccessful bank expropriation by the George Jackson Brigade.[1] The Brigade had been conducting acts of armed propaganda such as bombings and financed itself through bank robberies. Convicted and sentenced to two consecutive life terms by the state of Washington on two counts of first-degree assault against police officers (because of a shootout at the bank), I was sent to the Washington State Penitentiary at Walla Walla. It was there that I organized Men Against Sexism.

After serving eighteen years, I was released in 1993. For nearly a decade I have worked as a network administrator for a nonprofit in San Francisco.

—Ed Mead
2003

Note

1. *Editor's note:* The George Jackson Brigade was a multiracial, armed organization that operated in the Pacific Northwest during the mid- to late-1970s. This guerrilla group took its name from George Jackson, an imprisoned black revolutionary and writer who was killed by guards at San Quentin on August 21, 1971. According to ex-brigade member Rita Bo Brown, the group was composed primarily of working-class exconvicts who engaged in acts of armed resistance in solidarity with antiracist, antiimperialist struggles. See *Imprisoned Intellectuals: America's Political Prisoners Write on Life, Liberation, and Rebellion,* ed. Joy James (Lanham, MD: Rowman and Littlefield, 2003), 216–26.

Men Against Sexism
2003

It was the summer of 1977, and I'd just been released from the hole and was entering the population for the first time. I moved from the segregation unit into cell B-6 of Eight Wing, a four-man cell located on the flats that was "owned" by a comrade named Danny. Yes, cells were owned by individual prisoners and bought and sold much like real estate on the streets. One had to be approved by the owner in order to move into a cell. If the administration moved a fish [a new inmate, among those most vulnerable to sexual assault] into a cell, he would generally be permitted to stay for two or three days while he looked for another place to live. Beyond that his stuff would be thrown out on the tier and he'd have to fend for himself. In any case, I was fortunate enough to be moving into a cell already owned by a friend. I did not have to play the musical cage game so many other prisoners were subjected to. A guy I will call Joe was already in the cell when I moved in. He was the first of us released from the hole, and shortly after I was turned lose, Danny and his friend Mark followed. The cell itself was designed for two men but contained four beds, two bunk beds along each of the dingy cobalt blue walls.

Joe was the cell's sound man. The noise outside the cell was a cacophony of loud radios and blaring televisions, all playing on different stations and channels. On top of that, prisoners added to the general sense of pandemonium by yelling at each other between tiers; trading coffee, insults, and gossip in loud voices. What Joe would do is set his portable tape deck near the bars at the front of the cell, with the speakers aimed inward, and then he'd crank up the volume until there was a virtual wall of sound that drowned out all other external noise. The effect of Joe's artistry in this regard was awesome. The tape deck was not playing uncomfortably loud, yet there was not another sound beyond its sensitively balanced speakers. Of course Joe's choice of music was such that there were few silences, either between notes or between songs—not unlike the heavy metal of today. And while Aerosmith and the absence of any silence was stressful, it was far better than the noise it replaced.

There were sixteen or seventeen hundred prisoners in the population at Walla Walla and only enough jobs for a portion of them. I did not have to work and thus was able to devote the bulk of my time to prison politics; talking to fellow convicts and trying to learn more about local concerns. I was also trying to adjust to this very different reality. Rape was clearly an issue. Prisoners were being routinely bought and sold by each other; the young and vulnerable ones were raped and then subjected to forced prostitution. While there was general agreement that this was wrong, there was no support within the population for a group like Men Against Sexism. Straight prisoners were not going to put their prison status and personal safety on the line for gays, and for the most part the gay population was too demoralized or defeated to stand up for itself.

While our decisions were not as conscious and straightforward as I might tend to make them sound, those of us in the cell did manage to slowly develop an agenda of sorts. We were going to work with the existing Resident Government Council (RGC) toward forming an RGC-sponsored subgroup called the Prison Justice Committee (PJC). The Seattle branch of the American Friends Services Committee (AFSC), an offshoot of the Quaker Church with a long and progressive tradition of involvement in prison issues, agreed to support our organizing efforts.

Building the Prison Justice Committee was not a very difficult task. We were to some extent leaders of the recently victorious forty-seven-day strike. If we believed that an arm of the RGC should be formed that called itself the Prison Justice Committee, then influential members of the population would be more than happy to support the proposal. Most prisoners agreed that it was important to build upon and to consolidate the gains and promises achieved as a result of the strike, and that's what the PJC was trying to do. The PJC was led by a former segregation graduate named Eddwynn Jordan. He and his brothers were well-respected members of the black prison population, with long histories of struggle. I was the group's vice chairperson. So the PJC was organized and a schedule of meetings established. From the very start, attendance at PJC meetings exceeded that of its parent organization, the RGC. Within a month the PJC was *the* prisoners' group at Walls [Walla Walla]. One of the first things we did was to break ourselves down into much smaller subcommittees, each of which was assigned the responsibility for monitoring specified aspects of the prison experience. On top of that, we had outside guests coming in to the prison each week to hold joint meetings with us and to work with us around various prison-related issues.

Just as prisoners in general became increasingly involved in the activities of the PJC, so too did gay prisoners and some of the other more vulnerable prisoners. They did not become PJC supporters out of a need for protection, but rather because the group took a firm stand not only against racism, but also against all forms of sexism and homophobia. It was an organization that related to the special needs of gay prisoners. It provided hope for constructive change. Before too long the PJC formed yet another subcommittee, with me as its chairperson, which I called Men Against Sexism (MAS). The Resident Government Council (RGC) was an officially sponsored group; the PJC was an offspring of the RGC and therefore enjoyed some measure of respectability in the eyes of our captors. Similarly, MAS, because of its relationship to the PJC, while certainly not respectable, did possess a degree of legitimacy sufficient to keep the pigs' boot off our necks for long enough for us to stand on our own two feet. I don't think MAS would have survived that initial phase of development had it not been for the protective wing of the Prison Justice Committee.

The PJC did its work well and continued to grow; before too long the group was able to cut all of its ties with the RGC. Now formally sanctioned by the prison administration, and with the AFSC as its primary source of outside support, the PJC became an independent organization. The PJC held its weekly meetings in a room on the second floor of the admissions building. This is where our outside guests would come into the prison and regularly meet with us. At these joint gatherings each subdirector would have to give a report on the status of the work the subcommittee was doing. The subcommittee on visitation, for example, would report on the progress being made in that area, such as problems with the visiting room staff, expanding the visiting area, the conjugal visitation proposal, and so on. I think there were about six different subcommittees, each dealing with issues ranging from racism to legislative action. The MAS subcommittee started out like all the others, but then seemed to quickly develop a life all of its own. MAS membership soon grew to be half the size of the PJC, then grew some more until we slightly outnumbered our parent organization. This difference in growth did not at first create any problems, since we were all marching in more or less the same direction.

MAS started having its own separate meetings in the PJC's office (in addition to the weekly PJC gatherings), and at these smaller meetings we invited people from Seattle's gay community inside to talk with us. Before too long, firm friendships had been struck between the inside and out. At the same time we were busily conducting MAS types of activities, which in large part centered around building a sense of pride and community within the walls. This was accomplished through deeds.

While an occasionally published underground paper at the penitentiary called *The Bomb* usually printed only when someone in the population thought it necessary to make a sort of call-to-arms, we started a monthly newsletter and called it *The Lady Finger* (a very small firecracker). In addition to addressing general issues of sexism and containing news of interest to gays and the more or less advanced social prisoners, the newsletter was a broadside against the scum-bags who were involved in the ongoing rape and the buying and selling of prisoners. I also wrote to and obtained progressive film catalogues through which I was able to obtain documentaries with titles like "Men and Masculinity" and subjects of sexism and anti-Vietnam War themes. The film companies would loan us the films for free; we merely had to pay for the postage and insurance costs. Getting a room and projector was never a problem, as we'd use the PJC name on our authorization memos.

A typical MAS action during this period would be calculated to strengthen gay unity while at the same time working to isolate and expose those powerful elements within the population who believed it was their god-given right to rob, rape, and otherwise pillage their peers. The process was a slow one. If we stuck our collective neck out too far someone would chop it off. Here is an example of the type of action we'd do back then. There was a nationwide religious organization that primarily ministered to the spiritual needs of gays called the Metropolitan Community Church (MCC). Over a period of time we had managed to obtain authorization from the administration for the MCC to come inside the prison and to hold regular services in the prison's chapel. The Catholic priest had no problem with this, although the Protestant chaplain, who happened to be a right-wing, born-again fundamentalist preacher, stooped to petty acts of sabotage against the MCC minister and his congregation. One Sunday morning a prisoner came running up to me and said, chaplain so-and-so (I forget his name) is going to do a sermon this morning on the evils of homosexuality, specifically targeting the MCC services. I immediately sent runners out to spread the alarm to gays in every cell block; my message was that all MAS members were to attend Protestant services being held later that morning.

We were a pretty sight as about twenty of us quietly sat in the conservative church that morning, waiting for services to begin. I wore shoulder length blond hair, with lavender stars for earrings. Others wore facial makeup or were in full drag, including colorful dresses. Our quickly arrived at consensus, that our mere presence would be enough to restrain the preacher's bigotry, proved to be wrong. He started in on the MCC, and homosexuals in general, preaching what a travesty it was that queers would defile the house of the lord with their so-called religion. That was enough for me. He no more than got a good start when I interrupted his

Nazi diatribe with a speech on the value of religious freedom and toler- ance. The other MAS members chimed in with their support for what I was saying, while his congregation of protective custody candidates and would-be child molesters remained prudently silent, no doubt intimidated by the sight of so many angry faggots. When the issue was put in a rights context, rather than a religious or moral one, I managed to make the preacher at least pretend to see that his efforts to prevent our chaplain from coming in and conducting services was a denial of our religious free- doms. I made it clear that we would fight hard for that freedom. That con- frontation seemed to take much of the wind from his sails, as we had no significant problems with him from then on. After that incident gays seemed to walk around with their heads held a little higher, and with a bit more pride than usual.

As a communist, I am of course an atheist. But being a godless commie did not prevent me from defending the rights of MAS members to religious freedom. And I exercised that right myself by personally attend- ing each and every MCC service that was conducted at Walla Walla. Gen- erally speaking, whether it is workers striking for a fairer wage or peasants struggling for land, you will always find communists defending the rights of the poor and working people. We will be on the side of working-class justice, and exploitation in any form, be it racial, sexual, or economic.

Men Against Sexism continued to build in size and grow in strength. We found safe-cells for exploited people to move into and, while continu- ing with all of our regular political activities, moved more and more in the direction of what we called crisis intervention. A young pedophile had recently arrived at the prison and was promptly snatched up by the preda- tors. When they were done "using" him, he was sold into a different cell for three hundred dollars. Where before our intervention tended to come after the rape or related incident and would take the form of hand-holding types of support, now we were moving into the area of direct meddling with the behavior of the prison's tougheoisie (tough-wah-zee). With a com- bination of bluff and bluster, moral persuasion and dumb luck, we extracted the pedophile from his state of sexual bondage and moved him into one of our safe cells. There was much outrage over this in certain cir- cles. How, they wanted to know, could we possibly justify standing against real convicts over a stinking child molester? We stood on our principles and in the end managed to hold firm against the shifting tides of prisoner opinion. We'd won another round.

But the fight was an ongoing one. For every situation we were able to deal with, there seemed to be two others that were beyond our strength to resolve. There are two types of contradictions in the world, antagonistic and nonantagonistic. Antagonistic contradictions are like the one between us as poor and working people, on the one hand, and the ruling class and its government on the other. This is an antagonistic contradiction that must ultimately be resolved through the process of class struggle and revolution. Nonantagonistic contradictions, on the other hand, are those among the people themselves, and are resolved through nonviolent means such as persuasion and criticism. At least that's the theory. In practice it did not always happen that way. Our work had, over a period of time, developed to the point of confrontation with some predatory rapists; we were going to have to fight or back off—that narrow set of choices was pretty clear to everyone.

At the next Prison Justice Committee meeting, when MAS gave its weekly progress report, I asked for PJC support in a conflict that MAS was about to have with a group of obstinate prisoners over the rape issue. Some other prisoners had captured and enslaved some kid for sexual purposes. We'd talked and manipulated until we were blue in the face, without any success at all. Violence was the next option. It was my feeling that the more of us who confronted them, the less likely it would be that physical conflict would occur. The PJC would not back our play, saying it was a matter for us to resolve on our own. In retrospect they were probably right. Blacks must be their own liberators, just as gays must free themselves. We cannot rely on anyone else to do our fighting for us. But at the time we did not see it that way; we were outraged that our parent organization would cut us loose to fend for ourselves in the violent seas that surrounded us. MAS thereupon quit the PJC. The breakup was a rather acrimonious one. The PJC's demise was almost immediate; within a month they were completely dead. MAS was reduced to a more or less underground group. Our outside support network and inside membership were intact; we merely needed to relocate and reorganize.

The "breezeway" was a term I'd not heard of before my arrival at the Walls. There were a number of these roofed walkways at the penitentiary, only these, unlike those on the streets, had chain-link fencing from top to bottom on each side. Walking from block to the mess hall, for example, required one to traverse one of these open tunnels both ways. It was on these breezeways that much of the violence took place. In fact, there were so many stabbings in one area of the breezeway that it became known as "Blood Alley" by prisoners and guards alike. Because of the overpopulation there were far more men than there were jobs, and even those who did work were paid just pennies an hour. The breezeway was the place of choice for these unemployed or underpaid hustlers to hang out. They would sell used street clothing, drugs, and even pimp their punks from these areas. The breezeway was, in short, a commercial and social hangout for much of the joint's riffraff. And MAS was no exception. In the absence of an office, we met with each other and conducted the group's day-to-day business from the breezeway.

The entire prison was not dirty and ugly; there was a lovely island of beauty in the form of the Lifer's Park. Set on two sides by huge cellblocks, Seven Wing on one side and Eight Wing on the other, and a breezeway fence in front and the Lifer's clubhouse in the rear, the park was an exclusive island of manicured grass and carefully cultivated flowers. There was always an inmate guard at the gate leading to the park; no one got in unless they were a member or the escorted guest of a member. At the other end of their rectangular park was a large, two-story brick building. This was the Lifer's clubhouse. The Lifer's Club was run by a large black man named Tommy and his two white lieutenants, both of whom were young and tough. Tommy was a well-built ex-boxer who liked having sex with men. He pitched as well as he caught, meaning he would suck or be sucked, fuck or be fucked, although the public image he presented was one of "pitching" only. In the prison culture it is not considered to be homosexual behavior for one to stick his prick into another man's orifice; only the stickee was stigmatized with such labels.

Tommy fancied himself a progressive, on occasion going so far as to let it slip that he considered himself to be another George Jackson. While I knew better than that, I nonetheless tended to overestimate Tommy's level of political development. Tommy had ongoing problems with other elements of the population, like the Chicanos, but these were nothing he could not handle himself, should it ever come to that. Still, like any leader, he could always use additional strength. Tommy liked having sex with men and wanted more political and military strength. MAS consisted mostly of people who liked doing sex with men; it had some strength, and it needed a home. An implicit agreement was reached. The Lifer's Club soon became the new MAS headquarters.

MAS's eventual takeover of the Lifer's was not a sudden one, nor was it deliberate. We slowly started spending less time on the breezeway and more time in Lifer's Park. Tommy made us feel welcomed. At a subsequent Lifer's meeting it was proposed that MAS, who had been orphaned by the mean ol' PJC, be loaned just a tiny corner of the big Lifer's meeting room, and this only for as long as it took MAS to be recognized by the administration and given a space of its own. With MAS present and Tommy and his goons ramrodding the motion through, the membership was somewhat agreed. We set up an office and from under the protective wing of legitimacy offered by the Lifer's, started inviting our outside guests back into the prison to see us.

Lifer's and MAS members were also able to have sex with outsiders in a specially prepared downstairs room. It was a soundproof room that prisoners once used for reading books for the blind on cassette tapes. But at that point it was empty and unused, with only a mattress tossed on the floor. The members of the Lifer's would take their women friends into the little room; MAS would take their men friends. I was with one guy on the inside, and Robert on the outside.

As officers of the Lifer's were attritioned by release, transfer, or dismissal, they would most often be replaced by MAS members. This was not because of some grand conspiracy or master plan, but simply because we were hard workers who did have the interests of the Lifer's Club at heart. Gradually, the line between the Lifer's and MAS blurred, in our minds as well as in the thinking of the other officers of the Lifer's Club. I was the chairperson of MAS, and Danny Atteberry, Mark La Rue, and Carl Harp were my officers. I was also the treasurer for the Lifer's, and Danny, Mark, and Carl were all on the Lifer's executive board as well. While I had all but lost sight of the distinction between the two groups, others—those on the outside of our gate—had not. MAS had contributed a lot to the Lifer's Club. We implemented a candy sales program in which all prisoners could trade prison script money for our specialized candies. The candy business was highly successful. The Lifer's Club was making money for the first time in a long time. We bought a pool table for the members and made many other improvements to the club. I put an end to Tommy's looting of the club's treasury and made regular and accurate financial reports to the membership. Decisions on what to spend the profits on were democratically arrived at. The Lifer's Club was doing better than at any time in recent history. MAS was doing well too. We'd obtained lots of support from Seattle's gay community and were in the process of pressuring the administration, both directly and indirectly, to recognize MAS and to provide us with a space of our own.

The lifers were being agitated by two dope fiends, who I will continue to call Kevin and Andy, both of whom were in Curtis's rape pack in segregation, and who later stabbed that wanna-be boss rapist. Kevin and Andy agitated for the need to take the club back from the niggers and faggots (my inside lover and many of my friends and MAS members were black). Kevin was going to run for the office of Lifer president, and with Andy helping to stir things up, it did not take me long to see that the Lifer population was going to vote for Kevin. And it was also clear that once elected he would kick MAS out of the Lifer's Club. On the surface all was civil and polite, but beneath the surface the struggle was waging. The day-to-day pressure of this polite-to-your-face-stab-you-in-the-back became too much for Tommy. One night he and his two sidekicks went to the pigs and offered to hand over our shotguns and shells in exchange for a transfer to what was then the kids' joint at Shelton. The administration agreed. They were gone the next morning, as were our guns and ammunition. So there was MAS, weaponless and, by default, the only ones left in the Lifer's Club.

There's an old Kenny Rogers song about gambling that has a line saying "you got to know when to hold 'em, when to fold 'em . . ." It was time for MAS to fold 'em, to pack our bags, and to move from the plush comfort of the Lifer's Club and back to the harsh realities of existence on the breezeway. Nearly all the thirty or so MAS members came with me. Danny, Blue, and Mark, most of the leadership, stayed behind. They were not going to run in the face of danger. They were not concerned with whether it was right or wrong for us to be there or whether it was politically right for us to take a step back before advancing again. Mark and Danny were soon driven out of the Lifer's Park at knifepoint, with the loss of much face in the process. Blue quit MAS and became a part of the new Lifer's clique, or at least he was tolerated by them.

MAS went back to seeking sanctioning and its own meeting space. I gave up the position of MAS president, turning the job over to a more "respectable" person, a guy more likely to win the recognition than my friends and I would have been. Buying and selling of weaker prisoners had been stopped, and rape had gone from a traditional test of manhood to an occasional incident. An unarmed MAS would do fine, and most of us would continue to be active in the group's meetings and activities. What was permitted to develop was little more than a social club for gays. MAS started working on inoffensive projects like collecting newspapers for recycling, doing sewing and mending jobs for the population, and generally putting forward a harmless face.

Some thought we should have fought Kevin and Andy over control of the Lifer's Club, but most of MAS's membership consisted of nonlifers who didn't belong there anyway. Besides, I did not want to hurt anyone else. And the bottom line was that we were unarmed and without allies. After the Lifer's experience, the old MAS leadership, Danny, Mark, and I, quietly turned our attention to other matters, like rearming ourselves and getting out of prison. We also started to do some serious work on a new escape plan.

There was always a high level of tension at the Walls. People were unceremoniously tossed out of their cells, for one reason or another, and no other cells were willing to take them in. There were frequent fights; stabbings took place often; and occasionally these would lead to a death. Often the death could have been avoided had it not been for the incompetence of the prison's medical staff. I'll give you a brief example. On May 23, 1978, a black prisoner named Robert Redwine was stabbed in the side by one or more of his fellows. The stabbing was over nothing of consequence—another senseless act of violence. The victim went to the prison hospital where he was given a cursory examination by a doctor who diagnosed the wounds as "superficial." The treatment did not include the standard practice of x-rays or probing the depths of the wounds. Redwine was sewn up and then locked in a hospital isolation room and left alone. After awhile, the victim started to protest by banging on the solid door at the front of his room and yelling for help from the hospital staff. His demands attracted the attention of one of the hospital porters, an inmate who inquired about the problem. Redwine told the porter that he was in pain and needed to see someone on the medical staff. When the porter delivered this information to the chief nurse, Eva Nelson, he was told to ignore the victim's cries, as he was only "playing for drugs." The victim's cries went unanswered until hours later he lay dead. He died alone and ignored, from internal bleeding.

Anyway, our collective response to the ongoing prisoner-on-prisoner violence was to re-arm ourselves. Although largely unspoken, there was a clear sense of agreement that if our enemies attacked any one of us, the survivors would launch an immediate counterattack on the aggressors. We still had potentially deadly problems with the new leadership of the Lifer's Club. While we were physically out of the Lifer's, few believed our contradiction between Kevin, Andy, and their henchmen, on the one hand, and us on the other, was even close to being resolved. The gap between us was not measured by the mere yardstick of their tossing us out of the club or the pulling of knives on Mark and Danny, but by the resurgence of rapes, heroin use, murder, drug dealing, and gangsterism that characterized their stewardship of the Lifer's. Not only did they loot the club's treasury, use the place for a heroin shooting gallery, and mercilessly exploit and terrorize the membership, they ultimately left the beautiful Lifer's Park paved over. Thanks to their later escape attempt and getting caught concealing weapons in the park, the administration destroyed the only island of tranquility in a whole sea of violent turmoil.

After many long months of work, including the submission of numerous proposals, revisions of those proposals, pressure from outside supporters, the dogged persistence of MAS workers, and the passage of time, the prison administration finally sanctioned our organization. We'd been on the breezeway for about two or three months. Now we were official. We were given a meeting space, which just happened to be the air-conditioned offices of some counselors who'd moved to another area of the prison. We thought we were in fat city. MAS was the first openly gay prisoner's organization to be officially recognized by a prison administration. As far as I know, no such group has been so recognized since then. Our organized existence was the result of our determination as a group, the pre-AIDS era in which we existed, the strength of our community support, the good work we'd done on the inside, and, of course, the existence of the then relatively liberal prison administration. What official sanctioning meant to us, in addition to having a nice office to work from, was that we could once again invite our outside guests back into the prison. And bring them in we did. We'd have good meetings in our new office, with lots of singing together, hugs, and general closeness. One thing we did not do, however, is have sex in the office. There was always pressure from the social gays to exploit what we'd gained, using guests to smuggle drugs for us, or to turn tricks for the population in the club's office. We always had to guard against these opportunistic tendencies.

Prison is always a terrible place to be. But within the context, the degree of terribleness can vary considerably from day to day. On some days, particularly when MAS was doing well, the relative level of pain was not too great. At times we were almost happy. At other times the fear and tension were so heavy in the air that we never knew from one hour to the next if we'd continue to live. There would be senseless killings, racial conflicts, and other forms of violence. It was during one of these oppressive periods that Andy raped a young kid in the Lifer's office. Rape had all but stopped taking place, and now here it was again, being rubbed in our faces by our old Lifer foes. I began to wonder if the sickness of this place would ever be changed. We took the rape victim into our cell, as Mark's bunk was still empty. Joe, Danny, and I all tried to help heal him. I had a talk with Andy, who I found lounging about in front of the Lifer's Club. When I confronted him over the rape, he lied to me, saying the incident did not happen. Now what? I'd talked to the kid and knew all the intimate details surrounding the rape; I'd seen the youngster's bruises. He had no motivation to lie. I was still inadequately armed for a showdown with Andy and the growing gang of killer dope fiends who ran the Lifer's.

When tension built up in seg [segregation unit], I would try to aim or direct prisoner anger against their captors and to educate them about the nature of their real enemies. Our cell tried to do the same thing with the whole population. The drug dealing and murders were getting out of hand. MAS would escort older prisoners to and from the inmate store to keep them from being robbed by these narcotic users, but others were victimized. It was going to take more than a finger in the dike to slow this flood of predatory behavior. We organized a prisoner work strike, putting all our effort into making it a success, only to discover that Kevin and Andy had become the administration's first line of defense. They threw a vested interest in the status quo; their candy scam and other schemes were needed to support their growing heroin addiction. Their narrow self-interests led them to a consistent pattern of opportunism and collaboration with the

Ed Mead

pigs. Their old pattern of having a love-hate relationships with their captors continued from their seg days.

During this time period there was an incident in which the Chicano Club made a move on one of the joint's most attractive gays, a feminine appearing homosexual I'll call Sally. Sally was not a member of MAS and was one of the few gays who had not contributed anything toward the building of the group. The leadership of the Chicanos, who were allied with the Lifer's, said Sally had to leave the man she was living with by choice and move into one of their cells. They would not see reason. I called an emergency MAS meeting. With members assembled in our office, I explained the situation, saying we were going to fight and probably kill people, but did not of course tell them we had a revolver, eighty rounds of ammunition, and three homemade hand grenades. They probably thought we had knives.

Mark, Danny, and I were going to walk into the Chicano Club and start killing people. We had the gun and bombs with us. The members would march to the Chicano Club with us and wait outside while we took care of business on the inside. The membership did not know the true extent of the violence we were about to wage. We did not talk long. As we were getting ready to march, Blue said he wanted to give the Chicanos one more chance. We told him to be quick. He was. Upon his return he told us the situation was resolved. We packed up our weapons and went home. I never asked Blue what he told them. I didn't care. There was a near certainty in my mind that we would kill several people that afternoon. I saw it as necessary to deliver the message that rape and slavery would not be tolerated. I was fully prepared to write that message in the blood of my fellow prisoners. We escaped committing mass murder on that particular day, but there was always tomorrow.

During this event it was necessary to move bombs and to gather materials to make more. We briefly stored some empty pipe casings in Sally's cell. We would later learn that she reported this fact to the pigs. We were prepared to kill and perhaps die for her right not to be forced into sexual slavery, and she rewarded us by turning us in to the administration. This kind of thing happened more than once. Those were the ups and downs of organizing Men Against Sexism. I was subsequently transferred out-of-state for about five years, then served my last ten years at the prison complex outside Monroe, Washington. During that ten-year period there was not a single prisoner-on-prisoner rape at Monroe, nor did I hear of any happening at other facilities within the state. And I kept an ear pretty close to the ground for that sort of thing. I'm sure some rapes happened, but if so it was nothing like the brutality and volume that existed within the state prior to Men Against Sexism.

III. Revolt

13

Little Rock Reed

Little Rock (Timothy) Reed[1] was born in Illinois in 1961. Abused as a child, he became involved with drugs early in his life and was first imprisoned at age eighteen. In 1982, he was convicted of theft and burglary, and was sentenced to twenty-five years in the Southern Ohio Correctional Facility at Lucasville. While incarcerated, Little Rock, who identified as Lakota Sioux, began studying law and became an outspoken activist, writer, and advocate for Native American and prisoners' rights. In 1993, he co-authored a collective statement by Native American prisoners, former prisoners, and spiritual leaders entitled *The American Indian in the White Man's Prisons: A Story of Genocide.* Following his parole in 1992, he founded the Native American Prisoners' Research and Rehabilitation Project. Charged with a parole violation linked to his activism, Little Rock fled Ohio and settled in New Mexico, where he began working at the Center for Advocacy for Human Rights. Although Ohio authorities declared him a fugitive and hunted him down, New Mexico's highest court refused to extradite Little Rock. The U.S. Supreme Court overruled the New Mexico Court's decision, and Little Rock was returned to Ohio in early December 1998, but was released later that month to serve the remainder of his parole in the community. Little Rock Reed died in a car accident in New Mexico on January 15, 2000.

Note

1. "Little Rock" is the name the author took for spiritual and social purposes; "Timothy Reed" is his birth name.

References

American Friends Service Committee. "Little Rock Reed Released on Parole." Philadelphia: American Friends Service Committee, December 17, 1998. www.afsc.org/nrlr1217.htm (7 June 2002).
Higgins, Connie. "'Little Rock' Reed Killed in Auto Accident; He Spent a Decade in Ohio Prisons, and Became an Activist for American Indian Inmates." *The Columbus Dispatch,* January 16, 2000.

133

"Little Rock Reed Freed; New Mexico Judge Refuses to Extradite Him to Ohio," *Prison News Service,* No. 49 (January–February 1995).

Newell, Kara, American Friends Service Committee. *AFSC Statement on Little Rock Reed Case.* Philadelphia: American Friends Service Committee, December 11, 1998. www.afsc.org/news/1998/stlrreed.htm (June 7, 2002).

Reed, Little Rock, Lenny Foster, and Art Solomon. *The American Indian in the White Man's Prison: A Story of Genocide.* Taos, NM: UnCompromising Books, 1993.

The American Indian in the White Man's Prisons: A Story of Genocide 1989

. . . I am going to describe the spiritual significance attached to the immediate relief I am seeking. My reason for this is so that this court will possibly be able to understand how important these things are to me and my people . . . and the injurious effects the denial of these things are having on me and my people. I will describe, or explain, why the Defendants have no legitimate reason for continuing to deny us these things. I will begin with the sacred pipe, as to have an understanding of what the sacred pipe means to me and my people will make it easier for you to understand the other things I will describe. I am not a spiritual leader, and there may be some things that I am unable to elaborate on because of my little knowledge; but this is my personal testimony, and I speak from my heart.

The sacred pipe is at the center of my religion. We call it *caupa wakan*. It is a gift that was given to my people by the Great Spirit, through a messenger. This messenger instructed us in the meaning and use of the pipe. This messenger wasn't just a person, but a holy spirit woman. She told the people that this pipe was to be used in prayer. It is constructed like this: The bowl of the pipe is made of sacred *inyansha*, red stone. This stone is very sacred and it is only found in one place in the world, up in what is now Minnesota. A long time ago there was a flood, a great flood. This flood covered the whole earth because the Great Spirit was unhappy with the human race, the wickedness of man. So the Great Spirit cleansed the earth with this flood. The weight of the water crushed the people, and at that time my people were located in Minnesota. The blood of the people ran out onto the earth and over a long period of time it congealed and turned to stone. This is the sacred *inyansha*, the stone which we are to use to make the bowl of the sacred pipe. The bowl of the pipe represents the blood of the people, and it represents the earth, which we think of as our mother, our true mother, because she sustains us with all the nourishment we need to stay alive and healthy. The bowl of the pipe reminds us that we

135

are of the earth, we are tied to the earth, and we must love and take care of our mother just as she does us.

The stem of the pipe is made of wood, and it is long and straight. . . . It represents all that grows upon the earth: the trees, the grasses, the flowers, and all that grows upon the earth. It also represents the straight path that we want to walk in this life: the straightness of character and the virtuous qualities we strive to achieve in this life, and which we know the Great Spirit wants us to strive for.

There may be animal parts, such as the hide of a deer, or perhaps an etching on the pipe that is of an animal. These represent all the animals on the earth: the deer, the buffalo, the coyote, the wolf, the snakes, the insects, the fish, and all the other animals of the earth.

There may be an eagle feather attached to the pipe, or perhaps some other bird feather. This, as well as the smoke of the pipe, represents all that lives above the earth: the winged creatures, the sun, the moon, the clouds, the air, and all that resides above the earth. In my own way of perceiving, I believe this also represents all the waters, the rivers which are the lifeblood of our mother earth, because the clouds represent the rain which nourishes and purifies.

When we place the tobacco into the bowl of the pipe, each tiny grain represents some aspect of the universe: There is a grain in there for you and for me, and for all peoples, the rocks, the grasses and trees, the animals, the winds, and every living thing in the universe. And when we smoke the pipe we are praying; the smoke carries our prayers to the Great Spirit. We are praying for the coming together, the harmony, the healing of all peoples, and of all parts of the universe. And we are giving thanks for all that we have. . . .

These things are all very important to us; they are our way of life, our religion. I need the spiritual guidance—as do the other brothers in the prison here—which can come only from a Native American spiritual leader who is able to understand my culture, my religion, my way of life. I feel like an alien in here because this whole prison system is created in such a way as to cut me off from my culture, my religion. There is no way I can describe the effect it has had on me to be forcefully separated from my very way of life. The values of the white man, I don't understand. I don't understand a culture that believes that it is good to fight one another for wealth, for material things. I don't understand the white man's philosophies, which believe that we are superior to the earth, our mother, and that we must destroy her so that we can get rich with material things, or that we are above the other animals, or that one race is superior to another. These things I don't understand, but it is the way of the white man, and it is the way these prisoners are taught to be so that they can function properly in the white man's society when they are released. But I don't let these things touch me, because I know in my heart that the way of my people is the way the Great Spirit wants me to be. But it is hard on me in here to be deprived of an opportunity to join with my Brothers so that we can worship the Great Spirit [together], and so that we can help each other to renew our spirits. None of us were walking in balance when we were out there in the free world, otherwise we wouldn't be here now. We need the guidance that can come only from our spiritual leaders, and from our spiritual rites.

Imagine that you are a Christian and that you are placed in an environment where nobody but a small handful of people are Christians, and that those of you who are Christians are separated from one another because the officials don't want you to have an opportunity to ever see one another, and that all religious leaders in the free world are invited to come into the prison with the exception of any who are Christian, and that they are barred from entering, and that you are prohibited from having a bible or a crucifix. Imagine what that would feel like, and let the feeling sink down into your bones, your heart, your mind, your guts, and that it is with you every day, every night, every minute. And that you are constantly ridiculed or punished for any attempt to practice your beliefs. If you can realize how that would feel, then and only then can you have any idea of how it is for me and my people in this Iron House. But even if you have an idea, it is only a small idea, because you could never know what it is like until you have lived it. It is hard, and every single day before I go to sleep at night I pray to the Great Spirit, Wakan Tanka, and I ask that some miracle take place so that the officials in this prison system will become enlightened enough that they can someday know that my people are human beings who deserve a little bit of freedom. You have taken our land; you have taken our children forcefully from the reservations and placed them in the BIA [Bureau of Indian Affairs] boarding schools and punished them for doing anything Indian, and have set them loose into your cities after programming them into being ashamed of their heritage; you have murdered our women and children and our elders after smoking the sacred pipe in friendship; you have broken and continue to break your treaties with my people so that your oil companies can come onto the little bit of land that is left to us—we don't "own" the land. It never did belong to my people. We belonged to it and it is our duty to take care of her for the generations to come. We must take care of her if she is to take care of us.

Your people have caused much suffering to my people. The least you could do is live up to your laws by letting us worship God in the way God has instructed us to. You will all always be in my prayers, even though you usually do such wrong to me and my people. May Tunkasila Wakan Tanka have pity on you after all you have done and all you condone today. May he forgive you for destroying the earth he has given us to share as Brothers. May he forgive those who feel they are so superior that they even stand between God and those who wish to worship in accordance with God's will. I pray for you.

I sincerely believe everything I have told you in this affidavit. The religious beliefs I profess to have are my true beliefs, and I should not be deprived of the right to my religious practices. They are sacred, and the Great Spirit gave them to me. Who is so superior that he will take away that which the Great Spirit has given me?[1]

◆ ◆ ◆

As a result of humanitarian outcries in the latter nineteenth century, the United States shifted from the policy of outright military extermination of Indian peoples to that of forced assimilation. While there could be hundreds of volumes written about the actions of the United States government to serve its assimilative intent, I will only briefly touch upon how the United States has attempted to achieve this end through the suppression of tribal religions.

Early on in the assimilation campaign, it was apparent to U.S. political and Christian leaders that the political and religious forms of tribal life were so closely intertwined as to be inseparable, and that in order to successfully suppress tribal political activity it was imperative to suppress tribal religious practices as well. To that end, nearly every form of Indian religion was banned on the reservations by the mid-1880s, and very extreme measures were taken to discourage Indians from maintaining their tribal customs. The discouragement usually came in the form of imprisonment or the withholding [of] food, thus starvation. As observed by [Peter] Matthiessen, "on pain of imprisonment, the Lakota were forbidden the spiritual renewal of traditional ceremonies; even the ritual purification of the sweat lodge was forbidden. They were not permitted to wear Indian dress or to sew beadwork. . . ."[2] And as stated by [Vine] Deloria:

> Even Indian funeral ceremonies were declared to be illegal, and drumming and any form of dancing had to be held for the most artificial of reasons. The Lummi Indians from western Washington, for example, continued some of their tribal dances under the guise of celebrating the signing of their treaty. The Plains Indians eagerly celebrated the Fourth of July, for it meant that they could

often perform Indian dances and ceremonies by pretending to celebrate the signing of the Declaration of Independence.[3]

In 1878 the first Bureau of Indian Affairs (BIA) boarding school was founded, which marked the beginning of a systematic attack on Indian religions and cultures through the de-Indianization of the children. Many of the "children were captured at gunpoint by the U.S. Military and taken to distant Bureau of Indian Affairs boarding schools."[4] English names were assigned to replace [Indian] names and even [Indian] hairstyles were forbidden under penalty of criminal law.

> Those [Indians] who resisted this colonial rule were labeled "Hostiles" and were subjected to arbitrary criminal punishment, including imprisonment and forced labor, as determined by the [BIA] agent. Mass arrests of "Hostile" leaders were ordered and many served lengthy sentences at the U.S. prison at Alcatraz and elsewhere. . . .[5]

Thus Tullberg indicates to the reader that we are not talking about ancient history here, since Alcatraz prison was not erected until 1934.[6]

The speaking of tribal languages was a physically punishable offense in the boarding schools and continues to be so in some of the schools.[7] Christianity was forced upon the children and continues to this day to be stressed over tribal religions in the boarding schools. The predominant purpose of the schools has always been to Americanize Indians and to make them ashamed of their people and their heritage. In an 1897 letter to the Secretary of the Interior, the Commissioner of Indian Affairs, E. A. Hayt, observed that the best results of this objective are achieved "by a removal of the children from all tribal influence during the progress of education."[8] As stated by Peter Farb:

> The children usually were kept at boarding school for eight hours, during which time they were not permitted to see their parents, relatives or friends. Anything Indian—dress, language, religious practices, even outlook on life—was uncomprisingly prohibited. Ostensibly educated, articulate in the English language, wearing store-bought clothes, and with their hair cut short and their emotions toned down, the boarding school graduates were sent out either to make their way in a white world that did not want them, or to return to a reservation to which they were now foreign.[9]

[And as explained by Grobsmith:]

> Children living in boarding schools during the year were some-
> times sent to work as domestics in non-Indian homes during the
> summer to keep them from their relatives and traditions, a policy
> that became known as "legalized kidnapping."[10]

Many children would climb out the windows of the boarding schools
in an attempt to return to their families; many died of exposure during
their attempts. Punishment for recurrent runaways commonly included
being placed in dark, locked closets, or having balls and chains attached to
their ankles so as to humiliate them in front of the other children and to
discourage the children from further attempts to return to their families.
The runaways—and consequently, the deaths from exposure—became so
numerous that many of the schools barred their windows to keep the children in.[11] Powerful tranquilizing drugs such as Thorazine were also used
for disciplinary purposes.[12] Supreme Court Justice [William O.] Douglas
pretty well summed it up in 1973:

> [T]he express policy [of the schools was] stripping the Indian
> child of his cultural heritage and identity: "Such schools were run
> in a rigid military fashion, with heavy emphasis on rustic voca-
> tional education. They were designed to separate a child from his
> reservation and family, strip him of his tribal lore and mores,
> force the complete abandonment of his native language, and pre-
> pare him for never again returning to his people."[13]

In recent years, Indian people have had a little more say about how things
should be run at the boarding schools, and the conditions are improving,
albeit slowly.

In 1978, the United States Congress passed the American Indian Religious Freedom Act, stating that "the United States has traditionally
rejected the concept of a government denying individuals the right to practice their religion" and recognizing that "the religious practices of American Indians (as well as Native Alaskan and Hawaiian) are an integral part
of their culture, heritage, and tradition, such practices forming the basis of
Indian identity and value systems."[14]

Although the United States pays lip service to the rights of Native
Americans to religious freedom, those rights are drastically interfered with
in practice. For example, for many American Indians, America's prisons
have replaced the old boarding schools. Indian prisoners around the country have been fighting a long, hard battle for religious freedom in the last

two decades, and the battle will not end until the Indians have prevailed in forcing the administrators of every prison, reformatory, and jail on this land to recognize and comply with the American Indian Religious Freedom Act and corresponding laws. The battle has thus far cost the taxpayers millions, perhaps billions, of dollars in litigation; and although the litigation has resulted in generally consistent victories for the Indian prisoners, many officials persist in denying Indian prisoners their established rights, and the senseless litigation continues.[15]

Let's take the Southern Ohio Correctional Facility (SOCF) for example.[16] Before we continue, however, let's clarify the law. In 1972, the United States Supreme Court established that "reasonable opportunities must be afforded to all prisoners to exercise the religious freedom guaranteed by the First and Fourteenth Amendments without fear of penalty."[17] There is not a warden, superintendent, or administrator of any prison or jail in the United States who is not aware of the decision in the above case, and this is because American tax dollars are spent to pay government attorneys to keep such officials appraised of the laws.

The Indian prisoners in the Southern Ohio Correctional Facility are denied all reasonable opportunities to practice their spiritual beliefs, even to the extent that all Indian spiritual leaders are barred from entering the prison for any religious purposes. The Indian prisoners are prohibited from using the SOCF religious service facility for congregational worship and are systematically separated from one another so that they may never meet, even informally, for any religious activities. They are denied access to and use of any and all sacred objects or herbs for purification. Their hair, which is sacred and should not be cut, is cut by physical force if necessary, and such necessity results in one's being placed in solitary confinement for a minimum of six months, as does any other attempt to practice Indian religious beliefs—even when the prison chaplain is in absolute support of the Indian prisoners.

In the end of May 1988, *The Cincinnati Enquirer* published an article related to litigation pending in the federal district court in Cincinnati concerning these issues at SOCF. In that article, the Assistant Attorney General, Christian B. Stegeman, was quoted as stating that the Indian prisoners in SOCF were permitted to meet on a weekly basis for pipe ceremonies and that any Indian spiritual leaders wishing to do so could enter the prison to conduct ceremonies provided they are granted prior approval by Dr. David Schwarz, the Religious Administrator for the Ohio Department of Rehabilitation and Corrections. When the Indian prisoners wrote to *The Cincinnati Enquirer* informing them that David Schwarz refuses to grant approval of any Indian spiritual leaders to enter the prison, and that the Indian prisoners are in fact prohibited from meeting for any

ceremonies, they did not receive a response to their correspondence, and
The Cincinnati Enquirer made no effort to correct the misinformation it
had published, or even to investigate the veracity of the Indian prisoners'
claims. For these reasons, the readers of *The Cincinnati Enquirer* to this
day believe that the Indian prisoners at SOCF have weekly ceremonies
with spiritual leaders. The Indian prisoners have also submitted documen-
tation to the Associated Press in Columbus verifying these allegations, as
well as allegations that the Ohio Attorney General's Office has used a
fraudulent Indian chief of a nonexistent Indian tribe as an "expert" witness against Indian prisoners in previous litigation in Ohio.[18] These
attempts to gain support by and through the Ohio media have been futile.
The Indian prisoners in SOCF have no support in the state of Ohio
because they have no access to the media and the public is unaware of
what is taking place.

The Ohio officials have been claiming for several years now that any
interest the Indian prisoners at SOCF have in the freedom of religion is
miniscule in comparison to the state's interests in maintaining security and
order within the prison. For several years now, this author, a mixed blood
Indian prisoner in SOCF who is the elected representative for the Indian
prisoners at SOCF, has been asking the officials of this state for some
explanations as to how any of the requested religious practices can possibly present a threat to the security and order of the prison. An example of
his inquiries is as follows (a letter to the Director of the Department of
Rehabilitation and Corrections, copies of which were sent to the Ohio
Attorney General's Office, the governor, the Associated Press, and various
prison officials):

> For the past couple of years I have made repeated attempts to
> practice my religion, as have several other American Indians in
> the Southern Ohio Correctional Facility. The officials here, as
> well as Dr. David Schwarz, refuse to permit any Native Ameri-
> can practices in this institution, and the officials have not yet
> made one attempt to give me any reason or justification for this
> absolute deprivation of our religious freedom. I have been
> through the grievance procedure also, and no official in the state
> of Ohio has yet responded to my questions: 1) Why are the
> Native Americans in SOCF not permitted to have any spiritual
> leaders enter the prison to conduct religious ceremonies on a
> parity with the religious leaders of the other religious denomina-
> tions at SOCF? 2) Why are we not permitted a designated time
> and place to meet for prayer meetings and other religious activi-
> ties as the groups of other religious denominations are permitted

to do so? 3) Why are we not permitted to have access to any sacred objects for personal or group use as the prisoners of the dominant religions are permitted to do? 4) Why are spiritual leaders not permitted to send cassette tapes of religious teachings, as contributions to the SOCF Religious Services Department, when this is permitted for the other religious denominations at SOCF and when the prison chaplain, O. Franklin Johnson, has stated that he would be willing to inspect any such tapes to assure that they are of a religious nature, and when such tapes would become property of the SOCF Religious Services Department?

Supposing that these practices and activities are viewed by the administration as a potential threat to security within the prison, how is a threat presented? Chaplain O. Franklin Johnson has stated that he would be willing to hold any and all religious objects in his office while not in use for religious services, and that he is willing to supervise the use of all the objects. This being as it is, the practices and objects we are requesting are very similar to the objects and practices that are permitted for the dominant religious groups, and there is no security risk involved. I fail to see how a threat is presented in permitting American Indian spiritual leaders to enter the prison to perform functions on an equal basis with the religious leaders of the dominant religions, especially in light of the fact that Christian denominations are permitted to have guests enter the prison to entertain them with music when said guests are not even spiritual leaders, and said guests are permitted to bring with them objects such as electric guitars—and there is no religious object we [N]ative Americans have requested access [to] which presents a threat to security as an electric guitar would. Moreover, guests are permitted into the institution for recreation activities such as baseball, and they are permitted to bring in with them baseball bats, and certainly there is no object we have requested which poses a threat to security as a baseball bat would. . . .

There are various other religious practices we would like to undertake and which we believe we are entitled to, but I have limited this request to only those practices and objects which in no way present any security problems for the administration. I would also like to bring to your attention that these practices and objects are permitted in the majority of the maximum security prisons in the United States and Canada, and while I have read numerous cases that have arisen around the country concerning these specific practices, I have not yet seen one case in which the courts have not granted every bit of the relief sought in this request.[19]

To date, the Director of Corrections, the Religious Administrator, the governor, the Attorney General's Office, and the prison officials at SOCF have refused to respond to the questions set forth in the above letter and to various similar letters, and the Director of Corrections and the Religious Administrator have never acknowledged receipt of these communications addressed to them, and generally fail to respond to any correspondence from Indian spiritual leaders and organizations who support the Indian prisoners at SOCF. Without a doubt, there is no logical explanation for their failure to offer reasons for the absolute deprivation of any and all Indian religious practices at SOCF [other than] that these officials are racists, ethnocentric, and still hold fast to the policy of forced assimilation of American Indians.

A number of prisons around the country have established adequate spiritual/cultural programs for the Indian prisoners. At the Sioux Falls maximum security penitentiary in South Dakota, for example, the Indians had formed a group ten years ago called the Native American Council of Tribes (NACT). The NACT is permitted to have a "Voice Class," the purpose of which is "to help the younger inmates to learn to express themselves, voice their feelings, learn more about the traditions of their people, the importance of setting good examples, learning through education, and discouraging the use of alcohol and drugs."[20] They are also able to have language classes on a weekly basis which help the inmates to improve communication skills in their traditional Indian language. The NACT also holds a pow-wow at least four times a year that is held outdoors (weather permitting), and outside guests—friends, relatives, guest speakers, etcetera—are invited to attend. They have singing, drumming, traditional and fancy dancing, a traditional meal, and a craft giveaway to honored guests. The pow-wows generally last for four hours, but have been held for much longer periods on special occasions. The NACT "is also involved in efforts to provide instruction on alcoholism and drug abuse through the Red Road Approach to Recovery, an AA [Alcoholics Anonymous] type of program geared to Indian prisoners."[21] Indians with trustee status are sometimes permitted to take furloughs to attend the annual sun dances on the reservations. Many traditional items of religious significance, including eagle feathers, the sacred pipe, hobby craft items to make traditional objects such as beads, feathers, teeth, claws, etcetera, are permitted for the Indian prisoners in Sioux Falls. Herbs such as cedar, sage and sweet grass are allowed for ceremonial use, as are traditional clothing items. The NACT has a sweat lodge for purification ceremonies that is available on a daily basis. Medicine bags are allowed to be carried anywhere but to contact visits, and headbands are allowed anywhere. The Indian prisoners are allowed to make their own drums of buffalo or elk hide, constructed in the traditional way, and to use the drums at pow-wows and during recreation periods.[22]

Many other prisons have similar programs for the Indian prisoners. Such programs have proven to be a success in the rehabilitation of Indian prisoners.[23] For example, almost all Indian prisoners are in prison because of alcohol- and/or drug-related offenses.[24] There is a consensus among experts in the field of alcoholism treatment that the standard AA program is generally a failure where American Indians are concerned,[25] and many believe that the most effective treatment for Indians with alcohol and drug problems are those programs that integrate a variety of traditional Indian activities and elements into their treatment strategies.[26] "Increasingly, evaluators, treatment personnel, and potential clients deplore the Anglo cultural bias of existing alcoholism intervention programs and call for the integration of more traditional (American Indian) forms of healing practices into programs with . . . Native American clients."[27]

In the mid-1970s, when the people involved in the Seattle Indian Alcoholism Program recognized that over 90 percent of the Indians in jails and prisons in the state of Washington were there for alcohol-related offenses, they set up cultural-specific programs in the four major prisons in the state. These programs are much like the program at the Sioux Falls prison, and consist of tribal religious practices as the main intervention strategy, and counseling with medicine men and Indian spiritual leaders. Within four years after these programs were established in Washington's prisons, the proportion of Indian prisoners in the state's prisons had dropped from 5 to 3.5 percent.[28] With statistics like this, the relevance of and need for spiritual/cultural programs for the Indian prisoners can hardly be refuted. In fact, it would seem that such statistics would encourage prison officials to actively seek the establishment of such programs with the tax dollars they are currently wasting in their attempts to defend the suppression of the Indian religious practices that could be accommodated through the programs. Such action would be consistent with the asserted concerns of the high recidivism rates. As observed by [Richard] Seven in the *Seattle Times*: "For prison officials, the [purification ceremony of the sweat] lodge and other religious programs are ways to reduce the high rate at which released inmates commit crimes."[29]

Robert Lynn, religious program manager for the Department of Corrections, says inmates in Oregon prisons who were actively involved in religious programs over several years in the late [19]70s had a recidivism rate of 5 percent, compared with the national rate of close to 75 percent at the time.[30]

It should also be noted that in the prisons where these religious practices and activities are permitted, there is general agreement among the officials that such programs and activities present no more of a threat to the security and order of the prison than do the Christian programs and activities, and as the Washington [S]tate [C]orrectional [P]rogram administrator has stated, such programs and activities are "good for the institutions and [are] good for the offenders."[31] And as stated by William Hoffstetter:

> It has been my experience based on twenty years of juvenile and adult correctional work, both as a clinical psychologist and program administrator . . . the more an inmate is involved in his own rehabilitation process the more effective will be the outcome.[32]

We Indians think that's pretty sound logic, especially since the prison officials around the country who deny us our religious freedom do so because they lack any knowledge about our ways of life. How can a prison official know what rehabilitation process will be effective for any inmate when the value systems and beliefs held within the cultural background of the inmate are contrary to those of the culture to which the prison official belongs? It is impossible unless the official is willing to sit down with the inmate in an attempt to bridge that cultural gap. Repeated displays of insensitivity and indifference to the laws and to the needs of the Indian prisoners by prison and government officials such as those in Ohio serve only to make the prisoners more bitter toward the society those officials represent. I know for a fact that this is detrimental to everyone concerned—and everyone unconcerned.

In closing, I'd like to reiterate a message from the California Supreme Court:

> [T]he right to free religious expression embodies a precious heritage of our history. In a mass society, which presses at every point toward conformity, the protection of a self-expression, however unique, of the individual and the group becomes even more important. The various currents of the sub-cultures that flow into the mainstream of our national life give it depth and beauty. We preserve a greater value than an ancient tradition when we protect the rights of the Indians who honestly practice an old religion. . . .[33]

We feel that to do less than to help us preserve our traditional ways is no less than forced assimilation. The United Nations General Assembly has a word for that. It is called genocide.[34]

Notes

Originally published in *Humanity and Society,* Vol. 13, No. 4 (1989): 403–20.

1. Timothy Reed, Affidavit attached as Exhibit-A to Plaintiffs Motion for a Temporary Restraining Order and/or Preliminary Injunction, filed January 10, 1989. *Reed v. Celeste et al.,* Case No. C-1–88–1048. U.S. District Court for the Southern District of Ohio, Western Division (January 10, 1989), 6–8, 16–18.

2. Peter Matthiessen, *In the Spirit of Crazy Horse* (New York: Viking, 1983), 21.

3. Vine Deloria, Jr., *God is Red* (New York: Dell, 1973), 252.

4. S. M. Tullberg, et al., "Violations of the Human Rights of the Hopi People by the United States of America," in *Rethinking Indian Law,* ed. National Lawyers Guild Committee on Native American Struggles (New Haven: Advocate, 1982), 163.

5. Ibid.

6. *Editor's note:* Alcatraz Island, 1.5 miles off the coast in San Francisco Bay, California, began its life as a prison in 1868 when it was designated as a residence for military offenders. In 1934 Alcatraz was reopened as a federal prison for those prisoners declared the most dangerous. Although legendary mobsters Al Capone and George "Machine Gun" Kelly were held on the island, most of its prisoners were unknown convicts. The island was the first large-scale, super-maximum security prison in the country, and later served as a model for the federal prison at Marion, Illinois. Alcatraz Prison was closed in 1963. In three separate occasions between 1964 and 1969 the island was occupied by groups of Native American Indians, who claimed rights to the island based on historical (unhonored) treaties between American Indian tribes and the U.S. government. For more information on Indian occupations of Alcatraz, see *American Indian Activism: Alcatraz to the Longest Walk,* eds. Troy Johnson, Joane Nagel, and Duane Champagne (Urbana: University of Illinois Press, 1997).

7. Ann H. Beuf, *Red Children in White America* (Philadelphia: University of Pennsylvania Press, 1977), 32.

8. William E. Coffer, *Sleeping Giants* (Washington, D.C.: University Press of America, 1979), 5.

9. Ibid., 8.

10. Elizabeth S. Grobsmith, *Lakota of the Rosebud: A Contemporary Ethnography* (New York: Holt, Rinehart & Winston, 1981), 15.

11. Coffer, 8.

12. Robert Burnette and John P. Koster, *The Road to Wounded Knee* (New York: Bantam Books, 1974), 53.

13. R. Rice, "Native Americans and the Free Exercise Clause," *The Hastings Law Journal* (July 28, 1977): 1509–536.

14. Public Law 95 341, 25 U.S.C., Sec 1996.

15. As one example, in the state of Nebraska, "because of the wealth of litigation (initiated by) . . . Native American inmates, Judge Warren Urbom assigned one law firm to serve as a clearinghouse for complaints stemming from alleged violation(s)" of religious freedom rights (Grobsmith, in press, 9). Grobsmith's articles cited here will appear as chapters in her next book, *Indians in Prison: A Study of Incarceration among Native Americans*. [Elizabeth S. Grobsmith, *Indians in Prison: Incarcerated Native Americans in Nebraska* (Lincoln: University of Nebraska Press, 1994).]

16. While the Southern Ohio Correctional Facility makes for some dandy examples of the persecution of American Indian prisoners by government officials, it should not be construed as an exception to the norm. Indian prisoners are treated similarly in a great many of the prisons in the United States and Canada.

17. *Cruz v. Beto*, v. 405, US. 319 (1972).

18. The fraudulent Indian chief's name is Hugh Gibbs, alleged "Principal Chief of the Etowah Cherokee Nation." The actual Principal Chiefs of the Cherokee Nation have indicated that they do not know who Hugh Gibbs is, and have never heard the term "Etowah" except with reference to an animal mound in Georgia. Moreover, Gibbs has testified (or submitted affidavits) that being the Principal Chief of the Etowah Cherokee Nation, he has knowledge of all the laws and customs and traditions of "the various" Indian tribes and nations, which is absurd in itself, as there are as many Indian tribes and nations, each being distinct from the others, as there are member-nations of the U.N.—with several hundred extras! He had perjured in his testimony where he pretended to have the authority to speak on behalf of the Lakota Nation [and] concerning the Lakota religion, the authorization of which every Indian knows must come from the Traditional Circle of Elders, which Hugh Gibbs has never sought nor received. Gibbs has also appeared on Ohio's public broadcasting/educational station (Channel 34, Columbus, Ohio) under the guise of representing the view of Indian people in general, and has condoned the desecration of sacred burial grounds in such interviews—something *no* Indian condones.

19. Reed, Letter to George Wilson, Director of the Ohio Department of Rehabilitation and Corrections (October 27, 1988).

20. W. Coppola, et al., eds., *Thunderbird Voices Speaking* (Highbridge, NY: Thunderbird Free Press, 1988), 27.

21. Ibid., 25.

22. Ibid., 29.

23. This evaluation has been relayed to the author through correspondence with numerous prison officials and counselors, researchers, spiritual leaders, Indian prisoners, and exprisoners who have had contact with spiritual/cultural programs in prisons in at least twenty states.

24. Elizabeth S. Grobsmith, "The Relationship between Substance Abuse and Crime Among Native American Inmates in the Nebraska Department of Corrections," *Human Organization*, Vol. 48, No. 4 (1989): 285–98.

25. Dwight B. Heath, Jack O. Waddell, and Martin D. Topper, *Cultural Factors in Alcohol Research and Treatment of Drinking Problems* (New Brunswick, NJ: Journal of Studies on Alcohol, Center of Alcohol Studies, Rutgers University in cooperation with the Smithsonian Institution, 1981), 1.

26. See, for example, the results of the studies conducted by the Alcohol & Drug Study Group of the American Anthropological Association, which were observed by Weibel-Orlando (1985): 219–23. Native American involvement and staffing are essential to the success of substance-abuse treatment programs. See Provincial Native Action Committee, "Native Alcoholism Programs," unpublished report of the Provincial Native Action Committee (Edmonton, Alberta, Canada: 1974); E. J. Turner, unpublished testimony prepared for hearings by the State House Institutions Subcommittee on Alcoholism and Drug Abuse, 1977. For discussions on the success in the implementation of traditional Native American elements into the treatment modalities, see J. Albaugh and P. Anderson, "Peyote in the Treatment of Alcoholism among American Indians," *American Journal of Psychiatry*, Vol. 131, No. 11 (1974): 1247–50; L. Bergman, "Navajo Peyote Use: Its Apparent Safety," *American Journal of Psychiatry*, Vol. 126, No. 7 (1971): 695–99; J. Howard, "The Plains Gourd Dance as a Revitalization Movement," *American Ethnologist*, Vol. 3 (1976): 243–59; G. Jilek, "Native Renaissance: The Survival and Revival of Indigenous Therapeutic Ceremonials Among North American Indians," *Transcultural Psychiatric Research Review*, Vol. 15 (1978): 117–47; and R. D. Walker, "Treatment Strategies in an Urban Indian Alcoholism Program," in *Cultural Factors in Alcohol Research and Treatment of Drinking Problems*, eds. Dwight B. Heath, Jack O. Waddell, and Martin D. Topper (New Brunswick, NJ: Rutgers Center of Alcohol Studies, 1981).

27. Joan Weibel-Orlando, "Culture-Specific Treatment Modalities: Assessing Client-to-Treatment Fit in Indian Alcoholism Programs," in *Treatment and Prevention of Alcohol Problems: A Resource Manual* (Los Angeles: Academic Press, 1987), 264.

28. R. D. Walker, "Treatment Strategies in an Urban Indian Alcoholism Program," *Cultural Factors in Alcohol Research and Treatment of Drinking Problems*, eds. Dwight B. Heath, Jack O. Waddell, and Martin D. Topper (New Brunswick, NJ: Journal of Studies on Alcohol, Center of Alcohol Studies, Rutgers University in cooperation with the Smithsonian Institution, 1981).

29. Richard Seven, "Ritual of Rebirth; Sweat Lodge Reaffirms Indian Inmates' Heritage," *The Seattle Times/Seattle Post Intelligencer*, January 24, 1988.

30. Ibid.

31. "Native American Prisoners Seek Religious Rights Legislation," *Shaman's Drum* (mid-Fall 1988): 14.

32. Hoffstetter, *Criminal Rehabilitation . . . Within and Without the Walls*, eds. Edward M. Scott and Kathryn L. Scott (Springfield, IL: Thomas, 1973), 53.

33. *People v. Woody*, 40 Cal. Rprt. 69 (1969).

34. *Editor's note:* Little Rock Reed, Lenny Foster, and Art Solomon co-authored a book, that shares the title of this piece, to help promote collective efforts to convince Congress to pass legislation that safeguards the rights of Native American prisoners to freedom of religion and to culturally sensitive substance

abuse treatment. See Little Rock Reed, Lenny Foster, and Art Solomon, *The American Indian in the White Man's Prison: A Story of Genocide* (Taos, NM: UnCompromising Books, 1993).

Introduced to the 103rd Congress in May 1993, the Native American Free Exercise of Religion Act, which passed in 1994 as the American Indian Religious Freedom Act Amendments, grants, in law, Native American prisoners the same status, rights, and privileges as religious leaders of Judeo-Christian religions, access to religious facilities, and permission to utilize certain materials in religious ceremonies. See Dakota-Lakota-Nakota Human Rights Coalition, "Native American Free Exercise of Religion Act of 1993," www.dricoalition.org/related_issues/native_american_free_exercise_of_religion_act1993.htm (September 24, 2004).

14

Imari Abubakari Obadele I

Imari Abubakari Obadele I (Richard B. Henry) and his brother, attorney Gaidi Obadele (Milton Henry), convened a gathering of black nationalists in Detroit, Michigan to cofound the Republic of New Africa (RNA) in 1968. Members of the RNA, which was founded on principles of black self-determination, cooperative economics, and community self-sufficiency, referred to themselves as "New Afrikans," and named a provisional RNA government with I. A. Obadele as president. RNA demands included that the U.S. government cede the states of Louisiana, Mississippi, Alabama, Georgia, and South Carolina for an independent, all-black nation and pay $400 billion in reparations for slavery to African Americans. Currently based in Washington, D.C., the RNA continues to advocate the establishment of an African American nation in the southern United States.

Targeted by the Federal Bureau of Investigation (FBI), Obadele was first arrested, along with ten other RNA leaders, in Mississippi in August 1971, following a raid during which an FBI agent was killed. All of the RNA members present were arrested and charged with sedition and murder and the "RNA Eleven," as they came to be known, were convicted and sentenced to terms between three and twelve years. Although Obadele was not present at the raid, he was charged with sedition and murder and imprisoned from 1974 to 1976. While serving additional time in 1977, he filed a civil suit that revealed the FBI's COINTELPRO actions against the RNA.

Following his release from prison, Obadele received his PhD in political science from Temple University in 1985. He has taught at several universities and colleges and has published a number of articles and books, including *Revolution and Nation-Building, Free the Land!, America the Nation State, Foundations of the Black Nation, Reparations Yes!,* and *Eight Women Leaders of the Reparations Movement, U.S.A.* Obadele continues to speak on behalf of reparations and for black self-determination.

References

Meyers, Aaron. "The Republic of New Africa." *Africana: The Encyclopedia of the African and African American Experience,* edited by Kwame

Anthony Appiah and Henry Louis Gates Jr. New York: Basic Civitas Books, 1999, boxed edition, 1612.

Obadele, Imari Abubakari. *War in America: The Malcolm X Doctrine.* Detroit: Malcolm X Society, 1968.

———. *Revolution and Nation-Building: Strategy for Building the Black Nation in America.* Detroit: House of Songhay, 1970.

———. *Foundations of the Black Nation.* Detroit: House of Songhay, 1975.

———. *Free the Land! The True Story of the Trials of the RNA-11 in Mississippi and the Continuing Struggle to Establish an Independent Black Nation in Free States of the Deep South.* San Francisco: House of Songhay, 1984.

———. *Chokwe Lumumba and Nkechi Taifa. Reparations Yes! The Legal and Political Reasons Why New Afrikans, Black People in the United States, Should be Paid Now for the Enslavement of Our Ancestors and for War Against Us After Slavery.* Baton Rouge, LA: House of Songhay, Commission and the Malcolm Generation, Inc., 1995.

"Obadele, Imari Abubakari." *The African American Encyclopedia,* second edition, edited by Michael W. Williams and Kibibi Voloria Mack. New York: Marshall Cavendish, 2001, 1857.

A People's Revolt for Power and an Up-Turn in the Black Condition: An Appeal and a Challenge
1977

I

Something must be done about the black condition. About our poverty. About crime. About bad housing. And poor schools. And marginal health. About hunger. About the over-all decline of our race.

I am prepared to do something. With your help. I am prepared to lead a People's Revolt Against Poverty and For Power and a Good Life. And I am prepared to lead this Revolt to victory. With *your* help.

The groundwork is laid. For almost ten years We of the Provisional Government, Republic of New Afrika, have sacrificed to lay this groundwork, carrying on the labors of our fathers. Now, the future can be ours. All We need do is stand up on our feet—together—and *seize* it.

II

To begin all this We must take a cold, hard look at the political realities that are holding us back—the political ideas and concepts out of which the chains of our poverty and powerlessness are made.

Black people in the United States live politically in two worlds. On the one hand, We live and act as if We are United States citizens. This is more-or-less a matter of survival. Most lawyers and political scientists today would agree that blacks in America are not technically United States citizens, either under U.S. or international law. The simple reason is that our forefathers and ourselves, as the descendants of kidnapped Afrikan slaves,

153

had and have a right to choose our citizenship—but We have never been allowed to exercise that right.

Still, the United States government has *insisted,* officially, that We are United States citizens, and We have been made to serve in the army and pay taxes. In self-defense We have tried to use our votes to get something back for our tax money, to try to get a fair chance for ourselves and our children. We have elected sixteen black men and women to Congress. We have elected mayors in some cities and members of city councils and school boards. In 1976 our votes decided a U.S. presidential election, giving victory to Jimmy Carter in hope that he would do better by us than Gerald Ford.

All this has been very logical. It reflects one political world in which We live.

On the other hand, We also live in another political world. This is our Black World, the world in which We live as citizens of our own nation, our Black Nation, our *New Afrikan* nation. In this world We worry about how We are making out as a people, and We try to do something about it, *as a people.*

In a way the two worlds come together for us: for instance, although the sixteen black men and women in Congress are sworn in as *United States'* Congresspersons, and although they are elected to represent only about one-third of the black population, We all expect them to look out for *all* black people and to look out for black people *first.* And that is what they do.

But there are some things that We must do for ourselves as a people, as a nation—outside of the United States' political system. Only the *organized* government of the Black *Nation* can rightfully represent the interests of blacks in America at the United Nations—and We desperately need a voice in the United Nations. (Mr. Andrew Young[1] is not at the United Nations to represent the Black Nation. He represents the United States, the *white* nation.) Only the organized *government* of the black nation—in accordance with the history of international law—can rightfully demand and receive the *reparations* (the billions of dollars now owed us for the forty acres and a mule We never got) that the United States still owes us for slavery.

To carry out such work, the government of the Black Nation—even though our nation is not *independent* or free yet—must be well organized and strong. *It must be supported by the people.* (Remember: Indian governments exist in this land and have received *reparations* from the United States for their people, even though Indian nations and governments—like the Black Nation and government—are not independent.)

III

One of the worst problems facing us today as a people is unemployment and low income. Tied in with these is bad housing. Then there is crime. Crime, including the drug traffic, is doing terrible things to morality in our communities; it is breeding distrust, fear, and hatred, and it is robbing us, therefore, of good community life and safe, decent places in which to bring up and educate our children and in which to live happy, productive lives. Crime is causing us to lose the good minds of many, many of our young people down a useless drain, to a life of crime, to prison, to both, or to death.

All this is part of a war of genocide that the United States is waging—often as if she is unconscious of waging it—against our people. (The high unemployment and the drug traffic could not exist without the active help of U.S. officials.) This war of genocide is a carryover, a continuation, of the slave trade and slavery. And it is destroying our people—which is what "genocide" means.

Genocide also includes forcibly transferring children of one group to another group—which is what is happening to us when We are brought up in American schools and are taught that We are United States citizens rather than being taught that We have a right to choose our citizenship. It is what is happening to us when the United States government uses its power to try to destroy the organized Black Nation, the *New Afrikan* nation, and refuses to teach the fact that the nation exists, though subjugated, and that We have a right to be proud of our citizenship in our own New Afrikan nation just as the Navajo and other Indians have a right to be proud of their citizenship in their nations.

(Today the United States no longer tries to destroy Indian nations, like the Navajo. In fact, since 1968, the Civil Rights Act of that year has protected Indian governments, and the Indian Self-Determination Act of 1975 provides U.S. tax money to these governments for their strengthening and support.[2] The opposite has happened to us. The United States jailed Marcus Garvey, a leader of the Black Nation in the 1920s, and persecuted Elijah Muhammad and Malcolm X, leaders of the former Nation of Islam; now the FBI admits running an illegal program to "harass and disrupt" the present government of the Black Nation, the Provisional Government, Republic of New Afrika. I am President of the organized Black Nation, the Republic of New Afrika. But i am in jail, as are others, as a direct result of these illegal FBI efforts and their attempt to assassinate me and other RNA workers in Mississippi in 1971. All of this, to say the least, is discriminatory and very illegal on the part of the United States government. Today it is the black government—and not Eskimo or Indian governments (as distinguished from the Indian *sovereignty* movement and AIM [the American Indian Movement][3])—which the United States is trying to destroy.)

On the problem of unemployment and low income, Mr. Carter, the United States president, has proposed a plan—his welfare reform plan—as a partial answer. Some parts of the plan—like raising income for mothers of small children—are good. Some parts of the plan—like forcing people to work for low wages on almost useless jobs—are not good. To me one of the things most wrong with the plan is that it will have to be voted on each year, which means it could be stopped or cut back at any time. Also, in the end, black people will be left with nothing with which to make more jobs or help ourselves.

There is a way to avoid this. Since i became president of the Provisional Government of our black nation, *the Republic of New Afrika,* in 1970, i and those who have worked with me have insisted that the real—and permanent—way for us to end poverty is to have land and industry owned by the people. We insist that We as a people, as a *nation,* must have land for an independent nation (all of us won't have to live there, just We who want to) and that We must have the "forty acres and a mule" We are owed by the United States, which are now worth many billions of dollars. *With these billions—indeed, with just* some *of these billions—We would build factories and giant farms and New Communities, all owned by our people together, through our Land Development Cooperatives.*

I think it is wrong for the Carter plan—or any plan—to provide money to our needy people in a way in which all We can do is spend it with other people and have nothing left. That way We will never be able to help ourselves; what We need is factories and giant farms and good housing in beautiful New Communities owned by the people, *our* people. I say that part of the Carter "welfare reform" money must be spent for this. After all, the money being spent is *black* tax money—yours and mine—too.

IV

That is what i stand for. It is what i am fighting for—decent New Communities and fine housing, industry and giant farms owned by the people, top education, a bright future, and a good life for all, free of crime and the fear of crime. I am fighting for black people who live in the black counties and parishes of Louisiana, Arkansas, and Mississippi—the *Kush* District—to have political power over this magnificent, neglected land. I am fighting for the right of those who live in the ghettoes of the big cities to come to

Kush, *if they wish to,* where We shall build the New Communities and giant farms and industry, and live with us; all We ask is that those who come be serious and honest and want to help build a good life for all, a splendid place to raise one's children and live.

Already the Republic of New Afrika's Provisional Government—the government of our still-subjugated nation—has begun to organize *Land Development Cooperatives* to begin building the New Communities and industry using black people's own money, money from our own pockets. We need you to join this effort. We need you to join our cooperatives, *your* cooperatives.

But I also need you to help me make Mr. Carter and Mr. Thomas O'Neill, who is Speaker of the [House of Representatives] U.S. Congress, and other United States leaders understand that black people, *New Afrikans,* want our "forty acres and a mule" *now* and that no welfare reform program is complete unless it provides money to the Land Development Cooperatives for farms and industry and New Communities, so that We as a people will have something left in our hands in the end—or if anything goes wrong.

One way to make Mr. Carter and others understand this is to join the cooperatives. A strong membership in the Land Development Cooperatives will deliver that message very clearly. But another way is to vote in *the National Black Elections* in the fall of 1978. These elections will speak loudly not only to Mr. Carter but to the United Nations and the world— for We cannot win our battle without the help of the United Nations. *The National Black Elections* in the fall of 1978 are absolutely vital to our success in building New Communities and a better life.

The first National Black Elections were held in September 1975. Only about five thousand persons were able to participate; black people voted in cities from coast to coast, north and south, but most of the voting took place in Detroit, Washington, D.C., and Mississippi. It was the first time that black people had ever held *national* elections on our own, including at our own expense and pretty much without the help of the white-controlled newspapers, television, and magazines. It was very hard, but those who ran the elections learned a lot. This time, when We vote in the fall of 1978, We hope that it will be possible for black people in many more places to vote and vote in large numbers—because all black people born here and descended from slaves are *New Afrikans* and all, above a certain age, are entitled to vote for the officials of the black nation.

Almost anyone can run for office. This includes the national congress, called *the People's Center Council* (its members are called "Representatives"), and for the offices of President, Vice President (there are four), Justice of the black Supreme Court, and District Judge. Of course, those who run *for* office must be dedicated to the power and *independence* of the Black Nation as their highest, national, political commitment and must take an oath to this effect.

All this is part of what i meant in the beginning when i wrote that black people live in two worlds politically. You must vote in the United States elections, and We must support our black mayors and Congresspersons and other officials in the U.S. system. This is a matter of self-defense. But We must vote for and support the officials of our Black Nation, the Republic of New Afrika, also. Both things are necessary at the present time.

Remember, however, that it is the Provisional Government of the black nation, as i lead it—and as i would lead it if re-elected in 1978—which is conducting the fight for forty acres and a mule *now,* billions of dollars, to build fine New Communities, good housing, industry and giant farms, all owned by the people together. It is the RNA Provisional Government that is leading the struggle for independent land under black political power—in Kush, as the beginning. The basis of all economic power is *land* under sovereign political power.

Finally, i do wish to run again for the presidency of our nation. I think there is much to be done and, at this juncture, i think that i am best prepared to lead this work and get it accomplished. However, i must ask the support of my party and people like yourself, who believe in the work which i and others are attempting to do. Only through your help will the message which i am presenting here—a general statement of the *People's Revolt* We must have and how I see it and would lead it—get out door-to-door, meeting-to-meeting, to black people, *New Afrikans,* all over this land. So, I do request your support—your dollars, your time, and your work—to make a successful election and a successful candidacy for me.

Of course, i am in jail as i write this. i spent nearly two years in Mississippi jail cells from August 18, 1971 into 1973; then, for three years, from 1974 through 1976, i led the struggle in Mississippi while our convictions were being appealed and, when the U .S. Supreme Court refused to hear our case, i returned to jail in December 1976. I know that the press has hidden the important story of the black independence struggle in Mississippi, but it is a reality nevertheless. i am in jail because of my work in Mississippi, in Kush. i am in jail because i am leading a struggle against powerful people in the United States who do not want black people to control *anything* and certainly not political power over independent land. I am in jail because the Jackson, Mississippi police and the state's Attorney General, aided by J. Edgar Hoover and the FBI, tried to destroy the RNA cadre in Kush and one of their policemen was killed and a policeman and an FBI agent were wounded.

But We are going to beat them. I and the rest of the RNA-11 shall be free again—though the legal fight will take months more—and i, for one, shall return to Mississippi, to Kush.

V

So, if you will give me your support by joining the Land Development Cooperatives now and by passing the word among the black public during the next several months; if you will help to build the vote for the National Black Elections in the fall of 1978, you will be telling Mr. Carter and Mr. O'Neill, the United Nations and the world, that you—that *We* as a people—have come fully alive politically and that you, that *We as a people* want our forty acres and a mule *now*; that, moreover, welfare reform is not complete without New Communities, good housing, giant farms and industry owned by the people, *our* people, through our cooperatives. You will be telling them all, to the gratitude and cheers of the rest of the oppressed but awakening world, that We too are *seriously* in revolt against poverty, a revolt for a good life for everyone.

If you will say this by supporting me, supporting this program, this organized *People's Revolt*, We, together, will win this Revolt.

Help make it happen. Get involved.

Then if you feel that ordinary help is not enough, that you believe in the struggle for independence deeply enough to want to be a part of those who hold to and build upon the three elements of the Malcolm X Doctrine—*Land, Self-Defense,* and *Internationalization*—then you are urged to attend the convention of our Party, when it is announced in the coming months, and apply for membership.

But work with us, help us, whether in or out of the Party. And We shall win this Revolt. Without a doubt, We, together, shall FREE THE LAND!!

Notes

Originally published in 1977 as a pamphlet by The President Imari Obadele Revolt Against Poverty Campaign Headquarters (Detroit).

1. *Editor's note:* African American civil rights activist Andrew Young was executive vice president of the Southern Christian Leadership Conference from 1964 to 1970. He was elected to the U.S. House of Representatives from the state of Georgia in 1972. In 1977, President Jimmy Carter appointed him U.S. ambassador to the United Nations, making him the first African American ambassador to that

organization. He resigned from his post in 1979, following criticism of his contacts with the Palestinian Liberation Organization (PLO). In 1982, Young was elected mayor of Atlanta.

2. *Editor's note:* For accounts of repression faced by Native Americans, see Little Rock Reed, "The American Indian in the White Man's Prison: A Story of Genocide," in this volume; Ward Churchill and Jim Vander Wall, *The COINTEL-PRO Papers: Documents from the FBI's Secret Wars Against Dissent in the United States* (Boston: South End Press, 2002); Ward Churchill, *Struggle for the Land: Native North American Resistance to Genocide, Ecocide, and Colonization* (San Francisco: City Lights, 2002).

3. *Editor's note:* The American Indian Movement (AIM), founded in 1968, was a radical Native American Indian organization that struggled for the rights of urban American Indians, protection of the legal rights of all American Indians, economic independence of Native communities, revitalization of traditional cultures, and autonomy over tribal areas and the restoration of lands illegally seized by the U.S. government in treaties with Native American peoples. AIM was involved in the 1969–1971 occupation of Alcatraz Island; the 1972 march on Washington, D.C., to protest violation of treaties, in which AIM members occupied the office of the Bureau of Indian Affairs; and the 1973 occupation of a site at Wounded Knee. Along with the Black Panthers, AIM was a primary target of the FBI's COINTEL-PRO. See Ward Churchill and Jim Vander Wall, *Agents of Repression: The FBI's Secret War Against the Black Panther Party and the American Indian Movement* (Boston: South End Press, 1988); Ward Churchill and Jim Vander Wall, *The COINTELPRO Papers: Documents from the FBI's Secret Wars Against Dissent in the United States* (Boston: South End Press, 2002). For an update on FBI/AIM involvement in the murder of Anna Mae Aquash, see Ward Churchill, "Agents of Repression: Withstanding the Test of Time," *Social Justice,* Vol. 30, No. 2 (2003): 44–50.

To My Baby's Children 2001

Prince Imari A. Obadele (Shemuel ben-Yahweh)

Beloved children of my brother's children. I am your Uncle of many names: thief, armed robber, murderer, pimp, pusher, drug addict, revolutionary, political prisoner, man of God. I hope you are well and that you take the time to read this demonstration of Love.

If I preach to you, forgive me. I mean you no disrespect, but I am a preacher. If I come off like a boring teacher, forgive that too, for I am also a teacher. Above all, though, I'm just trying to reach you . . . before these folk (whom I call the Devil) get you. Because once they get you, they are going to hurt you—like never before! And, if you live through it at all you'll be so fucked-up that only the mercy of God will keep you halfway stable. You'll only stare into space a couple of times a day as opposed to being out in space all the time.

I am sending you this drumbeat because The Most High sent an angel blowing a shofar in my ear, calling me to arms, because it seems that a couple of you may be headed for trouble. Don't trip. I'm not going to tell you to "be good" because that's the "right thing to do." I know you don't want to hear that shit. But, there truly is such a thing as "right" and "wrong," and "good" and "bad," and "divine" and "evil." Nor am I going to tell you, like my father[1] told me, that you don't want to be forty years old trying to start a life. I know you don't want to hear that either. But, I will tell you this:

In prison, the belly of the Beast, I see the little boys, fourteen and fifteen years old, in prison with me! And, they are going to grow up here. Some are going to grow up into stark-raving lunatics. Some are going to grow up into being someone's "bitch," turning tricks for soup, or just to

---

Prince I. A. Obadele's biographical sketch appears on page 151.

stay alive. Some will grow into predators taking what they want and prey-
ing on the "bitches" and "hoes" and the otherwise "weak" and vulnerable
until they get their heart right, or someone kills their ass.

Some will die in here and some will make it out relatively intact—
physically, anyway. Aw, man, it ain't no joke and it ain't no video, or Sega
game. You can't turn this shit on and off and if you die in this movie, you
won't play in another. And, fuck what anyone else tells you, this is not a
school you want to graduate from. You never graduate, it never leaves
you, you're permanently scarred. And, those scars are going to be your
only diploma and your only award for your bit part in this drama.

Damn, I said I wasn't going to tell you what you didn't want to do,
didn't I? Sorry about that. But, on the other hand, you can take it any way
you want; either I'm wrong, or, like my father, it's just that I love you.
And, if you can't dig that, if you're lucky enough to see me in the next
couple of years, you can test your boxing game and we can get Our bang
on. And, I'll kick your ass and make you like it. You'll like it, appreciate
and love it because I won't be trying to destroy you like these folks will.
I'll just be laying one of those good Detroit Old School ass-whippings on
you. Catching you before the Devil does. The Devil doesn't love you; your
parents and I do.

It will take me another drumbeat to explain to you how a society can
be so rotten as to imprison its babies with its dregs, let alone imprisoning
them at all. But understand this: This country was conceived in the egg of
genocide with the sperm of slavery and it spawned a vicious monster. Dig
what I'm saying? Put another way, look at this country in terms of plants:
Poison ivy was planted. Poison ivy is what grew. It is impossible to plant
poison ivy and cause it to grow into a rose bush. Didn't happen.

It is that poisonous monster who is out to get you. It is constantly
passing new laws to capture you and building new dungeons to keep you.
You think I'm bullshitting? Dig this: "After peaking in 1994, juvenile violent crime arrests, which had increased substantially since the 1980s,
declined significantly. The juvenile arrest rate for murder *decreased* sixty-
eight percent—its lowest level since the 1960s."[3] "Crime," period, among
juveniles has decreased despite an 8 percent increase in the juvenile population during the period from 1994 to 2000! Despite this decrease in crime
among a juvenile population that has grown (dispelling the myth of the
inherently "bad" black juvenile), the Devil has consistently passed more
laws criminalizing your activities, increasing the punishment for the same,
stripping you of your right to defend yourself at trial and appeal, and
building more prisons to make sure they have room to keep you. Naw, this
ain't no joke; ain't no game. The Devil is out to get you. Believe dat.
Respect dat.

The Devil is out to kill you. That's what these prisons are designed to do: kill you—either through the outright cessation of heartbeat, or the destruction of your will, self-respect, self-love, and the ability to even think for yourself. And, those are all the things that define you as alive.

If you live through the years of resisting the attempts to break you, you'll be little more than a soulless golem. You'll just be alive—a soulless, will-less muthafucka that your master will push, twist, and shape into any direction, function, and thing he/she wants. Or, you'll become a beast—hopefully an alligator, hippo, or lion. But, just as likely, a hyena or a rat. If you somehow manage to transform into the 'gator, hippo, or lion it will most likely be because you were imprisoned because of your political beliefs, or you had a political awakening. Either of which are the same as true religion or a religious awakening. Anyway, it is a life experience and condition that your parents and I would rather you not experience.

Now, just because I'm "old school" and a minister it does not mean that I am stupid, cowardly, lame, or square. Nor am I some jack-leg, stuffed-shirt preacher. I've played from New York to L.A. and Michigan to Mississippi. And, I'm not talking about being a pussy-chaser, or "player" as y'all call it when I say "played." So, I know what you're going through. I know that if you have all of a sudden turned mean and vicious it's a good bet that someone has tampered with you sexually, or someone has pulled some other power play on you that has awakened you to the viciousness of humanity and your relative powerlessness. Or, it could just be that you're at that stage where you're interested in the opposite sex and the "finer" material things in life and you know you have to place yourself into a cold-blooded psychotic state of mind because you know that's what it takes to survive this corrupted life. Ain't that right? I mean, who are We kidding? You and I know that Master P and Jay-Z got their money the same way the Kennedys and the Rockefellers got theirs.[4] You got the message.

You also received the message that you are only worth how much money you've got and being black you've got to have ten times more than the white boy to get half the respect the poorest "white trash" gets just because they're white. So, you're probably going on that paper-chase. Being like most of Us you'll be on a path of destruction; of lying, stealing, robbing, and killing—that's the amerikkkan way. But, it's just like the NFL [National Football League] or the NBA [National Basketball Association]: Millions are slinging that ball, but few make it to the big leagues and fewer get rich. Remember, there are almost three hundred million people in Mystery Babylon and all of Us are watching the same program; the same illusions and realities that some white person wants you to see. Our reality is, beloved, that most of Us end up broke, busted, disgusted, and can't be trusted; on dope-down, or locked down; spaced-out in the head, or in a pauper's grave dead. Them's the facts, jack.

The deck is stacked against you, black child. The current regime is white supremacy. By definition there has got to be black inferiority. Dig it? In this world you are considered inferior by birth, so your struggle is, partly, proving that you are not. It is a daunting task. That is why so many beautiful black women and some black males, too, spend so much time and money frying their hair to make it straight like their white master, dying it pink and blue and green like a clown to be accepted by their white master.

In other words, We've been trained to hate and fear Ourselves and everyone else has been taught to hate and fear Us too. Unless We're entertaining them, or serving as their hitman, like Colin Powell; their maid, like Condoleezza Rice; or their "yes-man," like Clarence Thomas.[5] That's why nonblack people panic in your presence: follow you around their stores watching you while the nonblack steals them blind. It is also why you are ten times more likely than a white person, six times more likely than an [Asian American], and twice as likely as a Mexican/Chicano(a) to be killed by the police, stopped by the police, and sent to prison; to not have a job or health insurance; to not complete high school; to be the last hired, first fired; to be murdered; to live in poverty; to have your children die at birth; to suffer from drug addiction, including alcohol, diabetes, prostate cancer, lung cancer, heart disease, and stroke. In other words, in all areas of people activity this childhood ditty is manifested: "If you're white, you're alright, if you're yellow, you're mellow, if you're brown, stick around, if you're black, get back."

What I'm trying to tell you is this: I understand the forces that can drive you. The Lord knows I've been riding them. I'll also understand whatever it is that you might get involved in; you can't miss me. I may not dig it, but I'll certainly understand and won't get on your case about it. That doesn't mean that I won't try to get you to see another perspective, though. It means I will understand, keep your secrets, and love you. Because I know that the revolutionary nationalist, as it concerns you as young black people, has dropped the ball. The revolutionary nationalist has been so destabilized that it is difficult to distinguish between destabilization and defeat. So, I know you have no idea of your true history in this country, or your history, period. You probably think "american" history is your story. That, in and of itself, will cause you to stumble because "my people suffer for lack of knowledge."

Unfortunately, I cannot help you from here. I can only tell you what has happened to me, and millions like me, and give you some advice:

Attach yourself to the kingdom of Yahweh, or the New Afrikan Independence Movement, or the National Black United Front, the New Black Panther Party, the All-Afrikan Peoples Revolutionary Party, or even the Workers World Party. Or, the Maoist Internationalist Movement—something revolutionary where you can get some help and support and be of some help and support. If you're going to put your life on the line at least let it be for something that measures you as worthwhile just because you're you. And not because of how much your footwear costs.

Much love,
Uncle Shem, January 2001

Notes

1. The author, Prince I. A. Obadele, is the son of Republic of New Afrika founder, Imari Abubakari Obadele I.

2. *Final Call Newspaper*, February 26, 2000, 3.

3. *Editor's note:* Jay-Z (Shawn Carter) and Master P (Percy Miller) are hip-hop artists who combine business ventures with their music and have subsequently become multimillionaires. Like the deceased patriarchal Kennedys and Rockefellers, their early careers are purported to have been financed by illegal activities. See Alan Hughes, "Hip-Hop Economy," *Black Enterprise*, May 2002, 70; John Leland and James Gill, "The New Gangsta on the Block," *Newsweek*, June 1, 1998, 66; Kelefa Sanneh, "Getting Paid; Jay-Z, Criminal Culture and the Rise of Corporate Rap," *The New Yorker*, August 20, 2001, 60. For more information on the origins of the Rockefellers's fortune, see Gerard Colby and Charlotte Dennett, *Thy Will Be Done: The Conquest of the Amazon: Nelson Rockefeller and Evangelism in the Age of Oil* (New York: HarperCollins, 1995).

4. *Editor's note:* Colin Powell, Condoleezza Rice, and Clarence Thomas all came to prominence during the presidency of George Herbert Walker Bush. Powell was appointed Chairman of the Joint Chiefs of Staff by Bush in 1989; Rice served on Bush's National Security Council as a specialist in Eastern European and Soviet Affairs from 1989 to 1991; Thomas was appointed to the Supreme Court by George Bush in 1991. During George W. Bush's presidency, Rice served as National Security Adviser, Powell as Secretary of State, and Thomas as Supreme Court Justice. Rice replaced Powell as Secretary of State during the second term of George W. Bush.

16

Antonio Fernandez (King Tone)

Antonio Fernandez (King Tone) began keeping an oral diary during the latter part of his house arrest in the fall and winter of 1998. On January 15, 1999, he was sentenced to thirteen years in prison for "bagging" $100 worth of heroin for someone working undercover for federal narcotics agents, and is held in the Federal Penitentiary at Pollock, Louisiana. King Tone is a member of The Almighty Latin Kings Nation, a predominantly Latino and/or Chicano organization founded in Chicago in either the 1940s or early 1960s. Today, the Latin Kings exist throughout the United States, with chapters in Ecuador, Peru, Puerto Rico, Mexico, the Dominican Republic, and Europe.

Originally, the Latin Kings formed small coalitions to protect and preserve their cultural identity and to pursue the "American dream" of prosperity. However, racial assaults led to the formations of protective units that employed violence, which police now refer to as "street gangs." In the late 1980s and early 1990s members of the Connecticut chapter broke away from the main organization and developed the "All Mighty Latin King and Queen Charter Nation."

Members of this Latin Kings formation, to which King Tone belongs, self-identify as political organizers dedicated to the development of the Latino/Chicano community. Law enforcement, though, has identified the Almighty Latin Kings Nation as one of the most organized, violent, and powerful criminal organizations and drug operations in existence, and has imposed severe sentences on its leadership.

King Tone's writings appear in *Gangs and Society: Alternative Perspectives,* edited by David C. Brotherton and Luis Barrios (New York: Columbia University Press, 2003).

References

Alpert, John, Director. *Latin Kings: A Street Gang Story.* HBO, 2003. Video-cassette.
Brotherton, David C. and Luis Barrios. *The Almighty Latin King and Queen Nation: Street Politics and the Transformation of a New York City Gang.* New York: Columbia University Press, 2004.

King Tone's Diary
1998

You know, I come to think of a lot of things. Maybe I could've done things different as a leader . . . but I'm very much satisfied that within all this I have found that you must believe in yourself and the road that you choose to take, and you must stand up for that belief and you can't let nothin' deter you from what you wanna do because this society has got strong influence over what you wanna become, who you should become, and how you should become it. . . .

I feel our youth of today need to hear their own ideas, explore their own mistakes, and achieve their own goals. You know, it's kind of sad that I gotta go do a bid for something that I really didn't take part in, but that's not what I'm so sad about. I'm sad about facin' this with a smile and knowin' within my heart that when you start to fight and buck against this system, they will come after you in an effort to end you and your movement and your ideas, your thoughts. We are now one of the biggest countries in the world with the most prisoners, the craziest laws in the land. In Texas, it's not a felony to have a pistol; in New York it is. The same land has divided the law and made it different to each one. . . . The government has put laws in effect to torture the youth of this country instead of exploring new avenues to help them, and all we are saying, the Latin Kings here in New York State, is that we got an idea, we've got a method of dealing with these kids and it's nonviolent, it's constructive, and it's a way of hope—lettin' 'em explore what they wanna become, very much changin' the organization into something that they could join, explore, and advance. Well, it's kind of sad because I still didn't put together pieces of my heart in my life, but today is gonna be a better day. You know, I'm ready to go to bed now and I just want them to know that there is no sleep within the world of activism. There is no sleep in the world where a man who's sleepin' by your house is dyin' of hunger. There's no sleep in a place where the Latino and the black youth are being shipped constantly to a dead end future where they feel that they cannot accomplish the goals that are set forth by all of those who live in this free country. So, once again, I lay down tonight thinkin' of all the things I could've done, all the things I would've done. Most of all, all the things I wanna be. So remember, people, never, never lose sight of what it is that we're doing, and, most of all, be ready to face all of those things that are thrown before you. Amor de Rey, and a crown up high to the Almighty Being who chooses the path of all Kings, for it is not my will, it is His, and that's how I'm leavin' it for tonight. May His will be done in my life and in yours.

Well, today is Saturday night and it was a rough Saturday—a lot of fighting. . . . This Saturday it occurred to me that many people would not even comprehend what's goin' on in the midst of this city, why they just gradually work their way into a system that's "Get up, go to work, eat, sleep, go back home." It's gotta be a little more to life than that. Today I was really down and out because I was thinking of how I could make this a different system . . . when I'm being sentenced. Of course, I'm very confused and sad tonight, for every time I seek a moment of silence, a moment of peace, a moment of truth, I find the devil activating little situations within this house to distract me from what's the real cause and what's the reality of my situation. Like I tell everybody, I don't need no pity from nobody—nobody. I don't want nobody to feel sorry for me cuz pity is not what I seek. Understanding is what I seek, and understanding will give you the whole picture . . . when you're ready to rocket off into a positive . . . truth, you know? How could I say, you know, it's getting lonely at the top?

Today, the Kings from the Dominican Republic came. They wanna be recognized in the books, so that was happy of them to understand that some of my teachings have reached the Dominican Republic and it's good to know that regardless of what goes on in my life, people continue to believe a little bit of what they heard of my ministry and what's goin' on. The ministry of youth that defends and protects the ideas of their congregation, their movement. See, the Kings is a body, and we got a mind and we got a heart, we've got a soul and we got a God, and Kings all pray and confess and bow down only to that supernatural being that roams amongst us and gives us that spirit-filled way of a King to accomplish and to succeed in the things that each has to do within the realm of the five-point crown. It's a really sensitive issue of Kings comin' to the second stage of Kingism, leaving the primitive stage and entering the service stage. They start to learn who they are, what is the meaning to life. Like kids, a nice dinner, a nice wife, a bank account, a house. Accomplishing these things in the ghetto is so very hard for these kids. What's regular for a gentleman upstate who's got his college degree. . . . [T]hey got all these YMCAs, these police leagues and all that. New York has abandoned their children, has left them out on the corner, in the cold to find out for themselves how is it that they get to the top of a corporate world that doesn't want you there. How is it you get a dollar from a man that doesn't wanna give it? How is it you ask a man for a cup of water, when all he wants to do is sell the water? So you supply his profit and the basis of his profit is always to have you in need, never let you stand upon your own two feet so that you could succeed and feel the equality of the human race, that we are all equal and we all deserve to have the same thing at the same time. It's a shame when America holds so many riches of the world. . . . They have cornered the market and all the money. It's right there on Wall Street. For any country like Fidel Castro's Cuba to ask or to try to say, "We wanna stand on our own two feet. We wanna progress with our own identity," they will surround you, blockade you, starve your kids and your country. They'll demonize you. It's a different level but what they did to the Kings they did to Fidel. What they did to Fidel they tried on Mandela when he first came up and he revolted against apartheid. Malcolm X. I could go on down the list—great men of God, great men of the movement, great men of difference that stood upon this earth, that stood up to every system, from Jesus down to Moses, who came and stood up and screamed and became a radical like John the Baptist, who spoke against all these people and the oppression. It was their destiny. "Fear not the man who could destroy the body, but fear the man who could steal your soul."

So that's what I tell my own mighty Nation, "Fear not those that are screaming and yapping and making mistakes. Love them. But fear those who sit back and scheme on how to destroy and take this back to a place where hate and pain is accepted and betrayal is common. No longer make me follow that road of deceit and the fruits of death that live amongst my crown. The five points of the diamond, the Almighty Sun that shines upon me that gives me life and gives me the guidance to look up to the skies and know that there is a greater being that will judge all those who judge us and He will be oh, so merciful to them. . . . One of the things that I've noticed in this crisis was, spiritually I have disconnected myself from God, from the crown. I have, in my own way rebelled, and really listened to His voice to see what the crown would say and where I must go now to complete this mission that has been set forth by my forefathers. It isn't easy when you pick up a mission that you know few are called to do. I mean, there's people maybe who could understand what I say, some that are gone, some that are here in the present that lead struggles. It's unfortunate that spiritually you start dyin' cuz you start hurting more and more because in the struggles you see nothin' but pain and defeat so many times, especially when the struggle's against this system, a system called America, corporate America. It's a losing battle lots of times because in their God they trust the dollar bill and the poor man does not have that God, can't reach that God, can never obtain that God. That God is not our God. So that's why I laugh at the Latin man and the other men who say, you know, "The dollar's gonna get us. Yeah, on this earth and this time that God will do some good."

But the God we seek is not in the almighty dollar, it's in the crown's essence if we stick together as a people. The God that serves us will always give us what the earth asks for so we may live. So in essence of "in God We Trust," we should trust again in the sand, in the soil, to produce the fruit that gives life. We have destroyed everything around us and depend solely on corporate America to give us our food, give us our shelter, give us everything we need to survive. So, in essence, am I really going to jail, or have I been locked up all my life and just haven't noticed it? Barrios and his congregation gave me that faith to stand before my crown and my God and say humbly, "I kneel down before you," and I always do, but it's hard now because I could see Jesus up there sweatin' it, pacin' up and down sayin' "What the hell is gonna fuckin happen now?" I've done everything he asked me for, I've tried everything he said, and yet I find myself here.

17

Yaki (James Sayles)

James Sayles (Owusu Yaki Yakubu)[1] was born in 1949. Jailed for almost his entore adult life, he was first convicted at age seventeen, spending eighteen months in a juvenile facility. In 1971, he and friends went into a white neighborhood in Chicago in an attempt to foment and fuel a race battle that seemed to be on the verge of occurring in Chicago at that time. The plan went awry, leaving two white people brutally murdered. In 1972, at the age of twenty-three, he began serving a 200-year sentence in Illinois state prisons for the double murder.

In his struggle to be a political activist despite incarceration, Sayles has been involved in the New Afrikan Independence Movement (NAIM) and is the Minister of Information for the Provisional Government of the Republic of New Afrika (PGRNA).[2] However, he states that, "Real leadership can't be simply proclaimed—it has to be earned through the practice of those claiming responsibility."[3] Quoting Malcolm X's formula that "dialectically combined theory and practice, study and struggle,"[4] Sayles asserts that to be a *political* prisoner or a member of the NAIM or the PRGNA, one must *act*.

Within the struggle to create a sovereign socialist New Afrikan nation, Sayles stresses the need for connections between actvists and organizations.[5] To this end, he is affiliated with NAIM, PGRNA, the Freedom Network, the Crossroads Support Network, and the Spear and Shield Collective. He is the founding editor of the *Crossroad Newsletter,* which is coordinated by the Crossroads Support Network and published by the Spear and Shield Collective. Sayles has written prolifically and his writings have been published in English, French, German, and Italian. He wrote the introduction for the fifth edition of *Can't Jail the Spirit,* a collection of biographies of political prisoners held in the United States. Through his work with organizations, he emphasizes the importance of political education.

Sayles appealed his conviction for murder and connected armed robberies and applied for parole over twenty-three times.[6] In 2004, Yaki (James Sayles) was released from prison.

Notes

Research and draft for this biography were provided by Samuel Seidel.

1. Yakubu is also known as James Sayles, Atibe Shanna, and Atiba Shanna.

2. For more information on NAIM and the PGRNA, see Sundiata Acoli's essay, "An Updated History of the New Afrikan Prison Struggle," in *Imprisoned Intellectuals: America's Political Prisoners Write on Life, Liberation and Rebellion,* ed. Joy James (Lanham, MD: Rowan and Littlefield, 2003).

3. Khalfani Khaldun, "Definitions in Transition: Moving Towards a Collective Understanding," *LA RED,* No. 8 (Fall/Winter 1998), charm.net/~claustro/la_red/definitions_in_trans.html.

4. Owusu Yaki Yakubu, "The Legacy of Malcolm X: Carry It Forward by Taking Up His Political Stand," *Black Radical Congress News,* May 20, 1999, members.aol.con/freedomwk/febinspiration.html, 3.

5. Owusu Yaki Yakubu, "Notes For Those With Eyes and Ears," *Prison Activist Resource Center,* www.prisonactivist.org/pubs/crossroads/6.3/notes.html, 2.

6. Unknown, "James Yaki Sayles Profile," *Sayles v. Brierton,* Nos. 76 C 2751, 76 C 3886, 76 C 4471.

References

Khaldun, Khalfani. "Definitions in Transition: Moving Towards a Collective Understanding." *LA RED,* No. 8 (Fall/Winter 1998), charm.net/~claustro/la_red/definitions_in_trans.html (March 1, 2002).
Sayles v. Brierton, Nos. 76 C 2751, 76 C 3886, 76 C 4471.
Sayles v. Thompson, 99 Ill. 2d 122; 475 N.E.2d 440.
Unknown. "James Yaki Sayles Profile," illinoispoliticalprisoners.org/James%20Sayles%20C-01656 (March 1, 2002).
Yakubu, Owusu Yaki. "Fade From Black." *Crossroad Newsletter,* Vol. 7, No. 3 (October/November 1996).
———. "The Legacy of Malcolm X: Carry It Forward by Taking Up His Political Stand." *Black Radical Congress News,* May 20, 1999, members.aol.com/freedomwk/febinspiration.html (March 1, 2002).
———. "A Spear & Shield Look at the 'Name Debate.'" *Crossroad Newsletter* (March 8, 2001), afrikan.identity.com/deforum/DCForumID10/30.html (March 1, 2002).
———. "Notes for Those with Eyes and Ears." *Prison Activist Resource Center,* www.prisonactivist.org/pubs/crossroad/6.3/notes.html (March 1, 2002).

Let's "Gang-Up" on Oppression: Youth Organizations and the Struggle for Power in Oppressed Communities 1994

I cannot disassociate myself from the future that is proposed for my brother.

–Frantz Fanon, *Black Skin, White Masks*

Introduction

Soon after the original version (parts 1 and 2) of this piece was published in *Crossroad* in 1994, members of our Collective began discussing the possible need to revise and expand the piece.[1] We felt that certain points could be more clearly and forcefully made, and that We should set out more of the political perspective of the Collective and of the New Afrikan Independence Movement (NAIM).

We became more determined to revise and expand the piece after Larry Hoover and members of the Gangster Disciples/Growth and Development were indicted by the United States in 1995. We felt that We had to make a public statement about these indictments as they relate to the themes of this piece, that is, that the United States will target any sector of the Afrikan community (and other oppressed communities) that seeks to acquire power in order to develop the community in a revolutionary manner.[2]

We think that note should first be taken of similar indictments, brought by the United States little more than ten years earlier, against Abdul Malik Kabah Khalifah (Jeff Fort) and members of the El Rukns, a street organization on Chicago's south side. To us, it is significant that both sets of indictments were brought as the targeted organizations were involved in a process of political transformation, and each had engaged in

175

actions that directly challenged U.S. interests, on local and/or international levels.

Subsequent to the original publication of this piece (and, after the
indictment of Hoover and other members of Growth and Development),
people throughout the United States and the world became more aware of
the role played by the United States in creating the flood of drugs into
Afrikan communities—in this instance—*via* the CIA, in the 1980s.[3]

◆ ◆ ◆

We close this introduction as we began it, standing on the words of Fanon:
We cannot disassociate ourselves from the fate proposed for our brothers
and sisters. We urge all members of the Afrikan community, in particular,
and other oppressed communities, to also take a stand on these words.
Our entire community—but especially the (nationalist) activists of our
community—must intervene in the struggles of the "street force" to join
the entire people in the war for our independence and progressive national
development.

Our Collective also takes a stand upon the New Afrikan CREED,
which affirms our belief in the community and in the family . . . our belief
in the community AS a family. The CREED affirms our belief in collective
struggle, and in fashioning victory in concert with our brothers and sisters—whom We must love as We love ourselves; with whom We must be
patient and uplifting—and work to bring into the community and into the
Movement—on pain of disgrace and banishment.

An attack upon "gangs" in our communities by the United States is an
attack upon us all—and we must intervene. We must protect our brothers
and sisters, and We must encourage and assist them in their continued pursuit of new values, new ideas, attitudes, and behaviors that are more con-
ducive to our collective survival and development.

Point of Departure

There's an urgent need for the Afrikan and other oppressed communities
to develop new ways of viewing and interacting with "gangs" in our communities. (This should be seen as part of a larger process of changing the
perspective We have of ourselves, as We accept that We are a distinct
people—an oppressed nation—suffering neocolonial domination and not a
mere "national minority" suffering the racism of a few misguided individuals or institutions.)

Most of our current thinking and behavior toward the young people in our communities has been shaped by the media and other U.S. institutions—all of which are inherently opposed to the real needs and interests of "gangs" and the communities (oppressed nations) of which they are a part. From the seventeenth to the mid-nineteenth centuries, it was never in the interest of the colonizer (the "slave owner") to paint a true picture for the colonized people (the "slaves") that would depict the truthful relationship between them, thus allowing us to begin to see ourselves as a people, held in colonial bondage by a new form of settler-imperialism, and to begin pursuing our independence as a new, Afrikan nation state in the Western hemisphere.

The same holds true in the 1990s, as the modern propaganda arm of the "mother country" creates an anticrime hysteria to mask its program of destabilization and genocide. In creating this hysteria, the United States has equated "crime" with "gangs," and created an image of "gangs" that is meant to inspire fear and hatred within us, so that we will react with hostility and violence toward our own children and other members of our communities (oppressed nations). The United States and its media would have us believe that we must rid our communities of "gangs" because, allegedly, they are the *causes* of the crime and violence in our communities, and the obstacles in the paths of our social, economic, and political development, rather than the system of U.S. control under which We live.

Rather than look upon some of our young people as enemies that we should attack and destroy, We must be mindful that members of "gangs" are our children and grandchildren, our brothers, sisters, cousins—members of our families. We must love them unconditionally; We must protect them and work to help them along righteous and productive paths. Above all, We must recognize that negative images of "gangs" are created and used by our real enemies, as they seek to divide and confuse us, to undermine our collective strength, and to divert us from our proper path.

What Is a "Gang"?

The United States and its media would have us believe that there is only one way to define "gang" and "gang activity." They say that a "gang" is a "band of antisocial adolescents" that engages solely in illegal activity.

However, a quick look at *Webster's Dictionary* tells us that a "gang" is, first and foremost, *a group of people . . . with close social relations . . . that work together.* In essence, a "gang" is actually *any* group of people that shares close social relations, and works together toward a common goal, that is, a "gang" has common identity, purpose, and direction. More-over, a "gang" has actual and potential *power*—and it's the actual and potential power of groups within our communities (and thus, the actual and potential power of the community as a whole) that is feared by our common enemy. The United States fears us because We have power, and because We can use our existing power to acquire more power—a collec-tive power that, if used in our interests, can't help but be used to oppose the interests of the United States.

The United States actually aims to define the entire Afrikan commu-nity as "criminal," seen for example when a proposal was put before the Chicago city council, seeking an ordinance that defined a "criminal gang" as a group in which three or more members have been convicted in U.S. courts! Such an ordinance (definition) is clearly intended as a weapon in the war upon the entire Afrikan community—where today, 33 percent of males between the ages of eighteen and twenty-four have been convicted of "crimes" in U.S. courts! (A similar law was passed in California, which makes it a criminal offense not only to be a member of a so-called criminal street gang, but for merely being an associate of such a group!) It's not hard to see that by such laws, *any group of people* whose membership includes those with criminal convictions would be considered a "criminal gang" to local, state, and federal authorities operating a sinister agenda relative to the Afrikan and other oppressed communities.

Hopefully, We don't need to point out that there's really nothing "new" about such laws and their underlying purposes. Such laws—and their purposes—can be traced as far back as the beginning of the colonial relationship between Afrikan people and what would become the U.S. set-tler-imperialist state, with new forms appearing as changes took place in the forms of our oppression (i.e., laws applied to Afrikans prior to 1865, after 1865, e.g., "runaway slave" laws, "vagrancy" laws, "Black Codes," "Jim Crow" laws, etcetera).

We need to do one of two things with regard to the word "gang": 1) abandon the word to those who have defined it so that it now has a purely negative connotation; 2) redefine the word—or create a new word or phrase to describe organized youth/groups in oppressed communities.

However, new concepts must be developed to accompany whichever choice We make, and new forms of activity should begin to appear on the basis of the new concepts. The people in the community must begin to work collectively, to transform "gangs" into progressive organizations of Afrikan people, which struggle for freedom and development.

Our problem is not that there are "gangs" in our communities—our problem is that our communities are colonized territories that suffer from arrested development caused by the U.S. settler-imperialist state. Thus, we have no need to attack "gangs"—that is, ideally, we have no need to attack any organized groups of our people that work to free the process of our collective development. What We must do is make sure that all organized groups in our communities have this as their goal—and so long as We deal with members of our communities (i.e., members of our families), the means that We use should be education and persuasion, rather than physical force. However, even if stronger means are called for, they should be ones created and employed by forces within our own communities and not those of U.S. local, state, and federal governments. The transformation of "gangs" into progressive groups within our communities is part of the process of acquiring the group power that will enable us to control every aspect of our lives. Our problem is that too many people in our communities—old and young—lack the identity, purpose, and direction required of us if We are to acquire the kind of power that we need to truly free ourselves and begin to pursue the development of our ideal social order.

Why Was the Anticrime/Antigang Hysteria Created?

The anticrime/antigang hysteria was created for several interrelated reasons, which include, but are not limited to: 1) the United States and local governments needed a smokescreen to cover and divert attention from the worsening conditions of ever-larger numbers of people; 2) the United States and local governments needed to undermine actual and potential bases of contending power within oppressed communities; 3) the United States and local governments needed to test new tactical genocidal initiatives (new forms of colonial violence) in the on-going war between themselves and oppressed peoples inside U.S. borders.

Those who rule the United States and who operate its propaganda machine have a long history and much experience in diverting the attention of those under their control, manipulating them so that their real problems and their underlying causes go unchallenged, while they are led to chase "ghosts" and shadows. The real problem of all peoples under capitalist domination is capitalism itself—which creates the alienation that is driving people into madness, the pursuit of illusions, and the embrace of the commodity fetish.

The "criminalization" of Afrikan youth (e.g., lowering the age at which juveniles can be tried as adults and sentenced to long prison terms—including life without possibility of parole, and the death penalty) is actually about the United States trying to protect its power and the privileges of empire. It's using its legal system as a major weapon in the war to destabilize the entire Afrikan community, while turning the prison system into a new economic appendage (e.g., the privatization of prisons).

Rather than trying to "rid" our communities of "gangs," We should definitely try to assist them as they themselves engage in a process of transformation into community groups that aim to combat some of our real problems, for example: homelessness (the leading cause of which is the inability of poor people to find affordable housing—while housing costs are rising, the incomes of ever-larger numbers of people are declining); hunger; inadequate and decreasing access to health care (43 million people in the United States lack health insurance, while hospitals and clinics are closing, and plans are being made to decrease the number of doctors and other medical personnel). Eighty-five million people in the United States today live below the poverty line (over 21.5 million of these are Afrikan people, constituting 34.8 percent of the Afrikan population), and the U.S. job market is shrinking at the rate of 100,000 per year![4]

"Youth Organizations"—Afrocentric and Revolutionary

We can take at least one step toward power—one critical step closer to a new sense of collective identity, purpose, and direction—by using the power that We already have, to define ourselves, name ourselves, and speak for ourselves—instead of being defined and spoken for by others.

Let's begin to transform part of the reality in our communities by defining so-called gangs as organized groups of people in our communities who are essentially misdirected and who need our help getting on the right track. We should stop referring to these organized groups as "gangs," and instead refer to them as "youth organizations in need of adult supervision"—that is, supervision and assistance from adults who are themselves Afrocentric and revolutionary (nationalists).

Some of you like to say (usually only when it's convenient and won't cost you anything) that "it takes an entire community to raise a child"—well, you are part of the community, and We wanna know what *you* will *do* to help raise our children. Rather, the question is: What will *you do* to help fight the system that turns our children into criminals and victims?

All of the people in our communities must come to share the responsibility for providing a new, broader sense of collective identity, purpose and direction—for our children, and for ourselves. We all suffer the same oppression, at the hands of the same oppressor. We all confront and react to the obstacles to our progress that are created and sustained by the United States and its local governments.

We must begin to promote new ideas about how We want to live and the kind of society We want to live in; We must begin to promote new definitions of the causes of our problems (e.g., "racism" or capitalism/ colonialism), and the real solutions to our problems (e.g., "empower- ment" or genuine independence). We must begin to *work together* as a collective, distinct community that is primarily engaged in the struggle for sovereign power.

We must promote ideas that encourage our young people to identify themselves as Afrikans; We must promote among our young people the idea that their purpose is not to merely seek quasicontrol over a few city blocks, but to share in our control of entire cities, entire states, and ulti- mately, to share in the control of our independent nation. We need ideas that promote the notion that the direction We must take is toward national independence.

Let's "gang-up" against oppression—and struggle for power!

Planting Seed—Building Bases

In the Spike Lee film *Malcolm X*, there's a scene that depicts a real event: Malcolm, without uttering a word, used his hand to direct a disciplined corps of the NOI [Nation of Islam] outside a police station, through the streets of New York City, to the hospital to which an injured member of the Nation of Islam had been taken—at Malcolm's insistence, and under the threat of the unleashed power represented by Malcolm, the NOI, and the community that surrounded them. A police captain says: "That's too much power for one man to have." Clearly, that was not an objective observation.

The officer in question would not object to *his* having that much power—nor would he object to any other "one man" having that much power—so long as it was a man with whom he shared ideological, politi- cal, and economic interests.

The officer in question was uptight because "that much power" had just been used against him, his fellow officers, and the interests of the state that they had pledged to serve and protect. He had been shocked upon seeing that a *kind* of power existed in an oppressed community—power that could force him to refrain from doing that to which he was accus- tomed, in a community in which he was used to having his way, with no fear of opposition or reprisal.

When the police captain spoke, he was speaking for the federal and local U.S. governments. And, he really meant that: 1) No person in the

Afrikan (or any other oppressed) community should have the power to
successfully act in opposition to federal, state, or local governments and
their police forces; 2) Organized power should not exist within, nor be
exercised by, the Afrikan or any other oppressed community—to realize its
interests, in opposition to the interests of the oppressive United States.

When that police officer witnessed and responded to the power of
Malcolm, the FOI [Fruit of Islam], and the Afrikan community, he knew it
for what it was—he knew, too, the possibilities of that power—*and that is
what shook his world*! Those who rule the U.S. *still* tremble at the thought
of "ALL POWER TO THE PEOPLE" and socialist revolution.

We witnessed a similar reaction by police and government officials
when youth organizations in Los Angeles and Chicago announced, on separate occasions, that they were initiating a *peace* that would end violence
between "gangs" in parts of both cities.

The police and government officials in both cities responded to this
news with anger and alarm. They issued hasty releases to the media, claiming that the peace initiatives were shams, and that the peace wouldn't last
(voicing, of course, their own desires). They made special attempts to discredit the youth organizations in the eyes of the communities to which the
organizations belonged, calling into question their motives, their sincerity,
and their integrity.

We would think that, in light of all of the calls from all quarters for
an end to fratricidal violence in Afrikan and other oppressed communities,
the police and other U.S. government agencies would have welcomed news
of a peace, and that they would have used their resources to support and
sustain it. Instead, they tried to undermine it, going so far as to create situations that they hoped would help to reignite hostilities (e.g., paying or
otherwise encouraging renegade elements within the organizations to initiate attacks, or to otherwise engage in activities that were contrary to the
rules and aims of the peace initiatives). Why would the United States and
its agencies want to undermine peace among so-called gangs?

Peace, Development, and New Contradictions

Power: The ability to act in a desired manner, or to produce a
desired effect. Legal or official capacity or *legitimacy*. Possession
of control, authority, or influence over others. Specifically, *a sovereign state . . . a controlling group*. Shared meaning element:
The ability of a group to perform in a given way, or its capacity
for a particular kind of performance.

Peace among youth organizations in our communities means much more than an end to violent conflict—it also means that young people *and adults* begin to reorder our priorities, redirect our energies, and assume new responsibilities—for ourselves, our families, our communities—our nation. Peace among youth organizations in oppressed communities *can* lead to the resolution of other problems in our communities that, in their turn, can help to pull the covers off of U.S. socioeconomic structural obstacles that block our path to genuine peace and development. Once exposed, these obstacles will present themselves as new problems to be resolved; We will find ourselves confronting long-standing enemies who are far more threatening to us than are some of the young people in our own communities.

When Youth Organizations End the Violence

The initiation of a peace process by youth organizations immediately brought to light one source of the actual/potential power of the community—power that We can use to solve *all* of our problems, ourselves. Fred Hampton often reminded us that there is "power, wherever there are people," and people in our communities stopped violence that the U.S. settler-imperialist state couldn't or wouldn't stop—even with its greater resources, skills, and its alleged greater will.[5]

When, on one day, it wasn't safe for children to sit in their windows, or to play outside of their homes—and, on the next day the entire community sat safely in parks and playgrounds that until then had been little more than free-fire zones—the people were relieved and thankful—but more was happening!

The end to the violence in parts of Los Angeles and Chicago generated new hope, and a new sense of community and *community power*, which had not existed in these areas for some time. While recognizing that this power had manifested itself initially through the actions of groups of organized youth ("gangs"), there was also a gradual realization among people that an even greater power lay dormant within the body of the collective community. As this realization spread, so, too, did the new *legitimacy* that was bestowed upon the youth organizations by the people in the communities. The existence of youth organizations taking a new course now provided a vision of new possibilities for comprehensive community development, and the people looked toward the organizations with new expectations.

It is this transfer of *legitimacy* by the community—from the police and their bosses, to itself and the youth organizations—that so alarmed the United States when the peace process was announced. It wasn't just that the state didn't want the youth organizations to be seen as "heroes"—the state doesn't want us to view the organizations as *responsible*—doesn't want them to be seen as legitimate actors for positive development . . . doesn't want them to become models for the process of transforming negative energy into positive energy. The United States doesn't want dependent people to become self-reliant and begin to determine their own destiny. The United States doesn't want Afrikan and other oppressed people to recognize that We can count on ourselves—and ourselves alone—for solutions to the problems of violence, inadequate health care, inadequate housing, unemployment, etcetera.

The police, and those that they truly serve and protect, do not want us to respect the actual and potential power of our young people; they do not want us to glimpse, through our youth, the power that lies within each of us: If the Crips and Bloods can bring peace to our communities, and the police can't or won't, then why do We need the police? If the Disciples, Vice Lords, Cobras, Latin Kings and other street organizations can serve and protect our children and our elders, and the state demonstrates that it can't or won't, then why should We continue to depend upon it and profess loyalty to it? If the power to end violence exists within our own communities, then We should be looking for ways to increase our power, and We should be looking for ways to exercise it.

When Youth Organizations Participate in the Development of the Community

Other social, political, and economic implications arise as a result of youth organizations ending fratricidal violence in our communities. For example: The United States can't then use the occurrence of such violence as a justification for increased expenditures on police personnel, equipment, and prison construction; politicians can't then use the occurrence of such violence as a pretext for additional repressive measures in our communities and as planks in their campaign platforms.

For these and other reasons, an end to fratricidal violence would mean that We could then push for the attention and funds of the United States to be redirected toward the development of our communities—even though this would be a demand that the United States can't fulfill. That is, the United States *won't* promote the kind of community development

that We want and need, because it *can't*—the United States is not structurally designed to do so! Under the U.S. system of capitalist-imperialism,
for example, a significant number of people must *always* be unemployed,
uneducated, ill-fed, ill-housed, and in all other respects, oppressed and
exploited. Capitalism *means* development and prosperity for a few and
underdevelopment and poverty for the many. If we put more pressure on
the United States to house the homeless, to feed the hungry, to hire the
jobless (at wages above subsistence level), to educate and to provide adequate health care for *all* of the people—if we pushed for all this, the
United States would come up short. Contradictions would sharpen. Consciousness would rise and consolidate. People would organize to struggle
for their real needs. Lines would be drawn and people would choose
sides. Interests would be distinguished and fought for—*and this is what
we want to happen*!

When the youth organizations in Los Angeles and Chicago announced
their plans for peace, they subsequently announced plans for their participation in the development of their communities. The plan drafted by the
Crips and Bloods in Los Angeles, proposed activities in five defined areas:

1. Community Face-Lift: to get abandoned buildings, and to
   encourage the city to purchase and to build community centers
   upon the property; to repair pavements and sidewalks, plant
   trees, increase lighting, and clean up vacant lots—all with
   community involvement and financial assistance from the city.
2. Education: to implement accelerated learning programs; to
   increase and upgrade school bathrooms and provide new landscapes for schools.
3. Health and Welfare: the construction of three new hospitals,
   forty health care clinics and dental clinics; the establishment of
   day care centers. Eliminate welfare, and provide full employment, with the construction of new plants and facilities to
   service the city—provide welfare only for the invalid and the
   elderly.
4. Law Enforcement: the creation of "buddy patrols" whereby
   members of youth organizations are paired with police,
   trained, and patrol the communities. Those who police the
   community must live there, and commanders of the districts
   must be ten-year residents of the communities they serve.
5. Economic Development: loans must be provided to all Afrikan
   small businesses at 4 percent annual interest, and they must be
   security-free; 90 percent of the people employed by the businesses in the community must be residents thereof.

The Chicago plan, which focused primarily upon the Cabrini-Green area,[6] was drafted by the King David Black Disciples, the King Cobra Nation, the North Branch Gangster Disciples, and the Magic Insane. It was endorsed by a coalition of other community organizations, religious institutions, political activists, and elected officials. It was presented to Chicago's mayor, Richard M. Daley, and to the equally infamous housing authority chairman, Vince Lane. This plan called for:

1. The provision of educational, job training, and recreational activities to all youth and adults.
2. U.S. Representative Cardiss Collins to convene a congressional hearing on "what led to the destruction of Cabrini-Green and the entire Near-North Black community."
3. U.S. Housing and Urban Development regional administrator Gertrude Jordan to "cite Metroplex, the owners of Town and Garden Apartments, for gross violation of their contract with HUD, and to reclaim the property and turn them into scattered site housing" for Cabrini-Green residents.
4. The repair of all vacant Chicago Housing Authority units and their occupation by homeless families.
5. The turning of the 1117–1119 Cleveland Ave. building into a multipurpose service center including an alternative high school, drug program, library, and a shelter for youth and adults.
6. The construction of a theatre, bowling alley, and a recreational arcade.
7. The support of existing agencies, churches, and community organizations that already provide services to the area residents.
8. The provision of additional resources and support to all area schools.
9. The establishment of food and clothing cooperatives for the area. The establishment of a 24–hour trouble-shooter hotline.
10. The holding of elections for Local Advisory Councils. The establishment of community-wide Governing Councils that represent all groups in the community. And, the holding of monthly community accountability sessions and status reports.

Above our discussion of these plans, We tried to emphasize the fact that *violence in the Los Angeles and Chicago communities in question was stopped by the people in these communities*, and not by the police or other U.S. government agencies. The people in these communities made a decision to harness and exercise some of their power, and their action resulted in a victory that can have far-reaching possibilities. However, in order to realize any of these possibilities, We must be sure about what We're fighting for, and We must think through the tactics and strategies that We use in the fight.

We fight so that We can become the masters of our own destinies. We fight so that We can seize the power to freely determine and fully benefit from our productive capacities, and to shape all productive and social relations in our own society. In this fight, We will unavoidably choose methods and employ tactics that will be called "reformist"—but such methods and tactics must be chosen and employed on the basis of a strategy that seeks to fundamentally change the socioeconomic order according to which We will live. In other words, ours must be a revolutionary strategy, that is, a "revolutionary-democratic program," designed to transfer *all* power to the people. We must remember that the state was alarmed when peace was announced because of its understanding of the *possibilities* of the power of the people: The United States was alarmed because it feared that the people would exploit their potential *to go beyond reform*, and to pursue a revolutionary-democratic agenda. (A "democratic" agenda, in simple terms, is one that seeks to satisfy all of the basic rights and needs of the people. Such an agenda is "revolutionary" for us, because its realization will require the overthrow and junking of the present U.S. socioeconomic order, and the construction of a noncapitalist, i.e., a socialist, society.) These points are raised because both of the plans discussed above exhibit a dual character, that is, potentially harmful (mere reformist) and potentially beneficial (revolutionary-democratic) tendencies.

The primary reason for offering any proposal to local and federal U.S. governments should be that We want to further expose to the people the unwillingness and/or the inability of the United States to solve our problems. We need to use all opportunities to show to the people that these governments are not righteous, that they are illegitimate, and that they have no right to rule over us. Every struggle that We engage in must have the dual purpose of undermining U.S. power, and of transferring that power to the people. We must gradually dismantle the oppressive state apparatus, and begin to build a new, people's state apparatus, creating its embryonic structures in our communities as We build people's organizations and institutions that end the violence, house the homeless, feed the hungry, heal the sick, and educate and train our people for their responsibilities in a new society. Each time the people themselves create and develop an idea, build an organization, solve a problem, We show through practice that We can create new structures, and new ways, that satisfy our needs. Otherwise, our needs will go unsatisfied.

We must understand that by appealing to the state with a belief that it will satisfy our needs, We end up hampering the development of the people's self-confidence, their class and national consciousness, and their power. When We call upon the oppressive state to solve our problems, We promote the idea that it is not necessary to struggle against it and to replace it. This is a principle that should be stressed as often and in as many ways as possible. However, none of this is to say that demands should not be made upon the state: it is only to say that We should have no illusions, and We should allow none to be cast.

Once put under pressure, the state will make cosmetic changes—changes designed to lessen, or to give the impression of lessening, certain contradictions, or the resolution of certain problems. Some of these changes will be made on the state's own initiative, but most of them will come as a result of the pressure applied by organized groups of the people. No matter what form the inspiration takes, the purpose of reforms by the state is to preserve its rule, to distract and disperse the groups of people that challenge its legitimacy, its power, and its privilege.

All demands made upon the state by people's organizations should be widely exposed, and each step in the process should be analyzed, discussed, summed up, and the lessons shared with the masses. This is part of the process of mass political education, and part of the process of creating responsible organizations and leadership that emerges from within the masses. The people will learn when, why, and how the United States is failing them and, at the same time, they will learn that their own organized strength is working to serve their interests. The state will make a concession here or there, and soon the people will realize that the concession meant nothing—that daily struggles and victories over single issues aren't in themselves decisive. But more covers will be pulled off, more consciousness will develop; people will see more clearly just how far they will have to go in order to fully realize fundamental change—in themselves, and in the world.

The plans discussed above provide us with good, concrete examples of how the process We're describing can and should unfold; that is, make your appeals to the state, but build upon the power of the people—use existing resources to meet existing needs. Find out exactly what the people need, and organize them through the process of serving those needs.

To begin with, We should take special note of the fact that the youth organizations were not alone in the initiation of the peace, the articulation of the plans, and the daily activities in the communities. They were encouraged and joined by other community activists, organizations, and institutions (e.g., churches, businesses, local elected officials, educators, health care providers, etcetera). This is an example of unity in the community that should not be wasted.

We see varied groups and strata representing the entire community binding together and pursuing particular, shared interests. Rather than *march against* the youth, some responsible and conscious adults decided to *march with* youth and other organizations, to challenge the real criminals and to regain control of the colonized territories that are commonly referred to as "inner cities." Let's talk less about marching against our children, talk more about marching with them, to take back our communities from the colonial powers, which have arrested our creative and productive capacities. Now, let's look briefly at other examples in the plans discussed above, to check out some of the elements of a people's program for self-reliance, self-determination, and independence.

Both plans called upon U.S. federal and local government forces, placing little emphasis upon a reliance upon the people in the communities to address their own needs. For example, the "community face-lift" of the L.A. plan could surely be taken up by the people and institutions in the Afrikan communities, using presently available resources and, within the process of instituting comprehensive development of the community (economic, political, sociocultural), create the means of acquiring/creating new resources.

We know that We can't complete the development of the community in one day. . . . We can't repair or replace all of the abandoned housing overnight—but We can select one site, and use this as a model, a starting point. The entire community can be involved in such a project. Or, several sites can be selected, one in each of the areas where certain organizations predominate, or where certain churches or businesses are located, or which are represented by certain local, state, or federally elected officials. Youth organizations may decide to get into the business of housing construction or rehab. The point, however, is that if appeals are made to the city, asking it to pave sidewalks or to clean up vacant lots, and the city fails to respond—what happens when the people in the community take on the tasks themselves? *The people in the community should take on the tasks themselves!*

What does it really take to repair sidewalks, plant trees, increase lighting, or clean up vacant lots in our communities?! How much money? How many people? What kinds of examples or models? Again, We don't have to start big—We can start on one block, learning "how to win judiciously, step by step." Poor, colonized neighborhoods *can be clean* neighborhoods—if enough of the people therein assume the responsibility for making it so—and it doesn't take "hundreds" of people to begin or to complete such projects! We *can* do this; We can take pride in it, and We can use the sense of accomplishment that We will derive from it as a springboard for greater accomplishments.

The people in the communities can harness available resources (financial and human) to do such things as clean up and upgrade the bathrooms in the public schools. Some of the conscious and responsible adults who worked (and continue to work) with the youth organizations in Los Angeles and Chicago were educators. The coalitions that spring up in each of our neighborhoods should include educators, and they must help us develop *our own* "accelerated learning programs." There's nothing wrong with making demands upon city governments and upon city, state, and federal educational agencies—but our primary objective must be that WE seek control of the institutions that must educate our children—and educate them so that they can become fully developed, and so that they can help us to serve *our interests*. What can WE do to create programs that combat illiteracy within our communities and nation? What can WE do to provide an adequate number of textbooks (as well as develop new textbooks) for our children? What can WE do to "put a computer in every home" as well as a sufficient number in every school? What can WE do to insure that those who help to develop the minds of our children are themselves psychologically and ideologically "stable"? Who do the schools belong to? Who do the teachers work for? To what community (of interests) do the teachers belong?

Our communities do not lack experience in providing health care to the people therein; that is, We know how to assist one another, and We know how to develop health and dental clinics, how to create preventive health programs, how to develop programs to test for sickle cell anemia, etcetera. We've done it before, and We can do it again. There should be no insurmountable problems in the process of our developing our own day care centers, which can not only adequately provide for the needs of our children and the parents who need such service, but can also provide employment for people both young and old!

Moreover, We must begin to challenge the profit motive (in this case, with particular reference to the health care "industry") and raise the question of society's responsibility to provide for those who are unable to provide for themselves (as well as the more basic principle of society's responsibility for *all* of its members)—especially when, under U.S. capitalism, jobs are structurally eliminated, the health care system is consciously dismantled, and insurance companies and not health care providers are calling the shots over the health delivery system.

Those who control the United States talk out of both sides of their mouths—from one side they say that they want to put people to work;

from the other side they say that they need to keep an unemployment level of at least 6 percent in order to insure the stability of U.S. capitalism! The people of our communities will *never* be "fully employed" so long as U.S. capitalism remains in place. We will not receive adequate health care so long as insurance companies and corporate boards are in control of the health care system and place more value on profits than they do on people.

We don't need to receive permission from the state in order to hold elections or otherwise select people from within our communities to lead and represent us. The creation of our own governing councils is a needed step toward the creation of leadership that is truly accountable to the people who are served. It is also a prerequisite in the establishment of "dual or contending" bases of power, in the hands of the people, in the fight to create a new social order.

Very important: We don't and shouldn't rely upon our enemies for the creation of or assistance in the development of "food and clothing co-ops." Such institutions are essential as models or starting points in the process of economic development—especially as we look toward the future, where we will have to feed and clothe ourselves. The hundreds of billions of dollars that we cite as the "wealth" of Afrikans in the United States does not actually represent "wealth"—because we don't control the means of production, nor do we control the means of distribution—we are mere consumers (and this is part of our role as neocolonial subjects in the twenty-first century).

The economic development of the Afrikan communities should start with basic education in the science of political economy and a clear under-standing as to the commodity that We know as "money." We must under-stand that . . . social wealth is actually created by us, by people, through our labor, and not by investments in money market funds or the stock exchange. Fundamentally, social wealth originates through a combination of the labor of people, upon the land that they control, through produc-tion and distribution of the material resources that flow from that land (and the sea). Do you get the drift?

New Contradictions

As stated above, peace in our communities, and our struggle to develop our communities, will place new demands upon us, and will take us to new levels of confrontation with our real enemies.

We must first wage battles within ourselves—as individuals who want to be better persons, and as communities that want unhindered develop-ment. We must develop new values, abandoning individualism, petty envy,

and jealousy. We must abandon fear of the enemy and fear of change and
sacrifice in service to collective interests. We must truly love ourselves, love
our sisters and brothers as We love ourselves. We must "believe in the
family and the community, and in the community as a family," and work
to make this concept live. We must believe in the community as more
important than the individual, because no individual interests can be realized apart from realization of the interests of the community. Through all
this, and more, new contradictions will arise—most notably those that will
stand us in opposition to the United States.

The United States is an oppressive, exploitative state. It seems all-
powerful because We do not have the kind of power that We need; the
power that we do have is not yet fully exercised in the proper manner,
toward the proper ends. The more we exercise our power, the more antagonistic our relationship to the United States will become. This antagonism
is both part and consequence of our struggle to become more socially
responsible, more politically conscious and active, more economically
powerful and self-sufficient.

ALL POWER TO THE PEOPLE THAT DON'T FEAR FREEDOM!

Notes

Originally published in *Crossroad Newsletter,* Vol 5, No. 2/3 (May/September
1994).

1. The journal *Crossroad* is published in Chicago by the Spear and Shield
Collective.

2. *Editor's note:* Introduced to Congress by Senator Charles Schumer (D-NY)
in 2004, the "Criminal Street Gang Abatement Act" allows more juveniles to be
charged as adults and allows prosecutors to seek the death penalty without having
to use the RICCO Act. For more details about the act, see www.theorator.
com/bills108/s1735.html.

3. *Editor's note:* See Peter Dale Scott and Jonathan Marshall, *Cocaine Politics: Drugs, Armies, and the CIA in Central America* (Berkeley: University of California Press, 1991); Alexander Cockburn and Jeffrey St. Clair, *Whiteout: The CIA,
Drugs, and the Press* (New York: Verso, 1998).

4. *Editor's note:* According to 2003 statistics from the U.S. Census Bureau,
the number of people in the United States living below the poverty line increased
1.7 million between 2001 and 2002, to 34.6 million. Poverty rates for blacks
increased from 1.2 percent to 1.4 percent, such that 24 percent of the U.S. black
population lives in poverty. See www.census.gov/hhes/www/poverty.html.

5. *Editor's note:* Fred Hampton, Chicago Black Panther Party leader, was
assassinated by Chicago police, assisted by the Federal Bureau of Investigation, in

December 1969 in a predawn raid at Panther headquarters. The U.S. government awarded a $1.8 million settlement to family and friends of the survivors.

6. *Editor's note:* Cabrini-Green in Chicago is a high density public housing complex plagued by poor services, low maintenance, drugs, and violence.

18

Mumia Abu-Jamal

Mumia Abu-Jamal (Wesley Cook) was born in Philadelphia on April 24, 1954. After being attacked by a police officer during high school, he became involved in the Black Panther Party. As a result, he was targeted and monitored by the Federal Bureau of Investigation's (FBI) domestic counterinsurgency program, COINTELPRO. Abu-Jamal remained a Panther until 1970, when factionalism and FBI deception crippled the Party.

While working as a cab driver on December 9, 1981, Abu-Jamal saw his brother, William Cook, being assaulted by a police officer. He was shot while intervening, and a police officer, Daniel Faulkner, was killed. Abu-Jamal was charged with and convicted of Faulkner's killing, and was subsequently sentenced to death following a trial presided over by pro-prosecutorial Judge Albert F. Sabo. Consistently maintaining his innocence for over two decades on death row, he is appealing his imprisonment and continuing his advocacy for social justice through journalism.

Abu-Jamal has authored: *Live from Death Row, Death Blossoms, All Things Censored,* and *We Want Freedom: A Life in the Black Panther Party.*[1]

Note

1. Mumia Abu-Jamal, *Live from Death Row* (New York: Avon, 1996); Mumia Abu-Jamal, *Death Blossoms: Reflections from a Prisoner of Conscience* (Farmington, PA: Plough Publishing House, 1997); Mumia Abu-Jamal, *All Things Censored* (New York: Seven Stories Press, 2000); Mumia Abu-Jamal, *We Want Freedom: A Life in the Black Panther Party* (Boston: South End Press, 2004).

References

Bisson, Terry. *On a Move: The Story of Mumia Abu-Jamal.* Farmington, PA: Litmus Books, 2000.

Cleaver, Kathleen and George Katsiaficas, eds. *Liberation, Imagination, and the Black Panther Party: A New Look at the Panthers and Their Legacy.* New York: Routledge, 2001.

A Life Lived, Deliberately
1999

Welcome, students of Evergreen, and thank you for this invitation. On the MOVE. Long live John Africa.

I feel privileged to address your chosen theme, not because I'm some kind of avatar, but because a life lived deliberately has been the example of people I admire and respect, such as Malcolm X; Dr. Huey P. Newton, founder of the Black Panther Party; like Ramona Africa, who survived the hellish bombing by police of May 13, 1985; or the MOVE Nine, committed rebels now encaged for up to one hundred years in Pennsylvania hell-holes despite their innocence, solely for their adherence to the teachings of John Africa. These people, although of quite diverse beliefs, ideologies, and lifestyles, shared something in common: a commitment to revolution and a determination to live that commitment deliberately in the face of staggering state repression.

No doubt some of you are disconcerted by my use of the term "revolution." It's telling that people who claim with pride to be proud Americans would disclaim the very process that made such a nationality possible, even if it was a bourgeois revolution. Why was it right for people to revolt against the British because of "taxation without representation," and somehow wrong for truly unrepresented Africans in America to revolt against America? For any oppressed people, revolution, according to the Declaration of Independence, is a right.

Malcolm X, although now widely acclaimed as a black nationalist martyr, was vilified at the time of his assassination by *Time* magazine as "an unashamed demagogue" who "was a disaster to the civil rights movement." The *New York Times* would describe him as a "twisted man" who used his brains and oratorical skills for "an evil purpose." Today, there are schools named for him, and recently a postage stamp was even issued in his honor.

Dr. Huey P. Newton, PhD, founded the Black Panther Party in October of 1966, and created one of the most militant, principled organizations

American blacks had ever seen. J. Edgar Hoover of the FBI targeted the party, using every foul and underhanded method he could conceive of to neutralize the group, which he described as the "number one threat to national security."

Sister Ramona Africa of the MOVE organization survived one of the most remarkable bombings in American history, one where Philadelphia police massacred eleven men, women, and children living in the MOVE house and destroyed some sixty-one homes in the vicinity. She did seven years in the state prison on riot charges, came out, and began doing all she could to spread the teachings of John Africa, the teachings of revolution, and to free her imprisoned brothers and sisters of MOVE from their repressive century in hellish prison cells.

These people dared to dissent, dared to speak out, dared to reject the status quo by becoming rebels against it. They lived—and some of them continue to live—lives of deliberate will, of willed resistance to a system that is killing us. Remember them. Honor their highest moments. Learn from them. Are these not lives lived deliberately? This system's greatest fear has been that folks like you, young people, people who have begun to critically examine the world around them, some perhaps for the first time, people who have yet to have the spark of life snuffed out, will do just that: learn from those lives, be inspired, and then live lives of opposition to the deadening status quo.

Let me give you an example. A young woman walks into a courtroom, one situated in the cradle of American democracy—that's Philadelphia—to do some research for a law class. This woman, who dreams of becoming a lawyer, sits down and watches the court proceedings and is stunned by what she sees. She sees defendants prevented from defending themselves, manhandled in court, and cops lying on the stand with abandon. She saw the judge as nothing more than an administrator of injustice and saw U.S. law as an illusion. Her mind reeled as she said to herself, "They can't do that," as her eyes saw them doing whatever they wanted to.

Well, that young woman is now known as Ramona Africa, who lived her life deliberately after attending several sessions of the MOVE trial in Philadelphia. After that farce she knew she could never be a part of the legal system that allowed it, and she found more truth in the teachings of John Africa than she ever could in the law books that promised a kind of justice that was foreign to the courtrooms she had seen. The contrast between America's lofty promises and the truth of its legal repression inspired her to be a revolutionary, one that America has tried to bomb into oblivion. What is the difference between Ramona Africa and you? Absolutely nothing, except she made that choice.

Similarly, Huey Newton studied U.S. law with close attention when he was a student at Merritt Junior College in West Oakland, California. His studies convinced him that the laws must be changed, and the famous Black Panther Party ten-point program and platform proves, then and now, that serious problems still face the nation's black communities, such as all the predominantly white juries still sending blacks to prison, and cops still treating black life as a cheap commodity. Witness the recent Bronx execution of Ghanaian immigrant Amadou Diallo, where cops fired forty-one shots at an unarmed man in the doorway of his own apartment building. Huey, at least in his earlier years, lived his life deliberately and set the mark as a revolutionary. What was the difference between Huey Newton and you? Absolutely nothing, except he made the choice.

Each of the MOVE Nine—including the late Merle Africa, who died under somewhat questionable circumstances after nineteen years into an unjust prison sentence—members of the MOVE organization whose trial initially attracted the attention of a young law student named Ramona decades ago, was a person who came to question their lives as lived in the system. Some were U.S. Marines, some were petty criminals, some were carpenters, but all came to the point of questioning the status quo, deeply, honestly, and completely—irrevocably. One by one, they turned their back on a system that they knew couldn't care less if they lived or died and joined a revolution after being exposed to the stirring teachings of John Africa. They individually chose to live life deliberately and joined MOVE. And although they are individuals—Delbert Africa, Janet Africa, Phil Africa, Janine Africa, Chuckie Africa, Mike Africa, Debbie Africa, and Eddie Africa—they are also united as MOVE members, united in heart and soul. What's the difference between the MOVE Nine and you? Absolutely nothing, except they made the choice.

Now, unless I miss my guess, Evergreen is not a predominantly black institution, and my choices heretofore given may seem somewhat strange to too many of you, for far too many of you may identify yourselves by the fictional label of "white." In truth, as I'm sure many of you know, race is a social construct. That said, it is still a social reality formed by our histories and our cultures. For those of you still bound by such realities however, I have some names for you like John Brown, like Dr. Alan Berkman, Susan Rosenberg, Sue Africa, Marilyn Buck, for examples. Each of these people are or were known in America as white. They are all people I know of, who I admire, love, and respect. They all are or were revolutionaries.

John Brown's courageous band's attack on Harper's Ferry was one deeply religious man's strike against the hated slavery system and was indeed considered one of the opening salvos of the U.S. Civil War. Dr. Alan

Berkman, Susan Rosenberg, and Marilyn Buck were all anti-imperialists who fought to free black revolutionary Assata Shakur from an unjust and cruel bondage. They are the spiritual grandsons and granddaughters of John Brown. Dr. Alan Berkman, Marilyn Buck, and Susan Rosenberg were treated like virtual traitors to white supremacy and thrown into American dungeons. Buck and Rosenberg remain so imprisoned today. [Susan Rosenberg was released in 2000, granted clemency by President Bill Clinton.] They lived lives deliberately and chose liberation as their goals, understanding that our freedom is interconnected. They chose the hard road of revolution, yet they chose. And but for that choice they are just like each of you seated here tonight, people who saw the evils of the system and resolved to fight it. Period.

Now, the name Sue Africa may not be known to you. She's what you may call white. Yet when she joined the MOVE organization, the system attacked her bitterly for what was seen as a betrayal of her white-skinned privilege. On May 13, 1985, she lost her only son because the Philadelphia police bombed the house she was living in. She served over a decade in prison where the guards vilely taunted her in the hours and days after the bombing. When she came out, she went right to work to rebuild the MOVE organization in Philadelphia. She lives her life deliberately by promoting John Africa's revolution each and every day. Except for that choice, she's just like you.

Now, some of you are sure to be wondering, "Well, if this guy's gig is with revolutionaries, why is he saying this to us?" The answer of course is "Why not?" Okay, I know you ain't supposed to answer a question with a question, but do I expect you guys and gals who've just received your degrees to chuck it all for so nebulous a concept as revolution? Nope. I ain't that dumb. The great historians Will and Ariel Durant teach us that history in the large is the conflict of minorities. The majority applauds the victor and supplies the human material of social experiment. Now, I take that to mean that social movements are begun by relatively small numbers of people who, as catalysts, inspire, provoke, and move larger numbers to see and share their vision. Social movements can then become social forces that expand our perspectives, open up new social possibilities, and create the consciousness for change.

To begin this process, we must first sense that (1) the status quo is wrong, and (2) the existing order is not amenable to real, meaningful, and substantive transformation. Out of the many here assembled, it is the heart of he or she that I seek who looks at a life of vapid materialism, of capitalist excess, and finds it simply intolerable. It may be one hundred of you, or fifty, or even ten, or even one of you who makes that choice. I'm here to honor and applaud that choice and to [tell] you that, though the suffering may indeed be great, it is nothing [compared] to the joy of doing the right thing.

Malcolm, Dr. Huey P. Newton, Ramona Africa, the MOVE Nine, Dr. Alan Berkman, Susan Rosenberg, John Brown, Susan Africa, Marilyn Buck, Geronimo ji Jaga, Leonard Peltier, Angela Davis, and others, all of them people just like you, felt compelled to change the conditions they found intolerable. I urge you to join that noble tradition.

I thank you all, and wish you well. On the MOVE. Long live John Africa.

From Death Row, this is Mumia Abu-Jamal.

Note

Delivered on June 1, 1999 as the Evergreen State College Commencement Address, "A Life Lived, Deliberately" was originally published in *Radical Philosophy Review*, Vol. 3, No. 1 (2000): 41–45.

IV. Dialogues in Resistance
(Interviews)

19

Charles Baxter, Wayne Brown, Tony Chatman-Bey, H. B. Johnson Jr., Mark Medley, Donald Thompson, Selvyn Tillett, and John Woodland Jr. (with Drew Leder)

Charles Baxter was born in 1960, in South Baltimore, as the oldest of three boys. He spent his early years engaged in criminal activity and was incarcerated for first-degree murder and handgun violations. Baxter entered prison with only a fourth-grade reading level, but has spent his sentence of life plus ten years obtaining a BS in business sciences. He is also an imam of the Sunni Muslim religion.

Wayne Brown was born in 1958, into a family of eleven children, which was held together by his mother and aunt. He was convicted of rape and is serving a life term, but maintains his innocence. A devoted Christian with a theological degree, Brown is studying for ordination.

Tony Chatman-Bey, born in 1959, was raised in Beaumont, Texas, by his grandmother. He was jailed for two counts of armed robbery when he was twenty-two, but enrolled in college and worked three jobs after serving his five-year sentence. Later, he was incarcerated for robbery and rape (he alleges that the rape charges stemmed from a case of mistaken identity). Chatman-Bey is serving a life-plus-twenty-years sentence and has completed a double degree in psychology and criminal justice.

H. B. Johnson Jr. was born in 1946, into a strict Baptist home. He rebelled against his minister father, engaging in armed robbery and drug use. Johnson Jr. was incarcerated for short terms until he shot an employee in an insurance agency robbery. Johnson Jr. entered prison with an eighth-grade education, yet became a nationally recognized writer during his incarceration. He won the WMAR-TV Black Playwrights contest in 1992 and 1994, was profiled on the *Today Show*, and was twice recognized by PEN (Poets, Playwrights, Essayists, Editors, Novelists). Contracting HIV through a dirty needle while in prison, he died in 1996 from complications from AIDS.

Drew Leder, MD, PhD, is a professor of Eastern and Western philosophy at Loyola College in Maryland. He has authored *Games for the Soul: 40 Playful Ways to Find Fun and Fulfillment in a Stressful World, Spiritual Passages: Embracing Life's Sacred Journey*, and *The Absent Body*.

Mark Medley was born in 1954. He is serving two life sentences without parole for murder. Medley studies ancient civilizations.

Donald Thompson was born in 1957. An exemplary student as a child, Thompson changed at age twelve when his father was murdered. Convicted for armed robbery, attempted murder, and murder in the first degree, he is serving a life-plus-100-years sentence and has converted to Islam. Thompson has completed a degree in management science during his incarceration, and a 12-step program to overcome his previous heroin habit.

Selvyn Tillett was born in 1960, in the country of Belize. Although raised as a Jehovah's Witness, he became involved in crime. While serving a life sentence plus twenty years, he has pursued his college degree. A poet, essayist, and editor of a prison journal, Tillett is a Muslim and Black Nationalist.

John Woodland was born in 1956 into a professional African American family. After the premature deaths of both his parents during his teenage years, Woodland began selling drugs. He was attending Morgan State University, and had been accepted to law school, when he was convicted of first-degree murder related to drugs. While serving a life sentence, he has obtained a degree in management science and directed Project Turnaround, which counsels "at-risk" young men; he also tutors and teaches within the Muslim prison community.

References

Bowler, Mike. "Death Before Probation." *Baltimore Sun,* March 29, 1996, 19A.
Leder, Drew. "Live from the Panopticon: Architecture and Power Revisited." *Lingua Franca* (July/August 1993): 30–35.
————, et al. *The Soul Knows No Bars: Inmates Reflect on Life, Death, and Hope.* Lanham, MD: Rowman and Littlefield, 1999.

Live from the Panopticon: Architecture and Power Revisited 1993

The following transcript is drawn from class discussions in a philosophy course that Drew Leder, a professor at Loyola College in Maryland, teaches on a volunteer basis at the maximum-security Maryland State Penitentiary. The course began with questions of justice and imprisonment, suffering and liberation. The students discussed the crippled slave Epictetus's stoic approach to adversity, the sufferings of Christ, the trial of Socrates, the Book of Job, and Martin Luther King Jr.'s "Letter from Birmingham Jail." More recently, they have turned to non-Western traditions, studying the *Tao Te Ching,* Indian Hinduism, the shamans of Bali, and various African philosophies. The following excerpts are taken from two class sessions [in which] the topics at hand were prison architecture and what Leder calls the phenomenology of confined space. The reading assignments were Joseph Kupfer's essay, "Architecture: Building the Body Politic" (from *Social Theory and Practice*) and Michel Foucault's *Discipline and Punish: The Birth of the Prison.*[1]

◆ ◆ ◆

Drew Leder: Let me just run through a few central points of the first article. When Joseph Kupfer uses the term "architecture," he means buildings, structures, the spaces within buildings, streets, courtyards, the whole laying out of a city or building or prison.

The first point is that architecture helps determine the individual's sense of autonomy, which means something like freedom, power, the ability to control one's own life. The second is that architecture is crucial in determining the possibility of social interactions because, after all, as an individual, you only have so much freedom or power unless you associate with others and form communities to accomplish things in the world.

I was thinking that what we might do in class, instead of just focusing on the examples that Kupfer uses, like malls or classrooms, is to talk a little bit about how that plays out in a prison setting, possibly also in a kind of a street setting—an inner-city street or where we grew up.

John Woodland: Two things come to mind. One is that in prison the structure is designed to control, to be able to separate one part of the prison from another part. You can lock a tier down, you can lock a section of the jail down, you can lock part of a yard down, without interfering with other operations in the jail. The design is in cubicles, which makes it easier for prison authorities to have control. One thing I noticed when I first came to the penitentiary is that the penitentiary design is similar to the high-rise projects in West Baltimore or East Baltimore or wherever. In prisons it's the tiers; in the projects it's different floors. You have this limited space between a fence and where you live, and the room that you live in is also kind of confined—you know, big enough for maybe a couple of people. In prison, the cell is not really big enough for one person, but they put two in there. Same thing with projects—they're not big enough for entire families, but they put entire families in there.

It seems like they tried to make as efficient a use of space as possible. It's just enough room to live in. No more. Nothing for relaxation. Nothing for feeling comfortable. Just enough room to live in.

H. B. Johnson Jr.: Some people say that the prison question is a political question; some say it's a social question; some say it's an economic question. But at the hem of all three is the question of size. When we drive by a church, we may not think about it, but it dwarfs us. Drive by a prison and it's the same thing, plus a sense of fear, apprehension, revulsion—even, with some people, shame—and submission to a power outside of yourself.

When you drive past this building on the street, and you see the barbed wire, the tall wall, and you think of all the horror stories you've heard about the place, then you know you don't want to go in there. And if you drive a little farther down the street and you see an old Gothic structure, a church, and you've just passed this penitentiary, which is also a Gothic structure, it creates a relationship in your mind.

They're both symbols of authority, one being an authority that protects you from the bad guy and the other being an authority that's supposed to protect you from yourself.

Woodland: I want to look at this other aspect: the projects in the inner cities. It seems to me like the U.S. government is trying through these structures to control us. Because wherever you go, east or west, you see African Americans and low-income people packed in on top of one another, with no real space. When you walk down the streets of most inner cities, you feel indifference to everything: "This isn't really part of me. I'm just existing here. This is not something I should care about or protect or build up. This is something I gotta deal with until I get out." I guess that's the same way we look at prison. There's nothing in this building that we particularly care about or we think is precious or should be taken care of.

Leder: One of the points Kupfer makes in his essay is that to really form a bunch of individuals into a community, you need a public space. One of the ways to maintain political power over people is to prevent that from happening, to keep people isolated in cells or in housing projects. Also, as Kupfer says, if you don't have that kind of public space, you don't have any sense of the value or worth of your community, so it can lead to things like vandalism or throwing your garbage on the street because you don't feel the public space is your home, your place.

Donald Thompson: I agree the community should be structured so as to bring people together. By bringing them together you create a sort of political power. All right. But at the same time, there's a kind of trick hidden there. An example is the courtyard in the projects in Baltimore, which has all the doors, all the houses facing each other. But instead of giving people some sort of common power, it actually takes power away from them. When they come in and out, people can see them. The people in the project town houses that I have been around, they talk all day about how Miss So-and-So is sittin' at her window watchin' and waitin' to see who Miss Sally comes in with. And they end up using the back door.

Leder: So part of having autonomy is not only having a public space where you can come together with others but also having some privacy where you can be protected from the gazes of others.

Several Voices: Privacy. Exactly. Uh-huh.

Woodland: There's a degree of privacy, I think, that everybody needs and must have. In prison the degree of privacy you have also determines the degree of safety you feel that you have. If I'm in a single cell, I can lock the door and lay down and I'm cool. The only time I feel threatened is if the door's open. Then I know that I have to be on my toes. But if I'm in a cell with another person, and me and this person aren't friends—I don't really know him, we don't get along—then I'm not as relaxed because I don't know when I'm going to have to get up to deal with this guy. He might bring a personal problem in here or touch some of my private property or be on my food and I have to deal with him about that.

Thompson: In the yard and in the dining room, you are always around a lot of people. You may just want to socialize with one or two at a time, but you'll always find yourself in a situation where—even though it may be people you like and would want to talk to later—you're literally forced to say "Hi!" all day long. That's because the yard is the main thoroughfare. Just sitting right here, right now, I'm around the people I want to be around at this time, talking about things I want to talk about. I can really feel a sense of power. As soon as I walk out into that yard, that power is gone.

Johnson Jr.: You don't even have a sense of control over your speech. Since I've been in here, my speech has been affected, because I always have to hurry up and say something. And I'm a person who likes to think things out before he speaks.

A guard walks in to announce that the second prisonwide head-count of the day will take place shortly and that the class must adjourn.

Tony Chatman-Bey: That's exactly the point. You sit here, and you're beginning to get something, and boom!—*he* comes through the door. You've got five minutes. You're doing something that you want to do, that may help you, that in the long run may even help them; because if you're more in tune and relaxed, you're going to make their job easier. But you've got to do everything you've got to do, and you've got to stick it into a two-and-a-half-hour click.

Woodland: Another thing about the architecture of the building that has an effect on me, and maybe on other people: It makes you loud. You've got to holler because it seems like you've always gotta talk over somebody or talk to somebody at a distance or that there's something separating you from that person. It kind of makes you feel different than normal, I mean from everyday people.

Leder: It sounds like there's a way in which the structure makes people feel so powerless, they almost have to exaggerate any attempt to protect personal power—like talking loudly or being a badass or whatever.

Wayne Brown: I was going to say, when we were comparing the jail to the church, that I'd compare the jail to a school. In school you got the principal and the assistant principal; here you got the warden and the assistant warden. It's just like the classroom setup. They're always keeping you looking at the teacher, just like in here, when you come out of the cell, they're always keeping you looking at the officers. And the officers work for the warden and assistant warden and so forth. And no matter what you do you need to ask the officer for keys, just like when you come inside the school, you have to stop at the desk. You're always seeing that teacher who's there to try to correct you and try to guide you.

Leder: It's a perfect lead-in for our next session's reading, because Michel Foucault will say the same essential structure of discipline is used in the school, the prison, the church, the hospital, the psychiatric unit, the factory, etcetera.

◆ ◆ ◆

Leder: In the reading for today, Michel Foucault talks about some of the primary tactics that these disciplinary institutions use. The first one he talks about is the examination. These might be the examinations you'd take at school, or they could be putting soldiers or prisoners on inspection. Or it could be a factory foreman keeping his eye on his workers, seeing how much they produced that day.

He says there are a number of things that come out of an examination. One is that everybody has to be visible. Everybody is kept under surveillance. So, for example, if I were running a real course for credit here and I started to get the sense that you weren't doing the reading, I'd say, "Okay, students, take out a piece of paper. Now explain to me Foucault's notion of a panopticon." By making you take that examination, I would render visible what you have been doing for the past week, when I haven't been able to see you directly. I've rendered it visible by testing you and seeing what you know. So examination is compulsory; it makes you become visible and therefore disciplined.

So then Foucault asks: What is the form of architecture associated with such surveillance? Think back to when we talked about how the architecture of public spaces is a key mechanism for enacting power relations and keeping control over individuals. Foucault describes how a British philosopher named Jeremy Bentham came up with the idea of a panopticon, a building in which certain individuals can see everything, have absolutely 360–degree vision. And if you look at the picture, you can see that there is a kind of central control tower in the middle where you have a guard or a warden, somebody keeping surveillance, and then surrounding the central tower are the prisoners' cells arrayed in a circle.

It's an architectural setup for the kinds of disciplinary mechanisms that we were talking about when we talked about the examination. You have that structure of compulsory visibility, because everyone in the cell knows that they can constantly be seen by whomever is in the control tower. The light is sort of coming in from behind the prisoners so they're visible, silhouetted, but, inversely, the prisoners can't see into the central control tower. Why would that be important? That the people inside can see out but the prisoners can't see in?

Selvyn Tillett: So they don't really know when they're being watched. They have the sense that the guard or the warden may actually be looking in a different direction, but the prisoners don't know for sure when they're being observed. That in itself might keep them from doing something, trying to escape or whatever.

Woodland: Even in this prison—you might not notice this—but the chief of security's office sits right up here in the corner of the facility. And if he wants to stand and look out his window and look down at the yard, he cannot have a total view of the yard but about 50, 65 percent of it covered. He can sit there and monitor individuals' activity: *What's this guy doing over there on that bench? Who are those two sitting together, and why are they sitting together? Are these two getting ready to start a fight?* And from there he can get on the walkie-talkie: "Check those guys out." And nobody in the yard is aware that this man is sitting up at the window and giving instructions.

Leder: The privilege of being in power is that you get to be invisible, whereas the people subject to the power are made visible.

Thompson: I wasn't really aware of that window until I came off lockup one day and the security chief called me into his office. When I went in there first thing I did is look out at everything. And I thought, in retrospect, about the times I was in the yard trying to get into the kitchen and the officer was sweating me, pressing me about how I wasn't supposed to go in there. I couldn't understand why. I mean, I was just trying to get something small, a milk or some cereal, and this officer was going crazy. Then, after I went in, she shook me down, she knew I didn't have anything. But now, after I've been in the security chief's office, I see that the officers know how much of the yard the chief can see. And as a result of that, they apply more pressure and act out roles they wouldn't normally act out.

Leder: In a panopticon, not only are the prisoners under surveillance but somebody might be watching the guards as well, all the employees of the institution.

Thompson: I was also thinking about the visiting booth. That's like a panopticon. Not only is it structured like a panopticon, but it has three or four mirrors in it that the officers sit behind. So when I go in there for a visit, I'm very self-conscious, even though I know most of the officers who work here and I know they will not really watch me unless I do something to stand out for some reason. But, still, I'm conscious of them. When my son comes in, or my family, they may touch me, and that's frowned upon. These officers, they won't write you a ticket; they'll just tell you, "Don't do that!" But I'm so conscious of them that I'll hold back from my son. When the kid will try to touch or play, I'll hold back. It'll take a while before I, like, interact, and even once I begin to interact, I'm still conscious of that officer. And I can look up and see the mirror, but I don't see the officer. The officer may not even be paying attention to me. He may be watching somebody else. And most of the people who're visiting me, I like to touch, whether they're male or female or my kid. I'm a touchy kind of guy. But my hands are tied. As a matter of fact, I'll hold my hands on the counter, and as soon as I see someone reaching for them I'll look to the officer—automatically.

Johnson Jr.: When you asked how the theme of the panopticon plays out in this particular prison, I immediately thought about what Foucault said about the docile subordinate creature that they try to turn a human being into, and I began to think that it's no longer just by way of an architectural structure. Human beings serve the same purpose. You have more informers in the prison system today than ever before, because it's more widely accepted today than it used to be. There was a time when being an informer was considered totally corrupt. But now it's acceptable. It's not even necessary to build a guard tower in the center of this particular yard, because there are so many informers. Some of them do it simply because they don't have anything else to talk about. They don't have any ideas handy, so they start talking about people. You've heard the expression "Big men talk about ideas. Little men talk about each other." The human being becomes a machine, serving the same purpose as that guard tower serves.

Another weapon used to promote and sustain docility in prisoners is the kind of ticket that they put into your record that keeps you from getting transferred out of here. Even if it's for something like oversleeping. Say you've never had a ticket in ten years and you're going up tomorrow and everything is in place. You're getting ready to get transferred out of here or make parole, and then somebody comes around and gives you a ticket. Perhaps you were sick all night last night, so you overslept a little bit this morning. You were supposed to make count at the house and you didn't make it, and the guard comes along and gives you a ticket for it. Then, when you go up for your transfer hearing or your parole hearing, you're turned down because of this ticket. And they will overemphasize this ticket. They will take this ticket, which was given to you on your darker day, and they will use it like a scouring pad during the entire interview, rubbing away all of your brighter days over that five- or ten-year period. That's how you get your docility.

Thompson: Well, I want to talk about some other psychological aspects of the panopticon. When I first came here, I was very violent. It didn't take much for me to strike another person—with a baseball bat, a brick, a gun. Since I've been in here, I've had one fight. I haven't been that violent. I think the effect of knowing that I'm being watched and that somebody's going to tell has acted in a way to make me control that violence. I think the fact that I'm in a panopticon, that I'm visible and that if I do something, somebody is going to see it, served as a control mechanism. At first. As time went on, it became a kind of discipline. It helped me discipline myself. My intellect eventually kicked in.

Tillett: Different people might react to it differently. Some might rebel. Some might submit to it, like you did. It all depends on how the person reacts. It might reform people, or it might break them.

Woodland: It becomes your third eye. You become very crafty. You can time the times when the police walk their shifts at night. If you want to do something, you become familiar enough with the routine around here to know, well, I got fifteen minutes or I got an hour before someone's going to come by my cell. Being observed like this can enhance your ability to observe. Most of us who came to prison didn't know how to observe people the way we do now.

Mark Medley: I would say that in a total panopticon environment, where you're virtually under twenty-four-hour surveillance, like at the new prison they've built in Jessup, Maryland, one way a man can resist the reforming idea of this system—the sort of feedback where the panopticon simulates the person's consciousness—is with autistic thinking, or total absorption in fantasy for an extended period of time. A person can just absorb themselves in creating a fantasy, can say, "I'm building an island, and this is what my island will look like, and this is what my water source will be, and these are the kinds of plants or fruits I'll have on my island." It's like a resting period for the mind, almost like sleep, but it can be used in a sense to resist being conditioned.

Charles Baxter: I was in the Supermax [super maximum-security prison], and a lot of the brothers in there escape by doing a lot of reading and studying. A lot of them read African history or the Bible or the Koran. So they realize they're being watched, but that way they don't have to deal with the prison setting. They deal with something that gives them some hope, inspiration, motivation, some type of stability.

Johnson Jr.: I think the way to escape is by living the kind of life where you feel that you don't have anything to hide. You don't care whether the state's looking at you or not—you've done nothing wrong.

Woodland: I have to agree. One of the ways they have of monitoring a person in prison is urinalysis—what they call a piss test—to determine if you've been using any drugs. When I was using drugs at one time, that piss test was one of my greatest fears. I'd get high, and then I'd say: "Wow! I've been high twenty-four hours. If they don't come piss me in two days or forty-eight hours, I'm safe—I don't have to worry about it." But for that period of time, I was in a state of anxiety. I didn't want anybody to see my eyes, my dilated pupils, because I was in a position where all I needed was a piss test and I was gone. So I came to the realization that, man, you got to stop playing games with yourself and with these people. Leave this stuff alone.

And, now, because I don't do drugs, I laugh at them when they come and try to bother me. It makes me feel a lot better as a person. You know what I'm saying: Man, you're not doing anything wrong, so you got nothing to fear.

Johnson Jr.: You really burst their bubble when they come after you and there's nothing there for them to catch you on.

Leder: I do hear a lot of people say that if you're not doing anything wrong, at least according to the institution and according to yourself, you can relax. They can't get anything out of you, and in a way you have a certain power because they can't get a hold of you.

But I think Foucault would also say that that is the way that the institution also operates most effectively, because if they can really get people like John, for instance, to say: "I better go clean, so I can relax about the piss test," they've gotten you to internalize the standards of discipline. There are certain values, like getting off drugs or not behaving violently, that you can internalize in a positive sense as a part of your own self-discipline. But there are other values that I'm hearing are negative because they are turning humans into something machinelike.

Thompson: Or lower. You have to ask: What are the goals of the administration? Was it actually their goal to get this man to stop using, or was it their goal to do something else, or don't they care? Or maybe they want him to stay on the drugs but they want to use the piss test to control him in another way—for placement from one cell to another, from here to Supermax or lockup, for instance, so they can use his cell for another individual.

Woodland: A lot of times they play musical chairs with the cells because they don't have enough space. Some of us get phony tickets. We get sent to high security not because we did anything wrong but because they need cells. They've got guys in a punishment situation who finished their punishment; they're coming back so they need cells to bring them back to. So they got to move us out. A lot of times we see these fool games they play, and we say, "Man, these people, what they're doing is a joke." There's nothing reformist or anything else about what's going on in this prison.

Medley: It's just that they have to liquidate their inventory as a matter of storage space.

Several Voices: Yeah, yeah, that's right. That's it exactly.

Woodland: There's human beings in here

Notes

Originally published in *Lingua Franca* (July/August 1993): 30–35. The biographical introduction to the interview is an edited and revised summary taken from *Lingua Franca*.

1. Michel Foucault, *Discipline and Punish: The Birth of the Prison* (New York: Vintage, 1979); Joseph Kupfer, "Architecture: Building the Body Politic," *Social Theory and Practice*, Vol. 2, No. 3 (Fall 1985).

20

On Prisons and Prisoners
(with Leslie DiBenedetto)
1997

Angela Y. Davis

Leslie DiBenedetto: In *If They Come in the Morning*,[1] there is a discussion on defining political prisoners: Can you talk about that and also bring the discussion to today? What is different? What is the same?

Angela Davis: That's a really good question because during that period in the late 1960s, the early 1970s, the discussion around what counted as a political prisoner was very widespread. There were some who argued that political prisoners were only those who were in prison directly as a result of political beliefs or political activities. At the other end of the spectrum there were those who argued that virtually everyone in prison, particularly people of color and poor people, were political prisoners because their imprisonment was a function of a system of political repression as well as of economic exploitation and racist repression. As I think about that debate today I realize it was important not so much in its effort to arrive at a specific definition, but its importance resided more in the way we were grappling to understand the prison system as a whole. Out of that debate and the activism associated with it, the prison movement arose; we began to develop a vocabulary that allowed us to talk about the way in which state repression was centralized in the prison system. Eventually this movement gave rise to abolitionist strategies—radical notions of abolishing the prison system in its present form. But at the same time with respect to the actual effort to arrive at a definition of what counted as a political prisoner we did come up with different categories, including, of

---

Angela Y. Davis's biographical sketch appears on page 99; Leslie DiBenedetto is Chair of the Pelican Bay Committee of California Prison Focus, a San Francisco-based human rights group that advocates for the elimination of control unit prisons.

course, those who were in prison as a direct result of their political activities. And then because of intervention by people like George Jackson [see interview with George Jackson, this volume] we recognized that we had to take into account the fact that, particularly during that period, large numbers of prisoners were becoming politicized; they had become politically conscious while they were in prison and were subjected to another layer of repression precisely because of their politics. George Jackson was the most dramatic figure in that respect. Because of the connection with people who had sometimes spent long periods of time in prison and their efforts to analyze the conditions of their lives in prison, we came up with new ideas of how to engage in struggle around prison issues and relate those issues to the larger construct of racism and economic exploitation. By the time my own trial was over, a number of us established the National Alliance Against Racist and Political Repression [NAARPR]. There were a number of tasks within the organization that specifically addressed this issue. NAARPR was an attempt to keep people together that were working around my case as well as people who were working around other cases and political prisoners across the country. Work around political prisoners tended to be of an ad hoc character, which meant that if the person was in fact released then the committee disintegrated. Our effort was designed to keep all of the people who had gathered experiences in doing the work together so that we would not have to start from scratch each time we took on a case. Some of the first cases we took on were those of Reverend Ben Chavis and the Wilmington Ten, Lolita Lébron and the Puerto Rican Nationalists, and cases, including Leonard Peltier's, arising out of the occupation of Wounded Knee.[2] Ben Chavis was one of the founders of the organization, in 1973. As I think about it now I realize that this history has not been documented. Someone should take on that project. The organization still exists, by the way, but it is rather small. The headquarters are in Las Vegas, and there are active chapters in several states, but it is not really a national organization at this point.

DiBenedetto: How do you feel about the way we define and mobilize around political prisoners today; have things changed? Do we have a George Jackson?

Davis: There is a widespread international movement around the case of Mumia Abu-Jamal.[3] And I think it is important that we locate his case on a continuum of historical struggles around political prisoners. And of course activism around political prisoners did not originate in the 1960s. Before the efforts to free the Black Panthers there were the campaigns to save the lives of the Rosenbergs and Sacco and Vanzetti.[4] There was the campaign to defend the black communist Angelo Herndon and the international movements to save the lives of the Scottsboro Nine.[5] So we have a very long history of activist campaigns around political prisoners and against political repression. What was so striking about the period of the late 1960s and the early 1970s is the way in which the connection between political prisoners and the prison as a state apparatus of repression emerged. In the case of Mumia, of course, the focus is on the death penalty. Given the passionate and extensive activism around his case, we should be able to save his life. At the same time I hope that people's awareness about the fascistic character of the death penalty will be elevated. The Puerto Rican political prisoners and prisoners of war have received widespread support throughout the world. Even though we still have a lot of work to do in this country to popularize the campaign to free them, all over the world people are aware of the fact that there is a large group of Puerto Rican people in prison only because of their efforts to challenge the United States as a colonial power. I just read some literature about a conference that is happening soon in Cuba around the Puerto Rican prisoners. Of course there is a silence imposed here that continues to reflect the U.S. government's contention that there are no political prisoners. During the 1960s and 1970s, when there were popular movements to free political prisoners, the government insisted that everyone who was in prison was there because he or she was a criminal. At the same time we were arguing that despite the government's attempt to present a face to the world that the United States has no political prisoners, that was not the case. I think that argument is as strong today as it was then. What is different today is that the movement, as powerful as it is and as dedicated as many individuals are, does not have the same popular presence in the country today as it did then. Almost everyone knew about Huey Newton, Bobby Seale. And almost everyone knew about my case.[6] The political arena has substantively changed in the sense that there often tends to be a merging of conservative and so-called liberal ideas. There is an increasing class stratification, particularly in black communities and other communities of color and this has helped to create in part a presence of political conservatism in those communities that was not nearly as strong twenty-five years ago. The fall of the socialist countries—I'm speaking in very broad strokes here—has led to a kind of vacuum with respect to the enemies against which the nation tended to construct, so there is no longer a communist enemy, but there is the criminal who is constructed as the overall enemy. There is the immigrant, the welfare mother. So ideologically there have been very important changes that make it much more difficult to organize in the way that people were able to organize twenty-five years ago. Twenty-five years ago when crime was mentioned by the president or law and order was evoked, vast numbers understood that as a code word for racism, for repression. Today, [President Bill] Clinton, who is considered to be a liberal, deploys this notion and people aren't able to decode it in the same way.

DiBenedetto: You have been speaking about the notion of a prison industrial complex in the United States—briefly, what is the "PIC"? Why is it important?

Davis: First of all, I should acknowledge the fact that I encountered the term first in an article written by Mike Davis.[7] He argued that prison and the whole correctional industry were beginning to compete with agribusiness, particularly in the rural areas of California. John Irwin and James Austin in their book, *It's About Time: America's Imprisonment Binge*, use the term "correctional industrial complex." I think that many people have been trying to grapple with the way in which the punishment industry not only has expanded in a way that is clearly out of control, but that the penal infrastructure has connections with corporations on a whole number of levels.

Even during the period when the economy was experiencing a difficult time, there was a boom in prison construction. There is the privatization of prisons and multinational corporations, like the Correctional Corporation of America, which own and operate prisons not only in the United States, but in Australia and the United Kingdom. So the globalization of capital that is the economic characteristic of this era is also revealed in the way in which the prison industry is expanding. Then also there is a way in which prison labor is used not only in private prisons but in state-controlled prisons. The insinuation of private companies into state and federal prisons allows them increasingly to exploit prison labor. So the flight of capital toward ever-cheaper sources of labor is what has attracted some of these corporations to prison labor. When you combine these developments with the astounding rise in the numbers of people who are being sent to prison it becomes clear that the corporate structure has a material stake in the proliferation of imprisoned populations. These are some of the reasons it makes sense today to speak of a prison industrial complex. I should point out that the number of women being sent to prison is increasing at a greater rate than the number of men.

As I researched the expansion of the prison infrastructure, I discovered that as far as the state and federal prisons are concerned, between 1990 and 1995, 280,000 new beds were created and 213 prisons were added. And that actually represented a 41 percent increase in prison capacity. This is over a period of five years. And if you look at the number of people employed by these facilities from the same census, the Bureau of Justice Statistics, in 1995, 327,320 people were employed by state and federal prisons. In 1990 there were 264,201. Two-thirds were in custodial positions. And of course, when we are talking about this vast and expanding complex we should also include the county jails. In 1994 there were 9.8 million admissions to 3,300 jails; Irwin and Austin, in their book *It's About Time: America's Imprisonment Binge,* calculate that one out of every twenty-five adults goes to jail every year. And then of course we all know the information from the Sentencing Project regarding the fact that one-third of young black men are in prison or under the direct control of the criminal justice system.[8] Black women constitute the largest portion of women in prison. There are many more horrendous facts about the expansion of the penal system. What I would like to say, however, is that it is important to popularize the notion of an industrial complex so that people begin to understand that the stakes in the prison system are not just the ideological stakes that are represented in the wars against crime but that there are very material stakes. Corporations have economic stakes in the continuation of this mammoth prison industry because it becomes a source of profit, it becomes a source of jobs, in very much the same way the military has functioned historically. I would argue that just as we learned during the early 1970s to talk about a military industrial complex, we should learn in the latter 1990s to talk about a prison industrial complex. We appropriated the term "military industrial complex" from [President Dwight D.] Eisenhower and gave it a radical meaning.[9] The popularization of the notion of a prison industrial complex today will help to develop a contemporary radical political culture and will perhaps help to encourage people to identify with movements for radical change.

DiBenedetto: Your recent work has focused on women in prison. Why is this focus so important? Can you tell us about your work in countries outside of the United States?

Davis: A few years ago I decided that I wanted to integrate issues of women in prison in my research and I began to do a long-term project with Kum-Kum Bhavnani, who teaches at UC-Santa Barbara and is a former prison activist from England. Initially we decided we wanted to interview women in California to find out how the women thought about possibilities of alternatives to imprisonment. Our project is an abolitionist project in the larger sense. Historically prisoners have rarely been able to participate in debates about penal reform or even penal abolitionism. We decided initially to interview women in California prisons. We particularly wanted to do our fieldwork in the California Institute for Women. As it turns out they denied me entrance into the prison. As a matter of fact, I haven't been able to get into any California state prison at this point. So we decided to interview women in the San Francisco county jail, many of whom had been to prison or were going to prison. After publishing an article about these interviews, we decided to expand the project into a comparative, transnational examination of women in prison. We chose to visit a women's prison in the Netherlands because the Dutch penal system is considered to be the most progressive system in the industrialized capitalist world. We also chose Cuba because of the fact that Cuba is socialist and we wanted to see what was different about prisons in a socialist society. At this point we have completed all our interviews and have begun to work on a book. I can say that the last set of interviews in Cuba were so interesting and different from those in the other two countries, even as the set of interviews we did in the Netherlands was radically different from the ones we did here. What characterized the women in Cuba was the lack of the alienation we almost always associate with prison and the lack of a feeling of disconnectedness with the "free world."

DiBenedetto: Can you speak about the significance of the Critical Resistance conference being planned for the fall of 1998?[10]

Davis: The Critical Resistance conference being planned for the fall of 1998 will address the range of issues connected to the prison industrial complex. We want to highlight the marginalization of women, even in prison activism. People need to learn how to talk about women in prison as they do this work and to see the assault on women as having an impact that goes far beyond the percentage of women in the incarcerated population. For example, the dismantling of the welfare system is very much related to the prison industrial complex. So, we're trying to create these public conversations and to translate them into organizing efforts.

Notes

This interview, conducted in California in September 1997, was first published in *Prison Focus,* Vol. 2, No. 1 (Fall 1997/Winter 1998) and is reprinted with permission of Leslie DiBenedetto.

1. Angela Y. Davis and Bettina Aptheker, eds., *If They Come in the Morning: Voices of Resistance* (New York, Third Press, 1971; repr. Ithaca, NY: Cornell University Press, 1999).

2. *Editor's note:* In 1971, student protests of discrimination in Wilmington, North Carolina culminated in a week-long riot. Ten protesters, including Benjamin Chavis, were arrested and sentenced to prison. Their convictions were challenged and Amnesty International declared the "Wilmington Ten" political prisoners. Eventually, the convictions were overturned (Kate Tuttle, *Africana: Encyclopedia of the African and African American Experience*, eds. Kwame Anthony Appiah and Henry Louis Gates Jr. [New York: Basic Books, 1999, boxed ed.], 413).

Since the seizure of Puerto Rico by the United States government from Spain in 1898, Puerto Rican independence fighters, who contend they are fighting an independence war against a colonial power, have come into direct conflict with the U.S. military and justice establishment. Lolita Lébron and three men attacked the

U.S. House of Representatives on March 1, 1954, employing armed struggle as one component of a multifaceted revolutionary strategy. Since that time, other Puerto Rican nationalists have been imprisoned in the United States and have unsuccessfully fought to secure prisoner of war status. President Bill Clinton gave clemency to eleven Independistas in September 1999. For more information on current Puerto Rican nationalist prisoners of war, see *Can't Jail the Spirit: Political Prisoners in the U.S.,* fifth edition (Chicago: Committee to End the Marion Lockdown, 2002).

In 1975, Leonard Peltier and three other members of the American Indian Movement (AIM) were charged in the death of two FBI Special Agents. The agents were killed, along with AIM member Joe Stuntz Killsright, in a shootout on the Pine Ridge Reservation near Oglala, South Dakota, that involved more than two hundred federal troops, AIM members and Pine Ridge residents. Since AIM's ascension to national prominence several years earlier, it had become a main target of the FBI's COINTELPRO. This fact of FBI targeting of AIM, combined with questionable evidence in the state's case against Peltier and the acquittal of or dismissal of the case against the other three AIM members charged in the case based on evidence of large-scale FBI repression and misconduct, have led to an international movement of support for Peltier. The occupation of Wounded Knee to which Davis refers took place in early 1973 at the historically significant site of the 1890 massacre on the Pine Ridge Reservation. Although several AIM members were tried on charges connected to the Wounded Knee occupation (all of these charges were eventually dropped), Peltier was in fact not charged in this incident, and his indictment in the Pine Ridge shootout was not directly related to the Wounded Knee occupation. For more information on Peltier's case, on the history of AIM, and on the history of FBI repression of Native Americans, see *Can't Jail the Spirit: Political Prisoners in the U.S.,* fifth edition (Chicago: Committee to End the Marion Lockdown, 2002); Leonard Peltier, *Prison Writings: My Life is My Sun Dance,* ed. Harvey Arden (New York: St. Martin's, 1999); Peter Matthiessen, *In the Spirit of Crazy Horse* (New York: Viking Penguin, 1992); *Incident at Oglala,* with Robert Redford (Van Nuys, CA: Carolco Home Video, 1992), videocassette; Ward Churchill and Jim Vander Wall, *Agents of Repression: The FBI's Secret War Against the Black Panther Party and the American Indian Movement* (Boston: South End Press, 1988); Ward Churchill and Jim Vander Wall, *The COINTELPRO Papers: Documents From the FBI's Secret Wars Against Domestic Dissent* (Boston: South End Press, 1990); Paul Chaat Smith and Robert Allen Warrior, *Like a Hurricane: The Indian Movement from Alcatraz to Wounded Knee* (New York: The New Press, 1996); and Rolland Dewing, *Wounded Knee: The Meaning and Significance of the Second Incident* (New York: Irvington Publishers, 1985).

3. *Editor's note:* Mumia Abu-Jamal, former Black Panther and award-winning Philadelphia journalist, has been incarcerated since 1981. He was convicted in the death of a Philadelphia police officer and originally sentenced to death. Since his conviction (his past political activity figured prominently in the proceedings and the court appointed attorney he was assigned against his wishes was unprepared and failed to even refute basic inconsistencies), he has continued to maintain his innocence. His case has received international support from diverse sectors and he

has become an international *cause cèlébre* of the antideath penalty movement. For biography and references for Abu-Jamal, see chapter 18 in this work.

4. *Editor's note:* Ethel and Julius Rosenberg, members of the Communist Party USA, were convicted of espionage in 1951. An international campaign in support of the couple failed, and they were executed in 1953. Nicola Sacco and Bartolomeo Vanzetti were executed in Massachusetts in 1927, following a ten-year murder trial. The two men, Italian anarchists who had immigrated to the United States, were convicted despite a confession by another man that he had been involved in the murder. Supporters of Sacco and Vanzetti organized a massive campaign, decrying the conviction as politically motivated and unjust.

5. *Editor's note:* In 1932, African American communist organizer and labor leader Angelo Herndon was convicted and sentenced to twenty years of hard labor on charges of attempting to incite insurrection under an old Georgia slave insurrection law. He was arrested for leading a demonstration of African American and unemployed workers protesting cuts in relief rations, and later for possessing Communist literature. A movement on his behalf was formed by civil rights leaders and the Communist Party USA. See Charles H. Martin, *The Angelo Herndon Case and Southern Justice* (Baton Rouge: Louisiana State University Press, 1976).

In 1931, nine young African American men were charged with raping two white women in the infamous Scottsboro case. The men were given inadequate council, convicted hastily on scant evidence, and all but one were sentenced to death. The Communist Party USA's International Labor Defense (ILD) organized a massive political and legal campaign to exonerate the defendants, as part of a broader antilynching campaign. Although the legal campaign resulted eventually in only securing a lengthy plea bargain for the defendants, the case helped focus national attention on the unjust legal system of the South. In 1976, Alabama Governor George Wallace pardoned all of the nine defendants, although only one was still living at the time, and all had been released from prison by 1950. See James Haskins, *The Scottsboro Boys* (New York: Henry Holt & Company, 1994); Robin D. G. Kelley, "The Scottsboro Case," *The Encyclopedia of the American Left*, eds. Mari Jo Buhle, Paul Buhle, and Dan Georgakas (New York: Oxford University Press, 1998).

6. *Editor's note:* The cases of Bobby Seale and Huey Newton, cofounders of the Black Panther Party for Self-Defense, received national attention. Seale was involved in two high-profile cases: first in 1967, as one of more than thirty members of the BPP arrested in Sacramento, California for protesting a proposed bill that sought to outlaw the carrying of loaded guns in public; and then in May 1969, with members of the New Haven, Connecticut BPP charged with the murder of an alleged police informant. He was exonerated in both cases. Huey Newton became the national symbol of the BPP when he was arrested in 1967 for the killing of a police officer. Eventually, Newton's conviction was overturned. See Charles E. Jones, ed., *The Black Panther Party [Reconsidered]* (Baltimore: Black Classic Press, 1998). Angela Davis was imprisoned in California on false charges connected to Jonathan Jackson's use of weapons registered in her name to attempt to free two prisoners from a Marin County, California courthouse. See Bettina Aptheker, *The*

Morning Breaks: The Trial of Angela Davis (New York: International Publishers, 1975; repr. Ithaca, NY: Cornell University Press, 1999).

7. Mike Davis, "Hell Factories in the Field," *The Nation*, Vol. 260, No. 7, February 20, 1995, 229.

8. *Editor's note:* The information from the Sentencing Project to which Davis refers is most likely a report by the Sentencing Project released in 1995 entitled "Young Black Americans and the Criminal Justice System: Five Years Later," which states that "nearly one in three (32.2%) African American males in the age group 20–29—827,440—is under criminal justice supervision on any given day—in prison or jail, on probation or parole." The Sentencing Project also reports that "African American women have experienced the greatest increase in their rate of criminal justice control of all demographic groups in recent years." See The Sentencing Project, "Young Black Americans and the Criminal Justice System: Five Years Later" (Washington, D.C.: The Sentencing Project, 1995); Marc Mauer, "Young Black Americans and the Criminal Justice System," in *States of Confinement: Policing, Detention, and Prisons*, ed. Joy James (New York: Palgrave, 2000).

9. *Editor's note:* Dwight D. Eisenhower coined the term "military industrial complex" in his farewell address as President, warning against the growing collusion between and political influence of a massive arms industry and a professionalized military.

10. *Editor's note:* From the Critical Resistance website:

Critical Resistance (CR) was formed in 1997 when activists challenging the idea that incarceration is the panacea for all our social ills came together to organize a conference. The conference examined and challenged the phenomenon we have come to call the Prison Industrial Complex. Held in September 1998, the conference brought together over 3500 activists, academics, former and current prisoners, labor leaders, religious organizations, feminists, gay, lesbian and transgender activists, youth, families, and policy makers from literally every state and other countries. The three day event featured almost 200 different panels and workshops. The Conference also included a multitude of cultural events and a film festival.

In the years since the 1998 Conference, CR has continued to work building a movement of activists in opposition to the Prison Industrial Complex. A CR East conference was held in New York City in March 2001, and a CR South Conference was held in New Orleans in April 2003. See www.criticalresistance.org for more information about Critical Resistance.

21

George Jackson
(with Karen Wald)

George Jackson was born in Chicago, Illinois in 1941. Involved in frequent conflicts with police throughout his youth, Jackson was first imprisoned at age sixteen in a California Youth Authority Institution, for attempted burglary and possession of a stolen motorcycle (which he said he purchased). After his second release in September of 1960, he allegedly drove the getaway car after his friend robbed a gas station. He agreed to confess in return for a light sentence; the judge gave him one year-to-life, which became life imprisonment.

Introduced to radical philosophy by W. L. Nolen, Jackson read Marx, Lenin, Trotsky, Engels, Mao Tse-tung (Zedong), and other political theorists during his frequent solitary confinement. Jackson co-founded the Black Guerilla Family in 1968, and also served as a Field Marshall for the Black Panther Party. While in Soledad Prison in 1969, George Jackson, along with Fleeta Drumgo and John Cluchette, were indicted (despite a complete lack of physical evidence) for killing guard Opie Mills who executed Nolen and three other black inmates in the exercise yard. Attorney Fay Stender subsequently formed the Soledad Brothers Defense Committee, which eventually was headed by Angela Y. Davis, and arranged for the publication of the influential *Soledad Brother: The Prison Letters of George Jackson.*[1]

On August 7, 1970, Jackson's seventeen-year-old brother, Jonathan, entered the Marin County Courthouse—with weapons registered in the name of Angela Davis—in an attempt to bring attention to (and negotiate for the release of) his brother and the other Soledad Brothers. Law enforcement officers fired upon the parked van holding Jackson, the prisoners, and their hostages, killing Judge Harold Haley, prisoners William Christmas and James McClain, and Jonathan Jackson, and wounding prisoner Ruchell Magee and several hostages.

During an escape attempt on August 21, 1971, San Quentin guards shot George Jackson in the back of the head. The exact events of that day remain unclear. Stephen Bingham, Jackson's attorney who allegedly brought Jackson a gun on the day he was killed, eventually emerged from underground to stand trial and was acquitted in 1986.

Karen Wald, an activist-journalist who has lived in Cuba since 1973, conducted this interview as a reporter for the Liberation News Service.

227

Note

1. Fay Stender was shot in 1979, allegedly by an associate of Jackson. She committed suicide in May 1980. See Paul Liberatore, *The Road to Hell: The True Story of George Jackson, Stephen Bingham, and the San Quentin Massacre* (New York: Atlantic Monthly Press, 1996).

References

Durden-Smith, Jo. *Who Killed George Jackson?* New York: Knopf, 1976.
Jackson, George. "Toward the United Front." In *If They Come in the Morning: Voices of Resistance,* edited by Angela Y. Davis and Bettina Aptheker. San Francisco: National United Committee to Free Angela Davis, 1971.
Mann, Eric. *Comrade George: An Investigation into the Life, Political Thought, and Assassination of George Jackson.* New York: Harper & Row, 1974.

An Interview with George Jackson 1971

Karen Wald: George, could you comment on your conception of revolution?

George Jackson: The principal contradiction between the oppressor and oppressed can be reduced to the fact that the only way the oppressor can maintain his position is by fostering, nurturing, building contempt for the oppressed. That thing gets out of hand after a while. It leads to excesses that we see and the excesses are growing within the totalitarian state here.

The excesses breed resistance; resistance is growing. The thing grows in a spiral. It can only end one way. The excesses lead to resistance, resistance leads to brutality, the brutality leads to more resistance, and finally the whole question will be resolved with either the uneconomic destruction of the oppressed, or the end of oppression.

These are the workings of revolution. It grows in spirals, confrontations, and I mean on all levels. The institutions of society have buttressed the establishment, so I mean all levels have to be assaulted.

Wald: How does the prison liberation movement fit into this? Is its importance overexaggerated or contrived?

Jackson: We don't have to contrive any. . . . Look, the particular thing I'm involved in right now, the prison movement was started by Huey P. Newton and the Black Panther Party.[1] Huey and the rest of the comrades around the country. We're working with Ericka [Huggins] and Bobby [Seale],[2] the prison movement in general, the movement to prove to the establishment that the concentration camp technique won't work on us. We don't have to contrive any importance to our particular movement. It's a very real, very, very real issue and I'm of the opinion that, right along with the old, familiar workers' movement, the prison movement is central to the process of revolution as a whole.

Wald: Many of the cadres of the revolutionary forces on the outside have been captured and imprisoned. Are you saying that even though they're in prison, these cadres can still function in a meaningful way for the revolution?

Jackson: Well, we're all familiar with the function of the prison as an institution serving the needs of the totalitarian state. We've got to destroy that function; the function has to be no longer viable, in the end. It's one of the strongest institutions supporting the totalitarian state. We have to destroy its effectiveness, and that's what the prison movement is all about.

What I'm saying is that they put us in these concentration camps here the same as they put people in tiger cages or "strategic hamlets" in Vietnam.[3] The idea is to isolate, eliminate, liquidate the dynamic sections of the overall movement, the protagonists of the movement. What we've got to do is prove this won't work. We've got to organize our resistance once we're inside, give them no peace, turn the prison into just another front of the struggle, tear it down from the inside. Understand?

Wald: But can such a battle be won?

Jackson: A good deal of this has to do with our ability to communicate to the people on the street. The nature of the function of the prison within the [prison state] police state has to be continuously explained, elucidated to the people on the street because we can't fight alone in here.

Oh yeah, we can fight, but if we're isolated, if the state is successful in accomplishing that, the results are usually not constructive in terms of proving our point. We fight and we die, but that's not the point, although it may be admirable from some sort of purely moral point of view.

The point is, however, in the face of what we confront, to fight and win. That's the real objective: not just to make statements, no matter how noble, but to destroy the system that oppresses us. By any means available to us. And to do this, we must be connected, in contact and communication with those in struggle on the outside. We must be mutually supporting because we're all in this together. It's all one struggle at base.

Wald: Is the form of struggle you're talking about here different from those with which we may be more familiar with, those which are occurring in the Third World, for example?

Jackson: Not really. Of course, all struggles are different, depending upon the whole range of particular factors involved. But many of them have fundamental commonalities that are more important than the differences. We are talking about a guerrilla war in this country. The guerrilla, the new type of warrior who's developed out of conflicts in the Third World countries, doesn't fight for glory necessarily. The guerrilla fights to win. The guerrilla fights the same kind of fight we do, what's sometimes called a "poor man's war." It's not a form of war fought with high-tech weaponry, or state-of-the-art gadgets. It's fought with whatever can be had—captured weapons when they can be had, but often antiquated firearms, homemade ordinance, knives, bows and arrows, even sling-shots—but mostly through the sheer will of the guerrilla to fight and win, no matter what. Huey [P. Newton] says "the power of the people will overcome the power of the man's technology."

You know, guerrilla war is not simply a matter of tactics and tech-nique. It's not just questions of hit-and-run or terrorism. It's a matter of proving to the established order that it simply can't sustain itself, that there's no possible way for them to win by utilizing the means of force available to them. We have to prove that wars are won by human beings, and not by mechanical devices. We've got to show that in the end they can't resist us. And we will! We're going to do it! There's never going to ever be a moment's peace for anyone associated with the establishment any place where I'm at, or where any of my comrades are at. But we're going to need coordination, we're going to need help. And right now, that help should come in the form of education. It's critical to teach the people out there just how important it is to destroy the function of the prison within this society. That, and to show them in concrete terms that the war is on—right now!—and that in that sense we really aren't any different than the Vietnamese, or the Cubans, or the Algerians, or any of the other revolu-tionary peoples of the world.

Wald: In an interview with some imprisoned Tupamaros, urban guer-rillas in Uruguay, the question was raised about the decimation of the ranks of Tuparmaros; comrades killed or imprisoned by the state. Those interviewed assured me that there were far more people joining the ranks than were being lost to state repression, and that the movement was con-tinuing to grow. Do you feel the same confidence about the Black Panther Party, about the revolutionary movement as a whole in this country?

Jackson: We're structured in such a way as to allow us to exist and continue to resist despite the losses we absorb. It was set up that way. We know the enemy operates under the concept of "kill the head and the body will die." They target those they see as key leaders. We know this, and we've set up safeguards to prevent the strategy from working against us. I know I could be killed tomorrow, but the struggle would continue, there would be two hundred or three hundred people to take my place. As Fred Hampton put it, "You can kill the revolutionary, but you can't kill the rev-olution." Hampton, as you know, was head of the Party in Chicago, along with Mark Clark, the Party leader from Peoria, Illinois. Their loss is tremendous, but the struggle goes on. Right?

It's not just a military thing. It's also an educational thing. The two go hand-in-hand. And it's also a cyclical thing. Right now, we are in a peak cycle. There's tremendous energy out there, directed against the state. It's not all focused, but it's there, and it's building. Maybe this will be sufficient to accomplish what we must accomplish over the fairly short run. We'll see, and we can certainly hope that this is the case. But perhaps not. We must be prepared to wage a long struggle. If this is the case, then we'll probably see a different cycle, one in which the revolutionary energy of the people seems to have dispersed, run out of steam. But—and this is important—such cycles are deceptive. Things appear to be at low ebb, but actually what's happening is a period of regroupment, a period in which we step back and learn from the mistakes made during the preceding cycle. We educate ourselves and those around us from our experience. And all the while, we develop and perfect our core organization. Then the next time a peak cycle comes around, we are far readier than we were during the last time. . . . Ultimately, we will win.

Wald: Do you see any signs of progress on the inside, in prison?

Jackson: Yes, I do. Progress has certainly been made in terms of raising the consciousness of at least some sectors of the prison population. In part, that's due to the limited victories we've achieved over the past few years. They're token victories, perhaps, but things we can and must take advantage of.

For example, we've struggled hard around the idea of being able to communicate directly with people on the outside. At this point, any person on the street can correspond with any individual inside prison.

My suggestion is, now that we have the channels of education secured, at least temporarily, that people on the outside should begin to bombard the prisons with newspapers, books, journals, clippings, anything of educational value to help politicize the comrades who are not yet relating.

And we, of course, must reciprocate by consistently sending out information concerning what's really going on in here. Incidentally, interviews like this go a long way in that direction. There should be much more of this sort of thing.

Wald: [Inquiring to whether the life of George's younger brother, Jonathan, was wasted when he was killed on August 7, 1970 in a courtroom shoot-out.][4]

Jackson: Well, that's obviously a tough question for me because, emotionally, I very much wish my little brother was alive and well. But as to whether I think Jonathan's life may have been wasted? No, I don't.

I think the only mistake he made was thinking that all of the two hundred pigs who were there would have, you know, some sort of concern for the life of the judge. Of course, they chose to kill the judge, and to risk killing the D.A. and the jurors, in order to get at Jonathan and the others. It may have been a technical error. But I doubt it, because I know Jonathan was very conversant with military ideas, and I'm sure it occurred to him that there was a possibility that at least one pig would shoot, and that if one shot, they'd all shoot, and it'd be a massacre. Judge or no judge.

It was all a gigantic bluff, you know? Jonathan took a calculated risk. Some people say that makes him a fool. I say his was the sort of courage that cause men of his age to be awarded the Congressional Medal of Honor in somewhat different settings. The difference is that Jonathan understood very clearly who his real enemy was; the guy who gets the congressional medal usually doesn't. Now, who's the fool?

Personally, I bear his loss very badly. It's a great burden upon my soul. But I think it's imperative—we owe it to him—never to forget why he did what he did. And that was to stand as a symbol in front of the people—in front of me—and say in effect that we have both the capacity and the obligation to stand up, regardless of the consequences.

He was saying that if we all stand up, our collective power will destroy the forces that oppose us. Jonathan lived by these principles, he was true to them, he died by them. This is the most honorable thing imaginable. He achieved a certain deserved immortality insofar as he truly had the courage to die on his feet rather than live one moment on his knees. He stood as an example, a beacon to all of us, and I am in awe of him, even though he was my younger brother.

Notes

This interview with George Jackson was conducted by Karen Wald and recorded May 16, 1971 at San Quentin Prison in California. It was first broadcast on KPFA–FM, a Berkeley, California radio station. The interview was published in *Black Prison Movements USA: The NOBO Journal of African American Dialogue*, Vol. 2, No. 1 (New Jersey: Africa World Press, 1995) where it was misidentified as an interview done August 21, 1971 (the day Jackson was killed by prison guards). An edited version of the original interview was also published in the *Michigan Citizen*, Vol. 22, No. 38, August 13–19, 2000 as a Black August Memorial.

1. *Editor's note:* In May 1967, Bobby Seale and thirty other members of the Black Panther Party were arrested in Sacramento, California, for protesting a proposed California bill that sought to outlaw the carrying of loaded guns in public. (The Party, originally the Black Panther Party for Self-Defense, supported the carrying of loaded guns in public as a means to discourage the widespread police brutality against African Americans.) This confrontation catapulted the Party to national attention and attracted scores of new members in California and throughout the country. In October 1967, Huey Newton was arrested and charged with murder in the death of a police officer. Eldridge Cleaver (a former

convict and author of *Soul on Ice*) recruited Stokeley Carmichael, the former chairman of the Student Non-violent Coordinating Committee and a nationally known black power leader, and together they built a national "Free Huey" movement on behalf of their accused comrade. In September 1968, Newton was found guilty of manslaughter. His conviction was later overturned in August 1970. In the subsequent years, Party chapters were opened in prisons across the nation to politicize black prisoners (such as George Jackson). See Akinyele Omowale Umoja, "Set Our Warriors Free: The Legacy of the BPP and Political Prisoners," in *The Black Panther Party [Reconsidered]*, ed. Charles E. Jones (Baltimore: Black Classic Press, 1998).

   2. *Editor's note:* At the time of this interview, Bobby Seale was chairman of the Black Panther Party. In May 1969, he, Ericka Huggins, and twelve members of the New Haven, Connecticut chapter of the BPP, the "New Haven 14," were charged in the murder of an alleged police informant. The incarceration of these members forced the New Haven BPP to close. Although Seale and Huggins were eventually exonerated of the charges, several other New Haven defendants were convicted in the case. See Charles E. Jones, ed. *The Black Panther Party [Reconsidered]*, and Angela Y. Davis and Bettina Aptheker, eds., *If They Come in the Morning: Voices of Resistance* (New York: Third Press, 1971).

   3. *Editor's note:* "Tiger cages" were the five-feet by nine-feet cement cells of the Con Son prison in South Vietnam. The cells, built by the French in the 1940s, were used to hold political prisoners in the 1960s. See Stanley I. Kutler, ed., *Encyclopedia of the Vietnam War* (New York: Charles Scribner's Sons, 1996), 543–44. Under South Vietnamese, U.S.-supported leader Ngo Dinh Diem, U.S. Special Forces instituted the "strategic hamlet" program in 1962. The program, based on a tactic used to suppress anticolonial movement-building by the British in Malaya, relocated the South Vietnamese rural population into fortified hamlets in an attempt to stem the spread of Communist support and destroy the infrastructure of the National Liberation Front. The program created resentment and resistance among the population. See Gabriel Kolko, *Anatomy of a War: Vietnam, the United States, and the Modern Historical Experience* (New York: The New Press, 1994), 132–37.

   4. *Editor's note:* On August 7, 1970, Jonathan Jackson, George Jackson's younger brother, at age seventeen, stormed into the Marin County Courthouse in California in an attempt to free Ruchell Cinque Magee, William Christmas, and James McClain. Jackson, the prisoners, the trial judge, the prosecutor, and several jurors (whom Jackson had taken hostage) were fired upon by police and prison guards while inside a van. Jackson, McClain, Christmas and the judge were killed, the prosecutor was paralyzed for life, and Magee and the jurors were wounded but survived. See Bettina Aptheker, *Morning Breaks: The Trial of Angela Davis* (New York: International Publishers, 1975; repr. Ithaca, NY: Cornell University Press, 1999).

22

Geronimo ji Jaga (Elmer Pratt) (with Heike Kleffner)

Geronimo ji Jaga was born Elmer Pratt in 1948, into a family of Louisiana activists. Decorated Vietnam veteran and former leader in the Black Panther Party (BPP), he was imprisoned for twenty-seven years as a victim of the FBI's illegal COINTELPRO tactics. Throughout his incarceration, he maintained that he was framed for a Los Angeles murder that he did not commit, and that the State was aware of this given that it had him under surveillance in Oakland at the time of the shootings. Pratt was finally released in 1997, after winning a writ of habeas corpus in an Orange County Superior Court that threw out his conviction because prosecutors had withheld vital evidence regarding a witness who could have cleared him of the charges. In 2000, the U.S. government made a substantial financial settlement with ji Jaga for his wrongful imprisonment (although the government admits no culpability). Since his release, Geronimo ji Jaga has remained active in antiracist organizing and efforts to free political prisoners. He is the subject of Jack Olsen's biography, *Last Man Standing*.

Heike Kleffner, a journalist living and working in Berlin, profiled both Geronimo ji Jaga and Mumia Abu-Jamal for a 1993 *Race and Class* article, from which the following interview comes. (Elmer Pratt's name is spelled "ji-jaga" in the original interview; however, ji Jaga is the standard spelling.) This interview took place during Geronimo ji Jaga's second decade in prison.

References

Amnesty International. "United States of America: The Case of Elmer 'Geronimo' Pratt." New York: Amnesty International, National Office, 1998.
Baker, Karin. "Final Victory for Geronimo." *Against the Current,* Vol. 14, No. 3 (July 1999): 4.
———."The Legacy of COINTELPRO: Geronimo Pratt, Political Prisoner." *Against the Current,* Vol. 9, No. 3 (July 1994): 3–5.
Olsen, Jack. *Last Man Standing: The Tragedy and Triumph of Geronimo Pratt.* New York: Doubleday, 2000.

Pratt, Elmer Geronimo, Chris Harris and Myra Ming. *Elmer "Geronimo" Pratt: A Case of Injustice?* Los Angeles: Fox Television Stations, Inc., 1995. Videocassette.

The Black Panthers: An Interview with Geronimo ji Jaga Pratt 1992

Geronimo ji Jaga Pratt and Mumia Abu-Jamal were both members of the former Black Panther Party for Self-Defense which, from the mid-1960s to the early 1970s developed, in the ghettoes and inner cities of the United States, a revolutionary black politics. The organization, with its combination of practical social action, political self-education, and adoption of the constitutional right to bear arms, grew rapidly.

It was finally broken apart by the extensive infiltration of its local chapters, together with the virtual elimination of its leadership, who were either railroaded into jail or killed in FBI-instigated shoot-outs. Many former Panthers are still in prison on charges arising from that period; Geronimo ji Jaga Pratt served twenty-seven years in maximum-security prison before being released, because of prosecutorial misconduct.

Heike Kleffner: How did you get involved with the Black Panther Party (BPP) and what did you do before that?

Geronimo ji Jaga Pratt: I am from a small town in Louisiana, part of the national territory we feel should be liberated, and I grew up in a segregated situation. It was very much like you probably imagine a black nation to be. The situation was pretty racist, on the one hand; on the other, it was full of integrity and dignity and the pride of being a part of this community. So, I grew up witnessing lynchings and other activities that you have probably heard about, that the Ku Klux Klan performed. There was an atmosphere of fear like that, but, too, of a close-knit family—the values, the work ethic, very respectful to everyone. Eventually, I joined the U.S. army and ended up in Vietnam. This was during the '60s when a lot of change was taking place in the country. That change was interpreted to us down South in a different kind of way—because there, you grew up fighting; there was a constant state of warfare, because of the racial polarization. Martin Luther King, the civil rights movement, etcetera, was not that popular there, because we were raised on the self-defense principle of fighting and defending our people from those kinds of racist attacks. That stayed with me all my life through the service and back out and eventually in the BPP.

Kleffner: When did you first get introduced to the BPP?

Pratt: When I got out of the U.S. army, I enrolled at UCLA and I was befriended by a brother who was the Deputy Defense Minister of the Southern California chapter, named [Alprentice] Bunchy Carter. In fact, we ended up being roommates. We were both taking the same classes at UCLA and, as a result, I became very familiar with the BPP and the movement as a whole. Being fresh from Vietnam, plus being from the South, opened my eyes to a lot of things. At that time, I was not a member, I was just a friend of Bunchy's; everybody thought that I was a member because I was always with Bunchy. I had attended some meetings of the BPP with Bunchy—the national meetings in Oakland—and helped implement a lot of student programs in conjunction with the BPP. But I had not joined. When Bunchy was killed in January 1968, he left a recording that resulted subsequently in my helping to rebuild their Ministry of Defense.

So, when you say "joining the BPP" there was never really a formal joining. It was a coming together of different forces under the auspices of the banner of the BPP—it was not as cut-and-dried as people may think.

Kleffner: What did Bunchy's recording say?

Pratt: That if anything happened to him, he recommended that I take his place. It was a shock to me. I was blown away. I had already heard that he was dead and then, when I heard this. . . . He had never asked me to join; he knew my position on things. It was like a coming together of two different worlds, two different sectors of a field of struggle and I wasn't so eager to join anything. I had grown up in an organization that was based on the principles of liberation that the BPP were struggling to comprise. So, when he was killed and he left that recording, and Bobby [Seale] and Kathleen [Cleaver] and all heard it, and then asked me, would I do this—it kind of threw me off. After a while, I decided to help build the Ministry of Defense—the Party was made up of different ministries, the Ministry of Education, the Ministry of Culture led by [Emory] Douglass— and it became incumbent on me to take this task on.

Kleffner: What did your job entail?

Pratt: I assumed the role of the Minister of Defense because Huey [Newton], who was the nominal Minister of Defense, was incarcerated. And I became a member of the first cadre of the Central Committee, the highest decision-making body of the BPP. I had to go to various locations and organize classes on defense—self-defense—and things of that nature. Also, we worked on technical defense and theoretical defense. Theoretical defense was comprised of more intellectual dialogue between individuals, so that you could understand the basics of warfare; the technical was the actual implementation of defense techniques, defending our offices, etcetera.

Kleffner: Can you tell us a bit about the community programs of the BPP?

Pratt: That commitment was ongoing. You had to contribute a certain amount of hours to the breakfast program, to the clothing give-away program, to the medical programs. It was a constant thing, twenty-four hours, a full-time job. You had to maintain the political education classes, because those classes were primary, before anything we had to maintain political education. So, it was quite a busy time.

Kleffner: When did you first learn about COINTELPRO and when did you first become one of its targets?

Pratt: We began to feel the effects of COINTELPRO-type operations from the start. Even before I had gotten out here to California, those kind of things were being felt throughout the country, throughout the movement. But it became more intense at the end of 1968 and the beginning of 1969, shortly after J. Edgar Hoover issued his infamous proclamation that we were the greatest threat to their national security.

Kleffner: Can you describe when and how you felt the effects personally?

Pratt: When I was shot at in my bed, four days after the assassination of Fred Hampton in 1969. A very similar thing happened when a sister and I were in bed. They came and shot at the bed and they missed. Buckshots and an assassination attempt. A few months prior to that I had been shot at on the streets by unknown assailants—there were three whites in a car, in the ghetto on the East Side of LA. I was going through Memphis, doing some work there and was shot at. I had been shot at quite a bit in Vietnam, and when the bullets are close, they make a cracking sound. These were very close. I was just lucky that they didn't hit me.

Kleffner: Did you foresee then the split that was going to happen in the BPP?

Pratt: We had signs of it—not a split that actually occurred, but there were always some infiltrators, some agents, provocateurs, who were just omnipresent, who you had to try to weed out and identify, and who were constantly trying to provoke this kind of separation within the ranks. It would come from various directions. It might be played out through fratricidal warfare between other organizations and the Panthers, or the Peacetoll Nation and the Panthers in Chicago. Then you had the anti-Castro Cubans, who were known as the Guzanos and who were used pretty much against the Panthers; you had the Minutemen, and, of course, the Ku Klux

Klan and the John Birch Society. There was always someone, some kind of
force coming at you like this and it wasn't so clear during this period that
it was coming directly from the FBI or the CIA. But it became a serious
topic of our political education classes and studies. Quite a lot of the findings that came out of those studies were presented to the central committee. A few times they were laughed at, because a lot of the leaders didn't
think that we were that important; that the United States would waste
time using the CIA and the FBI.

Kleffner: Did you work with any white organizations and how did
you feel about those alliances?

Pratt: We had good relations with some white organizations throughout that period. In effect, we were criticized quite a bit by a more narrow
nationalist black organization for even working with organizations such as
SDS [Students for a Democratic Society], the Weathermen, the communist
New Left, the youth alliances, the labor parties—all the way to the Communist Party. There were problems. We had to find ways of working with
various forces moving in the same direction. And we understood that our
entire struggle was really based on a class struggle, and that our adver-
saries would try to use the race factor to manipulate and to divide and
conquer when all along those people of other nations, other ethnic backgrounds, are in fact our allies and our friends. We enjoyed good relations
with white people, brown people, red people and encouraged a united
front at all times. In fact, we had a couple of united front conferences that
were pretty successful—back in 1969.

Kleffner: At what point was the BPP split up nationally?

Pratt: We were growing like wildfire, so fast that the leadership really
had to slow down and try to see who was coming up. It was growing so
fast, it went national, then international when Eldridge Cleaver went over-
seas. We had chapters in Havana and Algiers and Copenhagen.[1] It just
spread all over. It wasn't that easy to try to provide the kind of leadership
needed to try to function properly.

Kleffner: Do you think that such an organization needed a hierarchical structure?

Pratt: That's a good question. I often brought that up for a topic of
discussion during that period and I was accused of being too militaristic,
of thinking too militaristically. But it was Amilcar Cabral who gave us a
lot of insight into vertical structures as opposed to more horizontal structures.[2] And that was discussed quite a bit—a lot of the formulas were actually put into practice in certain areas and worked pretty good. But there
was still the matter of hooking it all together, because sometimes you
would hook it together—say we hooked up the Boston chapter and the
chapter in Jamaica, NY—the link that you would use would actually be an

agent and you wouldn't know. That was the worst thing, being linked up through an agent who was directly working for J. Edgar Hoover (FBI director at the time). So we had problems in security screening that became harder because we were naive; agents would actually come and advocate blowing up buildings, shooting police, doing things radically, going out and shooting somebody. And you would say, "Oh, this guy, he is just crazy, but he is not an agent, just because he did some stuff like this." Yet they were the ones provoking it all. A lot of the local leaders were suckered because of that.

Kleffner: Did you think it was necessary to have hierarchical structures in order to control the organization or to make sure that it stayed together?

Pratt: What we called vertical structures were more popular, and I was one of the ones who dissented from that. I thought that, since we were widespread, we needed a horizontal structure, based more on a cell system, that empowered the local leadership. But, because of the fear and the paranoia so prevalent among the national leadership, they would opt for the vertical. Their strong advocacy of this though was continually opposed by the actual practices of the police, who were constantly arresting and removing the national leadership. So, you had to reverse and revise and develop other forms of organizational control.

Kleffner: What about the role of women in the BPP? It struck me in talking to different former Black Panthers and women, that sexism was right in there in the organization. What is your perception of it in retrospect?

Pratt: When I became a member of the central committee, I was always in support of women's liberation issues, but we didn't have to be in support of anything, because the sisters would make sure that you respected them and that their points got across and were adhered to. One of the first sisters who comes to mind is sister Afeni Shakur and, of course, the sister they called my wife, known as Sandra Pratt. She was killed. Or Kathleen Cleaver—you are talking about some strong sisters, sisters you may not have heard about—like Amantelaba—but who were very beautiful, who you would listen to. We had to face our sexism and our machoism because of them. They would educate us—Joan Bird, Assata Shakur—and you would respect and love them, because they made you look into yourself; you became a better person because of them. So, the credit starts with them, because they took the initiative to educate us, to teach us. I wish I could sit here and name all of them.

Kleffner: Can you describe how you ended up in prison, how you were framed and what the situation was over that?

Pratt: I was arrested on December 8th, 1970, in Dallas, Texas, on a warrant run out of what's known as the shoot-out in Los Angeles in 1969.

I was extradited back to California a couple of months later to stand trial for those charges. At that time I was indicted for a murder—I was indicted for quite a few things and one of them was the murder that I am convicted of right now. At the time that I was indicted, it was just another charge that they threw in to maintain a no-bail situation. It wasn't taken too seriously, because they had done this before. Eventually, it became more and more obvious to us that the murder charge was something that they were really going to try and press.

Kleffner: Looking at the rebellions in LA and speaking with young black kids, it seems to me that they are mostly concerned with the everyday struggle for survival. How do you reach out to them, or do you see any force at this point that is organizing these kids?

Pratt: There are quite a few forces out there that are organizing them—conscious organizers like, in some situations, "Educated Fools from Uneducated Schools," educating and organizing them to lean right back on the system. Most of those children have stated very clearly that they are tired of being always in the position of "we gotta ask him for a job; we gotta ask him for welfare; we gotta ask him for health care." It is almost innate for them to speak of autonomy, and, although they don't even really understand what sovereignty and independence mean, their deepest desire is to be on their own, to work for themselves. They are tired of asking the government. That is the strongest argument in favor of nationalism, national independence. Just listen to them, from the rappers to the ones that go to church every day. They want to have their own presidents or prime ministers, their own supreme courts, their own police forces, their own educational institutions. That is what I have been hearing every day. I get a lot of letters from them, and that is what they are looking for—someone who could help them build this vast nation of ours. There is kind of a rough, unrefined understanding that I sense from them, based on: they want theirs, not so much from the system, as from the hundreds and hundreds of years' wealth that was accumulated from slavery. I think there are a lot of ways that they can be organized and are being organized, whether we like it or not.

Kleffner: How do you perceive the support for yourself and other political prisoners and prisoners of war from the Black Liberation movement? A lot of young kids especially don't know about your case, or the cases of other Panthers.

Pratt: I think there is a conscious and systematic attempt on the part of the government to oppose any support that may be developing for us. The solution, I think, has to be based on our national efforts for liberation—that we are soldiers who fought for the liberation of our nation and our nation fights for the liberation of us. But if our nation does not realize it is a nation, then it's gonna constantly be victim of this kind of manipulation by our enemies. I don't now advocate so much "Free Geronimo" as "Free our Nation"; that our prisoners and our protectors and soldiers of that nation be provided for. The important thing is the freedom of our people. We were always sacrificial lambs for that, we understood that we were going to be killed, put in prison, or ostracized, because it is not a popular thing among those you fight against to fight for freedom and independence. And, in the process, support will come for Mumia Abu-Jamal and all other political prisoners and prisoners of war. One of the things that the white superstructure is afraid of is the coming together of various national forces such as the Native movement, the Chicano movement, what is called the white North American anti-imperialist movement, which are all based on the same principles, the principles of our independence. That is something I always try to make people aware of. We could talk about this a long time, but I know we don't have a lot of time.

Kleffner: Do you feel that the support for yourself has got stronger in the last few years?

Pratt: Yes, it is constantly growing. But, if I could, I would take every ounce of support that I have for me and give it to Mumia and other prisoners of war. Mumia is a very beautiful brother. He was framed, his life is in imminent danger and we can ill afford to execute Mumia.

Kleffner: Can you talk a bit about your prison conditions?

Pratt: My prison conditions are harsh. I am in maximum-security imprisonment, and, after twenty-two years in prison, it is not common to be maintained in what is called a level-four prison. The conditions are very punitive and repressive, ranging from the food conditions to the violence of seeing a person arguing and the guards shooting him from a tower, killing him. There are constant lies and manipulations. Just think of a COINTELPRO on a microcosmic scale. In fact, we found in some of the files the existence of an operation called PRISAC [Prison Activist] program; it is directed against prison activists and ranges over spreading rumors, falsely labeling you, taking your letters, poison-pen letters. It is a constant state of warfare.

Kleffner: What about the black elected officials—do they support the demand of freedom for black political prisoners at all?

Pratt: They like to individualize prisoners, because, by and large, they buy into the system's propaganda that there are no political prisoners. You have to understand that in the New Afrikan nation you have a class situation. Within this class structure, we have what we call the black bourgeoisie. Malcolm X would make the analogy that they were the house Negroes as opposed to the field Negroes. A field Negro lives in the field, hoping that something bad will happen to the master, whereas the house

Negro is hoping that master lives forever, because he lives in his house, eats of his table, etcetera. The house Negroes do all they can to try to preserve the very system that we try to get away from.

The black bourgeoisie individualize a lot—they might take an Angela Davis because it is fashionable to get behind Angela Davis to help her get out of prison and then they feel as though they have contributed; but they turned away from Ruchell Magee, who was actually shot and almost killed. So, a few may get behind Geronimo ji Jaga, because he knows Danny Glover or he has been to Vietnam, but they might oppose Sundiata Acoli, who is a very beautiful brother who should be supported a thousand percent and should be freed. They might get behind Dhoruba Bin Wahad and Mutulu Shakur and ignore Marilyn Buck and Laura Whitehorn. It is a matter of us trying to educate them to the reality, what is happening—so they could broaden their support and base their decisions on principles as opposed to personalities.

Kleffner: How about your parole hearings? Do they ask you to disavow your political beliefs?

Pratt: Ordinarily, you wouldn't find a person being kept in prison as long as I have because of what they say they are keeping me in prison for. To me, the parole hearing is only a formality. They have, by law, to review your case a certain number of times every few years. Since I have been in prison, I have known prisoners who have come in for heinous murders who have gotten out three times—not just once, but for three different murders and have gotten out. It is all a political machine comprised of ex-law enforcement individuals who are manipulated by their bosses. Every now and then you might run across one or two who seem to show a more humanistic understanding, but they are a minority.

It was a political situation that landed me in here, and it will be a political situation that releases me. And, after so many years, you cease to think so much about you yourself being released. Sure, I would love it. I love freedom, to be out of these places. But you don't dwell on that too much, you would go crazy. It is more broad; you think more about the liberation of society and your people, rather than this little, insignificant person who consciously joined a movement to struggle for liberation.

Kleffner: What do you think about the explosion of the prison population in the last twenty to fifteen years?

Pratt: It was predicted. Huey Newton gave a lecture on that one time and we had foreseen that this was gonna happen. After the leadership of the BPP was attacked at the end of the '60s and the early '70s, throughout the black and other oppressed communities, the role models for the upcoming generations became the pimps, the drug dealers, etcetera. This is what the government wanted to happen. The next result was that the gangs were being formed, coming together with a gangster mentality, as opposed to the revolutionary progressive mentality we would have given them. So, by eliminating or driving the progressive leadership—the correct role models underground, killing them and putting them into prison, eliminating them—all of these younger generations were left prey to whatever the government wanted to put them into. It is another form of genocide, of killing off populations of Third World and progressive people who pose a threat to their system. And this is one of the reasons why people like me are kept in prison. They don't want me out there, because people like me will go out there and struggle to bring home the truth to those youngsters. They know those youngsters have a lot of respect for us, because we haven't betrayed anything, because we have stayed firm to our principles. Like I said, it is not just me, it is people like us who adhere to the basic principles of liberation and basic humanism for all people—for the Mexican people, for Indian people, for all the struggling peoples.

We have the biggest prison population anywhere in the world and the next one is in South Africa. Of course, there is racism involved. Here, in California, you have a lot of Mexican and brown people in prison. It's just so pathetic. They are being railroaded into prison, a lot of them don't speak English, and when they come to prison they are just branded—either you're in this or that gang—and, basically, they don't even know what they are talking about. Then they end up shooting themselves. We have been struggling for years to get the [Crips] and the Bloods together in prison. We were successful in that a few years ago; it spilled out onto the streets and we are happy about that. Now, since the state and the government can't get the [Crips] and the Bloods to fight each other, what you see is them trying to get Mexicans and blacks against each other. It is all being manipulated from above, designed to keep that death factor high. The best way is to have them kill each other off. It is presenting again what existed when I first came in, which George Jackson and others struggled against, by trying to get the prisoners together across racial lines.

Notes

Originally published as "The Black Panthers: Interviews with Geronimo ji-jaga Pratt and Mumia Abu-Jamal," in *Race and Class,* Vol. 35, No. 1 (July/September 1993): 9–26.

1. *Editor's note:* See Kathleen Cleaver, "Back to Africa: The Evolution of the International Section of the Black Panther Party (1969–1972)," in *The Black Panther Party [Reconsidered],* ed. Charles E. Jones (Baltimore: Black Classic Press, 1998), 211–56.

2. *Editor's note:* Amilcar Cabral (1921–1973) was a founding member of the Popular Movement for the Liberation of Angola and also founded and became the leader of the African Party for the Independence of Guinea and the Cape Verde Islands. He was assassinated on January 20, 1973 in Conarky, Guinea, twenty months before Portugal was forced to grant independence to Guinea Bissau. See Amilcar Cabral, *Return to the Source: Selected Speeches and Writings* (New York: Monthly Review Press, 1974); Amilcar Cabral, *Revolution in Guinea: Selected Texts,* ed. and trans. Richard Handyside (New York: Monthly Review Press, 1970).

23

Viet Mike Ngo
(with Dylan Rodríguez)

Viet Mike Ngo was incarcerated at age seventeen for the murder of a four-teen-year-old rival gang member. Ngo, is a writer, activist, and political edu-cator who has participated as a guest speaker and lecturer in conferences, classes, and organizing sessions. While housed in San Quentin, he petitioned the Marin County Superior Court for a writ of habeas corpus regarding the prison administration's illegal racial segregation of inmates in housing and discipline. Currently held by the California Department of Corrections (CDC), Ngo is a prisoner at Soledad Prison. Ngo has nine cases or writs of habeas corpus against the CDC over such matters as racial segregation, institutional retaliation, religious freedom, and sexual harassment.

Dylan Rodríguez, assistant professor in Ethnic Studies at the University of California-Riverside, is a founding member of Critical Resistance and author of *Forced Passages: Imprisoned Radical Intellectuals and the Forma-tion of the United States Prison Regime*. The following interview was con-ducted by Rodríguez at San Quentin State Prison on May 24, 2002 and transcribed by Gabby Ocon.

"You Have to be Intimate with Your Despair": A Conversation with Viet Mike Ngo (San Quentin State Prison, E21895) 2002

Dylan Rodríguez: Mike, first introduce yourself to everybody.

Mike Ngo: My name is Viet Mike Ngo, and I'm a prisoner in San Quentin at this time, serving a life sentence for second-degree murder. [Electronic voice: "This recorded call is from an inmate at a California state correctional facility."] [Dylan and I] first got introduced through mutual friends; through the Patten College Program here. I met them because I felt that their politics were radical enough to really attack the program. So they hooked us up because we were both Asians, and there wasn't really many Asians involved with the college program . . . who were radical in politics and in thinking, and that's how we got hooked up, and I think its important because there isn't a voice for radical Asian intellectuals and activists.

Rodríguez: Now Mike, one of the ways that people talked about you before I even met you was that you were somebody that was inspired by a lot of radical intellectuals, including prisoners.

Ngo: Most definitely. George Jackson shaped a lot of my political theories and helped mold them the way my thinking is today. And so my, our mutual friends also told me that you were involved, or liked a lot of George's writing, and were interested in this type of political activity. That was another reason we got hooked up.

Rodríguez: Who introduced you to George Jackson?

Ngo: That's a good question. I can't say one person introduced me to him, but it was a growth process for me. The more I got involved in trying to understand my environment, the space I live in, the more I got involved with the history of prisoners and the history of the politics involved in prison. That's how I got hooked up with George. But it all comes from the will to understand your environment and to understand in a critical eye. Not just take it for granted and go with the flow. You have to be critical about the space you live in.

Rodríguez: What provoked you to start reading George Jackson, to start thinking about your environment critically?

Ngo: The first few years after I got locked up, I wasn't really involved with anything political. . . . And so I fell in with a lot of the gangsterism that's involved in prison; the cliquing and the racial segregation of prison makeup. Then I got in school. Fortunately, when I first came into prison, they had the Pell Grants still available for prisoners. That's where we were paid, or we were allowed to be involved in college programs in prison. And through that process, I got indoctrinated into critical thinking . . . just thinking in general, and history, and what have you. So that started my thinking process. Then I got here from Soledad. I got transferred from Soledad to San Quentin and they started up a program here. This is after the Pell Grants were shot down. So they started up a new college program that ran on a volunteer basis. And a lot of the students came from UC-Berkeley, the T.A.s, the professors, and UC-Davis, St. Mary's College. And these teachers that were, at least to me, in my point, were a little more critical of history and about the United States' part in history, in prisons too. And, so this made me think a little more and the book that really started kicking me off was Howard Zinn's *A People's History of the United States.*[1] That's when there was a time in my growing process that I really started being critical about everything I was taught, and it really opened up my eyes in a lot of things. Also, the church and religious [*beep*] entrenched in prison programs in California, and I got involved in this too, when I first got here, and this indoctrination process of religion, and how that co-opts or really stifles the way we think critically. And it really all came to a head [*beep*] at the major starting points of my political or my radical politics.

Rodríguez: Your movement from Soledad to San Quentin . . . [*"Your call will be terminated in two minutes."*] . . . follows the movement of radical prison organizers from the sixties to the present . . . including George, who was of course assassinated at the place where you're currently incarcerated.

Ngo: Right. That's why George impacted my life so much, because when I was reading it, I was thirty-one; his age when he died, and I followed his footsteps and coincidently, I went through the same process he did. I first got sent to Soledad, did time there, I did some funk there, and then went to the hole there, and was in the same wing he was in. Then I got shipped here to San Quentin. It was really a lot of coincidences and a lot of eye-opening things that really caused me to think more deeply about my life and my role here in prison.

Rodríguez: Do you think about yourself as trying to move in that same lineage, that same intellectual, political lineage as people like George Jackson and others?

Ngo: Most definitely. Although the context is different from then to now, I definitely, at least I hope I even fill the shoes of what that means. But yes, definitely, I want to create [*beep*] changes in prison. [*"Your call will be terminated in one minute."*]

Rodríguez: Mike, before I ask the next question, maybe we should hang up and can you call me back?

Ngo: I'll call you back.

Rodríguez: Okay, call me right back. . . .

Rodríguez: Mike, you there?

Ngo: Yeah, I'm here.

Rodríguez: Good. So we just finished talking about how it is that you struggle to work within the same tradition of activism and radical intellectual work that people like George Jackson, W. L. Nolen, and Yogi Pinell, who's still up there in Pelican Bay, and all these other people, and you were saying how you're in a very different context than those people were thirty years ago. . . . Thirty years ago, there was a critical mass of prisoners, prisoners of color. [*"This recorded call is from an inmate at a California state correctional facility."*] Black and brown prisoners especially, were trying to educate themselves and were trying to mount both resistance and radical opposition to not just the prison regime but to the structures of domination and oppression that define the United States. And you don't have that anymore?

Ngo: Oh, it's a total flip from the sixties and seventies. I still know some brothers here that were locked up then and they said they can't even explain it themselves and they were involved with that process of this depoliticization of prisoners. They [*beep*] a lot of this process to the TV. Before, back in the sixties and seventies, we didn't have TVs, and so people read. They read all the time, and during the political climate. . . .

Rodríguez: Say, hey, Mike. Say that again to these students, man. [Both laugh.]

Ngo: Do not watch TVs and read instead. But not just any reading. The readings that were going on in here were political reading. We were reading Mao. We were reading Marx. We were reading things that, thoughts that were contrary to the United States' ideology. So it allowed us to be more critical of our space and where we live. And so when they brought the TV in, the books fell by the wayside. People don't read anymore. And if they read, they don't read anything about politics. They read about Jackie Collins and Sidney Sheldon. I mean, I'm trying to get the guys here to read, but they ask me for those books instead of others, and I try to throw my jabs and then shoot them something [beep]. But even then the reading level of my peers is really poor, and I don't know how I can even start to tell them to read Marx or even George when they can't read, or they can't read well. So, it looks bleak, but at the same time, the people who are politicized, they're very radical to me. I feel like they're radical and they're solid in their foundation, and I don't worry about them switching in midstream. . . . But nearly everyone is ahistorical. They don't want to look at history. And when they do look at history, they're totally separated from it. They see no connection with themselves and history.

Rodríguez: One of the primary reasons that they want to abolish the Pell Grants for prisoners is precisely because of people like you.

Ngo: This is a great segue into what's going on with me right now.

Rodríguez: Let's talk about that.

Ngo: Me and about four other men here who are involved with the college program wrote a proposal, a very strong proposal, not even asking, demanding that we have freedom of speech in discussing issues in the program and what classes are taught.

Rodríguez: You had to write a proposal to ask for your freedom of speech in a college course?

Ngo: Right. Exactly.

Rodríguez: You know what? That sounds like the university too, actually. I should be quiet. [Ngo laughs.]

Ngo: So, these four or five guys who wrote this proposal asked for Ethnic Studies, asked to have freedom of speech as part of the discussion on prison grounds and through correspondence. So we submitted this proposal to the volunteer facilitator in here and she disseminated it through the student body and it finally got to the administration. Well, the administration came and searched the four to five guys's—who were on this proposal—cell, confiscated personal letters, their legal paperwork and then threatened to transfer us; threatened to retaliate against us for the signatures on this proposal that we submitted. I don't know if this is indicative of why they stopped the Pell Grants, but I know that historically, through the 1900s, that nationalist movements to get rid of imperialism in countries start with the leaders of the national movements being schooled in these [beep] schools. So yes, I want the college program here, I want the Pell Grants to happen here, because it allows us to critically think of our environment and this process, it has a radical tint to it when we're critical and it's just so evident that the United States is not all peaches and cream. [Both laugh.]

Rodríguez: But the point you're making to me is very similar to the way that we would argue for things like Ethnic Studies departments and programs in the university setting in the free world: It offers us a space to actually struggle.

Ngo: Exactly. And it's not all about how am I going to get a job. It's a problem of how am I getting a job. It's a process of how we shape how we get a job. It's at the very foundation of our society. It's not just about institutions and what kind of job can I [*beep*] paid.

Rodríguez: Right. [*"This recorded call is from an inmate at a California state correctional facility."*]

Ngo: It's about training, how I can think, and how this affects my life and those lives of people like me.

Rodríguez: So thirty years ago, you had radical, kind of semi-underground political education circles between prisoners that were happening totally outside the sanction of the prison. People were kind of getting together passing literature around, they were having conversations on the yard, between their cells, stuff like that.

Ngo: Study groups. They had, we had study groups.

Rodríguez: It was the same thing on the outside too. There were people who were doing political education, community-based political education, student-based political education, high school, elementary school, all the way on through, right. And then that gets crushed when they start assassinating people, when they start . . .

Ngo: COINTELPRO.

Rodríguez: Exactly. COINTELPRO, and everything else, and to reform the prison they create these college programs. And it's supposed to "domesticate" you.

Ngo: Co-opts you.

Rodríguez: Yet, a few people like yourself and like others actually take advantage of the college space to create a new front of opposition and radical resistance on the inside, intellectually and practically, which is why it is that you're facing this stuff now with the Patten College Program.

Ngo: Man, that's what's happening. We're trying to break containment and we're being retaliated against for it, and it's indicative of how prison administrations work, how prisons work.

Rodríguez: With you now, they're threatening to transfer you. Yet, the person(s) who actually chose to report you were not even prison authorities, they were actually civilians.

Ngo: That's right. See, this is a volunteer program. So the person that actually runs this program is a volunteer who is a graduate student at UC-Berkeley. She reported another professor to the administration saying that this professor on his own time is supporting my case against San Quentin and CDC racial segregation. And so she reported this to the warden and then the warden banned the professor from coming in.

Rodríguez: So the warden would have never known this if this civilian volunteer hadn't done the warden's job for him.

Ngo: Exactly. Now, the warden has full trust in her and the program.

Rodríguez: The problem of the reform mentality is that you actually become more protective of the institution you're trying to challenge.

Ngo: Yes. [*"Your call will be terminated in two minutes."*] You know, the issue of reform is a complex issue, but yes, that is a side effect of reform and I don't quite know how to address that. I'm still struggling, internalizing what that means, reform and revolution. But yes, that is a definite side effect.

Rodríguez: Let's talk about your writing, how you envision, or how you would fantasize political connections between people like you, right, and then the people who might be listening to this interview in this classroom. We started corresponding and I started looking at your creative writing and your kind of political, polemical writing. One of the grounds on which we've tried to form a political and personal relationship is through correspondence and through writing. . . . Talk a little bit about this struggle between the free world and the unfree world.

Ngo: Right, and our relationship, and how they interact. Okay. [*"This recorded call is from an inmate at a California state correctional facility."*] I think on the individual level, we just have [*beep*] with each other. . . . I'm not at the same political level as others, so you can't come in thinking that this is how prisoners are. You can't stereotype prisoners to begin with, nor should prisoners stereotype people who want to get in touch with them. So just start off as friends, just people who write each other and get to know each other. But always be on a political tip, always ask questions and let them ask questions about you and what your role is and what do you do, and you know, and this automatically helps us to internalize how we are helping or hurting whatever cause or whatever lifestyle we're trying to live.

Rodríguez: Well, Mike, you know what I'm thinking as you say that is that one of the strongest bonds that me and you have is the fact that we hate the state. When we actually get a chance to talk to each other in the visitors' room, we're always talking in hushed voices around those COs [correctional officers], because of what we're saying to each other.

Ngo: Right.

Rodríguez: And I know that that's the level at which I actually became your friend kind of immediately, was because I think we kind of sense from each other how much we hate this fucking country.

Ngo: Well, that was a big part of how we hooked up so quick.

Ngo: You have to read history and to understand the context that forms this place. Once you have a better understanding of that, then you're going to say what we can do within the context of prison now, because it's changed. So you can't use the same methods as George did back then. You have to be more creative in trying to find new ways of promoting change. So, for those inside, always encourage, always help with the resources and what have you. With me, I started with writing. I felt my only weapon was writing; being critical about this place. Within my writing process I moved over to legal work, because I feel like that's my next weapon. That's the only thing I can do and do over and over again, and hurt the system. So, you have to be critical and for those on the outside, you have to think of ways to promote this critical thinking and create a thinking of how the people, how the organizations on the streets tackle the problems: social problems. By trying to change the laws by getting involved with politicians, by running for office, by having grassroots movement organizing. Those are ways of doing it. . . .

We have to try to think outside of the box. That's very important. I feel like I'm hurting these people [prison authorities] because I thought outside of the box. What I'm referring to is that there are many policies and laws—the way we carry ourselves, we perceive that this is the way the law is. This is the way they enforce it. But if we think outside of the box and critique these laws and how they enforce polices, we could try to pick out where these laws and politics are unconstitutional.

Language is very important in this because it helps form our mentality, our attitudes. If we always say we're "inmates" and "convicts," we always put ourselves in a power relationship that is legitimizing our captivity.

They really don't know what to do with me and my comrades right now. I mean, one minute they want to transfer us, another minute they tell us, "We changed our minds"; because they don't know what to do with us, because we're thinking outside the box. We're fighting. We're actually standing up saying, "You know what? I have the right to challenge your policy, challenge the way you run things. Just cause you're a pig and I'm an inmate doesn't mean that I have to listen to what you say. That your word is law."

Rodríguez: One of the themes that we've spoken to throughout this course is this notion Marilyn Buck articulates in one of her essays, where she used the phrase: "The right to struggle." That seems a reflection of how reactionary the condition that we're living in actually is, where people are not even talking about the right to eat, or the right to live, or the right to reproduce, or the right to exist. They're talking about the right to struggle, which means they're talking about the right to struggle for those other rights. What you're talking about, what you're doing now, thinking outside the box, and acting outside the box is all actually above ground and perfectly legal stuff. And yet, people are having to fight just to do that.

Ngo: Hey man, the same things that the United States says about third world countries that have dictators, those are the same issues we're going through here. It seems like they become more repressive when we try to exercise this right. Like with China and in Cuba, they say, "Well, people can't go out and speak their mind." Well, that's the same thing that's going on here. We can speak our mind here, as long as it doesn't threaten their security. Or it doesn't threaten their ideology, or it doesn't threaten their prisons. You can say whatever you want, but you can't say it against them, basically. And so, yes, this right to struggle; we have to be able to voice our views, even if our views go up against those of our jailers.

I see my comrades sometimes. Like everyone, our energy is low. We lose hope sometimes and dwell in despair sometimes; a lot of times. But to me, I feel like you have to be somewhat intimate with your despair.

You have to understand it because it gives you a lot of strength; because once I no longer fear what these people do to me, I no longer worry about the repression they put against me when I struggle. When I exercise my right to struggle. So, I don't want to dwell in my despair, but I have to be intimate with it because some of my strength comes from this. So that's what I can say about [*beep*]. If you feel like the odds are against you, that nothing ever changes man, that we're fighting a mountain, always look at that and say, if that's the case, we have nothing to lose. We have nothing to lose. And once you have that kind of mentality, these people start becoming aware of you, and you promote change this way. Yeah. That in itself is a win.

Rodríguez: I try to think the same thing; that the hope is actually in the struggle. It's not even in the outcome.

Ngo: Exactly.

Rodríguez: It's in the struggle.

Ngo: Exactly. [*"Your call will be terminated in one minute."*] This is something me and my comrade talk about a lot. He thinks about strategies to hurt this place. And I'm cool with it because he knows the legal methods of doing it.

Rodríguez: Right.

Ngo: But I keep on [*beep*] that hey, you know, win or lose, it's a process that we need to find some meaning to our lives.

Me and my cell mate, my comrade that's involved with this legal stuff that we're doing, sometimes we sit at night, and after a hard week's work where all our time is spent on research, typing things up, filing motions, doing 602s,[2] and the appeals, and what we do in the future, sometimes we're drained and we sit there in our bunks and we're talking to each other of what our next strategy is. We ask ourselves, "Man, why are we even doing this?" And the answer we always get is that, hey man, we try to [bring] meanings [to the struggles] . . . as it is, we think that we're going to die up in here, because we have life sentences, the government isn't letting no one out; that's just the way it is.

So [*"This recorded call is from an inmate at a California state correctional facility."*], so the things that we're doing, we're trying to show our peers, and those people who love us, man, that our life is not wasted. That at least if we die, we're going to die trying to change this monster. And really, in essence, that's where all our energy and hope and despair and all of that comes from.

Rodríguez: And that's the thing that I think separates an individual like you from quite a few people who are locked into the logic of trying to just simply obtain their freedom; not even to escape, but just to be released from captivity.

Ngo: In some of my dialogues with my peers, this comes up because I'm so intimate with it; so during our political conversations, it automatically comes up. And they're kind óf taken aback by it, because they aren't intimate with it. They have hope that they can get out of here, and in the back of my mind, I do too, but at the same time, that can't take away from what we need to do here because of our fear of what they might do to us.

Rodríguez: If we take what you say seriously, then prison abolition is the only viable option.

Ngo: To me, if you're going to understand the context, if you read into the history, how can it not be? At the very least, stop any new building of prisons. Stop the inflow of new prisoners. Start a moratorium or stop any kind of growth of prison, at the very least.

And we could have a better understanding, a grip on this, of what's going on. But we have to admit . . . this is a monster man. If people can't see that, and they don't, all I can do, sometimes is just put my head down and run with what I have man, because I look around and see what's around me, I mean, I lose confidence. I lose faith in what I'm doing because it seems like I'm the only one. I'm the only one, and it's ugly.

That's why it's very important to find a group of people; comrades man, basically. You have to find people who love you man, and that's the biggest problem in here in prison. If we had more access to people who think and feel like us. . . .

It helps us do the work. Because we're so isolated in here and out there at least you guys have the opportunity to sit down and break bread with each other. . . . With people who love and feel the way you do. . . . That's where you get your energy from.

We get our energy from our despair and our hate and a lot of things that have to do with love too, and love of wanting to live. But it's overwhelming at times; so you have to use whatever advantages you have; and for a free person, that is your advantage. So definitely utilize it. That's something me and my comrades dream of. We dream of being around our family members, or even around just our comrades who love each other so that we can get some energy back. We could know that, hey, we're doing this not so that we have more time outside of our cell, or phone calls, or whatever; we're doing this because, man, our children, the lives of our children are at stake . . . the future.

Notes

1. Howard Zinn, *A People's History of the United States* (New York: Harper & Row, 1980).

2. *Editor's note:* According to the California Department of Corrections (CDC), a 602 form is used to file a "complaint by an inmate or parolee under the Department's jurisdiction" against a CDC employee.

24

Marilyn Buck and Laura Whitehorn
(with Susie Day)

Marilyn Buck was born in 1947, in Jasper, Texas. As a student at the University of Texas, she was involved in antiracist and antiwar organizing and worked as editor of the Students for a Democratic Society (SDS) national newspaper. In 1968, she moved to California to work with San Francisco Newsreel, a radical filmmaking collective. In 1973, Buck, a target of the Federal Bureau of Investigation's COINTELPRO, was imprisoned on charges of purchasing ammunition using a false identification. After going underground during a work furlough from the experimental behavior modification program at the Federal Women's Prison in Alderson, West Virginia, Buck was charged with aiding in the 1979 escape of Assata Shakur from prison, and the 1981 "Brink's robbery" case. In 1985, Buck was captured and tried in four cases, including the "Resistance Conspiracy" case. In 1987, she was convicted of conspiracy to commit armed bank robbery in support of the New Afrikan Independence struggle and was sentenced to fifty years in addition to twenty years of prior convictions.

A poet and teacher, she works with women in prison on literacy and HIV/AIDS education. In 2001, she received a PEN award for her volume of poetry, *Rescue the Word,* and her poetry also appears in *Hauling Up the Morning, Doing Time: 25 Years of Prison Writing,* and *Women's Prison Writings, 200 A.D. to the Present.* In 2004, *Wild Poppies,* a CD in her honor was released with readings by Marilyn Buck, poets Sonia Sanchez and Amiri Baraka, and author Dennis Brutus.

Laura Whitehorn was born in 1945, in Brooklyn, New York. She began organizing the civil rights and antiwar movements while studying at Radcliffe College (Harvard University) in the 1960s. She worked to support the Black Liberation movement, political prisoners, and Puerto Rican prisoners of war. In the late 1970s, Whitehorn moved to New York City and joined the John Brown Anti-Klan Committee to fight white supremacy and Zionism, and joined the Madame Binh Graphics Collective, an anti-imperialist women's art group. In 1985, after having gone underground to work at building a clandestine revolutionary movement, she was arrested by the FBI in Baltimore, and was eventually charged in the "Resistance Conspiracy" case for bombings of government buildings in which no one was injured. Placed under "preventa-tive detention," Whitehorn was denied bail on the grounds that she was deemed an escape risk and was held for five years, without sentence or bail, until her conviction in the "Resistance Conspiracy" case for which she was sentenced to twenty-three years. While imprisoned, Whitehorn wrote, pro-duced artwork, and worked on HIV/AIDS peer education. In August 1999, she was released from prison and now works as an associate editor at *POZ*, a national magazine for those affected by HIV, and is currently planning a cor-respondence course on HIV.

Susie Day, a freelance writer, lives in New York City and contributes to feminist and lesbian/gay publications, including *Sojourner, The Advocate, Z Magazine, LGNY,* and *Outlines.* She first met Susan Rosenberg and Laura Whitehorn in 1988 while interviewing the defendants in the "Resistance Conspiracy" case.

References

Baraldini, Silvia, Marilyn Buck, Susan Rosenberg, and Laura Whitehorn. "Women's Control Unit." In *Criminal Injustice: Confronting the Prison Crisis,* edited by Elihu Rosenblatt. Boston: South End Press, 1996.

Evans, Linda, Susan Rosenberg, and Laura Whitehorn. "Dykes and Fags Want to Know: An Interview with Lesbian Political Prisoners by the Members of QUISP." Reprinted in *Imprisoned Intellectuals: America's Political Prisoners Write on Life, Liberation and Rebellion,* edited by Joy James. Lanham, MD: Rowman and Littlefield, 2003.

De Vries, Sonja and Rhonda Collins. *Out: The Making of a Revolutionary.* New York: Third World Newsreel, 2000. Videocassette.

Resistance Conspiracy. San Francisco: Bay Area Committee to Support the Resistance Conspiracy Defendants (distributor); Oakland: Peralta Col-leges Television Production Company, 1990. Videocassette.

Whitehorn, Laura. "Preventive Detention: A Prevention of Human Rights?" In *Cages of Steel: The Politics of Imprisonment in the United States,* edited by Ward Churchill and Jim Vander Wall. Washington, D.C.: Maison-neuve Press, 1992.

Cruel But Not Unusual—
The Punishment of Women in U.S. Prisons
2001

Susie Day: You both were arrested and imprisoned in 1985. How have prison conditions around you changed over those years?

Marilyn Buck: They've become much more repressive, particularly since Ronald Reagan's presidency. Each year, there's been slippage. And certainly [President Bill] Clinton played a big role with the Anti-terrorism Act, which further limited people's legal rights.[1]

The balance of who is in prison has also changed. There's a much higher percentage of blacks and Latinos, and—at least in the Federal system—an enormous number of immigrants.[2] Not just immigrants but foreign nationals, who've been arrested for incidents in crossing borders. People are detained for years without ever being given any kind of judicial decision.

Laura Whitehorn: I think it's typical of Marilyn not to complain in an interview about her own conditions. When we look at the two million people now in the federal and state systems, the proportion of women in those numbers has gone way up. What that means to someone like Marilyn is tremendous overcrowding: You're living the rest of your life in a tiny cell that was built for one person and now houses three. It means you have no property, because there's no room. Little by little, they took away any clothing that was sent to you, and put down much more stringent requirements. It means that you have no desk. Marilyn Buck, like many prisoners who fight very hard to get an education, has to sit on a cot and write on her lap. The overcrowding means that people are treated like problems and like baggage.

The other thing is the federal conspiracy laws, which are particularly pernicious for women. In 1985, when people heard that I was facing thirty-three years, they were astounded. That seemed like so much time. In 1990, when I ended up with twenty-three years, people were less astounded, because the laws had changed and sentences were much longer. By then, my cellmate had a twenty-four-year sentence on a first offense. This was a drug conspiracy case where it was really her husband who had run this drug ring, and she was swept up in the indictment. Or there's our friend Danielle, who has a triple-life sentence for another drug conspiracy—her crime was basically refusing to testify against her husband. We found many more women with those kinds of sentences.

Day: How do you think these last fifteen years have affected you, personally?

Buck: Imagine yourself in a relationship with an abuser who controls your every move, keeps you locked in the house. There's the ever-present threat of violence or further repression, if you don't toe the line. I think that's a fairly good analogy of what happens. And imagine being there for fifteen years. . . .

To be punished, to be absolutely controlled, whether it's about buttoning your shirt; how you have a scarf on your head; how long or how baggy your pants are—all of those things are under scrutiny. It's hard to give a clinical picture of what they do, because how do you know, when you're the target, or the victim, what that does to you? But there's a difference between being a target and being a victim.

Whitehorn: The largest proportion of guards in federal women's prisons are men. That's who's in your living unit. That's who's looking through the window in your door when you might be using the bathroom or changing your clothes. There's the total loss of ability to defend your person.

For me, the hardest was the pat-searches. In the federal system it's legal for male guards to pat-search women prisoners. That means they stand behind you and run their hands all over your body. The point is not to locate contraband; it's to reduce you to a completely powerless person. If I had pushed a guard's hands away they would have sent me to the hole for assault. In fact, that did happen once. It reduces you to an object, not worthy of being defended. The message is, "your body is meaningless, why don't you want this man to put his hands all over you?" Very, very deeply damaging.

Marilyn talks about being "a target or a victim." She makes a distinction. That's really important because the struggle inside prison is to refuse to be victimized. Once you allow yourself to be a victim, you lose your ability to stand up and say, "I'm a person; I'm not a piece of garbage."

But over the years, when you have to put up with that again and again, you avoid situations because you just don't want to go through it. You have to exert an enormous amount of psychic energy to remove yourself from the situation, where this guy's running his hands over your body.

You end up exhausted at the end of the day, and your nerves are shot. Your only life is resisting these situations.

Day: Is there a portrait of a typical woman prisoner you could draw?

Buck: No, except in the broadest strokes. Typically, she's a woman of color. When she first comes to prison, she's twenty-three to twenty-four years old. Probably the median age of women here is thirty-five to thirty-six, which is much older than it used to be because women stay in prison much longer. Presently, in this particular institution, over 50 percent of the women are Latin American; a large percentage of that, Mexican. You could also say—and this is not news—a lot of the women here come from abusive relationships, whether parents or husbands. . . . If you look at the statistics, it says up to 80 percent.[3]

Whitehorn: I would also say that a huge number of the women are mothers. It means that, on the outside, there are basically a lot of orphans. I consider the prison system today to be a form of genocide. Prison has been used against third world populations inside the United States, in particular African American and Latino populations. These women are very young when they come to prison. They have sentences that will go through their childbearing years. Their children are either farmed out to relatives, or they become wards of the state. It means that the women, who would form some sort of collective bond when there's a need for struggle, are gone from the community. And it means that their children may well go to prison themselves. Those of us who grew up *with* mothers have complaints that we didn't get enough love. What does it mean to have your mother in prison?

One thing that would strike me whenever people came in from the outside for something like an AIDS health fair—we fought very hard to have those fairs—is that these straight, middle-America types would be sweating bullets, they were so scared. And they would be so expansive and warm when they left. They would say, "My picture of you all was so wrong. I pictured these killers with knives in their teeth, and I find you're just like my neighbors."

If you look at the number of women in prison, some of us are your neighbors. I don't care where you live. People who read [*Monthly Review*]: Your neighbors are in prison, okay? I must have met thousands and thousands of women over almost fifteen years, and I would have to say that, of the women I met, there are probably ten or fifteen who, in a socialist society, would need to be in prison.

Day: Do women ever get "better" after they go to prison?

Buck: Sometimes. I think there's the possibility of coming to terms with the fact that you were abused. Basically, you have two things happening. One is that you have this potential, because you're not running around, doing the things you had to do as a mother, a wife, a partner, or as someone who had to go to work. When that daily activity stops, then the potential exists to discover a sense of independence.

The other side is that we're in a situation where we're absolutely controlled. That sort of enhances another abusive relationship. It can limit your imagination and shut you down. So a lot of women become more creative here, in terms of arts and crafts, but it doesn't necessarily open them to their potential as human beings.

Whitehorn: Also, a lot of women who have been in abusive relationships get into lesbian relationships. And one of the things the chaplains do is preach against homosexuality, because they're terrified of it. I was once in a prison where there was a progressive chaplain who told other chaplains that for a lot of the women, these relationships were the first time someone looked at them and saw beauty and not something to be used and abused. There were also some horrible lesbian relationships that were a recreation of the worst in straight relationships.

Can we talk about medical care? The women are getting older. A lot of women in prison are going through menopause. Many have gynecological problems. I had surgery when I was in prison. . . . There you are: You're bleeding; you've had surgery a few hours before. You're strip-searched, shackled, chained, and you have to walk back to a van. If you're lucky they'll have a wheelchair for you to take you back to your unit.

I now work at *POZ* magazine, and a woman in Danbury Prison wrote a column for the magazine. She has HIV and goes to the male gynecologist to be told that she needs surgery on her cervix. She says to him, "I have to be completely sedated for this operation." And he says, "No you don't." And she says, "Yes, I do. I have a history of sexual abuse and I have a panic attack when I have to lie on my back with my legs spread open and chained in front of strangers."

And he laughs at her. He tells her, "Well, then, we can't do the surgery." And she writes, "I hate my doctor. And that's a problem. For me, but not for him." That's so profound. That relationship of being "cared for" by someone who sees you as their enemy is completely deleterious to your health.

I hope everyone who reads this interview is familiar with the medical crisis in the California women's prison at Chowchilla. "Health care" there is left to the guards: they are trained as low-level EMTs and they do the first stage of triage, deciding whether a woman should be seen by a doctor or not. Seventeen women died in that prison last year alone, and independent investigations concluded that medical incompetence or refusal of medical attention contributed to the deaths.[4]

The other thing I saw so much in women was the further erosion of already low self-esteem. What does it do to you to have to go stand in line and get a man's attention and ask him for sanitary napkins and then be asked, "Didn't you ask me for some yesterday?"

Day: How do you deal with the deaths of family and friends while you're in prison?

Buck: My mother died about six weeks ago. She became ill in September, so I went through a phase of real guilt that I wasn't there. And real sorrow and real anger. I think I've looked at the guilt a little more. I just couldn't be there. But the sorrow of not being able to hold my mother's little bird hand by the time she was starving to death from the cancer . . . just breaks my heart. And there's nothing I can do about it.

I could intellectualize it. I could have been on a ship halfway around the world, and we got stuck in the trade winds and couldn't get there in time. But I'm an extreme realist and understand who I am as a political prisoner. I knew that I would not be allowed to go to her bedside, nor to her funeral. That was just the reality. She died on a Sunday. And she was buried on my birthday. So it's just all very hard.

I talked to my mother every week I could. And she came to visit me once a year. It was hard for her to get here. My mom was seventy-four. She had to drive a long way and go through all the emotional turmoil that you can't avoid when you see somebody you can't do anything for. So I had to look at her anger, too.

In a certain way, I want to be able to lie on the floor and bang my heels and cry and scream, but that just hurts my heels. . . . So what can I say? I'm having a hard time. I'm having a very, very hard time. I . . . you know, it's grief. But it's grief under dire conditions. I'll always miss my mother.

Whitehorn: One of the hardest things about being in prison is losing somebody you love and being unable to be there with them while they're dying, or go to the memorial service afterwards. Being in prison through some of the worst years of the AIDS epidemic meant that I lost friends, both on the outside and the inside, very dear women who were among the best friends I've ever had in life.

My father died while I was in prison. I was very fortunate that there was a chaplain who allowed me to phone him twice, while he was in the intensive care unit. It's just an emblem of how families are destroyed by prison—the fact that Marilyn was not permitted to go; that I was not permitted to go to my father's funeral; that there was no question of ever being permitted to go.

Day: What kinds of internal resources have you developed to deal with these years in prison?

Buck: For me, the main thing is that I recognized, after the first five years of being imprisoned and on trial a lot, that one tends to build one's walls, which means that you begin to censor yourself, so that they can't censor you.

I censored how I spoke to people, how I interacted. It goes in tandem with, "If I button my shirt the way they want, they won't attack me for not buttoning my shirt properly." In some ways, I found myself trying to be a "good girl," because then maybe they'd see I wasn't a "bad girl."

When I got a handle on what I was doing, I was horrified, because how can you be a women's liberationist and worry about being a good girl or a bad girl? What I believed in my gut was being turned inside out by my actual life. And it made me understand a lot more about how any woman—it doesn't matter who you are or what you think—can get in a relationship with another person—generally a man, but not always—who can become your abuser, your owner.

So once I could begin to see that, I tried to find ways to tear down my walls, to protect myself less. It's always a risk, because when you open a door, you don't know what's going to come in, or what's going to go out. And everyone is needy in prison. When you're a prisoner, you're needy. It's emotionally, psychologically devastating. But I felt like, if I didn't take that risk, that I was going to smother the essence of who I was.

What I do is that I write. I write poems. Over the years I've moved from being a rhetorical, frozen writer to try to put out more of who I am, and how I feel. . . . I think that ultimately, if we want human liberation, we have to be able to be honest with ourselves and other people about our desires, our resentments; as we say these days, our "issues."

So I look to that as a little flame before my face. I can't say I'm there. But I can at least keep that in my mind.

Whitehorn: I think the hardest thing to maintain over the years, for me, was my sense of outrage. After a while, your heart hurts so continually, you begin to build a sort of padding around it. For example, one of the hardest things for me in prison was at the end of the visiting period, when you see children being led away from their mothers and they don't understand, especially the little ones are just screaming and crying. I got to a point where I would try to leave my visits early because I couldn't stand that any more.

I really started to disrespect myself for that. I felt like, the mother's going through it, how do you get the right to remove yourself from it? I think from that, I understood something of why people don't want to know about prisons, because it's too hard; there's something so painful about seeing a woman being removed from her baby. A woman who gives birth in most U.S. prisons gets somewhere between eight and twenty-four hours before she is taken back to the prison and separated from the infant.

When people say, "God, how did you survive prison?," I think the way I did it was by touching the lives and being touched by the lives of women around me. I mean, I was in prison with women who had been raped repeatedly by a stepfather when they were between seven and eleven, who had to go through pat-searches every day, through shake-downs where some man comes in your cell and paws through your under-wear. They would call home and find out that their daughter, who was thirteen, was again being abused by that same stepfather, who was back in the picture. They had to deal with the most intense levels of abuse, and yet were able to stand up through it, were able to survive.

I learned early on how people can communicate with each other on a really deep level without having to give up their own personal strength. I learned how to get emotional sustenance from the women around me and how to try to give some to them. That's the main thing I learned from prison. And it was easy for me because I knew I had a release date. For someone like Marilyn, or our friend Danielle, finding the strength to sur-vive is an enormous job.

Day: What reactions do you get as a political person from other prisoners?

Buck: Most people don't know my politics specifically. As I get older and tireder, and more beaten down by being in prison, I'm not out there as much with the population. I don't go to the dining room very much. I'm too tired to do that. So less and less, people know me.

But some people do understand my politics. You know, one woman who's twenty-two years old just left. A young black woman. We talked sometimes, and I have been supportive and critical of her in a couple of situations. When she left, she said, "Thank you. You helped me a lot."

So, to me, what your politics are in the abstract don't mean a damn; it's how you practice them. For myself as a white woman, I ask, how do you treat people; how do people receive you as a human being? Are people abstractions to you, in terms of racism? Or do you treat people as real equals, even given all the issues of privilege? Because they exist in prison, too.

Sometimes I'm treated differently by the administration. I know that my mail gets opened. That's not true of everyone else. So I end up getting envelopes without any contents. Every time you say anything about it, it's "Oh, it must be the post office."

Whitehorn: Marilyn's right that people knew us as political prisoners by how we dealt with people and situations every day. I remember feeling that the main impact I'd had was when I would intervene when a guard was picking on a woman, or help somebody get her privileges back when they'd been taken away unjustly. More than if I gave them a lecture on the history of something.

But Marilyn's also way too modest. When we were in prison together, all the other women knew she represented the politics of struggles for justice, human rights, liberation. Women would always approach her for help in understanding not only incidents on the news, world affairs, but also incidents of racism and hostility among different nationalities in the prison population. She may tire of talking about it, but I know for a fact she never tires of acting on all of it, treating people with respect, making peace in difficult situations, basically doing the right thing no matter how tired she is, how long she's had to do it.

One thing that changed while I was in prison is that there were many more women political prisoners. It was a shock to the prison system itself because they were terrified of us.

The government created a control unit. They tested it out on two of the Puerto Rican women, Lucy Rodríguez and Haydee Beltràn. Then they put Alejandrina Torres and Silvia Baraldini and Susan Rosenberg in an underground unit at the Federal Correctional Institution at Lexington. It was actually a basement unit and they were supposed to be there for the rest of their sentences, which were fifty-eight and forty-three and thirty-five years. It was a big mistake because it got international attention. It was one of the first times Amnesty International got involved in the conditions of incarceration in the United States. Part of it was that they were terrified we would revolutionize the rest of the prison population.[5]

A few years after that unit was closed down, I was in Lexington and working in the landscape crew, mowing grass, and my boss was a guard who had been assigned to that basement unit. She told me that they had been told not to speak to the prisoners there because they would brainwash them. I thought it was hysterical. I said, "You see after we've worked together, whether I brainwash you."

About three months later, that guard asked me, "Who's that guy who's the biggest mass murderer ever?" And I said, "George Bush [Sr.]." Then we got into a discussion about who is a mass murderer—someone who kills five people or a president who—?[6] And she says, "You know, you're making a lot of sense, Whitehorn. Uh-oh. I *am* being brainwashed."

Day: Some people say that political prisoners get more recognition and support than social prisoners. What's your reaction to that?

Buck: There's a misconception that political prisoners always get so much support. There are some who were in prison for years before they got any support at all, except for a few people they'd worked with in the world. We could look at [Nelson] Mandela. All these people worked to free Mandela. What was done about all the other [African National Congress] prisoners?[7] Probably ninety-nine out of one hundred political prisoners didn't join the struggle to become famous.

Also political prisoners tend not to get parole. Particularly men political prisoners, they're in isolation for years and years. There's a lot of things we don't get that sometimes other prisoners do get.

Whitehorn: If you want to understand prisons, you have to understand both political and social prisoners. They're two sides of a program of repression. One is, you terrify communities and tell them the law is all-powerful and people will lose their freedom for many, many years if they transgress. The other is, you give huge sentences to anyone who says, "There are such egregious social injustices that we have to go up against the government." You lock those people up for long periods of time, and that will prevent the rise of a new generation of leaders or activists. If you leave out one side of that equation, you'll never understand what prisons are. You'll think they're just about making money, which is ridiculous.

Having said that, I think the current building of a mass movement about the prison industrial complex began with political prisoners. There is absolutely no division between supporting political prisoners and fighting for an end to the prison system. Angela Davis has been instrumental in it. Who's she? She's an ex-political prisoner. [See chapter 10, this volume.] The people who have organized a lot of young activists in that movement are political prisoners or ex-political prisoners.

Every single political prisoner did prison work before they went to prison. We were the people who supported the Attica brothers; we were the people who were in the Midnight Special Collective back in the early 1970s in New York, which was a prison support collective. We're not the ones who don't think social prisoners are important.

And political prisoners often need extra support. Marilyn Buck has an eighty-year sentence and she has *never* been accused of actually hurting a single person. Or Teddy Jah Heath, who just died in prison. He had been convicted of a kidnapping, where a big-time drug-dealer was put in a car, driven around, talked to, and let out. No injury; no nothing. Jah did twenty-seven years in prison. After twenty-five years, he went to the parole board and was rejected. Two years later, he died in prison of colon cancer. Because his act was a political act. It was done in line with the programs of the Black Liberation Army, growing out of the Black Panther Party, to stop the drug trade in the black communities.[8]

Day: Marilyn, what do you need from people on the outside?

Buck: What I need from people is what we all need: to seize our human liberation as much as possible as women, as lesbians, as heterosexuals. To support the right of human beings to have their own nations, their own liberation, and their own justice. If we stopped police brutality; if black women and men were treated like equal human beings, that would make me feel really, really good, because I would be less dehumanized as a white person in this society. I would not be objectified as the oppressor.

I would like us to be more creative; to be the artists that we all are. I don't want to see child prostitution. That to me is oppression in the concrete; people having to sell their children to stay alive. Or watching their children in the clutches of the police. Or a woman standing on her feet as a waitress for ten hours a day when her veins are breaking and still not be able to pay the rent and be there for her children.

I was thinking about this the other day—I think about the vision I had when I was a nineteen-year-old of justice and human rights and women's equality. It was a wonderful vision. I think how it got implemented—how we became rigid and rhetorical within that—took away from that vision. But without a vision, you can't go forward.

Day: Laura, now that you're out of prison, what do you want to do?

Whitehorn: I don't ever want to forget. That would be like putting calluses over my heart. It would be forgetting the people I owe something to.

I guess the hardest thing for me about getting out was leaving so many people behind. I've been working in release efforts. We filed papers for clemency with Clinton for all the federal political prisoners. I try to do work for HIV-positive prisoners through my job at *POZ* magazine. And when people ask me, "How can I support your friends who are left behind?" that makes me feel whole.

It's made me sad that I've tried to interest different groups of women in supporting young women in prison on these ridiculous [drug] conspiracy cases. The "girlfriend crimes," like Kemba Smith.[9] There are hundreds of Kemba Smiths in the federal system. And I have been singularly unsuccessful in interesting any organized women's groups to fight for those women.

One thing that makes prisons so criminal is that they damage people over time. I'm very damaged, and I had tons of support. I did prison work for years before I was arrested, so I knew what to expect. Nothing could really catch me off guard. Yet I find I have places in me that I don't know how to go to, that are so filled with pain.

Especially late, in the middle of the night, when I think about some of my friends, these young women who are doing life sentences. They didn't kill anyone. They didn't hurt anybody. They gave a fucking message to someone, or maybe they didn't turn their husband in, and they knew he had killed someone. They're doing life, and they have very little chance of getting out. There's a pain in me that I don't know how to deal with.

You know, it's very difficult to carry on relationships with people on the outside while you're in prison. Your friends shield you from things because either they think you don't want to hear about the great dinner they had the night before, or you're going to think their problems are trivial because, after all, they're not in prison. It damages your ability to have human relationships. And I have to say that the people I've seen who carry on friendships with prisoners are few and far between, and I honor them.

So I need to continue to struggle for prisoners and to win their release. And to say, it's extremely important for people on the outside to understand what prisons are and who's in prison and to visit them. To bring that kind of humanity into the prisons—but most of all, to bring those prisoners out, back into the communities.

Notes

This interview was conducted by Susie Day in 2001 and printed in the *Monthly Review*, Vol. 53, No. 3 (July-August 2001). The *Monthly Review* introduction to the interview stated: "While it was possible to talk to Laura at length about her time behind bars, Marilyn was able only to make four long-distance phone calls, each summarily cut off by the prison after fifteen minutes. After reading Marilyn's words—and having known and lived beside Marilyn for years in prison—Laura added to what Marilyn wasn't able to say, as well as expressing her own experience and recollections."

1. *Editor's note:* In 1996, President Bill Clinton signed into law the Antiterrorism and Effective Death Penalty Act. Among other provisions, the act authorizes the government to deport immigrants based on secret evidence not disclosed to the immigrant or his attorney (known as "secret evidence laws"), and to impose criminal and immigration sanctions on those who provide humanitarian aid to any foreign organization labeled "terrorist" by the Secretary of State. See C. Stone Brown, "Legislating Repression: The Federal Crime Bill and the Antiterrorism and Effective Death Penalty Act," in *Criminal Injustice: Confronting the Prison Crisis*, ed. Elihu Rosenblatt (Boston: South End Press, 1996).

2. *Editor's note:* In 1980, black Americans made up 46 percent of the U.S. prison population (and 12 percent of the national population), while Latinos made up 7 percent of the prison population (and 7 percent of the national population). In 2000, black Americans made up 47 percent of the prison population (and 12 percent of the national population) while Latinos made up 16 percent of the prison population (and 13 percent of the national population). While in 1980 the incarceration rate for blacks was 551 per 100,000, in 2000 it was 1,815 per 100,000. In 1980, the incarceration rate for Latinos was 139 per 100,000, and in 2000 it was

609 per 100,000. (Mother Jones, "Debt to Society," Special Report, available online at www.motherjones.com/prisons/index.html; statistics from Bureau of Justice Statistics, Criminal Justice Institute, U.S. Census Bureau.)

3. *Editor's note:* For general information about the imprisonment of women, see notes in the preface of this volume. For information about women of color and the criminal justice system, see Juanita Díaz-Cotto, *Gender, Ethnicity, and the State: Latina and Latino Prison Politics* (Albany, NY: State University of New York Press, 1996); Beth Richie, *Compelled to Crime: The Gender Entrapment of Battered Black Women* (New York: Routledge, 1996); Luana Ross, *Inventing the Savage: The Social Construction of Native American Criminality* (Austin: University of Texas Press, 1998); Jael Silliman and Anannya Bhattacharjee, eds., *Policing the National Body: Sex, Race and Criminalization* (Boston, MA: South End Press, 2002).

4. *Editor's note:* For more information on the health care situation in Chowchilla Prison, see Joann Walker, "Medical Treatment at Chowchilla," in *Criminal Injustice: Confronting the Prison Crisis*, ed. Elihu Rosenblatt (Boston: South End Press, 1996).

5. *Editor's note:* In 1986, the U.S. Federal Bureau of Prisons opened a High Security Unit (HSU) at the women's federal correctional institution in Lexington, Kentucky. In its less than two years of existence, this control unit, which never housed more than six prisoners, became a focus of national and international concern over human rights abuses inside U.S. prisons. Susan Rosenberg and Alejandrina Torres, a Puerto Rican *Independentista*, were the first two women in the federal prison system to be transferred to the control unit. A short time after the HSU opened, a third political prisoner, Silvia Baraldini, an Italian national anti-imperialist convicted in the 1979 escape of Assata Shakur, was transferred to the unit. None of these women were transferred to the HSU as a result of disciplinary infractions. Rather, the Bureau of Prisons stated as its official criteria, "[a] prisoner's past or present affiliation, association, or membership in an organization which . . . attempts to disrupt or overthrow the government of the U.S."

Once sent to the HSU, prisoners were told they could not return to the normal prison population until they renounced their political affiliations and beliefs. The HSU was located in the basement of the Lexington prison, and its inhabitants were completely isolated from the other prisoners. There was no natural light, no fresh air, no educational or recreational opportunities. Prisoners held within the HSU lived under constant surveillance. They were permitted no privacy, only infrequent, no-contact family visits, and two ten-minute, monitored phone calls each week. Subject to sleep deprivation and arbitrary rule changes, they were exposed to sexual harassment and overt hostility by the mostly male staff. As a result of these extreme conditions, the women began to experience both psychological and physical effects, including vision problems, insomnia, exhaustion, weight-loss, and depression. The use of small-group isolation as employed in the HSU has been condemned as torture by Amnesty International and the United Nations. Following opposition from human rights groups and the Puerto Rican independence movement, the HSU was officially shut down in August 1988. But, the following year, the U.S. Court of Appeals overturned the court decision (*Baraldini v. Thornburgh*) that declared the HSU's political criteria for placement of prisoners unconstitutional. Moreover, in August 1988, the women from the Lexington HSU were simply transferred to the newly opened Shawnee Unit, a control unit with the same mission as the HSU, at the Federal Correctional Institution in Marianna, Florida. For more information, see Mary K. O'Melveny, "Lexington Prison High Security Unit: U.S. Political Prison"; Laura Whitehorn, "Resistance at Lexington"; and Silvia Baraldini, Marilyn Buck, Susan Rosenberg, et al., "Women's Control Unit," in *Criminal Injustice: Confronting the Prison Crisis.*

6. *Editor's note:* Whitehorn most likely refers to the domestic and foreign policies of the U.S. under George Herbert Walker Bush's presidency. Under that Bush administration, the U.S. government bombed and invaded Panama in 1989, bombed and invaded Iraq in 1990–91, and implemented an embargo on Iraq. That embargo led to severe malnutrition, disease, and hundreds of thousands of deaths among Iraqi women and children. See Noam Chomsky, *Culture of Terrorism* (Boston: South End Press, 1988).

7. *Editor's note:* First organized in 1912, the African National Congress (ANC) led resistance against South Africa's apartheid regime. In 1960, after decades of nonviolent protesting, and in response to increased police violence and government repression, the ANC concluded that it must meet government violence with armed resistance. It formed an armed faction. In the ensuing government retaliation, many ANC leaders, including Nelson Mandela, were imprisoned; yet the ANC continued to grow and attract support among the South African people and build international opposition to apartheid. As the ANC grew stronger, police repression intensified. The South African government was forced to the negotiating table. In 1990, Mandela was freed. He was elected President of South Africa in 1994.

8. *Editor's note:* For more information on the Black Liberation Army, see Evelyn Williams, *Inadmissible Evidence: The Story of the African American Trial Lawyer Who Defended the Black Liberation Army* (Brooklyn: Lawrence Hill, 1993); Assata Shakur, *Assata: An Autobiography* (Chicago: Lawrence Hill Books, 1987).

9. *Editor's note:* In 1993, at age twenty-four, Kemba Smith, a young African American woman, was convicted of conspiracy and drug trafficking, and sentenced to twenty-four years. She never actually used or sold any drugs, but was prosecuted for failing to cooperate with police who were pursuing her abusive boyfriend for his drug-dealing activities. She was pardoned by President Bill Clinton in 2000, following a national campaign on her behalf.

25

Shaka Sankofa (Gary Graham)
(with Larvester Gaither)

Shaka Sankofa (Gary Graham) was born in 1964, in Texas. Born into poverty, with a mentally ill mother and an alcoholic father, he dropped out of high school and became involved in petty crime. He was first arrested at age seventeen for charges of robbery and rape (the rape allegations were never proven) and sent to the Huntsville Maximum Security Prison in Huntsville, Texas. While incarcerated, he was charged with the murder of Bobby Lambert, a white drug dealer and police informant, who was shot outside a supermarket. Sankofa was convicted of the crime after a trial that lasted only two days, and in which his court-appointed attorney called no witnesses, despite the fact that at least two eyewitnesses to the murder contended that Sankofa was not the shooter. Based on the single eyewitness testimony of a woman who viewed the killing from thirty to forty feet away, Sankofa was convicted and sentenced to death.

In prison, Sankofa taught himself to read, studied the works of black liberationists, and became a political leader and active opponent of the death penalty and the U.S. criminal justice system. After a series of failed appeals, the state of Texas set Sankofa's execution date for June 22, 2000. Activists and political leaders called attention to the fact that his execution was a violation of international law, which declares it illegal to execute a person for a crime committed while under eighteen years of age. While prison authorities forcefully facilitated Sankofa's execution, hundreds of protesters gathered outside the prison opposition. Shaka Sankofa, who proclaimed his innocence to the very end, was the 135th person executed under the governorship of George W. Bush.

Larvester Gaither is a Houston, Texas-based journalist and social activist, and editor and publisher of the *Gaither Reporter.*

References

Abu-Jamal, Mumia. "A Man Called Shaka." *The Gaither Reporter,* Vol. 4, No. 6 (March/April 2000).

Mills, Steve. "Battle to the Death, Graham's Last Words of Anger." *The Daily Telegraph,* June 24, 2000.

Willett, Jim. "Eighty-Nine Executions; I Was the Warden. I Did the Job With Dignity. I Still Have Questions." *The Washington Post,* May 13, 2001.

25

An Interview with Shaka Sankofa (Gary Graham) 1996

Larvester Gaither: You have been in prison since you were seventeen?

Shaka Sankofa (Gary Graham): Yeah, and I was someone who was basically illiterate, who couldn't read. I've learned to read and write and sought to educate myself and really develop my own thoughts. One of the things I've tried to do throughout the years is be as true to my struggle and the struggle against the death penalty and oppression as possible. I think in order for me to be truthful to myself, I'm going to have to sit back at some point and analyze and look at what's real and not real: What's the real issue here? In my campaign I've had to constantly keep my eye on what was important for surviving that ordeal . . . the things we had to do and the people we had to get involved.

But I say that to say that when you look at this country and the way in which it is going, I think that our community leaders have been rocked by slavery and the rippling effects of that. So many of us are still vibrating from that today; we still feel the effects of that today. I think what we have to do, if we are serious—a lot of our leaders are serious—is come back and say, "Okay, let's back up. Let's not get caught in the rhetoric, let's not get caught up in the fact that there's a campaign coming up and we want to be involved in that or something. Let's not get caught up in that. Let's get a think tank off to the side, so to speak, and let's determine what is going to be the best thing we can do Monday morning."

One of the things that has always been a part of the Nation of Islam's program is the call for the allocation of certain states—unspecified—to be developed by black people in this country. That is something that has yet to happen, and I think we have to go a step beyond that. We have to look at the way they have created territory for the Palestinians. It's going to come from a demand. The masses, excuse me, the community is going to have to begin demanding that we want something if we want something better. We're tired of the same old games that are being played.

I think the Minister Louis Farrakhan and the Nation of Islam are certainly in a strategic position to help lead in that thought into the twenty-first century.[1] We're going to have to start seriously demanding some land for our own people. Seriously. Not just on paper. We're going to have to start organizing all of these brothers and sisters throughout these countries who are involved in different gangs and so forth. Let's get these brothers in our army because that's where they should be. Recognizing that they're basically firing their weapons and frustration at the wrong people. You're really being an adversary. You're killing yourselves, you're doing the enemy's job. The final job is that, in a sense. We have to educate and discipline these brothers and sisters. So I think the gang activity is serious. But it's a product of racism. Racism breeds gang activity. So we have to mold that untapped energy into activity that is productive for our community as a whole.

Let's bring the leaders together to discuss these issues. That's why I think the process Reverend Benjamin Chavis and a lot of them are going through right now is a very important process.[2] In my mind, of course, I think it's a process we should have went through a long time ago. The process is good because it's going to help us to realize that ultimately we're going to go to the United Nations (UN) with a strong petition dealing with this question of our self-determination and self-control. But in dealing with this issue I think what Farrakhan and Chavis are going to realize, and what Malcolm was going to realize, is that when we go to the UN, even that's not where we ought to be.

Gaither: So, the UN is a different institution than what it was?

Sankofa: It may very well be the same. The problem is that in that sameness, it has always been a body that was created and dominated by U.S. control. I have never known these people to create anything they didn't control and dominate into directions beneficial to them. It was created as an escape valve, in a sense, so to relieve that pressure and have an alternative to go to. But freedom is something I don't think anybody can give to you. They can't give that to Gary Graham. It's not what the UN gives to us. It's irrelevant, for instance, in my case what they do to the body as long as I keep my spirit intact, as long as I keep my mind intact. That's what our people are going to have to realize: Freedom is something you're going to have to demand. You can't lock Gary Graham into a cage. You haven't been able to do that in fifteen years and I'm not going to allow you to do that. What we have to do as a community is say we're going to demand our freedom. We're not going to the UN, the UN better come to us because we're going to go out and organize for control of our communities; we're going to organize our national political life. So I think the Million Man March[3] and the different organizing communities throughout the country now that are formulating a national agenda are going to be very helpful. I'm glad to see that the elimination of the death penalty was one of the issues on their agenda. They even crystallized it a little bit further than that in calling for a national moratorium, which is good. And hopefully more organizations will do that in the future.

But, ultimately, what I think we have to do as a black community . . . is to address the question of leadership. We have to be a lot more sincere about it. . . . We have to be able to develop strategies that are going to give us clear direction. We've got some serious problems out there, but there are some valuable solutions if they are going to be worked on and if we realize that it's not in the interest of this capitalist system for them to be worked on. That's why we have some of these problems that are really perpetrated from one generation to the next.

Gaither: Do you think that you were given an adequate and fair education growing up?

Sankofa: Absolutely not. I don't think I was and I don't think any of our kids are, today. The educational system is another thing that we must control if we are going to control our destiny. Our kids are being miseducated at such an early age. Anytime we have masses of scholars, anytime we have the best of our professional people. . . . I have a lot of friends of mine who are attorneys, journalists, and so forth, individuals that I have come into contact with, and they have all these different degrees and stuff, but when you ask them about their African heritage and their African languages, they're completely numb on the subject. So anytime a system teaches you so much about its culture and so little about yours, that's a problem. That's the basis, the beginning of genocide. And so we've got a lot of people out there beginning to sense these issues around what's happening in the educational system.

When we look at problems out there like teenage pregnancy, for example. If you go back and look at African civilizations, when our young girls were fifteen and sixteen, they were getting married. But the difference is that by then we had educated them to the process of motherhood and we had educated our young men to the responsibility of taking on those kinds of [parenthood] roles. So the problem isn't that teenage pregnancy is a problem, the problem is that the process of educating our daughters and bringing them up to that level of development by that age has been replaced by this European mentality most of us have been educated with. We have to break that cycle. When we look at what is being taught in the schools today, it's really death at an early age; it's cultural genocide.

There is only one way to change that. An Afrocentric curriculum is a part of that. But we have to go beyond that and begin to look at how we go about controlling the institutions that feed the minds of our children. Nobody allows the oppressor to educate their children and end up with some successful generations somewhere down the line. It's never been like that.

That's one of the things that Fidel Castro did when he [transformed] Cuba. The first thing he dealt with was the educational system.[4] To begin to educate a whole nation of people, to begin to recognize how they had been exploited and how the system of capitalism has basically taken over their land. And that's how it is here in America today. A small minority of people are controlling a large segment of the economy and the political system as well. At some point we have to ask ourselves: Who really owns the land and the soil? And we have to begin to realize that a part of our community would entail collectives in which people share in the wealth of the community. We have to look at that issue seriously. It's not a popular issue right now here in the United States but I believe we have to make it popular, and I think our survival depends on making it popular. I don't think we can continue to have people being turned away from hospitals simply because of the lack of money. There's no national health care plan. You're telling me you can put people on the moon but you can't guarantee health care for everyone in this country? What's the problem with that? The problem with that is that we put our progress before people. It's a mentality, a very capitalistic mentality, that is being propagated through-out the world that this is the best way to go about organizing our communities. It's not the best way. The results are plainly evident with the mass of homeless people and so forth in this country. It's not the best way for our community to be organized. We have to get serious about some of these issues. And a lot of this begins with having some land and being able to bring together representative councils who can direct policy that's going to be implemented to affect the lives of our peoples.

This might seem far out and abstract to a lot of people, but I remind people of some of the events I draw hope and inspiration from, of the Berlin Wall, the disintegration of the Soviet Union,[5] and those types of events that people thought would never happen. But all of a sudden they began to tumble down when peoples' thoughts began to raise up. And if capitalism has done anything, probably one of the good aspects of capital-ism in this country is that it has developed these production facilities to bring in socialism. What's lacking is the mentality of the city councils and governing bodies of this country. If we had this social mentality in place, we'd certainly have the lines of production, facilities, and so forth through-out this country to make sure that everyone has decent housing and health care. Some things should be guaranteed to humans. People, like [the CEO's of] Exxon and the Kennedys and so forth, who have amassed huge amounts of wealth should not be allowed to just take over certain airwaves and so forth. These are our airwaves. They belong to the people. Why are we paying water bills when the water waves belong to the people? Why don't we just pay a flat fee that's going to develop our plants, the water treatment plants, and then give the water to the people for free? That's who it belongs to you know. As long as we have these capitalistic mentalities dominating the productions and dominating every aspect of our lives, it's really an extension of slavery. It's come down to a slavery mentality. We have to change that.

Something is fundamentally wrong when we have people like Ross Perot making billions and people standing around on the corner unable to get something to eat. Something is wrong with that and it has to be seriously addressed. Once you start addressing the land issue, of course, you begin to address a lot of issues, and that's why it's so important for us to address the land issue, even now.

People like Malcolm have died, people like Sojourner Truth,[6] and so many leaders have come along and helped to keep us alive, and we're still here. That's a good and important sign. But as we go into the twenty-first century, we have to be very concerned about what's happening to us as a people in this country. We need to be very alarmed over the increase in incarcerations of our people and the mentality of our people in this country. If Malcolm knew that we accepted a lot of the things we do today, he would be totally outraged. If [Rev. Martin Luther] King [Jr.] could come back and really look at what's happening here, he'd really turn over in his grave because the "Dream" has still gone unrealized in all of these years.[7] If anything it has really become a nightmare.

How do we go about the creation of an internal control? We need to get some of our best minds and debate this issue, if necessary. One of things I'm studying right now is the rights of international people, the international minorities, and how the struggle for minority rights in Quebec for instance, led to an election where the people came very close to being able to control their destinies.[8] They haven't given up and I think eventually they're going to be able to bring it back up.

Gaither: Yes, indeed, I think they came within one hundred votes. It was close. Much of that had to do with leadership.

Sankofa: I think it's for us not to follow, to sometimes be renegades and say, "Well, we're not gonna go that way." In the spirit of Malcolm, some things you have to take a stand on. I sit back and make so much noise about this death penalty despite the fact that the attorneys constantly say, "Well, you need to be quiet about this, that, and so forth. You need to not draw so much attention to the larger issue. . . ."

I don't know how long we're going to live in this society or how long we're going to live in this world. Nobody is really guaranteed how long they're going to live. And I'm not really concerned about how long as much as with how well I live and how well our people are living. But in the spirit of Malcolm and Dr. King and Frederick Douglass[9] and so many of our leaders, I think we have to be truthful. If something is wrong, we have to have the courage to speak the truth regardless of the circumstances of the events. I think that's what's lacking now. We basically have a lot of politicians out there who have been caught up in this political system and have been spoiled by the comforts of it and are not really speaking truly to what they know to be right, what they know to be just, and what they know to be beneficial to the masses within their communities. That's what we have to be concerned about, not necessarily the few, but the masses out there and what's really affecting them out there. We see children all across this country who are dying. Little brothers are being shot and dying, drugs are being injected into our communities. It's tremendous, you know. So we have to stop it.

The only way we're going to really stop it is to get serious about elevating their pride, their consciousness of who they are and where they came from. When people recognize how important and special they are to their communities, they're not going to be out there mutilating their bodies with drugs and doing things like that.

Gaither: How long did you fast?

Sankofa: I liquid fasted for 149 days. I lost fifty pounds. And part of the reason for that was around the issue of the death penalty, trying to draw attention to the death penalty. And I had a lot of people, from Minister Farrakhan to Ben Chavis, and a lot of other brothers, who called in and expressed sincere concern about me individually. But I pressed on and went as far as I did because I was trying to send a message to all the brothers out there, and particularly people in the death penalty abolitionist movement who I've worked alongside for many years now, that we have to move in a new direction. Because the state is winning right now. We don't want to admit it but the reality is that the state is kicking our ass left and right. People are dying out here and we're sitting around talking about the innocence or guilt of Gary Graham. I think in my case the evidence is there and it's a legitimate issue but when you look at it, none of us are innocent and all of us are guilty if we sit back and allow people to be murdered like this in broad daylight. We have to get serious about this issue. And getting serious about it means that we're going to tell them that you can bring justice to our communities, but we're not going to let you continue to brutalize our community with the death penalty. We're not going to let you come into our communities and basically lynch our brothers and sisters with this death penalty you're not applying in a like manner to your own. There [have] only been three white people in modern history that have been executed for killing a black. The death penalty is seldom, if ever, sought whenever a black person is killed but yet it's used as a tool to victimize, in a sense, to get even, when it's a case of a black person committing murder. We have to get serious about those issues.

There are a lot of brothers that shouldn't be dying and could be saved if we were more serious. Also, we should recognize how fundamental this issue is to our people. The capital punishment issue is not an issue of crime and punishment that so many politicians would like to have you believe. It's about the lack of respect for our people that flows right out of the lynching in the South here. A lot of these judges . . . look at the judge in the Clarence Brandley case. What they said in the Clarence Brandley case is that racism was permeated throughout that whole prosecution throughout the state of Texas.[10]

Yet each and every one of the judges, as well as the district attorneys who were involved in that case were not disciplined or demoted—right there in Montgomery County. That's the reality of what we're dealing with here. And the only way to deal with it in a significant way and in a quantitative way is to deal with it where we begin to attack the whole system. We don't want reforms; we're beyond that. There is no such thing in our minds as a just or humane clemency process that leads to execution. We want the whole process eliminated, we want the whole process stopped. And the way that's going to happen is not with individual cases coming along where guys are innocent—their innocence should be proven, let's work on that and get us out of prison—but even in these cases where these guys are actually guilty of these crimes, we have to develop a plan that saves these guys from the political repression that is continuing. We can't allow it to continue as we go forward.

Gaither: So you see yourself as a political prisoner?

Sankofa: I think it is a very political issue. We have to understand that the death penalty is an issue that's about the political system. It's not as much about the judicial system as we're led to believe. It's a ritual, in a sense, in which it discharges our leaders, community leaders, elected leaders and so forth, of the responsibility and obligations to do something seriously about the crime problem. If the death penalty is the best that you can offer, then something is terribly wrong. But I think it is a very political issue. In my analysis, I see all of us as political prisoners. My case has really attracted attention, but all of us are political prisoners, and what makes us political prisoners are the political decisions that led to our incarceration. Look at the political decisions that lead to incarceration of persons on crack compared to those on cocaine.[11]

It's a political decision that's driving that. In that sense, we are all political prisoners. Not so much because of any ideology held by us, but because of the ideology of those who are incarcerating us. That's what makes us political prisoners. I think it's something America doesn't want to look at and doesn't want to recognize but that's what it is.

We have to look at what's happening in Texas where we have one of the largest incarcerated populations in the nation. A lot of people are making a lot of money off of us in these backwoods of Texas.

Notes

This interview, conducted by Larvester Gaither on February 14, 1996, was originally printed in *The Gaither Reporter*, Vol. 4, No. 6, (March/April 2000): 6–8, 11.

1. *Editor's note:* The Nation of Islam (NOI), founded in Detroit during the Great Depression, was based on the principle of black self-determination and Muslim and Christian religious beliefs. Following the declaration by the NOI's Supreme Minister in 1975 that whites would be allowed into the movement and the organization's move toward a more orthodox Sunni Islam, the NOI split into factions. In 1978, spokesman Louis Farrakhan organized a group that resurrected the original NOI teachings of Black Nationalism and separatism. Although publicly criticized, Farrakhan has also been credited with reaching out to diverse black leaders in an effort to organize for positive change in black communities. (Suzanne Albulak, "Nation of Islam," *Africana: Encyclopedia of the African and African American Experience*, eds. Kwame Anthony Appiah and Henry Louis Gates Jr. [New York: Basic Civitas Books, 1999, boxed ed.], 1399–1400).

2. *Editor's note:* Benjamin Chavis served as Executive Director of the NAACP from April 1993 to August 1994. An NAACP member since age twelve, Chavis was convicted of arson and conspiracy in 1972 and imprisoned for four years. A member of the "Wilmington Ten," Chavis was convicted along with nine others for his involvement in a student protest of discrimination in Wilmington, North Carolina, which culminated in a week-long riot. In 1980, his conviction was overturned. While Executive Director of the NAACP, Chavis was criticized for reaching out to Louis Farrakhan and the NOI and holding a gang summit in order to address black-on-black youth violence. Upon leaving the NAACP, Chavis went to work with the NOI, and helped organize the 1995 Million Man March. (Kate Tuttle, "Benjamin Chavis," *Africana: Encyclopedia of the African and African American Experience*, 413).

3. *Editor's note:* In 1995, Nation of Islam leader Louis Farrakhan called for a national "Day of Atonement" to draw attention to the social and economic problems plaguing black males. In response, the Million Man March was organized and, on October 16, 1995, approximately nine hundred thousand to over one million black men congregated in Washington, D.C. to hear speeches from black leaders, including Maya Angelou, Jesse Jackson, and Louis Farrakhan. The March was criticized for its sole emphasis on black male leadership, Farrakhan's reputation as anti-Semitic, and for alleged erasure of systemic racism within American institutions.

4. *Editor's note:* Following the triumph of the 1959 Cuban popular revolution, Fidel Castro established a universal, free, standardized system of education. An all-encompassing literacy campaign in 1961 and a complete reform of urban and rural schools gave Cuba the highest literacy rate (above 95 percent) and average educational levels of any country in Latin America. See Martin Carnoy, "Educational Reform and Social Transformation in Cuba, 1959–1989," in *Education and Social Transition in the Third World*, eds. Martin Carnoy and Joel Samoff (Princeton, NJ: Princeton University Press, 1990).

5. *Editor's note:* The Berlin Wall was erected as a barrier between East and West Germany in 1961. With the fall of the East German government in 1989, the border was opened and openings were made in the Wall. A restructuring of the political and economic system of the U.S.S.R. began in the late 1980s, and in 1991, following a coup, the Communist Party of the Soviet Union was abolished, and the republics that formerly made up the Union became sovereign states.

6. *Editor's note:* Sojourner Truth (Isabella Van Wagenen; c. 1797–1883) was born into slavery in Ulster County, New York. Inspired by a faith in God, she fled slavery, joined the American Methodist Episcopal Zion Church in New York City, and soon became known for her extraordinary preaching skills. At age forty-six, she changed her name and joined the abolitionist movement. During the Civil War she worked supporting black soldiers and freed people, and in 1864 she met with Abraham Lincoln. In her last years, disillusioned by the failure of Reconstruction in the South, she became an advocate of racial separation. See Arthur H. Fauset, *Sojourner Truth: God's Faithful Pilgrim* (Chapel Hill: University of North Carolina Press, 1938); Carleton Mabee and Susan M. Newhouse, *Sojourner Truth: Slave, Prophet, Legend* (New York: New York University Press, 1993); Margaret Washington, ed., *Narrative of Sojourner Truth* (New York: Vintage Books, 1993); Nell Painter, *Sojourner Truth: A Life, A Symbol* (New York: W. W. Norton, 1996).

7. *Editor's note:* At the August 1963 March on Washington, Martin Luther King Jr. delivered his famous "I Have A Dream" speech to over two hundred thousand civil rights supporters, in which he proclaimed, "I have a dream that one day this nation will rise up and live out the true meaning of its creed: 'We hold these truths to be self-evident, that all men are created equal.' . . . I have a dream that one day my four little children will live in a nation where they will not be judged by the color of their skin, but by the content of their character."

8. *Editor's note:* Organizing by the historically strong separatist movement in Quebec, a culturally and linguistically distinct province of Canada, led to an independence referendum on October 30, 1995. By a narrow margin, independence for Quebec was defeated in this vote.

9. *Editor's note:* Frederick Douglass (c. 1817–1895), the most widely known African American leader of his time, escaped from slavery in 1836. In 1845, he published his first autobiography, and in 1847 he founded the *North Star*, an abolitionist newspaper. During the Civil War, Douglass successfully opposed President Abraham Lincoln's policy of excluding African Americans from the armed forces. After emancipation, he advocated civil rights and political participation for African Americans, and was active in the Republican Party, under which he occupied a number of government posts. See Frederick Douglass, *Frederick Douglass: Autobi-*

ographies, ed. Henry Louis Gates (New York: Library of America, 1994); Frederick Douglass, *Frederick Douglass: The Narrative and Selected Writings*, ed. Michael Meyer (New York: Vintage, 1984); Arna Bontemps, *Free at Last: The Life of Frederick Douglass* (New York: Dodd, Mead, 1971).

10. *Editor's note:* In 1990, Clarence Brandley was released from Texas death row, where he had been held since his 1981 conviction for raping a white girl at the Texas high school where he worked (as the school's only black janitor). In overturning his conviction, the Texas Appeals Court ruled that the investigation was sloppy, racist, and a "subversion of justice." Among the evidence exonerating Brandley was hair found on the victim that could not have come from a black man, and the statements of a witness who recanted his testimony and said that police had pressured him into implicating Brandley. As of July 2002, 784 people have been executed since the death penalty was reinstated in 1976, while 101 people have been exonerated and released from death row since 1973. For up-to-date death penalty statistics, see the Death Penalty Information Center, www.deathpenaltyinfo.org.

11. *Editor's note:* For information on the racially coded sentencing differences between crack cocaine use and powder cocaine use, see: Marc Mauer, *Race to Incarcerate* (New York: The New Press, distributed by Norton, 1999); Dan Baum, *Smoke and Mirrors: The War on Drugs and the Politics of Failure* (Boston: Little, Brown, 1996); David Cole, *No Equal Justice: Race and Class in the American Criminal Justice System* (New York: The New Press, 1999); Jerome G. Miller, *Search and Destroy: African-American Males in the Criminal Justice System* (New York: Cambridge University Press, 1996); Human Rights Watch, "Punishment and Prejudice: Racial Disparities in the War on Drugs," *A Human Rights Watch Report*, Vol. 12, No. 2, May 2000; Human Rights Watch, "Incarcerated-America," *Human Rights Watch Backgrounder*, April 2003.

26

Alan Berkman

Born in 1945, Alan Berkman has been involved in resistance movements as both an activist and a medical doctor. Berkman treated wounded prisoners after the Attica Rebellion in 1971 and Native Americans at Wounded Knee in 1973; he also helped treat and defend several Puerto Rican *independentistas* and Black Liberation Army (BLA) militants. In 1982, he was imprisoned for seven months for refusing to talk with police about the treatment he gave to Solomon Brown, a BLA member. After his release, Berkman was indicted for providing medical treatment in a federal conspiracy case; he went underground until 1985 when he was arrested as one of seven white anti-imperialists who carried out a series of bombings to protest U.S. foreign intervention and racist domestic policies ("Resistance Conspiracy" case). While "locked down" in the segregation unit of the Chester County Jail in West Chester, Pennsylvania, Dr. Berkman developed Hodgkin's lymphoma. Knowing he could not survive if forced to serve a long sentence under prison health care, his codefendants (who included Laura Whitehorn and Susan Rosenberg) organized a public battle and engaged in a plea bargain for his medical treatment and parole.

In 1992, Berkman was released. He renewed his practice almost immediately, treating poor, homeless, and mentally ill people with HIV and AIDS. He now has a faculty appointment at Columbia University and is helping to promote AIDS treatment programs for developing countries such as South Africa, Thailand, and the Dominican Republic.

Engaged in Life: Alan Berkman on Prison Health Care (as told to Susie Day) 2003

There's a standard way to examine somebody under the armpit, whether it's for a lymph node or a breast examination. You tell the patient to put their arm on their lap so that the muscles relax. But instead, the doctor—who was an older man, retired—told me to put my arm up above my head—which is exactly the wrong thing to do because it tightens the muscles and makes it harder to feel up in the axilla. He said he couldn't feel the enlarged lymph node, and I knew that I was in trouble, because this guy had no idea how to examine a patient.

So I took advantage of the fact that I'm a doctor, and I said to him, "As a colleague, I would like to ask you to let me take your hand and show you where the enlarged lymph node is." Now, because I was a political prisoner, he was totally nervous and uptight, but I really tried, because I realized he didn't know what he was doing. So I lowered my arm, relaxed the muscle, and he allowed me to guide his hand, and said, "Oh, yeah. I can feel it." He assured me that he would get a surgeon to see me.

A few weeks later, they came. They wouldn't let me out to make any phone calls, then they cut off the water in my cell. That was the tip-off that I was going for surgery the next day—rather than tell me "don't drink anything," they cut the water off.

Counting for Nothing

When you're sick in prison, it's the security that dominates. You're scared there might be something seriously wrong. And, you're going to the hospital in chains with what we call a "black box"—which is a set of solid handcuffs that go over regular handcuffs that hold the hands directly to a

Susie Day's biographical sketch appears on page 260.

waist chain; also, there are leg irons—in a caravan of six cars with heavily armed Pennsylvania State troopers and U.S. Marshals who go with you into the operating room. The fact that you're sick and frightened, like any other human being, counts for nothing. I could tell you many stories about the inhumane treatment, always under the guise of security.

So the lymph node was taken out, and I was called to a nurse's office, and told that I had cancer.

Now, if I had been a young black man—which is who most people were in the Chester County Jail [in West Chester, PA]—the doctor never would have let me take his hand, and probably would have missed the lymph node. The fact I was a doctor got me diagnosed. If I weren't a doctor, I don't know how much longer it would have been, how much sicker I would have had to be, before the diagnosis would have been made.

Desperate, Dumb, Despicable

When I was a young doctor—this was in 1973—I worked at the Bronx House of Detention. The doctor I was replacing was a man in his late seventies. And the only antibiotic (this is the absolute truth) he knew how to use was penicillin, which had come out around 1945. He had not kept up with anything. He was working in a prison that was overwhelmingly black and Latino, and he used to call the young black men "boys," and couldn't figure out why they didn't like him. That's not a caricature of who works in prisons.

Usually, you get the desperate, the dumb, the despicable doctors in prison. Administrators use doctors who can't get hired any place else. Sometimes, people can't get hired for good reasons: They're bad doctors; they're old and their medical knowledge is out of date; and they can't get along with patients, so they work in prisons, because the opinions of the "patients" don't matter.

When I was in Marion Penitentiary—which is a federal prison and not a county jail like Chester County—there was one doctor there. He had been at this prison for ten years, and had never been able to pass a state licensing exam because, in the federal system, you don't have to have a state license. Yet, as far as the prison was concerned, he was competent to take care of men.

Guaranteed Worse Care

Unfortunately, it's not uncommon to hear some prisoners say, "Prisons saved my life," especially if they were using drugs on the outside and not taking care of themselves, or if they have HIV or Hepatitis C. But that's not the same as outside commentators saying that prisoners get *better* medical care. That is an outright lie. Commentators will argue, "Prisoners are guaranteed medical care." Well, under the law, a certain level of treatment *is* guaranteed, but that's because if you take people's freedom away and deny them access to their own doctors, you'd better supply some medical care, or you're just killing people.

Medical care in prisons is, by and large, below the standard for the community outside. When doctors work in the community, other doctors, in a variety of agencies, review their work. If your patients think you've messed them up, they have the right to sue you. For prison doctors, there's no peer review. And, while prisoners can file suits, the standard of malpractice a prisoner lawsuit has to reach is much higher than it is in the community.

It's not just that prisons try to save money by hiring the worst practitioners and the fewest doctors they can; it's that it's very important that the prisoners not be seen as human beings. Certainly, there are some doctors and nurses and physicians assistants who try to do a good job. But the security people will pressure them and say, "You're too sympathetic," and make fun of them. If you still don't capitulate and become "one of the boys" in looking down at prisoners, they can make it very uncomfortable for you to work there. It's part of the culture; the job of prisons is to dehumanize people.

Misfortunes in Prisoners' Eyes

I did know a doctor who broke through and was a decent human being. Much later, after the chemotherapy, I went for rehab out in Rochester, Minnesota. My doctor was a man about five years older than I—he was a much better doctor than most. He had, earlier in his career, worked in the Mayo Clinic. He was semiretired, then took this position at the prison to keep busy without having to run his own practice. Over time—I was there more than a year—we got to know each other, and he told me an interesting story.

When he was hired, he got sent to a two-week initiation, run by the Federal Bureau of Prisons in Virginia. Security is really what it was about. He said one of the hardest things for him was that they insisted that you, if you were working as a medical person, not look the prisoner in the eye. It was very important that the prisoner not be allowed to engage you directly, because *equals* exchange gazes.

Of course, it's exactly the opposite of what a good health care practitioner should do. Part of being a healer, that has nothing to do with the diagnosis per se, is that you share some humanity with your patient; it's in the gaze that you establish the fact that we're both human beings. "You can share your concerns, you can talk to me"—that's the core of the doctor-patient relationship. So the shared sense of humanity that makes medicine work is totally destroyed in the prison context, where it's about domination and inequality.

Worst Epidemic, Worst Doctors

Whenever you have severe prison crowding, and when the economy is collapsing, as it is now in the United States—you know that prison health care will be one of the first services to go. There's no constituency that's going to punish a politician for cutting back on that. It's hard to generalize, but I think, in most prisons, as the number of prisoners increases, the number of prison health people does not proportionally increase. So I imagine that the lines to see a doctor are longer, the lines to get your medication are longer. In most prison medical visits I had, nobody bothered to take your temperature or your blood pressure or feel your pulse, anyhow. But if anything, I imagine the medical visits are even shorter now, if that's possible.

Since I got out, I've been involved in a Legal Aid Society program, helping to monitor HIV care among prisoners in New York State. I do think there's been some effort to establish protocols and improve the HIV care. But generally, the proportion of people in prison with HIV and Hepatitis C is much higher than in the general population. So you have these prison health care providers, who are some of the worst doctors—they thought they were retiring someplace where they would see healthy, young people—and they find themselves in the middle of the worst viral disease epidemic in the history of the United States. They're also in an environment where you can't spend time; you're not really supposed to talk to the patient; you're never supposed to believe what the patient tells you.

What We Do for Each Other

Many of my patients in the ten years since I've been out have also been in prison, and I think I understand something about how they react to things. For example, when I got out of prison, I couldn't wait on lines. I would get totally angry and frustrated and upset and have to leave. I really had to think about it for a while, about why I was having such an emotional reaction to waiting, and I realized it was a flashback to being in prison, where I was just a number. It's never incredibly pleasant to be sick or in pain, but prison is a very dangerous place to be ill. When you know that nobody gives a damn about you, and they really don't care if you live or die, then it's a lot more frightening.

Sometimes, people who got out of prison would come to the clinic where I worked, and the doctors and nurses would say, "What's the matter with *them*? They have nothing better to do, why don't they just sit and wait?" I think I understood in a different way that it was an intense emotional reaction that had nothing to do with what was going on at the moment. I learned that from being in prison.

Another thing is that, when I first became a doctor—I think this is generally true—you get trained and become confident and in touch with all the things you can or want to do. Then, as you get older, if you have any sense, you get more humility. You realize that there are limits on what you can do to change serious illness. Mostly, you can help people, when they're sick, to figure out how they're going to manage their own illness. And if it's a serious illness, you may have to help them manage their own death.

The one thing I realized about being ill in prison is that I do not want to die alone. And I was thinking—because I was quite close to death on a number of occasions—that it would have been so nice when I was feeling sick to have somebody hold my hand, to have somebody who knew me look at me, care about me. It might not have changed the outcome, but I think it would have changed the reality for me. That's the thing that I learned the most—the role of what we do for each other as human beings.

So, when I was at the clinic, taking care of people with AIDS—and we had a lot of people dying in the early first years—I think I had a sensitivity to making sure that we spent time with the dying patients. We didn't just let them stay in their room. The doctors, the nurses, the social workers—all of us—would make sure we touched the person's hand and did something to make that human contact.

Chained, Paralyzed—Alive

I remember, toward the end of those rounds of chemotherapy, in December 1990, in the prison hospital, I was very sick, and pretty much paralyzed, and I was chained to the bed. And I started feeling myself going into shock. I remember quite consciously thinking, "Do I want to call the doctor? Do I want to get treated for this or should I just die? Maybe that's better than another ten or fifteen years of being in prison, paralyzed, in the hands of these guards who hate me."

But I went ahead and called the nurse and told her to get the doctor. So I don't know if there was a particular thing that kept me alive. I'm not

sure you could say that it was my commitment to the struggle or a vision
of my children or anything like that. It was feeling engaged in life and
wanting to continue to be part of it. I would wake up in the morning and I
still wanted to be there. So I was committed to doing everything I could to
get through the days.

I was fortunate that there was a campaign that demanded care for me,
and my friends and family were wonderful, and they had an impact. For
prisoners as a whole, it's much harder. The fundamental issue is, as long as
our society is a vehicle for racism and class domination, as long as deeply
exploitative relationships exist, I'm not sure that, other than in isolated
cases, we're going to improve prison health care. But we're all human
beings. We're all mortal. We get sick. We share that. And we have to
demand that prisoners be treated with respect as human beings.

27

Philip Berrigan
(with Amy Goodman and Jeremy Scahill)

Philip Berrigan was born October 5, 1923, near Bemidji, Minnesota. Ordained a Catholic priest in 1955, he soon became involved in the Civil Rights movement and the antiwar movement. For the next forty years, Berrigan organized grassroots action from inside and outside of prison, often working closely with his brother, Daniel Berrigan, S. J. Cofounder of the Plowshares movement and the Jonah House community of war resisters, Philip Berrigan spent over ten years in prison for over one hundred acts of antinuclear resistance. He wrote, lectured, and taught extensively, publishing six books, including his autobiography, *Fighting the Lamb's War*. Berrigan left the priesthood and eventually married peace activist Elizabeth McAllister. He died of cancer at Jonah House in Baltimore, Maryland on December 6, 2002.

Amy Goodman is Host and Executive Producer of Pacifica Radio's Democracy Now! She has won numerous awards for documentary work in East Timor and a 1998 radio documentary, *Drilling and Killing: Chevron and Nigeria's Oil Dictatorship,* which she produced with Jeremy Scahill. Scahill is a correspondent and producer for Democracy Now! who spent most of 2002 reporting from Iraq, where he coordinated www.iraqjournal.org.

References

Berrigan, Philip and Fred A. Wilcox. *Fighting the Lamb's War: Skirmishes with the American Empire: The Autobiography of Philip Berrigan.* Monroe, ME: Common Courage Press, 1996.
O'Grady, Jim and Murray Polner. *Disarmed and Dangerous: The Radical Life and Times of Daniel and Philip Berrigan.* Boulder, CO: Westview Press, 1998.

"It's Too Bad the Soil Couldn't Cry Out from the Blood Shed Upon It" 1998

Jeremy Scahill: Phil, beyond your having been in solitary confinement for ten days and your being isolated from your family and friends right now, there is a new kind of action on the part of the government that is facing Ploughshares activists as they are coming out of prison. That is that they are not being allowed to return home. Could you talk about this latest string of actions on the part of the government against Plowshares activists?

Philip Berrigan: Let me spend a moment on those measures taken by the government. They have attempted to infiltrate us. They have practiced intensive dirty tricks against us. They have kept us under off-and-on surveillance. It's like the sixties all over again. All of those measures have failed and Ploughshares continues, not only abroad but here in the United States. There have been about fifty-six or fifty-seven of these disarmament actions. So what they are trying now is to break up our communities. And they are taking it upon themselves to add to the sentences of these activists coming out of jail who not only nonviolently stood by for arrest but also went to court nonviolently and did their best to battle with these disasters that we call courts.

Amy Goodman: Before we talk about the first Plowshares action that took place in 1980, in King of Prussia, Pennsylvania, I wanted to ask you about the founding of Jonah House. Jonah House was founded in 1973 in Baltimore. What is it?

Berrigan: It's a nonviolent resistance community. We hold all things in common, we practice voluntary poverty, we work with our hands to earn what we need for our living and our work. And that means supporting any effort toward resistance and peace. We don't say one of our priorities is

Editor's note: For an audio version of the complete text, go to www.democracynow.org.

297

serving the poor, though we do an awful lot of work on behalf of the poor. For something like twenty-three years we bagged sizable amounts of fruits and vegetables and fish from wholesalers outside of Baltimore and then shared it with quite a desperately poor African American neighborhood. So we did do that, and we did it twice a week for twenty-three years. It's been that way now since 1973, and the community has paid a quite sizable price not only in actions but also in jail time. We speak about a revolving door between prison and what we call minimum security, which is living in this society. As you know the prisons have this term minimum security. That's a camp right over there, that's Petersburg camp, and that's a minimum-security institution. This is a FCI, a Federal Corrrection Institution, another level up.

Goodman: So where you are incarcerated is not minimum security. It's higher than that. Now you are clearly a nonviolent offender, well known by the courts and judges of this country. Why aren't you in minimum security?

Berrigan: Because for some aspect or another I'm a security risk. And because my chances for influencing others to the detriment of the government would be greater over there than here.

Scahill: I've heard you say before that an act of resistance does not end with your arrest but that the resistance continues in the prison.

Berrigan: We try to thrash out what we call "prison witness." You draw a lot of lessons from what we experienced during the Vietnam War; and you wonder at how a movement was built up outside, outside the walls, with all these young guys imprisoned who refused to fight in Vietnam, who were not interested in running to Canada or Sweden or any of those places. But the fact of the matter is that they were doing a hearts and minds and spirits thing. They were influencing their own constituencies outside. Which is to say their campuses, their churches, their neighborhoods, their relatives. So they were doing very valuable work and very often unaware of that. And meanwhile the so-called movement outside ran into perhaps fifty to sixty million who at least dissented from the war, and a large portion, too, resisted the war. And that of course brought about the downfall of President [Lyndon B.] Johnson. So this prison witness in American tradition, nonviolent tradition, has always been a very valuable and even central increment in the whole thing. People are not willing to forget that you are in prison and that you voluntarily sacrifice your physical freedom. I do perhaps much more good here than I do outside, and I work fairly solidly, as all of us do, against war and all its pomps and circumstances. So [Catholic Worker founder] Dorothy Day, for that reason, said, you know we have to fill up the jails. And you have to have the faith and you have to have the sense of justice and decency to do that.

Scahill: Now Phil, tell us how it was that you came to be kicked out of prison after your arrest at the King of Prussia.

Berrigan: Well, we determined to stay in [prison] in order to work out this business of prison witness. That was one factor. And then because we realized that middle-class folk like ourselves only identify with the poor when you're in prison. That's it. Not outside. You know, we can always go to a clean bed and decent food as the poor can't. So we were working all of that out and one of our number was a lawyer and he began to work with one of the jailhouse lawyers. And they began to pry the prisoners in that jail away from the clutches of the courts across the street because the jail was right across the street from the courthouse, the Montgomery County Courthouse. And these prisoners resolved to fight their cases, which meant trials. And the clones across the street did not want to go to trial, too much work, too much paperwork, to much expense, bla bla bla, too many lawyers had to be called in. So it got to the point where we became intolerable just by taking measures like that.

Scahill: Initially following your arrest the authorities hadn't set any bail on your head. Then as this trouble started to go on in the prison with you guys working with the other inmates and with a jailhouse lawyer, magically a dollar amount appeared on your head. Then slowly that was reduced and reduced until finally the authorities came to you and said you don't have to pay anything, you don't have to sign anything, you don't have to agree to anything, I just want you out of my prison.

Berrigan: It amounted to that.

Scahill: As President Clinton very nearly took us to the brink of war not too long ago, a lot of resistance was going on around the country. I've heard you talk about what we need in this country is the moral equivalent of war. Would you explain what you mean by that?

Berrigan: Well, the American philosopher, I guess it was, William James, wrote this brilliant essay where he said you know we'll end war when there's a moral equivalent of war. Which is to say all the energy and genius and money and everything somehow has to be matched on the other side of the ledger with moral investment. And just to give a simple example, when a young guy goes in military service he can be sent to far off lands, he can be sent into war, he can risk his life, he can lose his life, what have you. The risks for peace are negligible here in this country. Americans have a terrible fear of losing their physical liberty, a fear of jail. And there's a whole rhetoric, a whole volume of purple language passed on about what a horrible place jail is and so on. As though good, solid, middle-class, well-educated folk could not put up with jail as well as poor people do. In any event, some thought has to be given to this moral equivalent of war, because so much of what is wrong in this world is trace-able back to us, and we have to be responsible for it. And we have to find out what the moral equivalent really is and then implement that.

Goodman: Philip Berrigan, the prison authorities have just come over and said that we have to wrap this interview up. You're seventy-four years old. You've served more than ten years in prison for different actions at different times. [*Berrigan:* "A little bit less than that. It'll be about nine years when I finish this one."] Nine years. Some might say well, what has it accomplished, and especially that image of using a household hammer to pound a nuclear warhead? In the end, isn't this really just symbolic?

Berrigan: Well it's also real, you know. Some of our friends get charged with enormous volumes of damage simply because they're dealing with highly technical stuff, very sensitive stuff. It's also real. But we have to avoid maximum destruction because you have to preserve the symbol and what it can say to folks. . . . And the symbol of the hammer and the symbol of blood—because they're both universal elements—say very simply that we all have a responsibility to do this. We disarm, see, or we die. [President John F.] Kennedy used to make that clear. Martin Luther King [Jr.] did. We've been saying it repeatedly, my brother, myself, and other friends for thirty years now. We disarm or we die. We can't coexist with these weapons for much longer. That's fairly predictable. So that symbol that says that has to be preserved. You can't get into an orgy of destruction because the destruction becomes the issue and not the symbol of disarmament. So we are very scrupulous about that.

Scahill: How far have we come from since the Vietnam War and where do we go from here?

Berrigan: Things are going from bad to worse. Life in this country is becoming more and more ugly, to begin with. Outside of the recent upris-ing against the threat to Iraq, people were pretty dormant. They were hiding behind the woodwork. And a great deal of confusion is present about whether anything can be done at all. And that is a product of the way we live in this country, it's a product of lifestyle, it's a product of dis-information coming from the government. It's a product of moral confu-sion because the churches, the synagogues, the media, and the campus are not doing their work. So Americans are more and more helpless. To anyone thoughtful with their eyes open, things are rather dire. The econ-omy is booming, the Dow Jones is up, but that does not disguise what is really happening in our slums.

Goodman: What are your plans after this, Phil Berrigan, after you've served your time?

Berrigan: Well it's not too productive to plan, Amy. I guess what you do is hit the bricks, as they used to say, and start to listen to people who have been living with this mess for quite a long time while you were locked up, and then to plan with them. Do real communitarian work. In the Catholic Church we come from a tradition of community . . . fraught with defects and bad philosophical approaches, what have you. But it's still there and we need to build on it because that's what Christ did as a first public act. He built a community. And for us this means a nonviolent resistance community.

Note

This interview first aired on May 27, 2002, on Democracy Now! Radio; it was conducted from inside the Petersburg federal penitentiary in West Virginia on March 14, 1998.

Appendix 1

The Attica Liberation Faction Manifesto of Demands and Anti-Depression Platform

We, the imprisoned men of Attica Prison,[1] seek an end to the injustice suffered by all prisoners, regardless of race, creed, or color.

The preparation and content of this document has been constructed under the unified efforts of all races and social segments of this prison.

It is a matter of documented record and human recognition that the administration of the New York Prison System has restructured the institutions that were designed to socially correct men into the fascist concentration camps of modern America.

Due to the conditional fact that Attica Prison is one of the most classic institutions of authoritative inhumanity upon men, the following manifesto of demands [is] being submitted:

"Man's right to knowledge and free use thereof…"

We, the inmates of Attica Prison, have grown to recognize beyond the shadow of a doubt, that because of our posture as prisoners and branded characters as alleged criminals, the administration and prison employees no longer consider or respect us as human beings, but rather as domesticated animals selected to do their bidding in slave labor and furnished as a personal whipping dog for their sadistic, psychopathic hate.

We, the inmates of Attica Prison, say to you, the sincere people of society, the prison system of which your courts have rendered us unto is without question the authoritative fangs of a coward in power.

Respectfully submitted to the people as a protest to the vile and vicious slave masters:

The Governor of New York State
The N.Y.S. Department of Corrections
The N.Y.S. Legislature
The N.Y.S. Courts

The United States Courts
The N.Y.S. Parole Board
And those who support this system of injustice

The inmates of this prison have vested the power of negotiation regarding the settlement of the stipulated demands within the judgment and control of these men:

Donald Noble 26777
Peter Butler 26018
Frank Lott 26148
Carl Jones-El 24534
Herbert Blyden X 22480

All and any negotiation will be conducted by prison and state authorities with these five men.

These demands are being presented to you. There is no strike of any kind to protest these demands. We are *trying* to do this in a democratic fashion. We feel there is no need to dramatize our demands.

We, the men of Attica Prison, have been committed to the N.Y.S. Department of Corrections by the people of society for the purpose of correcting what [have] been deemed social errors in behavior. Errors that have classified us as socially unacceptable until programmed with new values and more thorough understanding as to our value and responsibilities as members of the outside community. The Attica Prison program in its structure and conditions has been enslaved on the pages of this manifesto of demands with the blood, sweat, and tears of the inmates of this prison.

The programs, which we are submitted to under the façade of rehabilitation, are relative to the ancient stupidity of pouring water on a drowning man, inasmuch as we are treated for our hostilities by our program administrators with their hostility as a medication.

In our efforts to comprehend on a feeling level an existence contrary to violence, we are victimized by the exploitation and the denial of the celebrated due process of law.

In our peaceful efforts to assemble in dissent as provided under this nation's United States Constitution, we are in turn murdered, brutalized, and framed on various criminal charges because we seek the rights and privileges of all American people.

In our efforts to intellectually expand in keeping with the outside world, through all categories of news media, we are systematically restricted and punitively offended to isolation status when we insist on our human rights to the wisdom of awareness.

Manifesto of Demands

1. We demand the constitutional rights of legal representation at the time of all parole board hearings; and the protection from the procedures of the parole authorities whereby they permit no procedural safeguards such as an attorney for cross-examination of witnesses, witnesses on behalf of the parolee, at the parole revocation hearings.
2. We demand a change in medical staff and medical policy and procedure. The Attica Prison Hospital is totally inadequate, understaffed, prejudiced in the treatment of inmates. There are numerous "mistakes" made. Many times, improper and erroneous medication is given by untrained personnel. We also demand periodical check-ups on all prisoners and sufficient licensed practitioners 24 hours a day instead of inmate help that is used now.
3. We demand adequate visiting conditions and facilities for the inmates and families of Attica prisoners. The visiting facilities at this prison are such as to preclude adequate visiting for the inmates and their families.
4. We demand an end to the segregation of prisoners from the mainline population because of their political beliefs. Some of the men in segregation units are confined there solely for political reasons and their segregation from other inmates is indefinite.
5. We demand an end to the persecution and punishment of prisoners who practice the constitutional right of peaceful dissent. Prisoners at Attica and other N.Y.S. prisons cannot be compelled to work, as these prisons were built for the purpose of housing prisoners and there is no mention as to the prisoners being required to work on prison jobs in order to remain in the mainline population and/or be considered for release. Many prisoners believe their labor power is being exploited in order for the state to increase its economic power and to continue to expand its correctional industries (which are million-dollar complexes), yet do not develop working skills acceptable for employment in the outside society, and which do not pay the prisoner more than an average of forty cents a day. Most prisoners never make more than fifty cents a day. Prisoners who refuse to work for the outrageous scale, or who strike, are punished and segregated without the access to the privileges shared by those who work; this is class legislation, class division, and creates hostilities within the prison.
6. We demand an end to the political persecution, racial persecution, and the denial of prisoners' rights to subscribe to political papers, books, or any other educational and current media chronicles that are forwarded through the United States mail.

7. We demand that industries be allowed to enter the institutions and employ inmates to work eight hours a day and fit into the category of workers for scale wages. The working conditions in prisons do not develop working incentives parallel to the many jobs in the outside society, and a paroled prisoner faces many contradictions of the job that adds to his difficulty in adjusting. Those industries outside who desire prisons should be allowed to enter for the purpose of employment placement.

8. We demand that inmates be granted the right to join or form a labor union.

9. We demand that inmates be granted the right to support their own families; at present, thousands of welfare recipients have to divide their checks to support their imprisoned relatives who, without the outside support, cannot even buy toilet articles or food. Men working on scale wages could support themselves and families while in prison.

10. We demand that correctional officers be prosecuted as a matter of law for any acts of cruel and unusual punishment where it is not a matter of life or death.

11. We demand that all institutions using inmate labor be made to conform with the state and federal minimum wage laws.

12. We demand an end to the escalating practice of physical brutality being perpetrated upon the inmates of N.Y.S. prisons.

13. We demand the appointment of three lawyers from the N.Y.S. Bar Association to full-time positions for the provision of legal assistance to inmates seeking post-conviction relief, and to act as a liaison between the administration and inmates for bringing inmate complaints to the attention of the administration.

14. We demand the updating of industry working conditions to the standards provided for under N.Y.S. law.

15. We demand the establishment of an inmate workers' insurance plan to provide compensation for work-related accidents.

16. We demand the establishment of unionized vocational training programs comparable to that of the federal prison system, which provides for union instructions, union pay scales, and union membership upon completion of the vocational training course.

17. We demand annual accounting of the inmates recreation fund and formulation of an inmate committee to give inmates a voice as to how such funds are used.

18. We demand that the present parole board appointed by the governor be eradicated and replaced by a parole board elected by popular vote of the people. In a world where many crimes are punished by indeterminate sentences and where authority acts within secrecy and within

vast discretion . . . heavy weight [is given] to accusations by prisons employees against inmates, inmates feel trapped unless they are willing to abandon their [right] to be independent men.

19. We demand that the state legislature create a full-time salaried board of overseer for the state prisons. The board would be responsible for evaluating allegations made by inmates, inmates families, their friends and lawyers against employees charged with acting inhumanely, illegally, or unreasonably. The board should included people nominated by a psychological or psychiatric association, by the state bar association, or by the civil liberties union, and by groups of concerned, involved laymen.

20. We demand an immediate end to the agitation of race relations by the prison administration of this state.

21. We demand the Department of Corrections furnish all prisoners with the services of ethnic counselors for the needed special services of the brown and black population of this prison.

22. We demand an end to the discrimination in the judgment and quota of parole for black and brown people.

23. We demand that all prisoners be present at the time their cells and property are being searched by the correctional officers of state prisons.

24. We demand an end to the discrimination against prisoners when they appear before the parole board. Most prisoners are denied parole solely because of their previous records. Life sentences should not confine a man longer than ten years, as a seven year duration is the considered statute for a lifetime out of circulation, and if a man cannot be rehabilitated after a maximum of ten years of constructive programs, etcetera, then he belongs in a mental hygiene center, not a prison.

25. We demand an end to the unsanitary conditions that exist in the mess hall: that is, dirty trays, dirty utensils, stained drinking cups, and an end to the practice of putting food on the tables hours before eating time without any protective covering put over it.

26. We demand that better food be served to the inmates. The food is a gastronomical disaster. We also demand that drinking water be put on each table and that each inmate be allowed to take as much food as he wants and as much bread as he wants, instead of the severely limited portions and limited (4) slices of bread. Inmates wishing a pork-free diet should have one, since 85 percent of our diet is pork meat or pork-saturated food.

27. We demand that there be one set of rules governing all prisons in this state instead of the present system where each warden makes the rules for his institution as he sees fit.

In Conclusion

We are firm in our resolve and we demand, as human beings, the dignity and justice that is due to us by right of our birth. We do not know how the present system of brutality and dehumanization and injustices has been allowed to be perpetrated in this day of enlightenment, but we are the living proof of its existence and we cannot allow it to continue.

The taxpayers who just happen to be our mothers, fathers, sisters, brothers, daughters, and sons should be made aware of how their tax dollars are being spent to deny their sons, brothers, fathers, and uncles of justice, equality, and dignity.

> Attica Liberation Faction
> Donald Noble 26777
> Peter Butler 26018
> Frank Lott 26148
> Carl Jones-El 24534
> Herbert Blyden X 22480

Note

1. *Editor's note*: The "Attica Brothers" were the sixty men charged with a total of over 1,400 felonies resulting from the September 1971 rebellion at the Attica Correctional Facility in New York. Prisoners at Attica rebelled in protest to the prison administration's failure to address the prisoners' duly issued complaints about the poor conditions in the prison. The uprising grew from solidarity among prisoners forged following the August 1971 killing of prison writer and Black Panther George Jackson by guards at San Quentin Prison in California. More than 1,500 prisoners cooperated, across racial lines, and seized the prison and held hostages for five days. Despite warnings by observers and prisoner-selected mediators, Governor Nelson Rockefeller of New York ordered that the prison be retaken by force. State troopers stormed the grounds, armed with high-powered rifles and shotguns, and fired some 4,500 rounds of ammunition at prisoners and hostages. Forty-three people were killed, including signer of the Attica Manifesto Herbert Blyden, and 150 shot—all from the fire of the state troopers. The sixty prisoners charged following the suppression of rebellion were defended by a team of volunteer lawyers and supported by a national movement, and by 1976 nearly all charges against them were dismissed. In 1974, a civil suit was filed against the state of New York alleging mismanagement and cruelty in the suppression of the rebellion. Following numerous delays by the state, which hired private lawyers, in a series of trials in 1991 and 1992, juries ruled that the state had engaged in cruel and unusual punishment and found that there had been violations of human and civil rights. In 2000, New York State was forced to settle for $12 million. See

30 Years After the Attica Rebellion, radio documentary (Freedom Archives, 2001), available at www.freedomarchives.org; *Eyes on the Prize Part II: A Nation of Law?* (Boston: Blackside Productions; Alexandria, VA: PBS dist., 1990); Tom Wicker, *A Time to Die* (New York: Quadrangle/New York Times Book Co., 1975).

Appendix 2

David Gilbert

David Gilbert was born in 1945 and raised in the predominantly white suburb of Brookline, Massachusetts. Gilbert, who traces the development of his political consciousness to the Greensboro sit-ins of February 1960, became active in civil rights organizing and resistance to the Vietnam War while a student at Columbia University. In 1962, he joined the Congress of Racial Equality; and in 1965, a month after President Lyndon B. Johnson began bombing North Vietnam, he started the Columbia Independent Committee on Vietnam. One of the founding members of Columbia's Students for a Democratic Society (SDS) chapter, he authored the first SDS pamphlet in 1967. In response to the war in Vietnam and domestic warfare against the Black Liberation Movement, Gilbert joined the Weather Underground, a militant formation of young, white anti-imperialists, in the early 1970s, and remained underground for ten years.

On October 2, 1981, Gilbert was captured by the police in Nyack, New York during an attempted Brink's bank robbery by a unit of the Black Liberation Army (BLA) and other white allies. A shoot-out ensued, resulting in the deaths of a guard, two officers, and BLA member Mtayari Shabaka Sundiata. Captured, charged, and convicted of felony murder, Gilbert was sentenced under New York State's felony murder law, which can place full responsibility for any deaths that occur during a robbery on all parties involved. His is serving a sentence of seventy-five years to life.

A writer and activist, Gilbert has been involved in AIDS peer education in prison since 1986 when his co-defendant Kuwasi Balagoon died of AIDS. His writing has been published in numerous journals and anthologies. In 2004, he published his memoir *No Surrender: Writings from an Anti-Imperialist Political Prisoner.* He is currently incarcerated at Clinton Correctional Facility in New York. David Gilbert is the author of *No Surrender: Writings from an Anti-Imperialist Political Prisoner* (Montreal, CA: Abraham Guillen Press & Arm the Spirit, 2004).

Attica—Thirty Years Later

The standard line among New York State prisoners is that the system, step-by-step, has been taking back all the reforms won in the wake of the heroic sacrifices of the Attica rebellion. In this case the truism is, unfortunately, pretty much true. A complete list of all the losses i've seen since coming upstate in 1983 would be long indeed. They range from the $5 fee (an average week's pay) added on to the isolation time for disciplinary infractions to the introduction of double-celling. One sad setback is the about 90 percent elimination statewide of what had been the most positive prison program—access to college education.[1] This example in particular belies the politicians' claim that their "law and order" campaigns are about protecting citizens from crime. College education was the program with the most striking proven success in cutting the recidivism (return to crime) rate in half.

Perhaps the most ominous change is how difficult it's become for prisoners to get redress in the courts for violations of Constitutional rights. In the late 1980s the courts, responding to political pressure, began interpreting away many of the rights they had discovered after 1971. Then in the 1990s it got qualitatively worse with new laws that gutted the courts' power to maintain ongoing oversight based on class action suits, which had been the most effective legal tool for challenging prison conditions.[2] That made individual access to courts prohibitively expensive for many prisoners. The way staff has been emboldened to regularly violate rights is already being felt. As with the particular example of college, these broader trends are completely counterproductive to the rationale of reducing crime. Sweeping ever more youth into a system that abuses and humiliates them is only a recipe for creating more and worse criminals. If crime were the demagogues' real concern, their cry would be instead for reducing unemployment and providing quality education for all, from the earliest ages up.

The negative trends are still going strong, and certainly at Attica. Since being transferred here in March, i've been shocked by how much worse it is than when i was last here, in 1990. While Attica COs (correction officers) were always aggressive, it is now out of control. Even i—a

313

veteran at navigating the harassment shoals—have been screamed on far more times in this five months than in the preceding five years. And behind the shouts and insults is the threat—and all too frequent reality—of beat-downs. I don't have a way to accurately assess how often beatings happen or to compare that statistically to other years, but it is certainly a palpable reality. I do know that there is a new form of humiliation of "pat frisks" that are nothing short of sexual molestation—which also serve as a provo-cation since a reaction can set off a beating and "box" (isolation) time.

Another change is the tenor of the civilian staff. While never exactly friendly, in 1990 they did their jobs in a fairly efficient way. Now many feel called upon to make our lives more miserable. There is considerable peer pressure among the COs and then toward the civilians not to be "inmate-lovers." Looking at these changes, it seems to me that twenty years of incessant media propaganda that criminals are scum who don't get punished nearly enough has taken on a life of its own. Staff have even become willing to make an extra effort to punish us more.

The conventional wisdom among prisoners that conditions are already worse than pre-1971 is probably an exaggeration. We still have access to more reading material (back then even a book on philosophy was contraband), recreation time, programs and family visits. But if current trends continue unabated, reality will outstrip our hyperboles.

In some important ways things are already worse. Sentencing struc-tures are now draconian and acts of defiance can bring many more years of prison time. There are many more housing units where prisoners are isolated, sometimes for years at a time. We are besieged by raging AIDS and hepatitis C epidemics. And the death penalty is back and looms over any future uprising.[3]

Perhaps the most discouraging aspect of the situation is the change in the consciousness and culture of prisoners. I want to guard against the old-timers' tendency to romanticize the past and condemn a new generation—which can be used as a rationalization for inaction. But there are very real setbacks. Prisoners have much less unity and much less willingness to fight for basic rights. The reasons for this deterioration include: the greater number of drug offenders (because addiction often promotes self-serving behavior), the individualist values of the dominant consumer culture, a much less politically conscious generation, and even the "benefit" gained of being allowed TVs in the cells. (TV not only serves as a direct means of pacification but has pretty much extinguished the flame of many prisoners' use of cell time to develop as readers and to grow into critical thinkers.)

In my opinion the number one factor—and this reality shifts the blame from simply "the youth of today" to very much include my genera-tion's failings—is the major setbacks to political movements in the wake of the government's vicious Cointelpro attacks of the late '60s and early '70s. It's no accident that as the Black Panthers, the Young Lords, AIM (American Indian Movement), and other revolutionary nationalist forces were cut down that drugs proliferated in the ghettos and barrios. It's no surprise that a generation that grew up with so few examples of successful political action, don't see themselves as organizers. It isn't a shock that with almost no visible examples of antiracist whites, far too many white prisoners remain mired in the prevailing racist values. To crystallize it in the starkest terms, prisoners feel that if something like Attica happened today the reaction would not include the strong push for reform generated by the civil rights and Black power movements. Instead, the public outcry would be "Why didn't the state kill more of those scum?"

As a prisoner, i'm embarrassed to ask concerned people on the outside to make us more of a priority when we—at least here at Attica—are doing so little for ourselves. But as a long-time activist who worked on prison issues when in the streets in the 60s and 70s, i will argue that criminal justice is a crucial arena for struggle. The negative synergy between the ebb in political movements and the current prison bleakness actually operates in both directions. Some basic questions can help illuminate the relationship. How did President [Ronald] Reagan carry out his frontal assault on the major gains for labor from the New Deal (won in response to the Great Depression of the 1930s) without major working class reaction? How could he remain a popular president to this day? Why do workers, despite relatively low unemployment, feel historically high levels of anxiety about losing jobs and about seeing ever more jobs defined as "temporary," without basic health benefits? Why, after such a long economic expansion, are unions still so weak and wage pressures so tame?

The genius of the rulers since 1980 has been the classic but still highly effective reactionary strategy of scapegoating: to shift white working people's focus from the corporations and government causing the anxiety and frustration to despised "others" of even lower social status—welfare mothers, immigrants, and prisoners. The disdain is built on the U.S. bedrock of white supremacy but without the indelicacy of using explicitly racist terms. The mobilization around criminal justice also serves to strengthen the government's repressive apparatus for potential use against future social upheavals. In short, there is a complete correlation between the greatest recorded shift ever of wealth from the poor to the rich over the past twenty years and the skyrocketing prison population under increasingly punitive conditions.

Naturally, our movements must organize around our positive vision: respect and empowerment for all those who are oppressed; humane social priorities and an economy based on both equity and ecological soundness.

But we won't be able to get many eyes to focus on these prizes when people are dazzled by the gaudily colored and overly inflated "war on crime." It's up to us to puncture that balloon.

—david gilbert, 83A6150
Attica Correctional Facility
Fall 2001

Notes

1. *Editor's note:* In 1994, under a provision of the Violent Crime Control and Law Enforcement Act, Congress eliminated inmate eligibility for Pell Grants. By 1995, despite the evidence that recidivism rates decline significantly with higher education, all but eight of the 350 prison college programs were closed nationwide. In New York State, public funds for college education in all prisons were eliminated.

2. *Editor's note:* Gilbert refers to such laws as the 1995 Prison Litigation Reform Act (PLRA), which was designed to "curtail the ability of prisoners to bring frivolous and malicious lawsuits." Under the PLRA, a prisoner must exhaust internal remedies before filing a suit in court, even if the prison administration fails minimum federal standards and refuses timely and effective remedies for the prisoner. The PLRA also terminates federal court supervision of local prison and jail systems that fail to maintain humane conditions unless the court makes detailed factual findings of current, on-going constitutional violations. For the text of the PLRA, see ojjdp.ncjrs.org/pubs/walls/appen-b.html.

3. *Editor's note:* For harsh sentencing structures nationwide, see The Sentencing Project, www.sentencingproject.org.

The Anti-Drug Abuse Act of 1988 extended the reach of the federal death penalty, allowing it in cases involving drug-related murders. In 1994, the Federal Death Penalty Act greatly expanded the number of crimes for which a defendant can be executed. These include: killing in the course of another serious offense such as treason or espionage; a prior criminal history of serious violent offenses; premeditated homicide; endangering the lives of others during a criminal act. Under Attorney General John Ashcroft's guidelines established in the U.S.A. Patriot Act, the federal government can seek jurisdiction to prosecute a capital case if a defendant cannot receive the death penalty under state law. For information on the expansion of the U.S. death penalty and executions since 1990, see the Death Penalty Information Center, www.deathpenaltyinfo.org/; NAACP Legal Defense Fund, "Death Row U.S.A.," Winter 2004, naacpldf.org/content/pdf/pubs/drusa/DRUSA_Winter_2004.pdf (5 July 2004).

For analyses of prison health epidemics, see Kimberly Collica, "Levels of Knowledge and Risk Perceptions About HIV/AIDS Among Female Inmates in New York State," *Prison Journal*, Vol. 82, No.1 (2002): 101–24; and the National HCV Prison Coalition, www.hcvinprison.org/ (5 July 2004).

Selected Bibliography

Abu-Jamal, Mumia. *Live from Death Row*. New York: Avon Books, 1996.
———. *We Want Freedom: A Life in the Black Panther Party*. Boston: South End Press, 2004.
All Power to the People! The Black Panther Party and Beyond. Directed by Lee Lew-Lee. New York: Filmmakers Library, 1996. Videocassette.
Amnesty International USA. *Allegations of Mistreatment in Marion Prison, Illinois, U.S.A.*, AMR 51/26/87, May 1987.
Amnesty International. *United States of America: The Death Penalty and Juvenile Offenders*. London: Amnesty International, October 1991.
Amnesty International, Rights for All. *Not Part of My Sentence: Violations of the Human Rights of Women in Custody*. New York: Amnesty International, March 1999.
Baum, Dan. *Smoke and Mirrors: The War on Drugs and the Politics of Failure*. New York: Little, Brown and Company, 1996.
Bennett, James R. *Political Prisoners and Trials: A Worldwide Annotated Bibliography, 1900 through 1993*. Jefferson, NC and London: McFarland & Company, 1995.
Berry, Mary Frances. *Black Resistance/White Law: A History of Constitutional Racism in America*. New York: Appleton-Century-Crofts, 1971.
Bin Wahad, Dhoruba, Mumia Abu-Jamal, and Assata Shakur. *Still Black, Still Strong: Survivors of the U.S. War against Black Revolutionaries*, edited by Fletcher, Jim, Tanaquil Jones and Sylvère Lotringer, New York: Semiotext(e), 1993.
Black Prison Movements USA. Trenton, NJ: Africa World Press, 1995.
Blackston, Nelson. *COINTELPRO: The FBI's Secret War on Political Freedom*. New York: Vintage Books, 1976.
Boyle, Robert. "Tribunal Urges Freedom for U.S. Political Prisoners." *Guild Notes* (Winter 1991).
Breitman, George. *The Last Year of Malcolm X: The Evolution of a Revolutionary*. New York: Schocken, 1967.
Brown, David J. and Robert Merrill, eds. *Violent Persuasions: The Politics and Imagery of Terrorism*. Seattle, WA: Bay Press, 1993.
Burns, Haywood. "Racism and American Law." In *Law Against People*, edited by Robert Lefcourt. New York: Bintae Books, 1971.

Burton-Rose, Daniel, Dan Pens, and Paul Wright, eds. *The Celling of America: An Inside Look at the U.S. Prison Industry*. Monroe, ME: Common Courage Press, 1998.

Can't Jail the Spirit: Political Prisoners in the U.S., fifth edition. Chicago: Committee to End the Marion Lockdown, 2002.

Chomsky, Noam. *The Culture of Terrorism*. Boston: South End Press, 1988.

Churchill, Ward and Jim Vander Wall. *Agents of Repression: The FBI's Secret Wars against the Black Panther Party and the American Indian Movement*. Boston: South End Press, 2002.

———. *The COINTELPRO Papers: Documents From the FBI's Secret Wars Against Domestic Dissent*. Boston: South End Press, 2002.

Cleaver, Eldridge. *Soul on Ice*. New York: McGraw-Hill, 1968.

Cleaver, Kathleen and George Katsiaficas, eds. *Liberation, Imagination, and the Black Panther Party*. New York: Routledge, 2001.

Davidson, Howard, ed. *The Journal of Prisoners on Prisons*. Ontario, Canada, www.jpp.org.

Davis, Angela Y. and Bettina Aptheker, eds. *If They Come in the Morning: Voices of Resistance*. New York: Third Press, 1971.

———. *Angela Y. Davis Reader*, edited by Joy James. Malden, MA: Blackwell, 1998.

Day, Susie and Laura Whitehorn. "Human Rights in the United States: The Unfinished Story of Political Prisoners and COINTELPRO." *New Political Science*, Vol. 23, No. 2 (June 2001): 285–97.

Deutsch, Michael E. and Jan Susler. "Political Prisoners in the United States: The Hidden Reality." *Social Justice*, Vol. 18, No. 3 (1991): 92–106.

Díaz-Cotto, Juanita. *Gender, Ethnicity, and the State: Latina and Latino Prison Politics*. Albany: State University of New York Press, 1996.

Dieter, Richard C. *The Death Penalty in Black and White: Who Lives, Who Dies, Who Decides*. Washington, D.C.: The Death Penalty Information Center, 1998.

Escobar, Edward J. "The Dialectics of Repression: The Los Angeles Police Department and the Chicano Movement, 1968–1971." *Journal of American History* (March 1993): 1483–514.

Faith, Karlene. *Unruly Women: The Politics of Confinement and Resistance*. Vancouver, BC: Press Gang Publishers, 1993.

Fanon, Frantz. *The Wretched of the Earth*. New York: Grove Press, 1968.

Fletcher, B. R., L. D. Shaver and D. B. Moon, eds. *Women Prisoners: A Forgotten Population*. Westport, CT: Praeger, 1993.

Foner, Phillip. *The Black Panthers Speak*. Philadelphia: Lippincott, 1970.

Foucault, Michel. *Discipline and Punish: The Birth of the Prison,* translated by Alan Sheridan. New York: Vintage, 1979.

Franklin, H. Bruce. *Prison Literature in America: The Victim as Criminal and Artist*. New York: Oxford University Press, 1989.

Goldberg, David Theo. *Racial Subjects: Writing on Race in America*. New York: Routledge, 1997.

Goldstein, Robert Justin. "An American Gulag?: Summary Arrest and Emergency Detention of Political Dissidents in the United States." *Columbia Human Rights Law Review,* Vol. 10 (1978).

Goodell, Charles. *Political Prisoners in America.* New York: Random House, 1973.

Gramsci, Antonio. *Selections from The Prison Notebooks,* edited and translated by Quintin Hoare and Geoffrey Nowell Smith. New York: International Publishers, 1985.

Grobsmith, E. *Indians in Prison: Incarcerated Native Americans in Nebraska.* Lincoln: University of Nebraska Press, 1994.

Gross, Samuel R. and Robert Mauro. *Death & Discrimination: Racial Disparities in Capital Sentencing.* Boston: Northeastern University Press, 1989.

Halperin, Morton H., et al. *The Lawless State: The Crimes of the U.S. Intelligence Agencies.* New York: Penguin, 1976.

Haney, Craig. "Infamous Punishment: The Psychological Consequences of Isolation." *National Prison Project Journal* (ACLU) (Spring 1993): 23.

Harlow, Barbara. *Barred: Women, Writing and Political Detention.* Hanover, NH: Wesleyan University Press, 1992.

Human Rights Watch. *Cold Storage: Super-Maximum Security Confinement in Indiana.* New York: Human Rights Watch, October 1997.

International Indian Treaty Council. "Violations of American Human Rights by the United States: Wounded Knee, 1973." In *Illusions of Justice: Human Rights Violations in the United States*, edited by Lennox S. Hinds. Iowa City: University of Iowa, 1979.

Irwin, John and James Austin. *It's About Time: America's Imprisonment Binge.* Belmont, CA: Wadsworth, 1997.

Jackson, George. *Blood in My Eye.* New York: Random House, 1972; repr. Baltimore: Black Classic Press, 1990.

———. *Soledad Brother: The Prison Letters of George Jackson.* New York: Coward-McCann, 1970; repr. Chicago: Lawrence Hill Books, 1994.

James, Joy, ed. *Imprisoned Intellectuals: America's Political Prisoners Write on Life, Liberation, and Rebellion.* Lanham, MD: Rowman and Littlefield, 2003.

———. *Resisting State Violence.* Minneapolis: University of Minnesota Press, 1996.

———. *States of Confinement: Policing, Detention, and Prisons.* New York: St. Martin's, 2002, revised paperback edition.

Johnson, Anita and Claude Marks, prods. *Prisons on Fire: George Jackson, Attica & Black Liberation.* Freedom Archives. Oakland: AK Press, 2002. Audio CD.

Johnson, Troy, et al., eds. *American Indian Activism: Alcatraz to the Longest Walk.* Urbana: University of Illinois Press, 1997.

Jones, Charles E., ed. *The Black Panther Party [Reconsidered].* Baltimore: Black Classic Press, 1998.

Kohn, Stephen M. *American Political Prisoners: Prosecutions under the Espionage and Sedition Acts.* Westport, CT: Praeger, 1994.

Levy, Howard, et al. *Going to Jail: The Political Prisoner.* New York: Grove Press, 1971.

Mancini, Matthew. *One Dies, Get Another: Convict Leasing in the American South, 1866–1928*. Columbia: University of South Carolina Press, 1996.

Marable, Manning and Leith Mullings, eds. *Let Nobody Turn Us Around: Voices of Resistance, Reform, and Renewal*. Lanham, MD: Rowman and Littlefield, 2000.

Marquart, James W., Sheldon Edland-Olson and Jonathan R. Sorenson. *The Rope, the Chair, and the Needle: Capital Punishment in Texas, 1923–1990*. Austin: University of Texas Press, 1994.

Massey, Douglas and Hajnal Zoltan. "The Changing Geographic Structure of Black-White Segregation in the United States." *Social Science Quarterly*, Vol. 76, No. 3 (September 1995): 533–34.

Mauer, Marc. *The Race to Incarcerate*. New York: The New Press, 2001.

May, John P., ed., and Khalid R. Pitts, associate ed. *Building Violence: How America's Rush to Incarcerate Creates More Violence*. Thousand Oaks, CA: Sage Publications, 2000.

Meyer, Matt. "Freedom Now." *The Nonviolent Activist* (November-December 1993).

Miller, Jerome G. *Search and Destroy: African American Males in the Criminal Justice System*. New York: Cambridge University Press, 1996.

Minor, W. William, "Political Crime, Political Justice, and Political Prisoners." *Criminology*, Vol. 12 (February 1975).

Nathanson, Nathaniel L. "Freedom of Association and the Quest for Internal Security: Conspiracy from Dennis to Dr. Spock." *Northwestern University Law Review*, Vol. 65, No. 2 (May-June 1998).

O'Hare, Kate Richards, Sometime Federal Prisoner Number 21669. *In Prison*. Seattle: University of Washington Press, 1976 (original 1923).

O'Reilly, Kenneth. "The FBI and the Politics of the Riots, 1964–1968." *Journal of American History*, Vol. 75, No. 1 (June 1988).

Oppenheimer, Martin. *The Urban Guerrilla*. Chicago: Quadrangle Books, 1969.

Oshinsky, David. *Worse than Slavery: Parchman Farm and the Jim Crow Justice System*. New York: The Free Press, 1996.

Owen, Barbara. *"In the Mix": Struggle and Survival in a Women's Prison*. Albany: State University of New York Press, 1998.

Parenti, Christian. "Assata Shakur Speaks from Exile: Post-Modern Maroon in the Ultimate Palenque." *Z Magazine* (March 1998): 27–32.

———. *Lockdown America: Police and Prisons in the Age of Crisis*. New York: Verso, 1999.

Prashad, Vijay. *Keeping Up with the Dow Joneses: Debt, Prison, Workfare*. Boston: South End Press, 2003.

"Political Prisoners in the United States," Washington, D.C.: Center for Constitutional Rights, September 1988.

Rosenblatt, Elihu, ed. *Criminal Injustice: Confronting the Prison Crisis*. Boston: South End Press, 1996.

Ross, Luana. *Inventing the Savage: The Social Construction of Native American Criminality*. Austin: University of Texas Press, 1998.

Sabo, Don, Terry A. Kupers, and Willie London, eds. *Prison Masculinities.* Philadelphia: Temple University Press, 2001.

Scheffler, Judith A. and Tracy Huling, eds. *Wall Tappings: An International Anthology of Women's Prison Writings, 200 A.D. to the Present.* New York: Feminist Press, 2002.

Shakur, Sanyika. "Flowing in File: The George Jackson Phenomenon." *Wazo Weusi (Think Black): A Journal of Black Thought,* Vol. 2, No. 2 (1995).

Sklar, Morton, ed. *Racial and Ethnic Discrimination in the United States: The Status of Compliance by the U.S. Government with the International Convention on the Elimination of Racial Discrimination.* Washington, D.C.: The Coalition Against Torture and Racial Discrimination, October 1998.

———. *Torture in the United States: The Status of Compliance by the U.S. Government with the International Convention against Torture and Other Cruel, Inhuman, or Degrading Treatment or Punishment.* Washington, D.C.: World Coalition against Torture, October 1998.

Smith, Jennifer. *An International History of the Black Panther Party.* New York: Garland, 1999.

Staples, William G. *The Culture of Surveillance: Discipline and Social Control in the United States.* New York: St. Martin's, 1997.

Theoharis, Athan. *The FBI: An Annotated Bibliography and Research Guide.* New York: Garland, 1994.

Tonry, Michael. *Malign Neglect—Race, Crime, and Punishment in America.* New York: Oxford University Press, 1995.

U.S. Commission on Civil Rights. *The Navajo Nation: An American Colony.* Washington, D.C.: U.S. Government Printing Office, September 1975.

U.S. Senate. *Final Report of the Select Committee to Study Government Operations with Respect to Intelligence Activities.* Washington, D.C.: U. S. Government Printing Office, 1976.

United Nations. *Standard Minimum Rules for the Treatment of Prisoners.* New York, 1984.

Watterson, Kathryn. *Women in Prison.* Boston: Northeastern University Press, 1996.

Wicker, Tom. *A Time to Die.* New York: Quadrangle/NY Times Books, 1975.

Zinn, Howard. *A People's History of the United States.* New York: Harper & Row, 1980.

About the Editor .

Joy James, Professor of Africana Studies at Brown University, is the author of *Transcending the Talented Tenth: Black Leaders and American Intellectuals; Resisting State Violence;* and, *Shadowboxing: Representations of Black Feminist Politics.* James is editor of *The Angela Y. Davis Reader* and coeditor of *The Black Feminist Reader.* Her current work on incarceration and human rights includes the anthologies: *States of Confinement: Policing, Detention, and Prisons; Imprisoned Intellectuals: America's Political Prisoners Write on Life, Liberation, and Rebellion;* and *Warfare: Prison and the American Homeland.* She is currently writing a book on the Central Park case.

Index

Massachusetts, xli, 3, 22, 44; Boston, 46, 235; Brookline, 311
Master P (Percy Miller), 163, 165
Matthiessen, Peter, 138
Mazolla, William (Judge), xli
McAllister, Elizabeth, 295
McClain, James, 99, 227, 234
McDonald's, 86
Mead, Ed, 117–130
Medley, Mark, 206, 214–15
Men Against Sexism (MAS), 118–30
mental illness, 40, 43; mental hospitals, 85; mentally disordered/ill, xxi, 48, 287
Metropolitan Community Church (MCC), 122–23
Mexicans, 245, 263
Mexico, 32, 167
Miami, Florida, 32
Midnight Special Collective, 269
military, xxviii, xxxi, xxxiv, 7, 45, 52, 138–39, 221, 231–32, 299
military industrial complex, 221
Miller, Percy. See Master P
Mills, Opie, 227
Million Man March, 278, 284. See also Farrakhan, Louis
Minnesota, 135; Rochester, 291
Minutemen, 239
Mississippi, xxxi, 89, 151, 155, 157–59, 163; Jackson, 158
Mississippi Freedom Democratic Party (MFDP), 89
Morgan State University, 206
Moore, Richard. See Bin Wahad, Dhoruba
Moses, 171
MOVE, 197–200; MOVE Nine, 199
Muhammad, Elijah, 155
Muntaqim, Jalil (Anthony Bottom), 27–36

Naeve, Lowell, 9
Nation of Islam (NOI), 155, 181, 277–78, 284; Supreme Commander of, 284. See also Islam
National Alliance Against Racist and Political Repression (NAAPR), 218
National Association for the Advancement of Colored People (NAACP), xxxix, 27, 284
National Basketball Association (NBA), 163
National Black United Front, 165

National Campaign to Stop Control Units, 44
National Coalition of Black for Reparations in America (N'COBRA), 116; Amistad-March chapter of, 116
National Football League (NFL), 163
National Prisoners Campaign to Petition the United Nations, 27
National Lawyers Guild, 67
Native Americans, xiii, xxv, 29, 33, 97, 133, 135–50, 154–56, 160, 287; caupa waken, 135; Cherokee, 148; Great Spirit, 135–38; inyansha, 135; Iron House, 137; Lakota Sioux, 133; Lakota, 138, 148; Native American Prisoners' Research and Rehabilitation Project, 133; Navajo, 155; (Tunkasila) Wakan Tanka, 137–38; Native American Council of Tribes (NACT), 144; Native American Free Exercise of Religion Act (1994), 150; Red Road Approach to Recovery Program, 144; Seattle Indian Alcoholism Program, 145; Seminoles, xxxvii; Eskimo, 156. See also American Indian Movement; Bureau of Indian Affairs (BIA); Peltier, Leonard; Pine Ridge Reservation; Wounded Knee
Nazism; concentration camps, 8; Germany, 53, 111; Adolph Hitler, 111
(neo)slave narratives, xiii, xxi–xxxii, xxxiv–xxxvii
New Afrikan CREED, 176
New Afrikan Independence Movement (NAIM), 30, 113, 165, 173, 175, 259; Declaration of Independence, 113; Provisional Government of, 113
New Afrikans, 30, 33, 151, 157–58; New Afrikan Nation, 154–55, 178. See also Republic of New Afrika (RNA); New Afrikan Independence Movement
Netherlands, 221–22; Dutch Penal System, 221
New Black Panther Party, 165
New Deal, 7, 10, 315
New Haven, Connecticut, 224, 234
New Haven Fourteen, 234
New Jersey, 77
New Mexico, 133; Center for Advocacy for Human Rights, 133
New York, xxii, xxvi, 3, 27, 57, 77, 79–81, 88, 163, 169–170, 269, 292, 303, 313;